HAWAIIAN
ISLANDS

OCEAN

9003209

STATES
TERRITORY
SIA

EQUATOR

ARCHIPEL
NEW
IRELAND

BOUGA

SOLOMON
SEA

MELA

SEA

Brisbane

PHOENIX
ISLANDS

TOKELAU
NESIA
WESTERN SAMOA
AMERICAN
SAMOA
GA OR FRIENDLY
ISLANDS
TONGA

---→— By Sea
...►...... By Air

Slow Boats Home

Books by Gavin Young

Return to the Marshes
Iraq: Land of Two Rivers
Halfway Around the World

Slow Boats Home

Gavin Young

Illustrations by Salim

Random House
New York

All rights reserved under International and Pan-American
Copyright Conventions. Published in the United States by
Random House, Inc., New York. Originally published in
Great Britain by Hutchinson & Co. (Publishers) Ltd., Lon-
don, in 1985.

Library of Congress Cataloging-in-Publication Data

Young, Gavin, 1928–
  Slow boats home.

   1. Young, Gavin, 1928–   . 2. Voyages and travels
—1951–   . I. Title.
G465.Y67 1986   910.4'1   85-25600
ISBN 0-394-52142-0

Manufactured in the United States of America
98765432
FIRST AMERICAN EDITION

This book is for Leueen MacGrath

ACKNOWLEDGEMENTS

As in the case of my earlier ship-hopping adventure, described in *Slow Boats to China*, I owe a great deal to many people, not all of whom appear in the book itself. I want to thank Mr Shi Zhi Wei and the China International Travel Service for allowing me to wander so freely about the backwaters of Shanghai. John Swire and his employees in the offices of the China Navigation Company in Hong Kong once again found space for me, this time on two of their ships. On my way across the South Pacific, Alan Grey of 'Aggie Grey's' in Apia, Western Samoa, had the humanity to open the doors of his famous hotel to Tolu's humble family; Michael Tinne and Tim Wilson introduced me to the strange world of the Melanesian copra plantations; and I shall never think of the daunting tract of ocean between Tahiti and Peru without offering up silent thanks to Raphael Tixier and Jim Hostetler of Papeete, and to Captain Vitaly Segal, master of the Soviet vessel *Alexander Pushkin*. I owe my sojourn on Alexander Selkirk's island of exile to Tony Westcott, that fine yachtsman of Valparaiso. And, without any question whatsoever, I should never have fulfilled one of my greatest ambitions – to spend days and nights on Cape Horn island – without the help and sympathy of Señor Don Hernan Cubillos of Santiago. I had invaluable advice from that considerable traveller, writer and diplomat, John Ure; from Brian Shaw of Furness Withy; and from Sir Ronald Swayne, formerly of Overseas Containers Ltd. The indefatigable Andrew Bell, founder of Curnow Shipping ('the greatest little shipping company in the West', I call it) saw me safely to St Helena, up the long South Atlantic seaways, and home.

My indispensable sea anchor in London, Gritta Weil, kept up my spirits in times of delay and frustration; the hard work she contributed to the production of this book is beyond appraisal. The same goes for much forthright advice from my friend Gill Gibbins; and for the unending encouragement of Roddy Bloomfield, my editor at Hutchinson.

Keep true to the dreams of thy youth.

Herman Melville:
Motto found glued to his
writing-box after his death

It's like a book, I think, this bloomin' world,
Which you can read and care for just so long,
But presently you feel that you will die
Unless you get the page you're readin' done,
And turn another — likely not as good;
But what you're after is to turn 'em all.

Rudyard Kipling:
'Sestina of the Tramp-Royal'

I am not yet born; O hear me,
Let not the man who is beast or thinks he is God
   come near me.

Louis MacNeice:
'Prayer before Birth'

Contents

Prelude   XI

Part One
A Dream of China Seas   I

Part Two
Isles of Illusion   75

Part Three
Uttermost Part of the
Earth   317

Part Four
Rolling Home From Rio 365

Landfall   429

Prelude

The SS *Shanghai* is in harbour again. I spotted her as I drove past the Star Ferry and recognized her immediately, though it is more than a year since I saw her here last. Then I had been sitting in this very room and she had been waiting to start me off from Hong Kong on the second stage of a ship-hopping adventure round the world. The adventure is over now. It is all in my head. I have come back here to write it down.

The second stage of that adventure, like the first, had its roots in my boyhood yearning to Run Away to Sea. It was a yearning born, as I have written elsewhere, during days spent lying on clifftops watching Atlantic breakers pound the rock-bound bays of North Cornwall's Wreckers' Coast, and dreaming – awake or asleep – of tall ships and thrilling places at the end of the horizon. The attic of my grandmother's ugly old house on Ocean View Road was full of dusty books by authors who had been my father's favourites when he was a boy – R. M. Ballantyne, Captain Marryat, Robert Louis Stevenson, and a dozen others. From the attic's high round window I could see a green, thrusting headland – it bore the Stevensonian name of Compass Point – that resembled the prow of a great ship riding up into a sky full of clouds like the billowing crests of giant waves; and beyond the headland the hypnotic glitter of the ocean itself, the mysterious, irresistible highway to Robinson Crusoe's cave ... cannibal islands ... the South Seas ... the remote, forested domain of the bird of paradise. Many years later, when the boy who had lain dreaming on those clifftops had long since ceased to be a boy, the opportunity came. I had finished a book about the Marsh Arabs of Iraq and was free. 'Now, I shall go,' I said to myself. 'If I don't go now, I never shall.'

There was no question of weeks on a cruise ship. I would take a series of ships at random – big ships, small ones, tankers, dhows, junks, whatever I could find – to take me wherever they happened to go. Well, not quite wherever – eastward, for choice. That was my decision, but decision was not enough. Was this kind of ship-hopping actually possible in these days of universal air travel and group tours?

The first London travel agent I approached to see if such a thing could be arranged by passenger ship threw up his arms and said, 'No can do,' quite snappishly, and even the Thomas Cook's men, though friendly, were no help. As I had suspected, the few passenger vessels that have escaped the breakers' yards are usually cruise ships carrying groups. You can control a group. Individuals are unpredictable, and so too much trouble. All the same, I managed to complete the first stage of what I came to think of as my private game of Traveller's Roulette, although it was eight months after leaving Piraeus, not the three or four I had imagined, before I found my twenty-third vessel that sailed me up the Pearl River to Canton for my last landfall.

The journey that completed my circle of the globe – the one I am about to describe – took even longer: exactly a year. The tangible relics of it that lie about me now would baffle the most experienced beachcomber were they all to be washed ashore in one place. A goose wing from the Falkland Islands; a whale-tooth dagger with 'Beagle Channel' inked on it; cowrie shell necklaces from Apia and a Bible in Samoan; a stuffed woodcock from a back alley in Hong Kong; an illustrated scroll from Shanghai; a set of Russian dolls; two ceramic vases from a ship's captain on Robinson Crusoe Island. The torn flag in the frame hanging on the wall flew on Cape Horn Island, the southernmost tip of the earth; it is signed by eight Chilean marines and a dog called Tony. The lump of obsidian like black glass comes from Ascension Island; the Gospel according to St Matthew is written in the pidgin language of the Solomon Islanders.... Enough to jog my memory of a good many places and people in the unlikely event of my forgetting. And then there are thirty-six notebooks that surround me now; big or pocket-sized, lined or unlined, somehow they managed to avoid what I always feared – obliteration by waves or rain squalls or the loss overboard of the bag in which I carried them.

The room I am in now is the one I set out from just over a year ago to join the *Shanghai*. It is a large room on the fourth floor of the Luk Kwok Hotel in Hong Kong, and I am fond of it. It is not in the least glamorous, but it is friendly and the hotel knows nothing of race or class; rather like the *Shanghai* herself. A homely old thing, ex-P & O, and before that Belgian, she used to transport Flemish colonial officials and their wives from Antwerp to the Belgian Congo, Conrad's Heart of Darkness. What a different world she has found here on the China coast.

The sun is shining, the harbour gleams and is full of life; a freighter carrying containers slides in from the eastern approach, bright as a freshly painted toy, and the Kowloon ferries move briskly back and forth. The sunshine makes the angular outlines of Kowloon softer and white, and seems to have brought the background of green hills closer. Below me, sunlight washes over the footbridge that spans Gloucester Road, on which a bow-legged old Chinese in baggy trousers is shuffling along carrying a tiny songbird in a cage. A boy overtakes him, running beside a small, happy dog with a curly tail; a plump little dog, the kind some Chinese like to eat – but these two are friends. The dog smiles up at the boy, and he, smiling back, flicks the dog's tail affectionately with the lead.

I had made up my mind early on that Hong Kong would be my starting point. It was the obvious place to complete my circling of the globe: Europe – China – Europe again, this second journey would take me across the Pacific, round the Horn, and the length of the Atlantic from the Falklands to England. But first, I wanted to take ships up the coast of China, if possible all the way to Dairen (Port Arthur in the days when the tsars of Russia owned it) at the head of the Yellow Sea. Hangchow was a port I particularly wanted to visit on the way. As a very small boy I discovered the name Hangchow one day in a heavy old atlas, full of must and weevils, that I dug out from the back of a cupboard in my grandfather's farmhouse in South Wales. The name was appealing in itself but there was more to it than that for me. It happened that my grandfather owned a large chow dog, a laughing, black-tongued specimen called Cheeko, with a curving fluffy tail and a most regrettable impulse to chase sheep. That impulse confined Cheeko to the neighbourhood of the house – he had to be restrained – and, thrown together thus, we became close friends. Childish illogic told me that Hangchow must be a chow's family home, and I made a vow to Cheeko as I gazed at that exciting name among the fly specks on the map of Cathay. One arm round his neck, I pressed my forefinger onto that big yellow patch and, with the force of every determined nerve in my body, I swore: I shall go there when I grow up!

All these years later I might reach Hangchow at last – but what then? Japan? Korea? First things first – although everyone seemed to be going to China these days I had no idea if the Chinese Government in Peking would permit a single traveller from the West to leapfrog between Chinese ports on Chinese vessels, leave alone from a Chinese port to a foreign country. Someone who knows China and me said, 'Don't go to the Chinese Embassy in London. Write direct to something called the Chinese People's Association for Friendship with Foreign Countries. It might do some good.' I still don't know if he was right or wrong; in any case, I wrote to the president of that organization asking permission to visit the ports of Xamen, Fuzhou, Shanghai, Quingdao and Dairen, on my way to Japan. Then I prepared for the long wait for a reply. A reply that never came. Instead, after two weeks – a remarkably short time, I thought – a friendly letter arrived from an Englishman, Mr David Crook, working in the Foreign Language Institute in Peking. Somehow he had seen my letter, and he advised me that the China International Travel Service might be a more useful organization for me than the Friendship Association, which 'is rather more politically inclined'. Accordingly, he had passed my letter on. 'I think that's about the best I can do,' he wrote. 'Good luck.'

I could do nothing without Peking's permission – and a visa. But it was pointless to write more letters from London or to wait for any. In any case, I was impatient to get away.

In the preceding months, there had been sudden deaths in my family, and the swift, successive shocks had thrown me into what now seems to have been an absurdly selfish sense of desertion. Unconsciously you trust those you love to last you out, and when one morning they are as lifeless as the black print in an obituary column, you feel betrayed. That, at least, was my experience. I happened to be reading Graham Greene's *Travels With My Aunt*, and I felt deep sympathy for poor Henry Pulling, the retired bank manager, as he coped with the disposal of all the trappings of his newly dead mother, the furniture and unwanted pictures, the unfashionable underclothes of an old lady, the half-empty pots of old-fashioned creams – and the dragging business with undertakers, estate agents, tax inspectors, solicitors.... I had had the same coping to do.

Eager to escape the Laocoön's coils of Lincoln's Inn Fields – and the circumjacence of death – I gave urgent thought to my departure for Hong Kong. I decided to visit in person the China Travel Service people there.

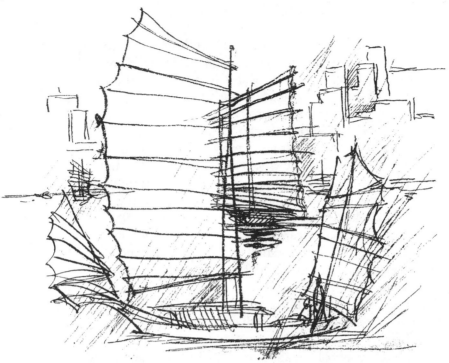

Perhaps I could bury my black dog mood in their branch in Kowloon.

I lost no more time. I dragged my Haliburton metal suitcase from a cupboard and looked at it with affection. It was dented and scarred by months of rude contact with Arab, Indian, Malaysian and Filipino jetties, and ships' decks from Piraeus to the Pearl River, but sea water had not rusted the tumblers of its combination lock as I had once feared it would. If it had, I would have had to borrow an electronic blowtorch (if there was such a thing) to open it. My old zipbag was still good for several voyages by the look of it and I fondly dusted that off, too. It seemed to wear its oil stains, the red smears of Borneo tanbark and the old curling labels like the medals old soldiers are given for long service and good conduct. The only other piece of luggage I needed was an overnight bag to hold my Pentax, films, binoculars and the essential Polaroid camera – as useful for breaking the social ice in remote places as beads and mirrors were to the first Europeans.

Then I bought a one-way ticket to Hong Kong, eagerly signed a number of letters giving my solicitors power of attorney over a number of (to me) utterly mysterious affairs, and raced off to catch the Cathay Pacific flight from Heathrow.

*   *   *

January 1982 was an ill-tempered month in which to be starting out again. There was no midwinter sun in Hong Kong. A cold smog accompanied my taxi from Kai Tak airport to the Luk Kwok. The windows of my room looked out onto the harbour, as they do now, but when I put my nose to the glass I found that the view, one of the most dramatic of the world's harbour views, had shrunk to practically nothing. All colour had drained away. A ferry or two crawled as though drugged across water the colour of dulled metal; a junk with sails like soiled brown paper barely moved at all, and through my binoculars I could see her crew, in baggy blue smocks, squatting under an awning on her deck, listlessly playing cards and smoking. Not far from her the white, blue and red squares of a Panamanian flag hung limply from the stern of a big, rust-streaked tanker. Lifeless at her moorings, she looked abandoned, set there to moulder for ever. Behind their grey veils of rain the white high-rise buildings of Kowloon were a mere jumble of decaying teeth; beyond, the green hills of the New Territories, that in sunlight climb with such radiant luminosity towards China, had vanished.

My nose was cold against the Luk Kwok's clammy windowpanes. My soul felt colder still. I took my Kümmerly & Frey map of the world from the metal suitcase and spread it on the bed. It gave me immediate comfort, confirming that without doubt Hong Kong was the right place to be. There it was, on the map: a magnificent wen on the convergence of two of the earth's grandest areas of land and sea – China (canary yellow) and the Pacific Ocean (a bilious, bluish green). In such a busy port, surely, I could find a vessel to start me off?

I shifted my finger on Kümmerly & Frey, south and eastwards. These were the objectives – to cross the Pacific (now my finger traced a path through the rash of islands that cover the map of the South Seas like chickenpox); to traverse the South Atlantic from Argentina to South Africa (my finger negotiated the lethal storms of Cape Horn without a tremor and moved up between Buenos Aires and the Falkland Islands before crossing the immense block of green-blue Atlantic to Cape Town); then to leapfrog up the coast of West Africa to Portugal, Spain, France and finally England (my finger wavered from the Bay of Biscay towards the knobbly leg of the West Country).

I hoped my last landfall would be Bude Haven, a tiny nick in a sweep of 700-foot cliffs which even in this century was a regular port of call for coastal ketches before they faded away in the 1930s. Now fishing boats and yachts creep in behind the old stone breakwater that at high tide shrugs off the huge Atlantic waves like a stranded but imperturbable whale. I suppose few people would want to end up, after months of sun and lagoons in the South Seas, in an insignificant Cornish resort miles from the nearest railway station; a place of generally unattractive Edwardian villas in a hinterland of ancient churchyards cluttered with memorials to generations of Cornish yeomen and drowned sailors; a place of beaches glorious in the summer sun, but in winter often battered by weather fit only for the Devil or Davy Jones. But my dream had started there, in that dusty attic with its tantalizing view of the ocean, and I hoped it might return after all these years, to rest there in peace.

I was setting off in search of what Henry James called 'the visitable past'. Robert Louis Stevenson, companion of my youth, was with me now – *The Master of Ballantrae* and the *Vailima Letters*, most of the letters he wrote to his friend Sidney Colvin from Samoa, as well as those written by his mother, staunch old Mrs Stevenson who lived to follow her Lou's Samoan pallbearers up the side of Mount Vaea to his tree-shaded grave. In the metal case I had packed Melville's *Typee*, Jack London's *The Cruise of the Snark* and Gauguin's *Intimate Journals*. Under socks and shirts lay a volume of Saki's short stories, a Conrad or two, a bunch of thrillers. And – at this moment of imminent departure for China, the most immediately exciting of all – a novel that described in words of fire the street terror which Chinese Communists and Nationalists brought to the international city of Shanghai in 1927 – André Malraux's *La Condition Humaine*, translated into English as *Man's Fate*. It was years since I had read it but I knew its opening by heart: 'Should Chen try lifting up the mosquito net? Or should he strike through it?'

Political murder in old Shanghai; Stevenson's Samoa; Cape Horn – my soul warmed a few degrees, and, resisting another look at the drowning harbour, I poured two fingers and a thumb of Black Label into one of the Luk Kwok's glasses. Feeling only slightly self-conscious, I drank to my immediate future.

Part One

A Dream of China Seas

The mass and majesty of this world, all
   That carries weight and always weighs the same
Lay in the hands of others; they were small
   And could not hope for help and no help came
           W. H. Auden: 'The Shield of Achilles'

One

The receptionist of the Luk Kwok Hotel had handed me a postcard when I registered, and I looked at it now. The picture showed a Chinese landscape with pagoda-like red-tiled houses, trees and grey hills. It was from Mr Crook in Peking. He said he had just received a note from the Chinese International Travel Service (Peking branch). 'They express their welcome to you,' he wrote, 'and have informed their European section. That looks moderately hopeful.' Once more he wished me luck.

Next morning I crossed on the Star Ferry to Kowloon and the office of the China International Travel Service. A Mr Cheung Chi Sing, a youngish, pleasant man, laid on the counter folders, airline schedules and tourist pamphlets. I explained I didn't want to go by air.

'I want to travel to Shanghai or other Chinese ports in a series of Chinese ships,' I said slowly and, I think, clearly, repeating what I had already written to Peking from London.

'It is not usual,' said Mr Cheung, gravely. 'No, not very usual.'

I showed Mr Crook's postcard to Mr Cheung, who looked at the picture of houses, trees and hills for some time before reading the back very carefully, more than once. 'Oh, I see,' he said, politely nodding, and once more silence paralysed our dialogue.

'You see, it says here' – I pointed to the postcard – 'that my name and the details of what I would like to do have been passed to the European section of your head office in Peking. They have acknowledged receipt. Look, they have even said "Welcome". Suppose you telephone from here and ask someone there what to do?'

Mr Cheung looked unhappy. The friendly smile that continued to lurk about his lips was sadly at odds with the helpless expression in his eyes.

3

'Maybe I will telephone there later.'

'Why not now?'

'All line are busy now.' I wondered how he could know that and doubted that he did. 'You leave address and telephone number in Hong Kong,' he continued. 'When I call Peking office, I will let you know. Okay?'

I knew there was nothing more to be done here. By now, I can usually recognize a dead end when I see one. To put it mildly, it was very frustrating. It might mean abandoning the idea of China altogether.

'Okay,' I said. 'Will you be sure to telephone me? This afternoon? Tomorrow?'

'Very soon.' Mr Cheung's smile was warm now; his relief at my imminent departure, polite and without truculence, was easily perceptible. 'As soon as I hear,' he said.

I thought, 'I'm not going to hear from Mr Cheung again.' Nor did I.

Nevertheless, I gave him that afternoon and the next day. After that I couldn't wait any longer, inactive by the Luk Kwok's telephone, watching American cops and robbers on TV while the depression that had accompanied me from London grew within me. I had had faith in the CITS. I had thought that tourism would be so important to China's economy that an organization set up specifically to smooth the way for Westerners seeking to admire the country and spend much-needed hard currency would be an efficient one. Crook's letter and postcard had been mildly optimistic, but Mr Cheung hadn't even known how to telephone his head office – or hadn't he dared to?

I had already telephoned an old friend, Donald Wise. With his crisply upturning moustache and upright, stalwart figure, Donald looked more like a colonel in the British Raj's Indian Army than the war correspondent he had been for a quarter of a century. He was an editor now with the *Far Eastern Economic Review* and had lived in Hong Kong some time; an Old Hand.

'Heaven knows what was in your Mr Cheung's mind,' Donald said. 'And frankly, I'm not sure what your best move is now. Why not do two things, though, for a start. First, contact someone in Jardine's travel department, and then the one in Swire's, too. Ask their advice. It's their world out here in more than one sense. It might get you somewhere.'

Jardine Mathieson is one of the two giant commercial houses in Hong Kong; John Swire & Sons is the other. Both had had intimate business dealings with China for well over a century, so they should know a thing or two.

4

'And the second thing?'

'Meet me at the Foreign Correspondents' Club for lunch.'

The Jardine's man was sympathetic when I explained my failure with Mr Cheung of CITS. 'Don't take it to heart. I'm sure CITS were not making it hard for you personally.'

'Oh, no. But I didn't imagine it would be quite like that.'

'They are just incredibly inefficient over there in some ways. Muddlers.' He gave me the name of a travel agent in Central Hong Kong. 'They should know the ropes. Try them.' And thanks to him I came face to face with Miss Angel Yip.

Dear Miss Yip. There was sunshine in her face, and she communicated it to me. She cut through all doubt as soon as I explained about the plans I had already laid before Mr Cheung and my would-be CITS benefactors in Peking. She considered briefly. Then she said: 'If you want to be sure to go anywhere by sea in China, you should take one of three Chinese passenger vessels from Hong Kong' – or, indeed, she added, all of them separately, one after the other. There would be no problem in that? 'Oh, no,' said Miss Yip, sweetly and confidently.

'Well ...?'

'Well,' she said. 'There are ships to Amoy, Swatow, Kwangzhou and Shanghai. All from Hong Kong. I can arrange.'

I thought quickly – and in a moment discarded my ambition to linger in the region. It was a long way to England. I couldn't spend weeks shuttling back and forth from Hong Kong to the Chinese coast. Shanghai was the port I wished to see above all others – Shanghai with its Bund and its old skyscrapers; the scene of the black dramas Malraux described; the scene of President Nixon's meeting with Chou En-lai, and of so much else.

'Miss Yip,' I said urgently across her desk, 'I'll take the ship to Shanghai and see what happens.'

'Right,' she said, businesslike. 'Perhaps you will be able to ask someone in Shanghai how to find a vessel from there to Dairen and the Yellow Sea.' I hoped so, I said.

I handed over my sea-stained passport. 'Expect the visa in about four days,' she said, adding that the ship was called the *Shanghai*, and that many Chinese would be on her going to Shanghai for the Chinese New Year holiday. 'The ship will be full up,' she said.

In the street, I remembered that I hadn't mentioned Hangchow once. I was going to betray my childhood promise to my poor friend Cheeko. Guilt padded at my heels all the way to lunch with Donald Wise.

Next day a letter arrived. Miss Yip supplied details of the voyage to Shanghai. It read exactly as follows:

ss. *Shanghai* – China Flag
Tonage: 13,500 tons
Speed: 18 mph
Totaly having 7 decks and only three main decks
take passenger with air-conditioned which have 115
cabins and she can carry 459 passengers.
  Facilities:- 1 dining room, ball room, bar,
cinema, swimming pool and hospital etc. Beside taking
passenger, she also carries cargo up to 2,500 tons.
  Sailing time: about 56 hours
  Check in time: 12.30 at Tai Kok Tsui Pier on 10th
Jan., the ship will arrive Shanghai on 13th Jan., at
0700.

I would be met in Shanghai by a CITS guide, Miss Yip said. Mildly elated by that information – anything that confirmed the existence *and* signalled the sailing of the *Shanghai* was good for my depression – I went for a stroll through the back streets behind the Luk Kwok. In the bars of Wan Chai bare-breasted Chinese girls, most of them remarkably devoid of allure, languidly invited one to buy them Coca-Cola for hefty chunks of coin. My guidebook to Hong Kong said that 'if nipples could yawn, those here would', and even the healthily lascivious spirits of some Scots Guardsmen I met drinking in the Pussycat Topless flagged before these lethargic displays of drooping flesh.

'Herpes are forever,' one of them said morosely into his beer.

An aura of drama hangs about Hong Kong at the most normal of times. This is partly because of its unusual appearance – the grouping of the steep-sided rocky islands round the headlands of China; partly because of the busy ebb and flow of countless vessels in and out of the harbour; and certainly not least because of the natural tension that exists where two of the world's most enterprising races are crowded together in a small space, the one economically a hundred times better off than the other. In physical terms, the cheek-by-jowl existence of the British and the Hong Kong Chinese is striking: on the one hand, the seedy, high-rise huddles of the Chinese residential areas; on the other, the gold, silver and ivory office blocks that soar, smooth and serene, from the water's edge and proclaim that that is where the billions of dollars are. Not far from the cosy simplicity of the Luk Kwok and the clamour of Wan Chai, the sun washes over the sleek snouts of Porsches, Mercedes and pink and yellow Rolls Royces in the parking bays of the rich Europeans and Chinese who have created this extraordinary capitalist pimple, and maintained it on the lip of Communist China, and dries out the laundry that hangs like the banners of a rag-tag army from the overcrowded tenements of the poor.

Now I found an extra element of drama – and might it prove to be the ultimate drama for Hong Kong? The year 1997 was on everyone's lips – it had become an even more emotive date than George Orwell's 1984. That year the British lease on Hong Kong would run out and the Communist Chinese would move in. Some in Hong Kong prophesied catastrophe ahead; but there was every chance that it would not change. Mr Deng Xiao-ping had insisted that it was in China's interest for Hong Kong to remain after 1997 the same successfully commercial concern. Although reincorporated into Mother China, Hong Kong would be allowed to retain its peculiar characteristics – it would become a privileged region where capitalistic business practices and the democratic freedoms of speech, press and justice would be allowed to survive. The difference would be that the Chinese would control Hong Kong and the British would depart. With the British gone, Hong Kong as an international centre of commerce and finance would continue as usual. Mr Deng's vision of the future was in many ways reassuring.

Yet doubt and anxiety prevailed. They focused largely on the fact that in 1997 Mr Deng, now in his eighties, would certainly not be able to supervise these very reasonable plans for Hong Kong. New men would be in control in Peking. Who could say if they would honour the undertakings of Mr Deng? Many, possibly most, Chinese in Hong Kong were voluntary refugees from China. Such fugitives were still coming in. On a recent visit to Hong Kong I had spent much of one night with the boat patrols of the Royal Hong Kong Police, watching young Chinese constables fishing from the freezing waters of Deep Bay young men and women swimmers from mainland China, risking sharks and currents to escape. A quarter of all Hong Kong Chinese in their twenties, I was told then, had come over in the past few years. Countless Chinese had found compelling reasons to flee to Hong Kong at various times since the armies of Mao Tse-Tung drove Chiang Kai-shek's Nationalists out of China in 1947. How would they feel about 1997, the year in which they might imagine their past lives would catch up with them?

I suppose many Hong Kong Chinese will accept whatever comes, resigning themselves in fatalism. Many others had come not so much to escape *from* Communism as to escape *to* relative freedom and affluence. The loom of Hong Kong's neon lights must have signalled El Dorado to many yearning Chinese watchers of the night skies, and proved as irresistibly alluring as the lamps of the fishing boats that draw the sea creatures of Deep Bay into the nets. Some of these might not care much who ruled Hong Kong in the future, provided the bright lights kept shining; for many, no doubt, Hong Kong's affluence had proved cruelly elusive.

At any rate, I imagined that for every inhabitant of Hong Kong who accepted the inevitable with a gay laugh and a shrug of the shoulders there might be one bowed down by doubt. The trouble was that doubts about the character of Hong Kong after 1997 could not be allayed until 1997 came. For fifteen years everyone could only hope for the best. Yet the best depended above all on the survival of the international financiers' confidence in Hong Kong as a place for making money. Suppose, for example, that the Chinese officers of the Royal

Hong Kong Police, aware of the sharply declining mystique of British authority, got cold feet and decided that to continue to arrest Chinese criminals or political troublemakers in the name of Her Majesty Queen Elizabeth was no longer worth the risk of terrible retribution? Who would hold back the subsequent chaos from which foreign businessmen and financiers would flee as from the Black Death?

Perhaps such gloomy speculation was unnecessary. Yet the fact remained that there would be no escape from Hong Kong for most of those from among the five or six million Chinese who wished to leave before 1997. Very few of them were entitled to receive a British passport, the *sine qua non* of a new life in Britain. I telephoned a friend in the police force – Lim, a Chinese sergeant I had met on an earlier visit; I had kept up with him and his wife. I found this brave and honest man in a sorry psychological state. Chinese sergeants like Lim, who was far from rich, are the backbone of this police force, as good warrant officers and sergeants are the backbone of a good army; they are indispensable because they were born here, know Hong Kong life at first hand and at many levels – *are* Chinese, after all. Yet, although as colonial policemen they are in the service of Queen Elizabeth as much as any bobby on the Piccadilly beat, the Hong Kong Chinese policemen have no right to follow their British officers to London. They do not qualify for a British passport. They aren't wanted. In London, people had told me: 'Britain is too full of immigrants'; it was 'standing room only' already. Responsibility was shrugged off like that.

Strolling in his British uniform along the harbour front of Kennedy Town on Hong Kong Island, Lim said, 'All I have is a Hong Kong passport. I have no United Kingdom right, and no China right either.' He shrugged morosely. 'Of course, I don't want to go to China.'

'I know, Lim. You belong nowhere.'

What a grotesque situation, I thought. Here we were, walking among Chinese men and women of his race who seethed around speaking his own language. Abrupt Cantonese shouts mixed with the squealing of the fat pink pigs being winched off a junk in long baskets shaped like wicker tunnels. There were many junks here. They had Chinese registration papers from Canton, and their decks were piled with tubs of fish and bulbous jars of vinegar for sale in Hong Kong. They would go home to Canton presently.

How could people belong nowhere?

Escaping famine, war or an uncongenial regime is a life's occupation for hundreds of thousands – no, millions – of Asians. In 1997 – God willing – there would be no famine here, no war either. Yet there might well be violence – bloody settling of scores, perhaps. No one on earth could rule out the possibility of an economic collapse. No wonder a creeping apprehension was already permeating Hong Kong like a bone-chilling fog in anticipation of the end of British rule. It came to me: Supposing I were a Hong Kong Chinese wanting to take my family to the West and had no legal way of escape....

Lim smiled. 'Who knows? 1997 will arrive and nothing bad will happen. It could be different from – what we fear.' I could imagine the familiar mental picture he would not express in words: the panic of Vietnam in 1975, the shocking scenes in Saigon. The photographs had made a deep impression on people in Hong Kong. There was still a camp full of Boat People in Kowloon.

'Of course it will be all right,' I said. 'It will be, Lim.'

'It had better be,' I added – but I added it to myself. By 1997, Hong Kong's population could be six million or more. If only a fraction of that number tried to escape by boat, there would be a lot of bodies afloat on the indifferent waters of the South China Sea.

In a day or two, a telephone call from Angel Yip summoned me to collect a ticket and my passport, and I hurried to her office. Shanghai Hai Xing Shipping Company, the green and white ticket said, had given me Berth No.2, Cabin No.10. I handed over 626 Hong Kong dollars, and warmly thanked Miss Yip. 'My pleasure,' she said demurely.

The next day, the day before sailing, I returned to the Luk Kwok to find a note from the telephone operator: 'Mr Young. Miss Amgel [*sic*] she tel to you please take warm dresses because Shanghai it is 0° very cold.' What warm 'dresses' had I? One sweater, an anorak and a scarf: that seemed enough. I was wrong.

The weather had not improved; a sulky drizzle still fell with a sort of despairing persistence. But that green and white ticket lay on my bedside table like a light in a dark room. I could hardly wait for the rendezvous at Tai Kok Tsui Pier.

Meanwhile I threw myself onto my bed, piled pillows behind my head, and opened *Man's Fate* again. At the top of the first page I read: '21 March 1927. 12.30 a.m.'

Ah, here it was! –

'Should Chen try lifting up the mosquito net? Or should he strike through it? . . .'

At first I thought, with a spasm of premature despair, that the ferry was taking me and what seemed like three hundred Chinese passengers to the wrong ship. Or maybe I had boarded the wrong ferry. A fine start for a journey from China to the West of England.

On the Tai Kok Tsui Pier in Kowloon a long, dense queue of Chinese men and women and a good many small children and babies had waited from shortly after noon until three o'clock. Under spits of rain, they gathered round a small trolley from which a man served Coca-Cola and cans of Yeo's chrysanthemum tea, or crouched patiently near small piles of hand baggage and large pyramids of hi-fi and radio equipment in boxes marked Sanyo and Sony. I saw only one other *gweilo*, a whey-faced young woman who sat on her suitcase and stared expressionlessly at the ground in a manner which certainly didn't invite conversation.

Out in the harbour a ship lay at anchor with the sand-yellow funnel of China ringed with a red band and waving hold lines on it. She had a trim white hull, but I couldn't see her name; she lay not far from Stonecutters' Island, quite a distance away. A nice-looking ship, I thought, the *Shanghai*. A knot of anxious passengers ran off to investigate when they saw a ferrry leave our pier and head in the direction of the white hull, thinking we'd all been left behind, and men in uniforms told them to keep calm and go back and wait because the white ship was going to Amoy, not Shanghai.

Our ferry, once we were finally embarked, headed towards the very part of the shore of Hong Kong Island I had left that morning. There, nearer to Hong Kong than to Kowloon, we found the old *Shanghai*. I say 'old' because when our launch came close to I saw patches of rust on her green side, and the general shape of her showed that it was some time since she had left her builder's yard. She had a mildly knocked-about look that made her more interesting. Up a narrow metal gangway we slowly edged — slowly, because quite a few of the Chinese were feeble and elderly, and some of the younger ones with trendy helmet haircuts were pushy. Vociferous bottlenecks blocked the steps. The ship's young stewards and stewardesses in white jackets came down into the melee, took the arms of the old people, lugged up the awkward boxes of stereo and hi-fi equipment, and huge gleaming radios, and electric fans. It seemed that only I had neglected to bring a folding aluminium baggage trolley with little wheels. These were useless on the gangway — the little wheels caught dangerously on protruding bits of metal and looked like tipping several old ladies into the harbour.

As my foot met the deck, relief flowed through me like electricity. A middle-aged steward politely took my bag and my ticket and led me to a cabin nearby. A bunk, a couch, a desk and a chair, a cupboard, a shower — a good cabin, hospital-clean. I looked for the all-important reading light over the bed, and found one. The steward gave me a smile, showed me how to lock the door, handed me the key and a card. It said: 'Restaurant sitting. Meal times: breakfast a.m. 7.30. Luncheon 11.30. Dinner p.m. 6.00.'

Later, I wrote in my notebook:

The steward evidently speaks no English. He signals to me: 'More bags?' 'No more.' He points to a piece of paper on the desk: 'Afternoon tea has been cancelled,' and slips away. I wash, and find it's 4 p.m. I'm hungry, suddenly remembering I've had

nothing to eat since breakfast at the Luk Kwok. A final message from Angel Yip tells me to declare exactly the amount of money I have, and what I change in China, and what I take out. 'If there's a discrepancy,' she warns, 'they may think you are helping to provide funds for someone to escape from China.'

The deck shifts slightly under my feet. The skyline moves across my porthole. Hong Kong's skyscrapers, as lights in them come on, are like romantic castles. *Shanghai* drops her pilot back into his launch; a man in a blue suit and a tie and brown shoes. A scattering of islands. The water widens. Our bows begin to lift.... The SS *Shanghai* is alive. The adrenalin stirs....

Foraging for food, I meet an old man on the stairs. He has a pleasant, round nut face, grey hair smoothed back, and is carrying a bottle of Tsingtao beer. 'I take beer to loom. Velly good beer,' he says. He points upwards. 'Velly good beer upstairs. Beer, whisky, blandy. Velly good.' He is right. There is a good, long bar and a pleasant bar-girl.

When I ask for something to eat, she serves me a sort of sweet pastry and eggs hard-boiled in tea from an earthenware bowl. People cluster round to explain with waving hands and even scribble on bits of paper napkin that the eggs are cooked in the tea for two or three hours and the tea turns their whites a darkish colour. They are very hot and taste of – eggs soaked in tea. You eat them cupped in a paper napkin. Stewards wheel crates of Black Label whisky and Martell VSOP into the spotless bar and arrange the black and gold bottles on the shelves under the eager gaze of Chinese passengers who nod to each other in appreciative anticipation of the heavy duty-free drinking to come.

The lounge next door, like the bar and my cabin, is austere and spotless. It has tall rectangular windows and pink plastic flowers in plastic vases on formica tables. Posters advertise 'Sprouting Tea Bags' and 'Chinese Feather and Down Products'. In a corner stands a Vita juice vending machine. Passengers take turns to fiddle with a television set that, despite them, continues to bellow like a monster in pain.

A poem is fixed to the wall over the TV set. I sit at a table and copy it – with great difficulty because my view is continually blocked by passengers who stand in front of me discussing what I am doing. It looks like an awkward translation from the Chinese, but I get it all down at last:

The Red Army fears
Not the trials of the Long March,
Holding light ten thousand crags and the torrents,
The five ridges like gentle ripples.
And the majestic rivers roll by globules of clay.
Warm the steep cliffs lapped by the waters of golden sand,
Cold the iron chains spanning the Tatu River,
Minshan's thousand li of snow joyously crossed
The three armies march on, each face glowing.

The ship was quite full but certainly not overcrowded. Most passengers were well dressed and cheerful, obviously looking forward to the New Year holiday and the waiting friends and relatives in Shanghai. They grinned at me and nodded their heads. It seemed that white passengers were not a common sight. Two young men, who had watched me copying down the lines in praise of the Red Army, waved and came over smiling – 'Oh-oh, oh-ho,' they said. 'Hell-o!' We might have been old friends meeting again after a year or two. One was short, round-faced, with hair cut relatively short – short, certainly compared with his companion, a handsome man whose hair fell, long and glossy, almost to his shoulders. Both wore well-scrubbed jeans and basketball shoes. They jerked my hand up and down with enthusiasm. The shorter one spoke English.

'So Wei Kuen,' he said, introducing himself. 'And this is my friend, Yeong Su Tse. Better you call him Ah Po. Ah Po means Little Treasure. He cannot speak English.'

'Ah-ha! Hee!' Ah Po said. When he laughed he showed good teeth and his eyes half disappeared, like gun muzzles in very narrow weapon slits.

Wei Kuen explained that Ah Po came from Nanking, and couldn't even speak Cantonese very well. His own family originally came from Canton, but he could cope, he said, with the Shanghainese dialect of Ah Po. He had been a merchant seaman for several years – that explained his English. I offered them a beer or tea, but they wouldn't hear of it, insisting that they should order and pay for beer; when it came they impatiently waved my money away. They both lived in Kowloon, Wei Kuen said. He himself was an orphan and had a job with Esso, delivering fuel oil to clients in the surrounding areas. Ah Po, whose widowed mother lived in Hong Kong too, worked in the Kowloon 7-Up bottling factory. Both were married – and here lay a strange twist in their circumstances. They had both married girls in Shanghai, and both wives were still living there with their parents. Yet the two husbands lived and worked in faraway Hong Kong? Yes, said Wei Kuen, this was not unusual. Every Chinese New Year they were reunited with their wives in Shanghai. They had been married two years. Maybe this year – they hoped so – the Chinese authorities would allow their wives to join them in Hong Kong. Bureaucracy. Permits. It just took a little time.

'You see your wives only once a year?' I was incredulous.

'Only.' Wei Kuen found my astonishment amusing. 'Not so bad. They will come to Hong Kong soon.'

As Wei Kuen talked, Ah Po's large, dark eyes widened or narrowed, flashing intermittent warmth and good humour like sunlight moving in and out of light cloud. His skin was unusually white, setting off the blackness of the long hair that fell in a heavy lock over the left side of his forehead, and on both sides framed his high cheekbones. His lips were wide and mobile, always poised on the brink of an uninhibited smile. His lack of English worried him, and he soon fell into a habit of giving me an impulsive thumbs-up sign and nodding vigorously, as if, in default of words, to assure me of his sincere friendship. I found this touching. Ah Po was clearly in the grip of irrepressible goodwill.

We went to the dining room together for the first meal aboard. The room ran the whole width of the ship. Its furnishings were utilitarian, uninspiring but inoffensive. Friends of Ah Po and Wei Kuen waved from a corner table, and we joined them; two women, a baby, and a skinny man with sagging cheeks and a brandy flush. The baby was blowing bubbles. The red-faced man filled three wineglasses from a bottle of Courvoisier brandy and offered one to me and the other to Wei Kuen. Ah Po pointed to his white cheeks and said something in Chinese. Everyone made tut-tut noises and looked concerned.

'Ah Po's skin cannot take brandy,' explained Wei Kuen. 'The pig – ah –'

'Oh, the pigmentation.'

'Pig-ment-tation, yes. Cannot take brandy, cannot take beer.'

Ah Po nodded several times and beamed at me. He must have understood something because his finger made a circle before his face and he said earnestly, 'Blandy, no good.'

Wei Kuen and I toasted our host and he refilled our glasses. There were several toasts, I remember; I didn't try to count them. The

Courvoisier bottle seemed inexhaustible, like the goblet in the Norse legend. The women smiled encouragingly at me as you do to a small child at an adults' party. At last an elderly waiter, like a kind uncle, brought a menu. Under the Chinese version I read:

Choose Two –
1. Diced Chicken with Tomato Sauce and Mushrooms,
2. Three-Colour Shrimps,
3. Shredded Pork with Fish Taste,
4. Jelly Fish.

I chose numbers 1 and 3. When the food arrived it was bland and tepid, with no chilli to enliven it. Wei Kuen and Ah Po didn't seem to care for the food either. They ate slowly, looking around at other tables as if they hoped to see better dishes there.

After dinner, pandemonium. An ear-shattering sound came from the lounge like that of strong men hammering a marble floor into dust. The evening mah-jong session had started. Old men, old women, with furious faces, slammed their pieces down on the table with what seemed an almost venomous delight. They might, Wei Kuen said, continue to do so till dawn.

We said goodnight and I went out on deck. To port, there were no lights to be seen. Either we had veered away from China or the coastline here was devoid of habitation. The rain had stopped. The sky now was a dark, starry blue with misty patches of near-white near the horizon – perhaps the moon was coming up. Faint music seemed to come from the sea. In reality it came from a speaker over the deck. A Viennese waltz twirled to an end, and was replaced by a genteel female soprano quavering, 'Come! Come! I love you o-onlee....'

I went to my cabin, undressed, and took up *Man's Fate* again.

The Communist workers' rising against the warlords and the subsequent near-destruction of the Communists by Chiang Kai-shek is the setting of Malraux's story of man's inhumanity. The revolutionary Chen was himself messily obliterated as he tried to blow up General Chiang's car in the Avenue des Deux Républiques. The warlords' gun dealer he had murdered was awaiting delivery of three hundred imported carbines from a government ship in the river – weapons the Communists needed for the rising in Shanghai they had planned for next day. They could only get their hands on the carbines with the delivery order Chen had found under the dead man's pillow.

17

Shanghai was threatened from without and within. Chiang Kai-shek's army was around the city; his unnatural allies, the Communists, were a Trojan horse within it – an unseen, organized host of workers waiting in the 'great tattered flank of the town'.

> The scrabbling of the myriads for their daily bread was giving place to another, a more vital energy. The Concessions, the rich quarters of the town, where the Europeans and Americans lived with their servants and cars and cocktails and guards, no longer existed as a menace; but in these nauseous slums, which provided the largest muster of Shock Troops, throbbed the pulse of a vast and vigilant horde.... Those crumbling walls hid half a million men; hands from the spinning-mills, men who had worked sixteen hours a day from early childhood, ulcerous, twisted, famine-stricken....

I read on and on. The staccato clatter of the mah-jong pieces in the *Shanghai*'s lounge, harsh and faint like distant gunfire, made an appropriate accompaniment to Malraux's account of how the revolutionaries slaughtered the occupants of Shanghai's main police station.

Sunlight. Too late for the 7.30 breakfast. I dressed and went down to look for more tea-boiled eggs in the earthenware bowl in the bar. The barman suggested a Black Label but I stuck to the eggs and green tea. A young Chinese couple were already at the whisky: newly-weds, by the look of their smart new clothes. The musak had changed from Strauss to a Chinese girl singer accompanied by harps. Behind the funnel a small, nut-brown man sat in a deckchair. When I said, 'Good morning,' he replied, 'Hi! Is this your first time in China?' Indicating a second chair, he held out his hand. 'My name is Thomas Dor. Tom.' He was small, bespectacled, with a creased, good-natured face, in his late fifties. 'That's my English name, of course. I won't bother you with my Chinese one, unless you're particularly anxious to know it.' He had an honest, friendly laugh.

Tom Dor taught engineering in Hong Kong, but he still had a room, a toehold, in the house he had once owned in Shanghai and he went back to it every Chinese New Year. The house had been confiscated by the Communists and eventually he had fled Shanghai for Hong Kong to escape from the terrible hardships between 1966 and 1972 during the Cultural Revolution in China.

'It's a good two-storey Shanghai house. The Communists left me two rooms for myself and my mother. They ransacked all my things, and took away eight cartloads of my beloved books. Books! None of them were political. That was the worst thing to take.' He shook his head, still smiling. 'They hated intellectuals. They just hated a mere *sign* of intellect. Books were a sign.' He had graduated in mechanical engineering and had had a high post in the maintenance department of a textile factory. 'The Communists have the factory now, of course.'

The sun came round the funnel and warmed us.

'You had a bad time, then, in the Cultural Revolution?'

Thomas Dor smiled in a self-deprecating way. 'I was horsewhipped. They horsewhipped me in front of the whole factory. They pushed a microphone into my hand and shouted, "Confess!"' He shrugged in his deckchair. '"Confess!" I said. "Confess what? I haven't killed anyone." What I didn't do, I didn't tell them to go to hell, and shout at them, "You're the killers. You're the guilty ones!"' He looked at me vaguely, reliving the scene in his mind's eye. 'I'm not a goddam hero. One thousand and two hundred men with one yelling ringleader on one side – and on the other – me!'

'Might they have killed you?'

'No, I guess not. That would have spoiled their fun. Well, they *did* kill people. Old men with high blood pressure died. They died instantly.' Dor didn't look very strong now, and he couldn't have been strong then.

'After the whipping what happened to you?'

'After the whipping, they just made a slave of me for six years. All the dirtiest jobs. Cleaning the toilets, that sort of thing.'

'Did you ever meet any of your persecutors when it was all over?'

Dor beamed at me over his spectacle rims. 'I met them, you bet! I got back *some* of the things they had ransacked, although, as we say in China, they took a cow and gave me back a mouse. I gave a dinner and invited them. One of the worst, one who had horsewhipped me, was my guest of honour. Oh, yes, indeed! I stood him a dinner!'

'Did he apologise?'

'No. He never said sorry. He wanted to, but he couldn't face it. He was a young man, twenty-five, twenty-six.'

This surprised me. But I know now that Thomas Dor is not a man who needs apologies or cherishes resentment. The dinner had been a sort of pardon.

'You may not like talking about it?'

'No, I don't mind.'

'Let me get you a drink.'

'It's quite hot here in the sun, isn't it?'

In the bar, Thomas Dor insisted on ordering: a beer for me, tea for himself. The clash of mah-jong pieces drifted from the lounge. 'Chinese people absolutely cannot live without mah-jong, I guess,' said Dor.

When the drinks came, he said, 'In those bad days, a lot of people in Shanghai preferred to be in jail. They felt safer there. Outside you could be beaten up, whipped in the street. I used to go home and lock myself in my room. With the two books left me, I'd found paradise in my own little nest.' He began to sing '. . . and let the rest of the world go by!' He laughed loudly. 'Know the song? My accent. How is it? Good?'

'Good, yes. American.'

'Well, how did I get it? Not from books, because they have no intonation.'

'Radio? No — movies.'

'Yes, at first I saw many, many movies from Hollywood. But after the Communists came — no more movies. So then the Voice of America broadcasts. And — just think — it was a criminal offence to listen to them! Yet I learned. How about that!'

The influence of the 1940s movies had survived the Voice of America. I had noticed that his conversation was sprinkled with phrases like 'I guess' and 'So what?' and anachronistic Americanisms I associated with Edward G. Robinson and James Cagney, expressions like 'No dice'. Pleasantly nostalgic, they took me back to fleapit cinemas of my own youth. It was like meeting a man in a grey fedora with spats and a cane, or hearing a recording of the Andrews Sisters or Rudy Vallee. But while the matter of *how* he spoke was of course trivial, Thomas Dor's daring, clandestine persistence with the Voice of America had shown real courage.

'You speak it excellently,' I assured him. 'No foolin'.' And he laughed, gratified. When I asked him for more reminiscences, he was pleased to continue, once he was sure I would not be bored. After Mao's death and the arrest of the Gang of Four, the Communists had looked at him differently. They had needed intellectuals, and found from his dossier that he was a university graduate. 'But, gee whiz,' he said, 'I had no ambition left by then. The best thirty years of my life were gone. I had been a happy-go-lucky young man. And, well, I had become . . . old.' He wiped his face with his hand, and for the first time I saw Thomas Dor downcast, almost in tears.

Was he a Catholic or – ? He fanned away the question with a hand. 'No, I ain't no Catholic; I ain't no Protestant; and I ain't no Buddhist. Pity. It would have helped me.'

Investigating the ship, I found a bulkhead plaque that said, 'S.M. Cockerell-Ougree – Chantier Naval, Hoboken, Belgique, 1957'. The Belgian Congo became independent in 1960, so the *Shanghai* had had no more than three years on that run. Most of the books and magazines in her library were in Chinese, but not all. There were books in English by, and about, the Chinese writer Lu Hsun, who had been called 'China's Gorki' – *Dawn Blossoms Plucked at Dusk, Brief History of Chinese Fiction,* and *The Opium War. Reader's Digest* lay on a table and a copy of *Newsweek* with a cover story about Sadat's murder. There were several leaflets, and photo-magazines with articles and pictures about the breeding of storks. Younger passengers tucked their feet under them on the cushions; older people simply slept in the comfortable armchairs.

The *Shanghai* – I realize it now – was the only vessel of all those on which I sailed round the world whose deck officers remained wholly invisible. No officers appeared for meals in the dining room. Looking up at the bridge from the foredeck, I could glimpse no face at the windows, nobody on the wing taking a sighting. Glass and metal stared inscrutably back. It was disconcerting. Perhaps if I had asked, I might have been allowed to have a look round. The purser, available each day in his office, was friendly, and once or twice he asked if I was comfortable. Near his office an advertisement showed concern for health. 'Rare Medicinal Herbs, Antler (of Young Stag), Nutriments and Tonics, Etc., for your good Health and Longevity'.

I had expected to find political slogans scattered around the ship, but there were very few. The dining room had one: 'Long Live the Great Unity of the People of the World', but the only other sign in the room said, 'Cockatoo Brand Woollen Piece Goods – Elegant Appeal'.

The *Shanghai* was a smoothly run ship. Yet there were times when it seemed that hijackers might have been fighting to board her. Night and day the mah-jong schools filled the lounge with the sounds of musketry on a nineteenth-century battlefield. 'Tak-tak... crack...bbrrak...tak.' Elsewhere young Chinese milled round the electronic games room, barking ferociously like extra-terrestrial invaders on the Star War-path. Tracing a different hubbub to its source on the promenade deck, I discovered Wei Kuen and Ah Po, in shorts and T-shirts, partnering two girls at ping-pong, battering the ball back and forth with wild inaccuracy.

In the dining room I was conscious of many passengers watching me, furtively but certainly without malevolence. When they saw me using chopsticks, they nodded and smiled. Even the ship's chefs showed an interest in me; inquisitive faces under tall white hats peered at me round the kitchen door and they, too, nodded and smiled when our eyes met.

In the bar, after dinner, when Black Label scotch came neat in a wineglass, I described a bigger glass with my hands and a young waiter ran for a tumbler. When I asked for ice and water a young Chinese waitress came with them, giggling, and together they chorused like kindly teachers to a backward pupil, '*Ping* – ice: *Soe* – water. *Ping*...*Soe*.' They led me up and down the bar, pointing and instructing. Telephone in Chinese was such-and-such; the Norris glass-washing machine was something else; a bar stool was *this*; the plastic flowers were *that*. We reviewed the array of bottles like generals inspecting troops – Beehive brandy, Tunghua wine, Tazhi Bailandi (brandy, that), Rémy Martin, Kaesong Konyo Insan wine.

Later that night an unusually swollen moon lay on the horizon. From the boat deck I saw, silhouetted against its wide, glimmering trail, two of the *Shanghai*'s crew exercising in the grave Chinese manner – coiling and uncoiling apparently boneless limbs in slow, soundless motion. I leaned on the rail for some time, watching these dark, silent figures at their martial shadow play.

Then I went below to the improvized disco in the ballroom and watched Wei Kuen and Ah Po, trying, as far as inexperience and crippling gusts of hilarity would allow, to teach their girlfriends the Twist.

Three

By the time we saw land, the seasons had changed. A wintry wind was whipping up the shallower coastal sea to the colour of *café au lait*. I would soon need a thick sweater – or a Chinese quilted coat. In the lounge, too, the season had changed. No more T-shirts and shorts. The women had pulled on cashmere sweaters and trousers, or jeans and Chinese jackets. Men wore the padded, baggy Chinese coats with bulging pockets, wide trousers and carpet slippers. Inflated by the extra clothing, old men wandered impatiently about, hands clasped behind their backs, their heads thrust forward, like inquisitive turtles. They talked in staccato barks.

The Chinese mainland appeared, bruise-black mountains against the darker sky. I saw what looked like a strip of beach or a sandbar and a few trawlers motionless in front of it. It was my first sight of China since my river trip to Canton two years before, and I was registering it in my notebook when I was startled by a putty-faced young white man with faded blond hair tied in a bun, who poked a sharp nose over my shoulder and said in an American accent, 'You keeping notes?' It was the first time I had seen him. He looked like an underfed governess.

'Yes,' I said.

From the sort of tasselled leather handbag that costs a few rupees in Pakistan and very much more in boutiques in London, Paris or New York, he drew a large notebook. 'I worry about my notes,' he informed me, showing me pages of very cluttered writing in an illegibly small hand.

'People have told me that the Chinese customs officers read foreigners' notes, and if they don't like 'em, they keep 'em.'

I said I doubted it. In any case, if they could read my writing they'd be lucky. That went double for his, I thought.

'I've written mine in Latin,' he said. 'That should fox 'em.'

I suggested that it might make the customs men very suspicious indeed – and infuriate them as well. They might confiscate the lot just to be on the safe side. 'Oh, my gosh.' He stared at me. 'I'd never thought of that.'

'It won't happen,' I said, soothingly.

Later I saw him in the ship's shop, where the Chinese passengers were doing the last of their New Year's shopping: silk ties, girls' cotton slips, Rowntree's fruit gums, shoelaces, soap.

'What's this?' the American was asking, holding up a small bottle.

'Dried plums,' the shopgirl said.

Before I left he had bought a glass jar with something in it that looked more like a marinated centipede.

Soon the mouth of the Yangtze River met the Huangpu in a great brown stain. Water thick with silt spurted up when I flushed the toilet in my cabin.

There were bundles and suitcases all over the decks. Passengers zipped up their jackets and wound scarves round their necks. Some, like Thomas Dor, had woolly hats with earflaps. All I had was my old green anorak and a sweater, which I doubted seriously would be enough. That sad, end-of-term feeling enveloped me – my usual feeling when a ship reaches the end of voyage, however short.

The barmen and waitresses wanted me to sign their book. They meant the large suggestions pad hanging on a hook over the bar. I wrote my thanks (genuinely felt) for their friendly service, and Thomas Dor translated it for them into Mandarin or Shanghainese.

'I hope this will get you a reward,' I told them.

Big grins all round: 'Oh, no. It's duty. We are please. Bye-bye.'

My sad feeling was alleviated by Ah Po who bounded up to me as I followed Dor to the boat deck. He looked smartly athletic in a white woolly sweater and a baseball cap with the word 'Australia' and a kangaroo in silver thread stitched over the peak. What on earth, I wondered, would the Shanghainese make of that? Now Ah Po signalled urgently and tugged me quite roughly towards my cabin. Was there a fire? No. In the cabin he yanked a tin of jasmine tea from his windcheater pocket, thrust it into my hands, clamped his arms round my neck, kissed me hard on both cheeks – and vanished with a final thumbs-up gesture round the door. I recovered my breath and packed the tin of tea into my zip bag.

Shanghai! Past the dim outlines of islands to seaward, we turned up the Huangpu. Rows of ships moored on either side, chimneys, gantries, derricks, smoke mingling with a light drizzle: the smoke and soot of industrial China.

The first sight of the Shanghai Bund – the former European business section on the riverfront – thrilled me as I was thrilled by Paris and New York years ago. 'The living heart of China', Malraux called it, and the waterfront I gazed at now was something I had seen in my dreams and imagination for a very long time. Imagination had not lied. I had taken a step into the past. With its old-fashioned skyscrapers, its neo-Babylonian towers and pinnacles, the Shanghai exposed by the river was exactly the metropolis I had expected; a city of the 1920s, architecturally paralysed by circumstance. To approach it by sea was as unreal as approaching it in my dream. I thought: I have been here before. Thomas Dor stood by me, saying, 'British people coming back here after many years say, "Oh, everything is the same. Nothing's changed. No new buildings." A city with no change for thirty years, that's very rare in the world today.' A petrified city like this was not merely rare, but unique. Here, two eras impinged – Yesterday and Today swirled together as the muddy waters of the Yangtze and Huangpu commingled at the entrance to the East China Sea.

I consulted my guidebook. Shanghai (it said) is among the two or three largest cities in the world, supporting eleven million people and resembling New York or Rome more than it does Peking or Canton. The only 'Chinese' element in the view I saw now were the junks that spread their brown sails like motionless fans on the lighter surface of the Huangpu.

I could remember earlier images of Shanghai – gruesome images from old newsreels and photographs in the *Illustrated London News*: huddles of burnt bodies after the Japanese air raids in 1932; living soldiers used for bayonet practice; political prisoners, about to be buried alive, posing by their graves for tomorrow's papers; refugees dwarfed by columns of smoke. A city of tragedy and melodrama.

The piped musak was interrupted by a girl's voice telling us that the captain and crew wished us a happy stay in Shanghai. We glided alongside a quay, close to a long warehouse. Sailors threw ropes to each other. The gangway went down.

'I'll come and see you at the Peace Hotel,' said Thomas Dor. 'Some time this afternoon. Say, 12.30 or 1 p.m. You're sure to be in that hotel. If not, I shall find you in another. There aren't too many.'

'I don't want you to waste your holiday time looking for me.' I hoped he would come.

'Oh, I will come.'

A jostling began around the tables in the lounge where immigration and customs men were examining passports and asking about currency. But there was no delay. I was soon free to go. Wei Kuen and Ah Po were in the queue. When I went to say goodbye Wei Kuen said, 'We will come to your hotel. Tomorrow.' Ah Po nodded his head until I thought he would shake loose the kangaroo on his cap.

I said, 'I hope so,' but I doubted that I would see them again; not here. They had given me their Hong Kong addresses, but I was sure they'd be too busy with their families in Shanghai to bother about me. In any case, I suspected that their in-laws, waiting for official sanction to leave China, would advise them against contact with a foreigner. Might they not be pointlessly drawing suspicion down on themselves? Or was I now the victim of paranoia?

'We will come,' said Wei Kuen.

We shall see, I thought.

I was met – though gathered up would be a better expression. Not only did a trim young man appear promptly at the dock gate, asking 'Mr Gavin?' but he had a car and a driver with him. Angel Yip had scored again. Mr Shi Zhi Wei of the China International Travel Service – he introduced himself with a smile and a handshake – wore a Mao suit and a long, wide, maroon scarf. 'My wife knitted it,' he said when I admired it. He was positively elegant, his suit distinctly stylish, tailor-made, I was pretty sure, in a soft, dark blue material, not just any old official uniform grabbed off a peg in a people's store. It fitted his slim and willowy figure to perfection; above it a pleasant, intelligent face, pale and heart-shaped with a quite large, curved nose, was lively and benign. His Chinese black hair was thick and wavy on top of his head and long over his ears. There was something rather aristocratic about him, as if he had been born the son of a mandarin. Now he asked me with the greatest politeness to wait a moment while he made some arrangement with the customs men – nothing to do with me, some unfinished business. I watched him move among the piles of baggage swiftly and nimbly, and saw that when he talked with the customs officers he fluttered his hands in graceful gestures. I waited by the car while a pressing crowd of men and women gathered closely round, silently appraising me. I might have been a giraffe that had been decanted from the ship onto the quay. I was certainly quite a bit taller than the tallest man there.

'This is our driver, Mr Jang,' said Shi, coming up. I shook hands with the driver, a stocky man of Shi's age, I guessed – about twenty-nine – in a brown zip-up jacket and dark blue trousers, with the top of a grey scarf showing over his collar. 'His name is Yu-long. That means Jade Dragon.'

I asked him what his own name meant.

'Stone of Wisdom,' he said, and laughed. 'We shall go to the Peace Hotel now. That is where you will stay. It is a good hotel with a very good view over the city and over the river.' His English was fluent and accurate; there would be no language problem between us.

The Peace Hotel on the Bund was the one Thomas Dor had named – it had been the Cathay in the old days – and on the river was where I wanted to be. On the Bund! – the Bund was the place for me. We pushed through the hotel's vast, high-ceilinged hallway, full of shopping counters and salesgirls, to the reception desk. We ascended in an antique lift and followed a porter into a seventh-floor room whose tall windows looked onto the Huangpu. I had not been allotted a broom cupboard. The immense room had black and gold William Morris-style wallpaper, romantic panelling (were there secret panels?), a 12-foot-high moulded ceiling and a ponderous baronial fireplace the colour of mahogany – perhaps it *was* mahogany. It was like a film set for a 1930s movie called, maybe, *Rendezvous Shanghai*, and starring Clark Gable and Carole Lombard. I wondered what Wei Kuen and Ah Po would make of it.

The thing now was to see what was possible and what was not. After all, I had not come to explore China, much though I would like to do so (but that would take several years and a course in Mandarin). I had to ask Mr Shi whether or not I could find another ship to take me to Tsingtao and Dairen. Or to Japan. The answer was short and simple. It was not possible to do that now, he said. There were ships plying between Shanghai and northern ports, and it should be possible to get on them – but only when dates and schedules had been planned in advance. Plans could not be made on the spur of the moment, Mr Shi said. The CITS was not yet geared to handle a sudden whim. If I had made an arrangement, in Hong Kong, to get off the *Shanghai* here, then to catch whatever steamer would take me to some place up the coast, he thought it could have been manageable. He thought so.... 'What a pity,' he said.

So one thing was clear. I could not go on from here in any direction except back – to Hong Kong, and by air. Miss Yip had warned me that I must have a confirmed ticket out of China and I had a place on a flight in four days' time. Mr Shi was consoling: Next year or the year after, he said, many more things would be possible. Meanwhile, he had one or two things to suggest. Would I like to see a commune? And the Garden of the Mandarin Yu? The Jade Buddha Temple? The Shanghai Industrial Exhibition? A factory? The zoo?

I hesitated. Was it *de rigueur* to see a commune or a factory? I've looked at factories in many countries, always with a barely tolerable feeling of bone-aching boredom. I don't understand factories; they all look the same. 'The guide may want you to see a factory,' Thomas Dor had said. 'Just say you've seen many factories.'

I said tentatively to Mr Shi, 'I've seen a great many factories....'

'I didn't think you'd be interested,' he said with a smile. 'You don't have to see one. Or even a commune, if you prefer to miss that out.'

'Then let's see the rest.' I like gardens and zoos. But I thought of Tom Dor and Wei Kuen and Ah Po. Supposing they did come for me, I needed time to see them. And was I going to be allowed to go out with them – outside the confines of an official itinerary? I needn't have worried. To my relief, Mr Shi pooh-poohed any thought of a problem there. 'If your friends come for you, make any arrangement you like. You can use the car.'

In the next few days we did visit all the other places Mr Shi had suggested, with the exception of the zoo. Under grey skies we shuffled about the Garden of the Mandarin Yu in a crowd of padded coats; over bridges spanning ornamental ponds; in and out of red and gold throne rooms and dragon-filled bedrooms in old buildings with winged roofs that might have been reconstructions from the Willow Pattern. There were no padded coats at the Jade Buddha Temple, where Shi had to find an old guardian to unlock the doors. By the time Mr Shi proposed a visit to the zoo, the conviction that not to have a padded coat in Shanghai's wintertime would lead to ice clots in the blood had taken unshakeable root in my mind. Although there was no snow, the wind

howled up the Huangpu and gripped me agonizingly, like the icy hand of the Snow Queen herself. I come from the Atlantic side of England and people there think the winters are cold, but I was not prepared for this and it was too much. So we skipped the zoo – luckily I had seen pandas before, in Canton – and instead paid a visit to the house in which the Communists held their first National Congress in July 1921. It was then a private house, explained Mr Shi, in what was at that time the French Concession. Thirteen Chinese had attended, two Russians representing Lenin, and a Dutchman. It was a pleasant room with whitewashed walls and a wooden floor and ceiling; at the back a staircase led away from it. Old photographs hung on the walls like ikons: groups of young men, now world-famous, looked down at us dressed more like bank clerks than violent revolutionaries – Chou En-Lai and Deng Xiao-ping, nattily dressed in drainpipe trousers, ankle bootees, ties, high white collars and white hats. Next to a framed page of the *Journal of the Young China Association* were pictures of a general strike, with soldiers in a tram-lined street between shuttered shops.

Mr Shi pointed to Chinese characters on the wall. 'It says, "To start something is very easy,"' he translated, '"but to finish it is difficult."' I couldn't argue with that. After a pause he added, 'The Communist Party of China has 39 million members.' There was no boasting in his voice, and I don't know why it seemed unacceptably personal to ask if he was one of them. Presumably, if Shi had been a member of the Communist Party, he would have been proud and quick to tell me. For now, it didn't seem to matter.

I found a note from Thomas Dor in the hotel saying he had been round there and found me out ('Looking at a factory?' the note asked) and that he would call again next morning. In the immense lobby, a middle-aged American was saying to his Chinese guide in unnecessarily loud, aggrieved tones, 'Mr Chong, why didn't you *tell* me those stamps I bought had no glue on them? I tried to stick them on the envelopes, I licked them, and they had no glue.'

Mr Chong's face registered nothing one way or another. He only said, 'The letter office puts glue on the stamps.'

'Yes, but look here, how could I *know* that? You didn't tell me.'

I went to the counter selling stamps and bought a set. When I returned, the American was still at it.

'Now, the stamps just fell off. Why didn't you *tell* me they had no glue on them...?' Would Mr Chong fell him with a karate chop? I didn't wait to see.

From my bedroom window I looked at the Huangpu. Strings of barges meandered upstream like slow-worms, ten in line behind their tugs. The light green of the *Shanghai*'s hull lay alongside down to the left with several smaller steamers. Four-tiered ferries honked up and down like agitated geese, and a junk passed slowly before the Peace

Hotel, one large sail and two small ones fore and aft, looking like a Chinese character in broad umber brushstrokes. Beyond the light brown water, the far bank of the Huangpu was a busy industrial wasteland — a flat expanse of jetties, cranes, slate roofs and cement factory walls. Big ports are exciting, particularly if they are old and look it. A port like Shanghai has seen many things: it is venerable, businesslike, quivering with life. It is of an ugliness, as Conrad put it, so picturesque as to delight the eye. The bending river, the water traffic creeping or darting against the background of funnels, masts and sails, wharves and chimneys, stirred me as much as the water scenes of Bangkok, of Hong Kong, of the Bosphorus at Istanbul or the Hooghli at Calcutta. In those precise, rather grimy, places, Past visibly melds with Present, and East with West. In the grime of Shanghai, too, I was aware how close past success and suffering lie alongside the self-absorbed vigour of today. It would be satisfying to carry home a bottle of such a blend and pour it out like a fine wine for discriminating friends. Taste that, one would say — it's Life.

Four

As evening fell, a few weak lamps went on among the leafless trees along the Bund. Crowded trolley buses, bicycles and hundreds of pedestrians in blue caps and uniforms surged through the pale, cold light of sunset; across the river the white and blue flashes of the welders' torches grew fewer and died out. The hubbub of sirens gave way to the sad, intermittent goose calls of the night ferries. The great strident loudspeakered voices on the river passenger boats – voices that boomed and rasped over the water as if the gods of the Huangpu were engaged in furious public debate – they, too, had called it a day.

I sat down in a deep armchair, happier than I had been for months. I had come looking for timelessness, and I had found it here under the William Morris wallpaper and the dark, romantic panelling. Above me, the white plaster moulding on the ceiling looked – of all things – Arthurian: sword belts and bucklers, shields with metallic-looking protuberances like studs, breastplates with chrysanthemum-headed nipples. How could I have expected to find Camelot in China?

The guidebook said:

In 1842, near the end of the Opium War, Shanghai's garrison surrendered to the British fleet. From that point on until 1949 the city developed largely as an enclave for Western commercial interests in China.... Residents of these infamous 'international concessions' were exempt from the laws of China. Numerous traders and speculators – French, US and Japanese – joined the British. By 1936, the Western population of Shanghai numbered 60,000.

Shanghai in the twenties and thirties had been one of the world's most sophisticated, cosmopolitan cities. Hadn't I read that Noël Coward had written *Private Lives* here in four days? Some of its dialogue seemed curiously appropriate in a city once renowned for its White Russian exiles.

> *Amanda*: Is that the Grand Duchess Olga lying under the piano?
> *Elyot*: Yes.... Delightful parties Lady Bundle always gives, doesn't she?
> *Amanda*: Entrancing. Such a dear old lady.
> *Elyot*: And so gay: did you notice her at supper blowing all those shrimps through her ear trumpet?

Sophisticated, cosmopolitan – and wicked. Malraux's Baron Clappique – decadent, facetious, bitchy, a humpless Punchinello, dealer in secrets and antiques – I could imagine him to the life, trifling with the Filipino and White Russian hostesses in the Black Cat nightclub.

> 'Not a word! ... the awful thing, dear girl, is that there's no imagination left in the world.... A European statesman sends his wife a little parcel; she opens it – not a word! ...'
> The finger laid across his lips:
> '... and there's her lover's head inside. Still the subject of conversation three years later.... A shocking business, dear girl! ...'
> Forceful:
> 'Waiter: Champagne for these two ladies, and for me ... a s-small Martini....'
> Severely:
> '... very dry.'

Shanghai, 1927: *Private Lives*, Dry Martinis – and severed heads. In 1927, the severed heads were Communist heads and swung in cages from telegraph poles. Their blind eyes gazed across at the luxurious quarters of European businessmen, at the studio, for example, of Monsieur Ferral, in *Man's Fate* the French president of the Chamber of International Commerce. It was a modern one, for Shanghai 1927. On the walls, some Picassos of the rose period, and an erotic drawing by Fragonard; a huge black Kwannyn of the Tang Dynasty (bought on the advice of Clappique, and probably a fake).

It was thrilling to be in that hotel room in Shanghai – to feel the city's grotesque past, to imagine Clappique and Ferral were in the bar downstairs. The bar too might have been a film set – it had soaring pillars, bottles, old-fashioned cocktail shakers, a polished walnut counter, a nickel bar rail. The middle-aged Chinese barman murmured: 'Gin-tonic?'

'Do you have a Shanghai Cocktail?'

'Shanghai Cocktail?' He seemed pleased I'd asked. 'Have!' he said, with satisfaction. He took a half-pint tumbler and sloshed into it what looked like equal measures of Chinese gin and chilled Chinese dry white wine. He stirred this briskly and then with smooth precision poured it neatly into a 1930s cocktail glass, triangular with a long stem. The drink was a pale straw colour, and cold enough to frost the glass. It tasted dry and innocuous. I put it back and had another.

'This bar is new?'

'No, not new,' the barman answered me, 'reopened one year. Cultural Revolution close it.'

I emptied my glass again.

He suggested a Panda Cocktail.

'A what?'

'Very nice cocktail from Shanghai.'

'As long as I can walk out of here,' I said.

He laughed, pleased to demonstrate. 'Not too strong. Take *mao tai* – Chinese rice liquor – half of one egg, and sugar.' He stirred all these things in a shaker. *Mao tai* is strong, like Polish vodka but sweeter. He added white wine, too, and a little finger of Parfait Amour. Too sickly, but I swigged it down to please him.

Mr Shi had left me. In the evening, he had said with a man-of-the-world smile, he had to think of his wife, and I did not detain him. I dined alone in a top-floor dining room full of golden dragons, and came down to the bar for a last beer. In a room next to the bar a handful of elderly Chinese musicians were playing on dented instruments the dance music of five decades ago. They played rustily but with gusto, and a group of dancers slow-foxtrotted sedately on a small dance floor. 'As Time Goes By' filled the room. How had the gleaming aluminium drums and brass cymbals survived the Cultural Revolution? Lovingly mothballed, under a bedroom floor? Perhaps only the triangle was left hanging provocatively over the washbowl: a daring snub to the Red Guards. You'd have to be quite old to remember the rumba in Shanghai, I thought, yet fat ladies and old gentlemen in Mao suits wiggled happily across the floor to 'South of the Border'. Young waiters tapped their feet to the paso dobles. Chinese girls danced with girlfriends or Japanese tourists, but they were not hostesses. They had obviously come in to practise the steps. This was an escape into nostalgia, not a time for flirtation. The waiter who brought my beer said, 'So happy.'

It *was* happy. I waited to the end, until the lights went down and 'Red Sails in the Sunset' drifted smoothly over the dancers, like the innocent memory of a distant era that had managed only here to survive.

Thomas Dor appeared next day; I was pleased to see his smiling walnut face. With Mr Shi and Jade Dragon the driver, we went to Dor's house. It seemed a long way away. Finally, in a ramshackle suburb, we walked in the cold down a lane between high walls to find ourselves in a small, bleak garden. Here was what had been his house. It was quite large, and had a neglected look.

'They took my father's furniture,' Thomas said, dimly. 'So what you see is odds and ends.' The rooms were adequately furnished – that was all you could say. Downstairs, young women stood about in white coats under charts of the human body on the walls. They looked at us and curtly nodded their heads. 'It's a government clinic for injection,' Dor said.

We stood in the wintry garden. Dor seemed smaller here, and sadder.

'Do you leave it empty?'

Yes, he had a nephew-in-law to look in now and again, clean it, and air it. 'I am lucky to have close relatives in the Housing Agency.'

Shi seemed to have no objection to Dor's temporarily taking over as my guide. When Dor mentioned once more his sufferings during the Cultural Revolution, Shi smiled sourly and made his own contribution. He had been ten years old at the time, he said. His mother, a teacher of the Chinese language, was beaten and forced to do 'dirty work'.

'Like me,' said Dor.

'Yes, like you.' Yet at least those who humiliated Shi's mother did say sorry later. '"It was orders," they said. "We'd have been beaten, too." That was their excuse.'

We walked back down the lane in silence.

Then again, in the official car, Past and Present wrapped us round. Thomas pointed out unchanged buildings he'd grown up with – Sassoon House, the King Kong ('Owned by Sassoon, too. Sassoon owned so much.'), the Shanghai Mansions, the old Grosvenor, Kiessling's Restaurant.

And when we went to lunch in the old restaurant of my hotel, he told me things about his father that surprised me.

'My father made a lot of money,' Thomas said. 'Smuggling.' He smiled. 'Smuggling arms, actually, through Shanghai to a warlord – a Mr Sun – in Hangchow. As a cover, he claimed to be the representative of IG Farben, the giant German arms manufacturer, but under that cover he really bought other arms. Mausers. German arms, but not Farben's.'

The klaxons and sirens rasped and whooped on the Huangpu. When the food came, Mr Shi, Thomas and I poked our chopsticks into the little dishes, aware of the encircling tables of foreign businessmen and representatives of Chinese trade agencies. In precisely such a setting as this, Dor Senior had discussed his clandestine consignments of machine guns and grenades to Mr Sun with ... surely not a Punchinello figure hissing – 'Not a word!'?

'At that time there were so many things to do under cover of the British or the French administration. Arms – and drugs. Opium, largely. In those days, opium houses were open to the public.'

I had read somewhere of one of the Al Capones of the Shanghai underworld – a notorious gangster called Tu Yueh-sheng, who dressed in silk and rode in limousines, and contributed his gunmen to Chiang Kai-shek's crackdown on the Communists in 1927. (Local American and European businessmen gave him armoured cars for the purpose.) Men like Tu provided millions of dollars each year to the French *propriétaires* – the Ferrals – of the Concession. All the rackets were here: protection ... kidnapping ... prostitution ... lotteries ... murder. And opium.

'"Swallows' nests,"' Dor said. 'That was the name we gave the opium houses. "Swallows' nests." It was comfortable there, you see, just like a nest.'

Shi and I sipped our Seagull beer and picked at crab in wine, and listened like two schoolboys at a history lecture. I wondered what Dor's father had looked like. To match this gentle, frail, honest Dor with a physically similar pre-war arms dealer was out of the question. But if he said his father smuggled arms, he had smuggled arms. Even then I realized Dor was a truthful man; I am more convinced of it all these months later. He himself could never be a racketeer. In him, as it does so often, innocence proclaimed itself.

A message came for Shi: wanted on the telephone. He excused himself. Dor went on: 'My father and mother – and so many others, of course – used to entertain guests with opium. Even after the Japanese, there were illegal swallows' nests until the Communists came in 1949.'

The party at the table next to ours began to break up. A big, red-faced European said, 'Thet vasn't bed, vaitress. You did zet kvite nicely.' Another man slapped a waiter on the arm – chummily – with a magazine. The waiter grinned and turned red. On a wall of the restaurant I read: 'Rules for Waiters – Polite Service, Smiling Face, Personal Hygiene, Good Attitude, Proper Posture, Enthusiastic Attention, Satisfactory Countenance, Warm Greetings.'

Dor said: 'When the Communists came in in 1949 – the day my ills began – the buses ran, I remember. Odd, but they ran. There wasn't much cheering. Disciplined troops. Until the Communists knew damn well what was going on in Shanghai there were few big arrests. Until 1951, I guess. Cabarets went on. Prostitution, even. I recall the buses going round the streets one night much later. Rounding up all the prostitutes, for rehabilitation!'

Rehabilitation: I remembered something. In Cuba in the early 1960s, Castro's guides took me to a camp in Camaguey to see how prostitutes, recently rounded up in Havana's red-light district, were undergoing 'rehabilitation'. Twenty buxom tarts sat in a classroom watching a young instructress chalking basic algebra on a blackboard. They had been fitted out in khaki fatigues that on their ample figures looked skin-tight, and the pants zipped up the back, starting at the waistband and curving provocatively down to disappear between the buttocks. What's more, they had been allowed to keep their make-up. The faces now turned in my direction from twenty desks were outrageously self-possessed. Exaggerated lips pursed into scarlet kisses. False eyelashes fluttered in a parody of seductiveness. I caught one or two long, deliberate winks. And then the whole class (with the exception of the teacher) burst out into good-natured laughter. Of course, that was Cuba. How the rehabilitation of prostitutes worked in China, heavens knows.

Wei Kuen and Ah Po had done as they promised. They and their wives and an in-law or two appeared one afternoon in the hotel lobby. I was standing at the reception desk when, to my delight, I heard a happy cacophony of chittering behind me. There was much smiling and embracing. Both families invited me to visit their homes. Ah Po's lived two or three miles down the riverbank; Wei Kuen's flat was in one of the most highly populated areas of central Shanghai. It was decided that

I should see Ah Po's first, the next day. A day or two later, Wei Kuen would come to the hotel to take me to his home. 'Very difficult to find,' he said.

Mr Shi raised no objection to this plan. In fact, he suggested I take the car to Ah Po's. He would come too.

Next morning we drove towards the sea through the industrial straggle of chimneys, power stations and silos that lines the north bank of the Huangpu. The road was bumpy with railway tracks running from dockside complexes to other parts of the city. In the end we reached a gate with a guard on it, who recognized Mr Shi's pass, and we drove into a deep, wide compound with trees and flowerbeds, and numerous three-storey houses of red brick grouped round an ugly red-brick church. There had been an American mission school here, Ah Po explained to Shi; now it was an engineering college. The mission's church was a store. Ah Po's wife, Ching Man, lived in a third-floor flat with her mother and father, both recently retired teachers, her sister and a brother. Ching Man was a tall girl, pretty and shy; she spoke very little Cantonese, and no English at all. This increased her shyness, and her shyness seemed to make her stooped. Her unmarried sister, even prettier, had the almost unnaturally healthy looks of girls on Chinese Government posters. She wanted nothing more, she said in weak English, than to go to Hong Kong. Mr Shi's expression remained one of cool benevolence.

The flat, not large, was bright – three rooms, I think, two or three people to each. The living room was stacked with Ah Po's New Year presents: hi-fi equipment, a television set, an electric mixing machine and a jumbo-sized thermos. I wished he had bought an electric heater.

His mother-in-law gave us all plates of sweet dumplings and cups of tea – and Ah Po's good news was revealed. Ching Man had been granted permission to leave Shanghai: she would join him in Hong Kong. The whole family was celebrating her good fortune. Even Mr Shi, eating his dumplings, looked as pleased as anyone else.

The hows and whys of permits to leave China are not easy to understand because they change so often. Ah Po's family, in China as fugitives from anti-Chinese riots in Indonesia, had been able to leave again as original expatriates.

Ah Po's mother-in-law said, 'Ah Po's family passed through Shanghai from Nanking to go to Hong Kong. So we arranged that Ah Po should come back, marry our daughter and take her to Hong Kong, too.'

I said, 'Ah Po, how good you are! You were doing a most charitable thing.'

Everyone laughed, and Ah Po patted his wife and giggled, 'I love, I love.'

In the afternoon, with Mr Shi and Thomas Dor, I crossed the Soochow Creek at the northern end of the Bund over a bridge near gardens where elderly men were concentrating on the slow-motion martial exercises I had seen the two crewmen practising on the stern of the SS *Shanghai*. The park had been exclusively European in the old days. The Soochow Creek had reeked of the hovels that lined it. We made our way towards the railway station at Chapei and, I forget why, to an austere building with tall windows looking down on a schoolyard. I think perhaps the building must have been a museum. What I know is that the schoolyard that Mr Shi pointed out had been the ante-chamber to a human abattoir. Here, the prototype of Malraux's revolutionary, Kyo, and the Russian agent, Katow – together with hundreds of other Communist prisoners – had had to wait in turn for their deaths in the Chapei goods yard nearby, to be thrown alive by Chiang's soldiers into the furnaces of the locomotives. Imagine lying prone on the floor of a schoolyard, and listening for the twin signals of the agonizing deaths of each of your comrades: the crack of his exploding skull, a single shriek of the locomotive's whistle. And then the bark: 'Next one – you!' I had read somewhere that human heads explode just like roasted chestnuts. Is there a worse death? The young prisoner next to Katow was sobbing, 'To be burnt alive! ... Even one's eyes.... Every finger and then one's stomach....' How could anyone's dignity as a human being survive a minute of such a situation? Mine might survive a second or two; no more.

Human dignity. Malraux's Kyo used the words to explain his presence in the ranks of the revolutionaries. Malraux's König, Chiang Kai-shek's police chief, bursts out:

'Dignity! In Siberia, I was taken by the Reds.... I had a lieutenant's star on each epaulette.... They drove a nail into each of my shoulders, through those stars. A nail as long as your finger.... I squealed like a woman, blubbered like a baby.... My friend, you would be well advised not to say too much about dignity. My own dignity consists of killing them off....'

When I told Mr Shi about the Chapei executions, the locomotive's whistle and what it had meant, he shook his head and said nothing for a time. Then he said, 'I suffered in the Cultural Revolution, too.'

'At least they didn't throw you into the fire.'

'Ha-ha! No, not that!'

We passed down a street I had wanted to see, remembering it from an old photograph of the early 1900s. In the picture banners hanging across the street had said 'Strike for a 12-hour day!' and 'No More Work for Children under Eight!' When I mentioned this, Thomas Dor said, 'Work! I tell people in Hong Kong, "Ease up. You work too hard. You'll die young." In Shanghai now, people live to seventy or eighty years old; they don't work so hard. No incentive.' Does that mean that dignity, so often said to reside in labour, can now coexist with taking it easy? An odd thing, dignity. In affluent Europe, among the industrial conflicts, the soccer hooligans and the 'Good Living' pages in glossy magazines, dignity is undoubtedly elusive. In less fortunate regions idealists can, in the name of dignity, liquidate one in furnaces or hammer three-inch nails into one's shoulders. Small, unassuming people like Wei Kuen wear dignity as easily as they wear the scarves their wives have knitted for them.

In appearance, Wei Kuen was commonplace; that is to say, his face was friendly, ruddy and wide-awake, but he had none of Ah Po's exuberant good looks. He was short and almost plump; he would grow into a roly-poly middle age. Despite his alert, blackcurrant eyes he conveyed an element of reserve and introspection that Ah Po lacked. He was thoughtful and observant. He was modest, too; his clothes were not shabby, but they were 'sensible' – sober in colour and hard-wearing – while Ah Po, in his fluffy white sweater and pale blue jeans, was something of a dandy.

Wei Kuen and his wife, Shun Ling, called to take me to their room on a terribly cold afternoon. A dark grey sky settled down over the frozen city as if intent on crushing it. The wind from the river slashed through my anorak and my scarf, and reached my bones. I had tried, with Shi's help, to buy a Chinese padded coat, but the shops didn't stock my size, or maybe the 'Outsize Foreign Visitor' range had sold out.

Mr Shi politely declined to come with me to Wei Kuen's. He said he had important things to do at home – and if I didn't mind. . . . I didn't mind at all. 'But take the car,' he said unexpectedly. So Jade Dragon drove us to Wei Kuen's.

The house was a long way away, tucked into a row of old, three-storeyed houses buried in the decrepit heart of the old city. Here Jade Dragon dropped us and drove away. We stumbled into a small doorway, then up an unlit wooden staircase. It was very narrow, ill-lit by a single bulb overhead, with a peeling wall on either side and jagged holes in the skirting. On the first floor, a wizened face peered out as our clumping footsteps approached, its wrinkles registering shock to see – what was this? – a tall European groping his way through the half-light, shoulders bent under the dilapidated ceiling. Other doorways revealed small, palsied rooms, lit with a single strip of neon. Wei Kuen and his wife had two small neon strips in their room. My anorak felt about as warm as a pair of silk pyjamas. I trembled from head to foot. It was below freezing by the feel of it, but, as at Ah Po's, I saw no heating of any kind. Perhaps body heat was enough, if you were used to nothing else.

Wei Kuen said his father-in-law and two brothers-in-law lived downstairs. His mother-in-law slept under a quilt behind a screen at the far end of the room. Clothes and blankets were scattered over the backs of the few chairs. Stacks of cheap suitcases filled much of the little room; the only luxury I recall was a Hitachi TV set under a yellow cloth. When I moved, the wooden floor snapped and creaked. Mildew spread greenish maps down the whitewashed walls.

'Sorry, so cold,' said Wei Kuen cheerfully, wrapping a blanket round my shoulders. I was annoyed with myself. Why hadn't I heeded Angel Yip's advice to bring warm 'dresses'? It was a great relief when Shun Ling began to make tea, warm in her blue padded smock as he was in his brown leather jacket and high-necked sweater. Shun Ling is pleasant-looking but not pretty. She has a goldfish look, the little pursed goldfish mouth of so many Chinese girls who wear large, round glasses – the glasses emphasize the mouth in that fishy way, or perhaps it's that the big, round lenses resemble goldfish bowls. More important, she is humorous and good natured. She talks in the same swift and decisive way as Wei Kuen, and together they present a four-square, quizzical, undaunted face to the guileful world.

But there were things I wanted to know. How had they met? After all, Wei Kuen is a Cantonese, born in Hong Kong, while Shun Ling is from Shanghai.

'My wife's brother was a seaman like me,' he said. 'We made friends when he and I were in Hong Kong with Blue Funnel Line.' So he had suggested that Wei Kuen might marry his sister....

'Arranging' marriages like this helped girls to leave China – but did it mean a happy marriage? 'We're lucky,' Shun Ling said (Wei Kuen translating). 'Girls who arrange to marry boys they've never met are marrying passports. Often very disastrous. Husbands sometimes cruel. Sometimes girls don't like Hong Kong. I'd advise girls not to do it – this arranging. Unless they love.'

All this trouble and doubt – about emigrating to Hong Kong. Was it worth it? Wasn't Hong Kong's special appeal strictly limited in time to its predetermined end in 1997? In a sense, yes, Thomas Dor had explained; but vulnerable people like Wei Kuen and Ah Po and their young wives must always live with hope. In any case, he said, Wei Kuen and Ah Po already lived in Hong Kong; naturally they wanted their wives with them. Apart from that, there was always the expectation of several years of the present opportunity to work overtime, to earn more money, to spend that extra money on better clothes, a better school, the cinema, and to be able – God willing – to save for their children's future. There might even be a chance to travel – some time. Who knew? And who knew, either, what really would happen in 1997? Maybe simply a change of ruler. Perhaps life in Hong Kong would go on as before. I could not argue with that.

The door opened and a man of about Wei Kuen's age came in and looked at me, taken aback. Shyly, he shook my hand. This was one of Wei Kuen's brothers-in-law from the room below, home from his shift in the Huangpu dockyard. He had brought a bunch of plastic flowers and put them into the plastic vase on the only table. Then he sat and watched us.

'You'll be glad to leave one day for Hong Kong?' I asked Shun Ling.

'Oh, yes ... I think ... but I'm not sure,' she said with a little smile. 'All those Cantonese people....'

When it was time to go, Wei Kuen and Shun Ling wrapped scarves round their necks in the doorway.

We groped our way down the ramshackle stairs into the blackness of the street, and it was like lowering ourselves into an icy flood. Shanghai was blacked out like wartime London and it was rush hour. A solid, pushing, human mass filled the pavements; people in dark blue tunics barely seen, identical shapes advancing silently, dark against the darkness.

I was suddenly frightened that I might get separated from Wei Kuen. He could be swept away from me very easily – and what then? I was utterly incapable of telling any of these blue-uniformed shapes where I wanted to go to. Claustrophobia! Alone in China's largest city, a freezing night coming on, inadequately clothed, deprived of speech.... For once I was grateful that I towered above the Chinese. Thanks to that I managed, with difficulty, to keep Wei Kuen in sight or in touch; time and again my desperate handholds on his arm were torn away by

the press. I could see his face, a pale buoy bobbing in and out of an ocean of inky waves, straining to keep me in sight. I saw reflected in it my own anxiety.

In the main thoroughfare the crowds surged round a bus stop like breakers round a rock. Buses came and went, but again and again the human turbulence swept me away from their doors. At last a likely one wallowed up – but stopped a hundred yards down the road. We fought our way towards it. 'Ha!' – Wei Kuen reached the door as it closed, banged on it with his fists and pointed to me. The door opened and I leaped in. 'Tell him where I go,' I yelled to Wei Kuen, but the door snapped shut sharply, blotting him out. Would I ever see him again? The bus moved jerkily away. My arms were pinned by mufflered strangers, and to avoid my head banging the low roof I was obliged to stand stooped like an old heron. I could imagine what a ludicrous sight I was, and suddenly I wanted to giggle. 'Mysterious disappearance of.... Last seen running for a bus in Shanghai.' I could see the headline now.

Someone tugged at my anorak. A woman had moved aside on her bench, pressing against her neighbour to make a tiny space for me. I squeezed in between her and a dark-skinned soldier with the narrowest slit eyes I've ever seen. His gaze for the next twenty minutes never left my face. It was as if he had dislocated his neck into a permanent eyes-right.

Much later the bus pulled up on the Bund, and of course now my semi-panic shamed me. The conductor patted my arm, and in a moment the warmth and light of the Peace Hotel washed over me.

I went to the bar and asked the barman for a Panda Cocktail.

'Panda, good,' he said, smiling encouragingly as I drank.

'Same again,' I said.

Whenever I heard the 'Chinese masses' mentioned in future, I would remember this hectic evening in the Shanghai blackout.

Mr Shi took me to a calligrapher's studio in an ornamental garden; famous, he said. The artist was a stubby, cheerful old man with white hair and glasses. After my introduction, he drew something on good white paper, wielding his brush with wide, confident sweeps. It was for me, Shi said. 'Beautiful flower; full moon; long life,' the old man said through Mr Shi, sitting back and indicating the wide or tapering ribbons of black ink. The writing was swift and delicate as a breath;

sublime. The ample bar of 'flower' thinned perfectly into a mere gossamer connection with the generous circle of 'full moon'; the sleek, trailing tendril of 'long life' led the eye to infinity.

'But flowers die, a full moon wanes,' I said to Mr Shi. 'How do they connect with long life?'

Mr Shi smiled. 'See – beautiful flower means good person: you. Full moon also means good because the moon is at its full size and without defects: you, again.'

I shook my head. 'That's too flattering.'

He continued, smiling, as if he had not heard me. 'Longevity is to wish you long life, live long time.'

'I see. Thank you.'

The old man made a remark and pointed to the character that signified 'beautiful flower'.

Mr Shi said, 'The artist suggests that the character looks like a dragon flying, or a phoenix singing.' I looked at the character again. It *was* a bit like a dragon on the wing. About the phoenix singing I wasn't so sure.

As we prepared to leave, the old man said to me: 'Chinese say music is sweet but the sweetest part is after the music ends. So your visit is very good for us, but the memory of it will be even better.'

All I could do was try to quote Keats correctly: 'Heard melodies are sweet, but those unheard are sweeter.'

The old man laughed when Shi translated this. 'I like that,' he said, screwing up his eyes. 'Oh, I like that.'

On my last morning I walked out along the twenties splendour of the Bund. I wanted to see how long the famous Long Bar really was. At the Tung Feng Hotel a banquet was in preparation. Men in white overalls scurried about carrying trestles, cloths and dishes. Long pointed chandeliers hung down like opalescent elephant tusks. What I supposed to be the Long Bar ran the length of the room, from the tall windows on the Bund to the back wall. A hundred feet? More?

'Welcome,' a young waiter said. 'Beer?'

When it came, I said, 'This may be the longest bar in the world.'

He looked indignant. 'Not "maybe". Sure!'

I strolled back along the river. The water traffic fidgeted; the mournful hooters called to each other. Lines of complacent barges lay along the riverbank, their crew's bicycles stacked on deck under their awnings. *Sen Hai, Ding Yang*: the names were painted in English under the Chinese characters.

A young man stopped me to say, 'I learn English from radio. Shanghai Radio. Do I speak with Chinese accent or Russian accent?'

A Chinese accent, I assured him, and he seemed pleased.

'I work in the Medical Centre,' he said. 'I am from Hangchow.'

My final rendezvous in Shanghai. Mr Shi and Jade Dragon were waiting at the hotel to drive me to the airport. Wei Kuen was there, bright-eyed. Ah Po nearly broke my neck with a mighty hug, and gentle Thomas Dor smiled his weary smile. We swore we would meet in Hong Kong. They would return there soon on the *Shanghai*. I was grateful to Mr Shi, and said I would write to tell him so. He laughed and smoothed his bouncy black hair with his butterfly hands. 'Ah-ha. Thank you.' With the flourish of a conjurer producing a dove, he took a small package from his pocket. Inside was a jar. On a label, in English, I saw: 'Essence of Chicken with Pearl'.

'For long life,' he said, smiling.

We reached the airport. The business of tickets and checking-in began. I shook Shi's hand warmly and said thank you to Jade Dragon.

Dreams cannot survive the bustle of airports. Under the departure boards, among the impersonal police uniforms and the businessmen's Samsonite briefcases, my dream of Shanghai, Past and Present, shivered like a dying reflection in the Huangpu River. At the passport counter, the first, sudden roar of a jet engine. The dream image faltered and grew dim. A loudspeaker rasped, 'Will all passengers for Hong Kong....' I moved through the glass doors into the departure lounge. Now it was gone.

Five

On the seventh floor of the Swire Building facing Hong Kong's harbour and its shipping sits a former acquaintance, Tim Bridgeman, of John Swire's China Navigation Company. I had met him two years earlier after sailing in one of the company's ships – the *Hupeh*.

As I knew, Tim said, Swire's had no passenger vessels going my way. Most ships of any kind crossed the Pacific from right to left, east to west, far more frequently than from left to right, which was my direction. But still ... wait ... yes, Swire's had the *Chengtu*, a container ship. She would leave in a few days for Papua New Guinea and the Solomons. To be precise, she would call at the little ports of Wewak, Madang and Lae on the north-east coast of Papua New Guinea, then Rabaul in New Britain, then Kieta on Bougainville Island. She would go on to Honiara, the capital and the main port of the Solomons, and return. Nearly two weeks' outward voyage, all told. Of course, I needn't go all the way.

There was no doubt about it. The *Chengtu* was what I needed – as far as Rabaul, anyway. After Rabaul, I could take my chance.

'Good idea,' Bridgeman said. 'Nice place, Rabaul. Volcanoes.' He himself had seen a number of the Melanesian islands and had even collected a few books about them.

'I don't know if you're interested, but I found a remarkable old book in England on my last leave; in a secondhand shop, hidden away, you know. It's a collection of letters written to a friend in England by an Englishman – an oddball, I suppose – who had run away to the South Sea islands in the early part of this century.'

'He liked the islands?'

'Sometimes hated them, sometimes loved them. An odd bloke, I should think. Educated, literate. You're going to be just about where he was.'

He brought the book into his office next day, and so I held in my hand for the first time one of the most interesting books I have ever read – *Isles of Illusion*, a most vivid and full-blooded account of rough-and-tumble, almost piratical life in the copra plantations of the south-west Pacific between 1912 and 1923.

'The writer of the letters was still alive when they were published,' Tim Bridgeman said, 'and he wanted to keep his real name dark. So he called himself Asterisk. Perhaps you will find out who he really was and what happened to him. Anyway, take it. Please don't lose it, that's all.'

As I stood there, I flipped through a few pages. Bits of enlivening sentences sprang to my eye: 'One sits at table,' I read, 'with known murderers.' And: 'It's the slavery business I cannot stand.' And '... shot 'im, of course I shot 'im, and I'd shoot again tomorrow. ...' It sounded promising. I thanked Tim, bore the book away and locked it in my metal suitcase as carefully as if it were a second passport.

'See David Walker in his office about details of when and where to board the *Chengtu*,' Tim had said. I had a few days to wait, but I wasn't worried. With my onward berth in my pocket, so to speak, I could relax, and time passed swiftly in a whirl of small events.

First, Wei Kuen and Ah Po returned by ship from Shanghai. They were in transports of joy because they had both been allowed to bring their wives with them. At the Luk Kwok that evening, Wei Kuen pumped my hand with little excited barks of 'Yes, yes. ... Good news, good news.' He trotted about the room, his round redcurrant face beaming. From Ah Po I got a hug and a wet kiss on the cheek. They were ecstatic.

Wei Kuen insisted that I go at once to see his home in a high, dilapidated building in the far, poor side of Kowloon, so high that I was panting by the time we reached his door down a narrow corridor. Shun Ling politely took my hand.

'We sleep here,' Wei Kuen said. They did everything there, except wash and cook. I saw a metal two-tiered bunk that filled one wall. A table with drawers, one dwarf wardrobe with three or four cheap suitcases on it, a plastic clothes bag and a smaller table with a modest television set on it took care of the remaining space. By way of decoration, a tin of Ovaltine stood on a shelf and a small plastic duck flew up a wall. The room – that is all their home was – was very clean. I can't even remember a chair; I perched on the lower tier of the bunk.

From a drawer, Wei Kuen took a photograph album of colour pictures of his wedding – he solemn, in a dark suit with a white plastic flower in his buttonhole; Shun Ling smiling, in sugar pink. Family and friends were red-faced from beer.

Now, Wei Kuen said, we were celebrating another happy gathering. 'Eat food.' We walked downstairs to buy a cooked duck at a street stall lit by a pressure lamp, watching the stall-keeper divide the duck into chunks with deft, short chops of a cleaver. Through her big glasses, Shun Ling blinked at the neon street lights like a cat blinking at the moon. 'The light!' she exclaimed at intervals. After the semi-blackout of Shanghai the lights of Hong Kong amazed her. She said something, laughing, and Wei Kuen, too, laughed, as he translated it. 'She says my duty now to help her have baby.'

Ah Po and Ching Man lived quite far away behind Kai Tak airport, in another peeling urban rabbit warren which, Wei Kuen told me, has the highest crime rate in all Hong Kong. Every door in his building had a heavy metal grille, he said, and every window had bars. Ah Po had to unlock so many padlocks that it took him ten minutes to get into his own house.

When we had arrived and waited to be let in through Ah Po's defences, he waved us in, switched on his beautiful smile and announced, 'We are to have a baby.'

'That is, he wants to have baby,' Wei Kuen explained. 'You will be grandfather.'

'Godfather.'

'Godfather, sorry.'

'I should like to be.'

'We want you gran ... godfather, too,' Wei Kuen added.

'I'd be proud.'

There didn't seem to be much room for babies here. Their room was just as overcrowded as Wei Kuen's, with one additional obstruction – Ah Po's goldfish bowl in which their small fish, more silver than gold, watched us, opening and closing their mouths as if trying to say something. Ah Po and Ching Man shared a tiny toilet and a poky little kitchen with seven neighbours and an army of oversized cockroaches.

Ching Man would work in a factory: her salary, with Ah Po's overtime, was needed to pay the rent. Even so, though they very much wanted a baby, they wouldn't be able to keep it here. A baby would prevent Ching Man's attendance at the factory. 'The baby will be sent back to Shanghai, to Ching Man's mother,' Wei Kuen explained. Thus disencumbered, Ching Man could return to work. What if Ah Po fell

50

sick? Of course, if Ah Po fell sick ... oh ... that would be disastrous. 'Ah Po cannot get sick,' Wei Kuen said. 'Not allowed.'

Everybody laughed. It was best to laugh at so serious a possibility. No work, no money – ha-ha! Ah Po put his arm across Ching Man's shoulders and laid his head fondly against hers. With his thick, long, black hair, sturdy limbs and big chest he looked like some handsome, exuberant animal. All he had to do was to stay that way. 'Also need money for roller skating,' he asked Wei Kuen to tell me.

When I told them of my imminent departure, Wei Kuen and Ah Po immediately agreed to forego a few days of precious overtime. Should we do some sightseeing, they asked.

'Good idea,' I said.

At about that time Thomas Dor returned from Shanghai. We were just setting off for the aquarium at Ocean Park. 'Oh, great. A nice day out,' he said with enthusiasm. 'So modern, eh?' He waved a hand from the taxi window at Central Hong Kong.

'My wife says Cantonese talk of money all time. Very strange,' said Wei Kuen. The high-rise flats and offices thrust up round us like imperial dragons' teeth of gold, silver and ivory – the late twentieth-century equivalent of the ziggurats of the Shanghai Bund. One was like an up-ended gold bar; another was drilled full of holes as if a gangster had tommy-gunned daylight into a marble slab; and there was an emperor's gravestone of wet obsidian. Somewhere here the chairman of the Hongkong and Shanghai Bank was building a house for himself – over a million sterling pounds-worth, they said.

'Quite a change from Shanghai, whaddaya say?' Dor said.

'You're glad to be back here?'

'Oh, I guess so. I like it here. Oddly enough, I like it there, too.' We walked towards the cable cars that carry visitors to the aquarium over a mountain, as skiers on their way to the slopes. 'Of course, you can do what you like here. I can't get books in Shanghai. Or see movies. That's boring. But even here, of course, I can't afford to go to the movies all the time.' He was teaching to make ends meet, he said, a few students on a freelance basis, and living in a small rented room.

High on the promontory, seagulls shrieked over our heads. Islands far below lay like dozing dragons soaking up the unusual sunshine. A public toilet disgorged a chain of Japanese men; a middle-aged couple, arm in arm, licked pink ice creams; Chinese children ran about with a

terrier straining at the end of a lead. The year 1997 and the Communist takeover seemed far away.

Ching Man felt that Hong Kong people ate too much food; and so much traffic, she said, made her feel nervous. Dor sighed: 'Shanghai could be really fine, but the Communists always must *interfere*, that's the trouble.' Again, he laughed. 'If only they would get lost, how beautiful and calm Shanghai would be.'

Suddenly he said, 'Watch me.' In mime he snatched something from his breast, clasped it in both hands, seemed to knead it as if it were a snowball. Then he tossed it – an invisible gobbet – to a seal that had reared up in the water begging to be fed. 'Ha!' Tom Dor laughed. 'There goes all my care and woe.' His hand patted my wrist. 'Now we'll have a real nice day out.'

We stared at the beautiful world of the underwater Atoll Reef, at wavering sea anemones, at seahorses arching their spiny necks, at the bitter mouth of a shark. We squeezed into a bus to the Botanical Gardens. White-headed sparrow-finches busied themselves among the peeling paper bark trees and the long pods of the purple camel's foot. The black earth of the flowerbeds was sheeted with camellias and leaves from dark copper bushes; fallen frangipani blooms lay like white stars on the grass. Tom Dor and Wei Kuen fed peanuts from a bag to an irritable macaw. Ah Po gazed at passing girls. 'Weee-eee-eee,' he cried as two European girls bounced chestily by. Ching Man was amused. She gurgled happily and rocked him back and forth by the arm. She was proud of him.

*   *   *

Ah Po took me on other adventures.

In the cold and damp, arthritic pains had moved into my neck and shoulders and settled there. When I turned my neck, I heard a sound like sand grinding around at the base of my skull. I asked Ah Po and Wei Kuen if they knew of a good massage place. Kipling's account of the massage Kim received at the hands of the Sahiba – a massage that brought him back from an exhaustion close to death – was an Asian luxury I had hoped some day to experience.

> Laying him east and west, that all the earth-currents which thrill the clay of our bodies might help and not hinder, they took him to pieces all one long afternoon – bone by bone, muscle by muscle, ligament by ligament, and lastly, nerve by nerve. Kneaded to irresponsible pulp... Kim slid ten thousand miles into slumber.

That was what I needed now.

'Not for games,' I told Ah Po firmly – he had winked at Wei Kuen and made lewd gestures. '*Proper* massage. Not playing.'

'No play-ing,' Ah Po agreed, violently shaking his head and assuming a severe expression. 'Ah Po wants to cure your aches in his way, as a personal present,' Wei Kuen said. 'Go with Ah Po.' So I meekly followed.

He didn't seem too sure where to go at first. At the top of a dingy stairway in Wan Chai he talked quickly in Cantonese to a surly young man with a squashed-in face standing behind a desk. Money passed. As instructed, I lay down naked on a hard couch in a gloomy cubicle, none too clean. I had stuffed my socks with my money, and my shoes with my socks. A tiny puce towel was no defence against the cold draught that blew in under the curtain, and I shivered alone until a plump girl in an inadequate skirt ambled in, said 'Hi', and began to pinch my stomach in a perfunctory way, as if to convey that she didn't think much of *that*. Was this massage? I wondered. Five minutes passed, then small black eyes peered querulously into mine. 'Masturbate?' she inquired.

I smiled at her politely. 'Only massage,' I said, and added, in what I hoped were commanding tones: 'On back.'

A few mild pats to the midriff later she snapped, 'Masturbate?' rhetorically, and this time she snatched impatiently for my groin with the attitude of a hard-bitten hospital nurse instructed by matron to administer an enema *and no shilly-shallying.*

53

'Never mind,' I said. I wriggled deftly out of her clutch, and sat up. 'Want only *massage*,' I told her, defensive and prim.

Ah Po soon appeared looking smug, and I assumed he had accepted the full bill of goods. Why not? Ah Po would go through life happily incapable of refusing anything like this.

'Good,' he explained.

'Ching Man will hear of this.' He pretended to look alarmed, repeating his wife's name fondly and making little soothing Chinese noises at me. It was all very well for him, but I had paid too much money for a few pokes in the stomach, my shoulders still ached, and when I twisted my head I heard the familiar sound of grating sand at the base of my skull. It seemed to have grown louder.

Ah Po was mortified. He was determined to do me some good. 'He wants to make you happy,' Wei Kuen said, encouragingly, on our return. 'He will take you to another place.'

Next day Ah Po came to the hotel bearing a surprising present – a stuffed woodcock on a wooden stand. It had a long beak and a crafty, though generally benevolent, expression. I thanked Ah Po profusely, stood the woodcock on the table, and followed him this time to an all-male sauna. I didn't mind that. Masseurs, I am inclined to think, are often better at massage than masseuses – a simple question of strength.

The sauna Ah Po chose was a bright, clean, crowded establishment in Kowloon – no doubt about its respectability – where brisk young Chinese led us to comfortable chairs in a darkened room. We were swaddled in towels and given pale tea with large green leaves floating on it. There were goldfish in bowls, racks of Chinese movie magazines, and a colour television set quietly gabbling Cantonese. People talked in low voices – unlike Westerners, Asians do not feel lack of noise to be a threat. I was the only foreigner. A nude Gulliver in a nudist Lilliput, I attracted discreet attention.

The social diversity of a sauna – or its lack of it – can be observed in its changing room. Here T-shirts, frayed jeans, suits and ties hung side by side. Pale clerks, businessmen wearing gold chains and spectacle frames, sun-darkened men straight from the nearest building site – 'a bath-house is a democracy,' a *Hammam* owner in Baghdad once said to me. He had that very day handled (literally) two ministers, the Iraqi national football team, several well-known singers, radio announcers, office and factory workers....

In this bath-house naked Chinese, ivory-skinned, almost hairless but for black, spiky tufts at armpit and groin, wandered languidly about,

54

plunged gasping into the near-freezing pool or lay floating in the hot one from which steam rose like marsh gas. The echoes of the waterfalls that fed them whispered round walls of white and blue fish-patterned tiles.

In the small, wood-lined sauna, I thought of the locomotive executions in Shanghai in 1927: twenty minutes of this heat and my own skull would snap. I watched the sweat spurt obscenely off a man who had spent a fortune on tattoos: red and blue dragons writhed over his chest, across his back and shoulders, and along his arms; their tails and wingtips disappeared up his neck into his long hair and down his legs to his calves, so vividly alive that you wanted to beat them off him. One serpent dived between his buttocks and seemed to disappear up his rectum. A crew-cut man nearby read a newspaper, uttering guttural gasps and groans of . . . anger, pain, amusement? His nose had a serious kink in it and his eye sockets had the puffy look of a habitual fighter. A secret society boss, a television wrestler? Over his shoulder, I saw on the damp printed page a photograph of a football match – sports news, not crime. Below me, a young man lay supine: a gold-coloured neck chain gleamed on an alabaster chest and a clump of pubic hair stuck stiffly up like black pampas grass.

As for Ah Po, he refused the hot-box, explaining with gestures that it brought his skin out in a rash, and crouched, hull-down in the warm pool, like an albino water buffalo. Around him, the sauna's clients abandoned themselves to the hot water and to the abstracted contemplation of the no longer private parts that floated before them like pale lotus buds in a painted pond on a Chinese scroll.

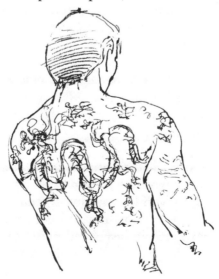

Only three massage room couches out of a dozen were occupied by dim, white cocoons. Kim could have expected no more of the Sahiba: the hands of my masseur were small precision instruments, expert crackers of joints and poppers of vertebrae. The half-moon Oriental eyes looked down, reassuring. Crack ... crack ... crack-crack! A clock ticked; someone snored. Soon, lips to my ear – 'Walk on back?' Careful feet began a promenade from pelvis to sand-filled neck, as if a tightrope walker was feeling his way along a dangerously frayed high wire. Vertebrae gave out sounds of roasting chestnuts, and aching muscles shrieked most satisfactorily. Kim's massage had brought him back from the exhaustion of death but, in its less drastic way, this was the most expert massage I have ever had. 'Finish,' the young acrobat murmured at last and sprang down to earth. Fingers moved diplomatically under the towels, and in my ear, faint as a breath – 'You like?...'

Mildly surprised but unshocked, I twisted my head towards the clock: 'No time ... very late ... sorry.' My second refusal of such services in two days began to make me feel unreasonably prudish – quite unnecessarily, because I had created no embarrassment or resentment. A friendly pat on the shoulder conveyed 'Okay', and the trim, tracksuited figure led me back to the darkened room, an armchair and more China tea. There, Ah Po sat mesmerized by an advertisement on the TV for a watch so encrusted with jewels that it might have made a Hong Kong millionaire blink. Swathed in toga-like towels, he looked like a young Roman senator from some Mongolian corner of the Empire. He waved to me flamboyantly, and other Chinese faces turned my way and smiled.

'Good?' Ah Po said.

'Good.'

We sat at ease, side by side, watching Chinese-speaking animated cartoons which eventually changed to football. Ah Po reached over and patted my hand. Now he was my proud and contented host.

But I was going to sea. I had to bring myself to say goodbye to Wei Kuen, Ah Po and their wives. To Thomas Dor I did so by telephone because he was tied up with his teaching schedules. 'So long,' he said. 'Don't wait too long to return. I'm too goddam old.' For our last evening, the others wanted to hear 'real' music for the first time, and Wei Kuen chose – in preference to the knockabout music hall spectacular I had suggested, not knowing what was best – a concert of popular Chinese orchestral music by the Hong Kong Philharmonic Orchestra.

The concert hall was as big as a large circus tent and nearly full; the music was evidently as popular as it claimed to be. Applause followed the vigorous cadenzas that flew from the muscular fingers of a Japanese lady soloist, who braced her short legs like a golfer addressing a long tee shot upwind. When the first chords of the 'Butterfly Lovers' violin concerto – a Hong Kong Chinese composition – flowed around us, Shun Ling dabbed her eyes happily, and Ching Man sniffed and was comforted by Ah Po.

The programme was full of butterfly words: 'Colourful Clouds Chasing the Moon', 'Fishing Boats at Night', 'Little Stream'. A programme note for 'Red Bean Song' said, 'A girl is thinking of her lover and hoping that, in his absence, he may be reminded of her by the red beans that grow everywhere.' The 'Red Bean Song' threw Ah Po into ecstasies of nudging and winking, his smile twitching rapturously; and a dab of moisture appeared under Wei Kuen's left eye during the harp solo in 'Fishing Boats at Night', which received an ovation.

It was a good way to round things off.

Arm in arm on the way back to the Luk Kwok, Wei Kuen said quite fiercely that we must do this again – I must return. Shun Ling's eyes blinked agreement behind her fishbowl glasses, and Ching Man turned up a beaming face. 'Rove-ree!' said Ah Po, imitating Wei Kuen's English, and banged his head against mine as a sign of affection. In my hotel room, Ah Po as usual immediately turned on the television: even the stuffed woodcock on my desk looked down its long beak disapprovingly. And so, as we said our farewells behind the windows with their sad, wintry view of the harbour, the TV screen showed an advertisement for an expensive French brandy. A delicate, disembodied female hand, its wrist encircled by a diamond bracelet, lifted a glass of rich, amber liquid towards the camera's eye....

At this moment of goodbyes and inappropriate brandy advertisements I realized that, since my arrival at Kai Tak airport in rain and gloom, I had strayed into lives as strange to me as scenes on a Chinese screen. Something of my dejection had left me, and I had the four smiling people before me to thank for that. But what was in store for them? Would 1997 prove to be for them the Year of Wrath? Or a year like any other? They, like Sergeant Lim, were poor and vulnerable and faced a possibly menacing and at any rate inescapable future in Hong Kong, yet their unconscious dignity had made my personal gloom feel trivial, even unseemly. Dogged courage, diligence, humour – those were the sparks of life in these four bright handfuls of dust. They had very little, but they had Character – 'the eternally valuable element' (I forget who called it that) beside which everything else wears out. They were going to need it.

I took them down to the front door. In the street, they looked back and waved. I waved in reply and went rapidly back into the hotel. But a feeling of loss made me run out once more and we waved to each other again, back and forth, until they turned the corner.

When they had disappeared I walked to a bar, the first bar I saw. It was called the Old China Hand. Among false beams, tobacco smoke and pint glasses of draught beer, white men looking like off-duty policemen or sailors on shore leave played darts with Chinese men who spoke with Anglo-American accents and might have been bank clerks or hotel receptionists. I ordered a beer. At the last moment of parting, Ah Po had slipped a scrap of paper into my hand. Now I sat down and read it: 'I will save to buy a flat in Hong Kong. If I have flat in Hong Kong, you need not worry about when you are old.' It was signed, 'Your son, Ah Po.'

Presently, I opened my notebook to write a close to this first phase of my new Odyssey. Flipping back through the pages, I came across a bar-room song I must have jotted down some time before in a Wan Chai pub similar to the Old China Hand. I read it again now, remembering that it went with a well-known hymn tune, although which one it was escaped me for the moment.

Me no likee Blitish sailor.
Yankee sailor come ashore!
Me no likee Blitish sailor,
Yankee pay one dollar more.

Yankee call me, 'Honey darlin'',
Blitish call me 'Fuckin' whore'.
Me no likee Blitish sailor.
Yankee, won't you come ashore?

Yankee always wear Flench letter,
Blitish never wear fuck all.
Me no likee Blitish sailor.
Yankee, won't *you* come ashore?

Yankee sailor fuck and finish,
Blitish fuck for ever more.
Me no likee Blitish sailor!
Yankee, *won't* you come ashore?

It wasn't Kipling, but it brought me back into the no-nonsense world of ships and seamen. It reminded me just how near I was to launching myself once more into a world unknown to me except in years of reading. Tomorrow – tomorrow! – my mid-sea course, like that of the south wind, would be taken

Over a thousand islands lost in an idle main,
Where the sea-egg flames on the coral
   and the long backed breakers croon
Their endless ocean legends to the lazy, locked lagoon.

That *was* Kipling and the recollection of it made me close my notebook, drink a last whisky for luck, and walk across Hennessy Road to the Luk Kwok, oblivious of the wet, greasy streets and the falling drizzle, my mind afloat on sunlit seas that stretched as far as imagining could follow.

Six

David Walker had written very clearly on a piece of office paper: '*Chengtu* Buoy A8, 1700 hours, 1900 hours, 2300 hours, Blake Pier.' This meant that the walla-walla, or sampan, that effected a water taxi service from the shore to the ship set out at those hours from that pier, almost opposite Swire House. But when I walked in the rain to the pier, a little before 1900 hours, I found a confusion of sampans bobbing and rolling in the darkness. Blake Pier is quite long and has a leg to it like a letter L. Sampans came and went from a number of waterlogged steps, where huddles of seamen of various nationalities waited to be taken off to ships in the harbour. A wind blew; it was raining hard. Where was the walla-walla for the *Chengtu*?

By 1930 I had decided that it wasn't coming or that I had misheard some instruction from David Walker. None of the Chinese whose unsmiling heads poked out of the office kiosks at the entrance to the pier knew anything about the *Chengtu*. So I searched around and found an old man and a boy on a sampan that danced alongside some slippery stone steps, bargained with them for a minute or two, agreed to pay 30 Hong Kong dollars, and at last we swayed away in a roaring cloud of oil fumes across the choppy waters of the harbour.

Buoy A8: *Chengtu* was there, only partly visible, her foredeck and the forepart of her accommodation and bridge wings illuminated by the arc lamps on her derricks, the rest of her in shadow. A modest-sized container ship with pleasant lines, she lay in the rain, nuzzled by barges like a sow with piglets. The walla-walla rose and fell at the bottom step of a steep gangway slippery with rain, and I wondered how I could lug my metal suitcase up there. Luckily, a Filipino seaman appeared almost at once, peering over the rail, calling 'Ok-aa-ee!' A dark, stocky figure in a lumberjack's plaid shirt descended the gangway, grabbed the case as if it were a matchbox and shouldered it up to the deck. I tossed some money to the old boatman and followed the Filipino up the gangway with my zipbag. The walla-walla disappeared in sheets of rain.

Ships at rest in harbour are cold, indifferent things. They can seem positively hostile to strangers. The first thing to do is to find the chief officer or the captain. You need to explain your presence. Probably you have to sign a waiver, exempting the shipping company from any responsibility should you fall down a companionway and break your neck. A cabin is a refuge to dump your bags in. Once you have a bunk, you somehow feel safe. Someone must show you to it, whatever it is – the owner's cabin, a pilot's cabin, or a cubbyhole somewhere to accommodate a supernumerary officer.

The trouble is that when a ship is in port a temporary chaos usually reigns aboard her. As I manhandled my suitcase from deck to deck, interlopers from the shore – large men made larger by padded windcheaters, their battered Chinese faces crowned by white or yellow hard hats, customs officers, watchmen – jostled me on the narrow stairways and blundered against me in the alleyways. As usual on a night before sailing, most of the stewards were ashore; there were dirty sheets on my bunk when I found it at last – steered there by a Filipino mess hand in a singlet with a 7-Up can in his hand – and used towels in the shower. At such times, you're relieved if a kind chief officer takes time from supervising the loading of the ship to offer you a beer from the refrigerator in his cabin, or in the ship's bar, if there is one. The chief officer appeared in his cabin – at last – wet, in white overalls. The *Chengtu* had her bar, and without hesitation he hurried me to it. 'Jim Bird,' he said, laying his hard hat and gloves down on one of three or four orange bar stools. The bar looked onto the foredeck; it had a settee and, on the bulkheads, prints of old Hong Kong and a wooden Papuan mask it would be better not to meet on a dark night. 'Glad to know you.'

Jim Bird was a good sort of man to meet on a rainy night in a strange ship. Dark-haired, relaxed, good-humoured and well-named – he was as chatty as a mynah. He looked a bit like one, too, hopping about, cocking his head to one side and fixing me with bright, friendly eyes. He talked rather like a ticker tape flashing out the latest stock market reports. Loading would soon stop – or at least it should – and resume early tomorrow morning. We should sail about eleven o'clock. Captain was ashore, but would be back soon. Julian Gomersall by name.

Filipino crew. Not a bad lot. What about a beer? A San Mig or an Aussie Four X? Make yourself at home. He left me with the beer and peace of mind, and soon I heard his quickfire voice addressing the Chinese stevedores on the foredeck among the containers.

I wandered out on deck myself and watched derricks swinging 20-foot-square containers onto the forepart of the ship. The rain pelted down; the decks were slippery with it. The open hatches gaped blackly in the dangerous shadows thrown by the huge metal boxes. Gently, meticulously, the Chinese stevedores eased them into their slots. How easy to be nudged down a hatch; or have a hand pulped. A slip on the greasy deck, a moment's inattention – that's all it needed. Why weren't people crushed to death all the time?

The captain came on board quite soon; a tall, youngish man, with a neat, fair beard and a pleasant, decided manner. He was welcoming. 'Weren't you on the *Hupeh*?' he said. 'With old Ralphie?' I admitted that, two years before, I had sailed from Manila to Hong Kong in the China Navigation's vessel *Hupeh*, and recalled her – and Ralph Kennet – with affection. It was pleasant to be on another ship from the same company; the same family, so to speak. Pleasanter still to know that in a few hours I would be on the way to the South Seas.

Not much later, lying on my bunk, I heard someone strolling down the alleyway outside, and a voice singing:

> Father's got an anal stricture,
> Mother's got a fallen womb....

The tune was that of a well-known hymn – the Old Hundredth, I think. I fell asleep happy, as I always am when safely in a berth and we sail next day.

Next morning, my notes recorded:

> Three blasts on a ship's hooter. The captain on the bridge: 'Hard a-starboard! Slow ahead!' We move. 11 a.m. as Jim Bird had forecast. The second officer said in a Geordie accent to the pilot: '*Chengtu*. Bound East to Wewak.' The pilot is a Chinese dressed in a dark suit and striped tie. He might be a commuter hitching a lift to an office, not a man taking an expensive ship out to sea through cluttered corridors of shipping.

Captain G. comes out to me on the bridge wing, pointing, 'There's the old *Hupeh*. Not ours any more. We've sold her.' Ah, yes; I recognize the long, satisfactory silhouette, the familiar high-flared bows I first saw in Manila harbour. A Panamanian flag flies at her stern now, I'm sad to see. Sadder still, she is getting a new name. I can see the last letters of her old one, U P E H, not quite painted over. 'Looks like a *real* ship, doesn't she?' Gomersall says. Yes, she does; because she's not a container ship. Say what you like, container ships, however sleek, are less like ships than floating boxes of red, yellow and blue children's bricks.

Chengtu – our sleek box of bricks – swings behind the *Ibn al Nafees*, a grey and white bulk carrier, registration: Doha. Once more, as I had so recently done from the old *Shanghai*, I watch the skyscrapers, the proud symbols of affluent Hong Kong, slide grandly by. Level with Star Ferry: 'Full ahead.' Is Wei Kuen, or Ah Po, or Thomas Dor looking out to see us pass? A crag with a Union Jack on a tall pole. A golf club with red roofs. Fishing vessels; sampans with cold men in greasy coats and chow-like dogs with curling tails barking at us from their slippery decks. Silently, the islands draw aside to let us pass, green with grey ribs of rock and scree, like Scotland. You expect to see sheep.

Now into the widening sea, heading S E. 'Midships steady.' *Chengtu* begins to nod her head, to quiver with excitement like a horse released from confinement in a paddock onto open down-land. The South China Sea, in friendly mood, meets us with a gentle swell, a strong hand, cradling and lifting our bows. The green water, frothing alongside, begins to hiss, 'Come south ... s-s-south ... s-s-s-south.'

When I introduced myself to the second officer he winced away, saying, 'Excuse me,' not offering his hand to shake but showing me instead a white lump of bandage over the tip of his middle finger. 'Caught it between a container and the spreader,' he explained, 'on the *Chengtu*'s last voyage.' A spreader is the rectangular metal frame that clamps onto container tops and lifts or lowers them.

'Nail gone?'

'Nail?' He held it up with a resentful expression. 'The whole tip's bloody gone.' He seemed remarkably unconcerned. He told me that the first officer had broken an arm and one or two ribs and damaged his left

leg in a fall down a hold on the same voyage. 'I thought he was a goner.'
The second officer's name was Ken Hindmarsh, a young Geordie with
rust-coloured shining hair and beard and appropriately pallid skin.

The *Chengtu* carried eleven officers and thirteen crew. At the first
midday meal I met the chief engineer, Tony Darby, a grey-headed man
with a belly like a cheerful Buddha, grey moustache and a Yorkshire
accent, who, like Captain Ralph Kennet of the *Hupeh*, came from
Don-caster, which is how he pronounced it. As the Filipino steward
carried in steaks, the conversation turned to what I came to recognize as
a familiar topic at sea — the dehumanizing of life at sea by containers,
computerization, cost efficiency. Ships don't linger in port as they used
to. Shore leave is minimal, perhaps merely time for a beer. Schedules are
calculated in hours, not days.

'No, sea life is not what it used to be,' said Tony. He shook his head.
In the old days, too, the senior officers had their own stewards, and
ships had crews of sixty men, not twelve.

'You could join the Merchant Navy and see the world once,' Jim Bird
said. He poured a liberal dollop of salad cream over his steak.

'Salad cream on steak! Christ Almighty!' Gomersall cried in mock
surprise. 'What an abominable taste!'

'Do you mind?' Bird said smoothly, and went on: 'Now a ship can be
into a port in the morning and out again in the evening. All sorts of
exotic-sounding ports and never a chance to see them. That's why
young men don't want to join as they used to. Join the Navy and what
do you see? You see the sea.' He poured more salad cream. 'We're
bloody tram drivers, that's what we are.'

'You'll be in bloody hospital if you go on eating like that,' Gomersall
said, winking at me.

I mentioned the second officer's mutilated middle finger. 'Caught by
the container,' said Gomersall. 'It came off in his glove. The mate – not
this one' – he flicked a thumb at Bird, who smiled and said, 'Oh,
thanks' – 'brought it up to him still in the glove, with ceremony like, as
if he were serving him a perfectly cooked boiled egg, and said, "Your
finger, I believe."'

Darby broke in, with relish, 'Down in Australia the other day they
were moving containers in a hold with a fork lift truck, and they didn't
see a young cadet between the side of the hold and the container.' He
brandished the ketchup bottle. 'A nice lad. It crushed him. *Cr-oo-shed*
'im.' Glog-glog-glog – the ketchup slopped thickly like blood onto his
plate. 'They heard the screams, but it was *too late*!'

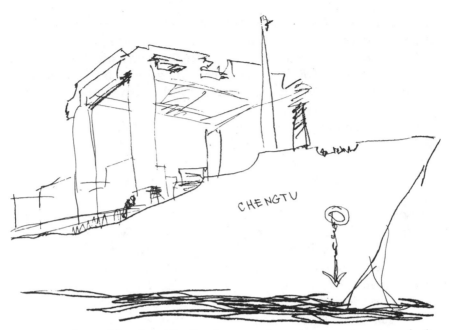

CHENGTU

Across the table the *Chengtu*'s second engineer, a young, dark, birdlike Sri Lankan called Rohan, winced and his Adam's apple yo-yo'd rapidly up and down. He glanced at the scarlet pool of ketchup on Darby's plate, gulped 'Excuse me,' pushed back his chair and left.

My cabin contained a table, settee, two chairs, a bunk and, most important of all, a good reading light. The ship's library was small but varied: Muriel Spark's *Memento Mori*, Patrick Moore's *The Story of Astronomy*, a Larousse *Encyclopaedia of Modern History*, a handbook on witchcraft. I took down *The Oxford Book of Short Stories*; it seemed ideal for the ten or twelve days to Papua.

As I lay down on my bunk to read it, a notice pinned to the cabin wall near the telephone caught my eye. It was printed in Japanese and English, and I read:

> The Sufscriber lifts the handset and diall-ng '2' then replaces the handset and wait when the subscriber and called hears ringing tone if called answers. Both ringing tones stop and speech starts.

The *Chengtu* had been built in 1977 in a Japanese shipyard, for (I think) a Dutch company. Odd that Japanese efficiency could result in gibberish. On the other hand, Japanese efficiency had got the ship herself just right. The *Chengtu* moved smoothly and most economically at thirteen knots, and she could do no more. Just as important – for me – she was built to accommodate tall men. Japanese often design ships like dolls' houses for half-pint Japanese seamen, but I was never threatened by the *Chengtu*'s deckheads, lintels and air-cooling outlets. I had no need to go about stooped like a miner at a coalface.

Across an empty sea we passed without incident down the west coast of Luzon, the northernmost of the Philippine Islands; then, with the long splinter of Palawan Island to our right, we entered the shelter of the Sulu Sea. The Sulu Sea! What memories were summoned up by that innocent-looking stretch of tropical water. Two years earlier I had crossed this region of piracy, rebellion and death in a Filipino launch bearing contraband goods from North Borneo to Mindanao Island. A very different experience from the *Chengtu*: then, men with tattooed bodies had relieved me of money and binoculars. I had been lucky. Very recently, men had walked the plank hereabouts. Others had been thrown overboard, and their slit throats quickly attracted sharks.

The sun shone now on a sea as immaculate as I remembered it had been then. I will never forget it. I carry like a snapshot in my head the beauty of the ancient domains of the old sultans of Sulu, where palm-lined bays have always sheltered the scudding outriggers of smiling, brown men who a hundred years ago, for the sake of plunder, killed with their curved krisses and brass cannon, and who now prefer machine guns. Better armed than ever before, the living descendants of the sea rovers of old Sulu have fired on, and even boarded, cargo vessels as big as the *Chengtu*. If you were the captain of any kind of vessel in these waters the important thing was not to stop. The mistake of anchoring for a night to shelter from a cyclone had led, in the recent case of the British master of a container ship, to his waking at midnight to feel the cold touch of a pistol on his neck, and to hear a whisper in his ear: 'Money, money, where's the money?' He must have heard the snick of the hammer before the whisperer shot him dead.

Around midnight, I was reading R. L. Stevenson's grisly short story, *Thrawn Janet*, with only the bunkhead light on.

An' then a' at aince, the minister's heart played dunt an' stood stock-still; an' a cauld wind blew among the hairs o' his heid. For there was Janet hangin' frae a nail beside the auld aik cabinet; her heid aye lay on her shouther, her een were steeked, the tongue projekit frae her mouth....

Could this chill, northern tale really have been written on the sun-heated beaches of Samoa? Something made me look across the darkened cabin to the door – a slight movement, no sound. The door handle slowly drooped; silently, the door began to open ... it opened halfway. What ...? I waited for the ghastly, hanged head of Stevenson's Janet to peer at me round it ... coyly. But as I sat up, rigid with utterly senseless fear, the door closed again as slowly and silently as it had opened, and the metal handle moved back into place without a click. I leaped for the door and looked out. No one. At the stairhead, no sound. The captain's and the second engineer's doors were closed. I returned puzzled to my bunk and my reading, but now I substituted one of Saki's lighter stories for the gruesome tale of how the 'auld desecrated corp' of the witch wife Thrawn Janet crawled back from the dead in the moorland manse under the Hanging Shawn, 'wi' the heid aye upon the shouther, an' the girn still upon the face o't', and how the devil in her drove to madness the Reverend Murdoch Soulis.

At breakfast I told the story of my opening door, and Julian Gomersall smiled. 'Maybe it was our ghost. Our last third officer swore he saw a phantom figure on the left wing of the bridge. He even spoke to it – well, so he claimed – but it disappeared.'

'The *Chengtu* was only built in 1977. Anyone die in her yet?'

'Not aboard her, that's true,' Jim Bird said. 'But all around her. Want to hear?'

'Yes please.'

And he began: 'In 1981, we were en route to Hong Kong and detoured to avoid a typhoon. North-west of Luzon – actually, we've just passed the place – near dusk, we saw a boat. A big wave suddenly threw it up or we wouldn't have been able to see it. It was really rough; Force 8, I should say. It was difficult to get alongside the boat, which was tiny – about 18 foot long, with just a sort of rabbit hutch on it where people were huddled.' I knew what was coming.

'Vietnamese.'

'Yes, Boat People. They must have been drifting for a month or two. Their engine had packed up; no fuel.' He shook his head, munching cornflakes. 'Well, we threw over a line. But, trouble was, the poor bloody Vietnamese were too exhausted to help themselves much. Only two of 'em managed to grab a rope ladder and begin to haul themselves aboard.' He shook his head again, even more mournfully. 'Yes, but a heavy sea swept one of them back into the water, and he disappeared. The other one just managed to get aboard. A girl ... an emaciated girl. What else could we do? We tried throwing down a net right over the boat, hoping they could at least fall into it and we'd pull them up. Like fish, you see.'

'Good idea.'

'Yes. But the seas were appalling and the ship was rolling and pitching something terrible. And then – good God! – the little boat was swept under our stern – and that was dangerous. We threw down lifebuoys and lines, and yelled to them to grab hold – "We'll haul you up," we shouted. But they were too weak for that. And they couldn't understand English – and we, of course, couldn't speak bloody Vietnamese. Only two youngsters did what we told them – jumped into the water from the boat and held onto our lifebuoys. Just two. And even they.... Just then, a huge wave slammed the whole loaded boatful up under our counter. Bang. And that was it.... The boat filled at once and went down with them all –'

'Except the two clinging to the lifebuoys.'

'No. If they'd clung on ... but they panicked ... scrambled back into the doomed, fucking boat. Of course, it took them down, too.' Jim Bird looked round. 'What else could we do? Even then, I sent a volunteer over the side with a line round him. He fished out another girl ... and then I called him up again or we'd have lost him, too, in that bloody awful sea. So we saved just the two girls – living skeletons by then.'

I thought of close Vietnamese friends – as close as part of my own family – I had said goodbye to in Saigon before it fell; of Shanghai 1927 and Saigon 1975 – and after; of Asians dying in the furnace of a locomotive, or in a Force 8 gale off Luzon. Over the *Chengtu*'s breakfast toast and marmalade an image arose of Wei Kuen, Ah Po and their young wives in that doomed boat under the *Chengtu*'s counter. I thought of 1997 and Hong Kong. It could happen to anyone.

Tony Darby reminded me of a portrait of Arnold Bennett in middle age, a comforting image.

'Foony thing happened once,' he said a morning or two later. 'We're at sea, y'see. And I'm in the engine room takin' the night watch at one in the mornin', havin' a cup o' tea and a sandwich down there, like. I'd sit there on a chair –'

'On a *chair*? Get away!' said Bird, winking at me.

' – and have me sandwich and cup o' tea. And for two or three nights, I'd look up and think I saw, above me, near the gangway' – he stared at us in turn and added with great dramatic emphasis – '*a figure.*'

'Go on with you,' Bird said.

Darby laid bacon on a slice of bread and poured HP sauce over it. 'A figure,' he continued, 'which sort of flinched away – and disappeared into nowt. Well, next morning I took my tea right by the door, to watch and wait. And the figure appeared – a little black man! – and I grabbed 'im. "Gotcher!" I said. "But you're not a bloody ghost."'

'A stowaway?'

'Ay. Hidden in the bilges somewhere and creepin' out at night to snitch food from the crew's mess.' He bit into the sandwich.

'Who was it then?'

'Some sort of refugee from Mombasa. Well, we took him halfway round the world. Had to. He'd no papers. Didn't exist, officially.'

'So he *was* a sort of ghost, then.'

Darby laughed. 'Ay, he *were* a ghost, an' all.'

A notice in the wheelhouse said:

Recently two stowaways were discovered on board *Asian Pearl* soon after she had left Hong Kong. These men were carried around Australia and Far East ports and were eventually landed on her return to Hong Kong. At one stage they leapt into the sea while the vessel was at anchor and were rescued from imminent drowning by a fishing boat. We would ask, therefore, that you have a thorough search before the ship leaves port. . . .

There would be others. Asia is full of human beings ready to risk death rather than stay where they are.

The *Chengtu* moved south through strings of islands, strangely shaped, some like green-gloved fists, some like brown teeth, and in one case something like a small pyramid riding on the back of a whale. On some I could see smoke rising from houses on stilts, and outriggers drawn up on a beach. The Malays of Borneo call this region the Land Below the Wind, below 10° north, above which lies the typhoon belt between Luzon and Japan. We were approaching the Equator.

The whaleback of Mindanao lay to starboard, and the long outline of Basilan Island; and then Zamboanga's white buildings with, alongside its wharves, several passenger ships bound for Singapore, Cebu City or Manila, and a congregation of kumpits, as they called local launches like the 80-footer in which I had crossed these waters two years before. Little fishing outriggers skimmed about with small, brilliant sails — green with chocolate brown stripes, pale brown and black stripes, turquoise blue stripes on white or the palest yellow; tiny, vivid moths on the placid blue sea. 'Zamboanga is a violent city,' the captain of my kumpit had said. 'Many grenades in markets and movie houses.' Muslim guerrillas had been fighting the Christian troops and police of President Marcos in these islands for years. A grenade went off near the main plaza when I was there, and I'd seen gunmen terrorizing customers in a cafe. But Zamboanga is a beautiful little city, full of flowers.

On the *Chengtu* we turned our backs to it: we had boat drill. The Filipinos, short, bronze-skinned, wearing hard hats and yellow life-jackets, paraded under the lifeboats and prepared them for launching. Long black Filipino hair and whiskers stuck out under the helmets. One had tied his hair into a pigtail. They were a cheery bunch. Europeans in the shipping business had told me that Filipino officers can be a problem. Filipinos, Koreans and Taiwanese have too often bought their certificates of competence — their 'tickets' — for a few hundred dollars in Manila, Seoul or Taipei. 'That's one reason why the sea is so bloody dangerous today,' Julian Gomersall said. But a Filipino crew works well, giving no trouble.

'Cheap labour,' I said.

'Good cheap labour,' said Gomersall.

Cheap labour. These giggling brown men in overalls would not have resented that description; they felt lucky to be any kind of labour at all. Cheap labour! An image arose in my mind of the shabby white hull of an old liner in a steamy Red Sea port. In 1979 the veteran Messageries Maritimes liner *Pasteur* had lain at anchor, a floating dosshouse, in Jeddah. Once she had plied between Marseilles and Saigon carrying French colonial officials and their wives, planters and legionnaires, dealers in gems and Buddha heads, spies and card sharpers. On her decks, in imperial times, white-suited Frenchmen in topees sipped *pastis*, and while chatting to their wives thought with inward lascivious smiles of their Tonkinese mistresses. When she became a dormitory ship, two or three thousand Filipino stevedores slept cooped up below those decks like battery hens and by day were ferried to the Jeddah docks, to perform the manual work that, in these booming days of

70

desert oil and gold watches, the poorest Saudis disdain to do. One of the *Chengtu*'s Filipinos told me that the going wage in Jeddah for a Filipino labourer was $280 a month. The Middle East has spawned a new working class of Asian serfs who are glad to get this humble work. Koreans sweep the airports of Arabia; Pakistanis clear the rubbish from its streets; Filipinos work its docks.

During inspection at sea European ships' officers often find Filipino seamen, who like most seamen these days have cabins to themselves, huddled in each other's arms three or four to a single bunk, like apprehensive puppies in a basket. The officers smile significantly when they talk about this, but in a tentative, uncondemnatory way. For what is it? Affection? Sex? A cringing need for comfort in an unsure world? Something of all these, no doubt – and especially the last. Luckily for them, Filipinos are born with a protective skin: their indomitable humour and an unmatchable sense of fantasy.

The Filipino with the pigtail turned out to have almost as many names as a European prince. People called him Sonny, but he told me his real name was Sebastiano José Generoso. 'I am also known as Sonngen III,' he confided, squatting half-naked in red tracksuit bottoms on his bunk and handing me a San Mig beer. 'Sounds like a king,' I said. His cabin walls were an eye-riveting photographic collage of topless girls. In one or two vividly coloured photographs he himself was prominent, his arms round a couple of nude shoulders. One girl sat astride a bicycle in tight leather pants and dark glasses. 'Good for wanking,' Sonny admitted, adding, 'Maybe I marr-ee the one at left, maybe not.' Maybe not is more likely, I thought. He had a pleasant, unserious grin and the typically white teeth of most Asians. His pigtail was released so that his long, black hair fell straight to his naked shoulders, and from the gold chain round his neck hung what looked like a small tusk. 'This is a tooth of a wild peeg from Luzon,' he said.

He looked – many Filipinos do – like a good-natured pirate. But what was this photograph of mushrooms?

'These mushrooms are very interesting, surr. They are like LSD.'

'You like LSD, Sonny?'

'Not any more. Before, I was injecting Nembutol, speed, coke, something like that. Now I like whiskee, beer, vodka. Not too much – I don't like fighteeng and troubles.' His expression, in repose, was oddly sad and drawn for a young Filipino. All those drugs seemed to have depleted him.

Over his bunk were two paperbacks, *Everything You Want to Know about Recreational Drugs* (recreational?) and a paperback western by an author called Louis L'Amour. Bursts of hi-fi pop roared and pulsed down the alleyway outside.

'That's Roger,' Sonny said. 'He beats on my door at midnight to get me to come hear his music. But I read books. I say, go away. Last treep, some guy try to steeek a knife into Roger in the mess.'

'A music lover, perhaps?'

He laughed.

Sonny would be paid off at the end of this voyage; the China Navigation Company had decided to replace Filipinos by Hong Kong Chinese – a matter of company policy: Hong Kong company, Hong Kong crew. Never mind, Sonny shrugged; some other ship would turn up. A tramp for preference; you get the odd day or two in a port on a tramp; a container vessel never seemed to stop. Filipinos need fantasies: this one had put together a royal-sounding name, for instance. With his friends he would laugh, but he was a touching figure at other times. With me, his laughter would stop and his smile fade. Filipinos are amazingly ebullient, but their homeland – so beautiful – is cursed with a degree of poverty beside which the ailments of affluent Europe seem trivial. Sadly swinging his legs from his bunk, Sonny-Sebastiano-Sonngen III-Rahja sighed, 'The Filipinos are despised by so many people,' and his expression, suddenly close to tears, wrung my heart. Like gypsies, the indigent Filipinos are condemned to roam this cruel world, scrounging menial jobs to keep their families alive – and their self-respect.

I read in my notebook:

Captain Julian Gomersall, 5 foot 5 inches, a Yorkshireman living in Sidmouth. Also a fitness freak. Although no teetotaller, he does look fit, one has to admit that. At dawn he appears on the bridge in swimming trunks, and starts pacing up and down silently, like a caged panther; deep breathing; back and forth. Thirty times a day he runs up and down the external ladders of the ship. Robert Lau ('Sparklet'), the young Chinese radio officer, another health fanatic, passes him, impassively, in the opposite direction. Risking broken ankles for the sake of their waistlines, they dart about the ship panting grimly, ignoring each other and everyone else. 'Daft,' says Tony Darby, complacently patting his Tweedledum stomach.

Lau is quiet, shy and teetotal, the son of a retired Hong Kong prison officer. Lau plays poker with Ken, the second officer with the missing fingertip. He eats alone in his own cabin, gobbling Chinese food from his own bowl, untempted by the Norwegian hash served to us by the Filipino cook in the dining room. Once he had wanted to be a priest. 'But I am a sinner – I think.' His girlfriend wants him to leave the sea and join the police. 'Sins don't much matter there,' he said, with no sign that he's joking.

The captain and Jim Bird get on well, despite non-stop back-chat. Bird talks very loudly. Gomersall shouts back, 'Jim, I'm two feet away from you. D'you see? *Only two feet away*!' And: 'I should've brought my bloody ear trumpet down to dinner, I should.' The second officer laughs and calls them the Odd Couple. There *is* an element of light-hearted, knockabout, music hall about them: Morecambe and Wise or Laurel and Hardy.

Like Jim Bird, the noise in Darby's engine room is a serious danger to your hearing. Darby handed me a pair of ear muffs, then shouted descriptions of the various restless bits of gleaming machinery that pumped, spun and oozed hot oil. To no avail. I couldn't hear a thing. Darby looked like an actor on TV with the sound turned off. When I pointed this out, he shook his head. 'You have to be a lip reader down there, you do.'

Into the Molucca Sea. Flat water. To port, the horizon disappears into the Pacific towards Guam and the thousand coral islands of Micronesia. I am in a new world, heading for a huge stretch of newness – thousands of unknown miles of it. What do I see ahead of me? Stern missionaries in pince-nez (or lapsed ones like Noël Coward's Uncle Harry), outriggers skimming blue lagoons, whales, fuzzy black heads and filed teeth, Sadie Thompson, unflagging sunshine, coconut wine, Gauguin's grave. The razor-like winds of Shanghai and the China Seas seem far away in time as well as space. But wait! Someone spots a white object in the water. *More* Vietnamese?

'A bit off-course if they're Boat People,' Julian Gomersall says, looking through binoculars.

'And it's not waving its arms.'

'An albatross?' Ken suggests.

'An albatross, he says!' Gomersall sniffs contemptuously.

It is — harmless, unharrowing, innocent — a fisherman's buoy washed away from some village on the coast of New Guinea. Perhaps I might take its innocence as a sign that, for now at least, refugees, war and political terror are behind me. Farewell then to the tormented shores of Asia!

Part Two

Isles of Illusion

The term 'Savage' is, I conceive, often misapplied, and, indeed, when I consider the vices, cruelties, and enormities of every kind that spring up in the tainted atmosphere of a feverish civilisation, I am inclined to think that so far as the relative wickedness of the parties is concerned, four or five Marquesan Islanders sent to the United States as Missionaries might be quite as useful as an equal number of Americans despatched to the Islands in a similar capacity.

Herman Melville: *Typee*

Seven

Salute to Melanesia!

Approaching our first port of call, Wewak (pronounced Wee-wak), we raised the flag of Papua New Guinea over the wheelhouse. A pretty flag, of an interesting design, it is diagonally divided with the bottom half depicting the five golden stars of the Southern Cross on black, and the upper half red with the golden silhouette of a bird of paradise on the wing. The bird of paradise is a famous local inhabitant.

Pointing to the beautiful bird, Ken, the second officer, said, 'Know what we call that? Kentucky fried chicken.'

'Legless chicken,' I said.

'I beg your pardon?'

'They have no legs.' I read out loud:

In these islands onlie is found the bird which the Portingales call pasaros de Sol, that is Fowle of the Sunne, the Italians call it Manu codiatas, and the Latinists, Pradiscas, and by us called Paradice-birdes, for ye beauty of their feathers which passe al other birdes; these birdes are never seene alive, but being dead they fall on the Islands; they flie, as it is said, alwaies into the Sunne, and keep themselvs continually in the ayre without lighting on the earth, for they have neither feet nor wings, but onely head and body and the most part tayle.

This description was written by a Dutch geographer, John van Linschoten (1563–1611), who was not alone in denying the wretched birds of paradise legs and even wings. A more reasonable man, Antonio Pigafetta, Magellan's lieutenant, described these shy birds: 'Big as thrushes, with small heads, long beaks and legs slender like a writing pen.' 'The most part tayle' of Linschoten's description is accurate enough: both the king and the red-plumed variety (among others) are very like multi-hued feathered waterfalls – their tails dwarf their bodies in such startling cascades of colour that you wonder if they really have strayed from Paradise, rather than from the leafiest recesses of the rain forests of New Guinea and the Malay archipelago. What a pity that their voices do not match their noble appearance. Alas, they are related to the harsh-tongued jays. Instead of the melodious fluting you might expect, their raucous shouts convey the impression that, feather by heavenly feather, they are being plucked alive. Or even Kentucky-fried, very slowly, by heartless emissaries of Colonel Sanders.

Nothing but sun from now on? Approaching Wewak, the sea was a stagnant-looking green, the radio said there was rain over Port Moresby to our south-west, and large logs began to appear in the water.

Dark ridges rose up on the western skyline of West Irian. On the chart, the names were becoming the names of explorers: Mount Bougainville to starboard and the Schouten Islands to port. Bougainville, who circumnavigated the world between 1767 and 1769, established a colony on the Falkland Islands, visited many Pacific Islands, named this one after himself, and somehow missed Australia. He also, of course, gave his name to a brilliant-coloured flowering creeper. The far more obscure Wilhelm Schouten – why were we never taught about him at school? – discovered what we know as Cape Horn Island and named it after his home town, Hoorn in Holland. Here, three of Schouten's other islands have attractive Dr Doolittle names – Bam, Mot Mot and Blup Blup. Otherwise names becoming unsmilingly Teutonic – Marienbad lay beyond Wewak, and so did Richthofen Point. The sea we moved on, as smooth and shining as a Prussian cuirass, was the Bismarck Sea; the colony on our right hand and ahead had been German New Guinea until the defeat of the Kaiser in 1918.

My notes say:

> Not much to Wewak. All I see is a promontory and behind it an open shore; smoke over attap roofs; palms; a mission church.
> Near us, on the shore: a meagre sprinkling of neat white bunga-lows with corrugated iron roofs some way away, a broad but

featureless meadow; a background of creeper-draped trees.

A causeway with a jetty crossing its head to form a T, at the end of which we must tie up and offload.

'If they'd looked hard they'd have found it difficult to find a worse place to put that causeway,' says Gomersall. 'Famous swells here. Daft.'

We approach the causeway dead slow and an Australian voice on the radio warns us of 'something of a swell', but there is no hitch. Black stevedores with the gnome faces of New Guinea quickly come aboard.

I went below and read the *South Pacific Handbook* – which people in Hong Kong had told me was an indispensable guide for an ignorant traveller like me. It had pages of down-to-earth information and sensible advice. It also contained some history. I read of the hard-handed rule from the 1880s of the Kaiser's Germans in the north-eastern part of New Guinea we were skirting and in the banana-shaped island of New Britain, which then they called Kaiser Wilhelm Land; its capital, Rabaul, was one of our ports of call. After the German defeat in 1918, Australia took control of this entire region until in 1975 it became the independent state of Papua New Guinea. In between the Germans and independence came the Second World War. From 1942, much of New Guinea was occupied by Japanese forces whose commanders set up a major base at Rabaul. The Americans and Australians fought them off before they could reach Port Moresby, the chief city of the territory. It took three years of carnage before the Japanese finally surrendered to the Australians at Wewak – after the American atom bombs had fallen on their homeland.

This little I learnt on my bunk on the *Chengtu*. The more dramatic events in the war against the Japanese – the fall of Singapore, the sinking of the British capital ships *Prince of Wales* and *Repulse*, the prisoner of war camps – were familiar, yet who in Europe knew much of the jungle and naval war Japan brought to Australia's doorstep, of the American counter-attack from Guadalcanal in the Solomon Islands to the Gulf of Papua, through the Philippines and, finally, to the atom-bombed shores of Japan? What was Guadalcanal but a noisy gung-ho film, starring John Wayne – or was it Errol Flynn? I was ashamed of my ignorance, and correspondingly glad that Guadalcanal Island was a stop on the itinerary I hoped to follow.

While the sun went down on little Wewak, I tried to imagine how it was here forty years ago – the smoke from bombed petrol dumps, the terror of the emaciated, fever-struck soldiers of Nippon, a tattered Rising Sun over the scorched tatters of jungle round the airstrip. But instead of the roar of propeller-driven warplanes, there were the short, sharp screams of the clouds of small bats that darted in and out of our deck lights. A few black men hung about the wharf, smoking, idly gazing while the stevedores worked. I was glad to hear Gomersall's 'Full ahead!' and to feel the current carrying us smoothly away from the wharf. Perhaps we all were. That evening, there was Australian champagne with dinner, and brandy in the bar.

My notes record a debate: Tony Darby claimed that Queen Elizabeth I spoke English with a Yorkshire accent.

'For a start,' Julian Gomersall said, 'she didn't even come from Yorkshire.'

'Her father did.'

'Her father was a bloody Welshman. Tudor. Henry VIII. Talked like Stanley Baker, the actor.'

'Don't say we were ruled by a lot of bloody Cambrians!'

Later, I found Tony on deck staring at the stars. 'Millionaires would spend millions of pounds to see this view,' he said. He told me his wife was Japanese and that she and their two children spoke *real* English – real Don-caster: 'The language in which – it's mah con-sidered joodgement – Queen Elizabeth spoke to Sir Francis Drake.'

Two books might provide useful preparation for the host of islands we were fast approaching. These were my 1923 edition of Robert Louis Stevenson's *Vailima Letters*, his correspondence from his Samoan home, and the old, mysteriously discovered book lent to me by Tim Bridgeman in Hong Kong, called *Isles of Illusion: Letters from the South Seas*. In its first few pages, *Isles of Illusion*'s anonymous author revealed himself as an opinionated Englishman of some education who, enchanted by Stevenson's accounts, had run away to the South Pacific before the First World War to escape the boredom of schoolmastering in England. The book is a collection of his letters home, pungent evocations of the South Sea islands on which he laboured and suffered. He saw plenty of white cruelty and the terrible evil of 'blackbirding', as slavery was called then in the Pacific. He worked on remote plantations from 1912 into the 1920s, at first for a German trader called Müller, who had set him up as manager in one of a handful of islands which were then known as the New Hebrides, and which became independent Vanuatu in 1980.

The recipient of these letters, his literary friend Bohun Lynch, arranged in 1923 for their publication. But Lynch was prudent. To conceal the writer's identity – he was still living among the people he commented on so uninhibitedly in his letters – Lynch gave him the pen-name Asterisk. Asterisk was intelligent and observant. His views were strongly expressed and sometimes interestingly contradictory. His character soon began to emerge in my mind as a rough diamond, a hard worker, brave, irascible, easily shocked by the cynical brutality of Australian plantation managers (he writes with an angry contempt of these 'Orstryliuns'), and by what he saw as the dishonesty of missionaries. Naturally, Asterisk was a man of his time: he used the term 'Kanaka' (the white man's word for Pacific Islanders that is as unacceptable as 'nigger' is today) without a second thought. Nor did he pull his punches when describing what he saw as the islanders' shortcomings: the dirt, the smells, the fecklessness. At the same time he showed great compassion for them; doctored them; eventually took a New Hebridean woman into his bungalow and had a son by her. He was a gruff romantic despite himself, and never ceased to admire Stevenson, who had died in Samoa twenty years before. Yet I suppose the 'illusion' in the title of his book was the illusion Asterisk had brought with him from England – that every South Pacific Island was a Stevensonian paradise.

Now, sitting on my bunk in the *Chengtu*, I looked from one book to the other. 'God's best, his sweetest work', was Stevenson's view of his beloved Polynesians, the Samoans, while Asterisk was feeling cheated in Melanesia:

> I wish I had gone to more beautiful islands ... a strict line divides the South Sea Islands of Stevenson flavour from the merely interesting islands inhabited by ugly semi-cannibalistic savages. This line is drawn from the south-west corner of New Zealand to Honolulu, and passes between Fiji and the Tongan Islands.... The eastern islands are ... the real lotos land....

Yet there was much more to it than beauty.

> I doubt whether the dreamed-of Pacific Isle exists now. The horrible octopus of missionary-cum-trader-cum-official has spread his tentacles everywhere.

He wrote that in 1913. I wanted to see if things had improved or worsened in seventy years.

The British Admiralty's *Pacific Islands Pilot* – I found a copy in the chart room – told me that the Sepik River, which we soon passed, is the largest in north-east Papua New Guinea: a mile wide at its mouth. The Sepik had been investigated in 1910 by a mixed Dutch and German boundary commission (West Irian, now Indonesia, belonged in those days to Holland), whose members penetrated thirty miles upstream in canoes. They found 'dense swamps, reed-beds, crocodiles, exceptionally troublesome mosquitoes, a malignant type of malaria, and natives eager to trade'.

Nothing in that daunting inventory, except perhaps for the trade-hungry natives, could possible by applied to Madang, which we came to next day, a small, bland place of green bays and inlets. 'All the best, Charles and Diana' was painted on the harbour wall. I remember a walk ashore through a kind of garden suburb, lunch at a pleasant restaurant, an Australian wine called Coolabah Riesling; and a colony of huge fruit bats hanging upside down in an avenue of eucalyptus trees. One Australian-owned hotel advertised rooms for the equivalent of £75 a night. It catered, I suppose, exclusively for well-paid expatriates – Australian plantation staff, technicians, traders, tourists. Tourists flew up here from Australia, Jim Bird said, on a local airline that could be the most expensive in the world. It was called Air Niugini.

*   *   *

'Julian, do you think you could lift my pilot boat from the wharf into the water? We have crines, but you could do it better, ya?' The harbour pilot at the port of Lae was Norwegian, but his accent had a lot to do with his years in Australian outposts like New Guinea. 'A cridle and slings are on her, ready to tike her out. Ok-eye?'

The pilot's name was Rolf Underdahl and, according to Jim Bird, who could do a clever imitation of him, he was an old-timer here. Tall, beaky nose, white singlet, shorts and sandals, peaked white cap, pale gold hair, friendly, pale blue eyes – he looked like Danny Kaye impersonating Hans Christian Andersen.

A ring of hills encircled a bay where the wide mouth of the Markham River ran into the Solomon Sea. We lay alongside a long wharf and warehouses, near bustling fork lift trucks and stacks of coloured containers. From the shore a stiff breeze brought a sweet, damp smell of vegetation, but failed to stir the heat and humidity. 'What a little shit of a gulf,' said Underdahl cheerfully, rotating his wrists over his head like a man winding two grandfather clocks at once. 'Reel in, reel in!' he called in the direction of Generoso and his mates near the winches of the bows. 'Ya!'

When the *Chengtu*'s cranes had swung his little pilot launch into the water, Underdahl used it to take Julian Gomersall, Jim Bird and myself to the Lae Yacht Club, an unpretentious little place some way round the northern shore of the 'shit of a gulf'. There, large blond men and athletic-looking women milled about interspersing energetic swigs of beer with shouts welcoming numerous small yachts which charged 'home' amid much cheering and clapping.

'Oh, there's a little race on, is there, Gordon?' Underdahl cried genially to a man in an eyeshade, and led us under a board marked 'Lae Game Fishing Club', announcing that the biggest marlin caught here so far had weighed 250 pounds, to the water's edge where we sat among a happy, raucous group of the Australians of Melanesia at play. Most of the men wore shorts and sandals or 'sensible' shoes, were large and hearty, and their upper lips disappeared under the thick waterfall moustaches favoured by the cowboys in the Marlboro cigarette advertisements and by Dennis Lillee, the Australian fast bowler. Some wore long socks with their shorts; they looked like members of a hockey team, or schoolboys at one of those English schools which keep boys in shorts well after the time has come for longs. Their hair on the whole was fair and short, and their hands large and clamped round cans of beer. Sweat ran down faces burned scarlet by the sun.

Against a burst of cheering that greeted the dashing arrival of a small yacht, first in its heat, Underdahl and his tall, blonde wife, Astrid, told a story of a recent holiday – a drive round part of the Highlands behind Lae with their children. It sounded exciting. 'Yes, and for that I wouldn't do it again,' Rolf Underdahl smiled. 'Well – we ran into this bush war up there. Ya, a *war*! With our kids!' They had turned a corner in wild country a few thousand feet up, and suddenly spears and arrows shot back and forth across the road. Dark figures with painted faces pranced ferociously out of the bush. Were they rushing down to massacre the Underdahls? No – despite their hideous grimaces, these wild warriors were in single-minded pursuit of another set of warriors fleeing down the precipitous hillside, and the road had had the temporary halting effect of a firebreak. In the bushes on either side of the Underdahl family fierce faces under hornbill feather caps, and grotesquely transformed by streaks of paint into masks of implacable fury, peered and scowled. Shrill, inhuman cries arose. Spears rattled. Another volley of arrows down the hillside seemed to be on the cards. To the terrified Underdahls, caught in the middle of a sort of Papuan Agincourt, an immediate detour seemed *de rigueur*. 'Well, I had Astrid and the children with me, eh? Of course, those fellows would never attack whites. But better be sife, ya?' He had turned the car and accelerated away.

It was safer in those Highlands than in towns like Port Moresby, someone said, what with the muggings there, the assaults on white people. 'Even on tourists.'

Astrid Underdahl said, 'We've turned the locals into Baptists, Methodists, Lutherans, Seventh Day Adventists, Catholics, all sorts. No wonder the poor devils are all muddled. What to believe? They take to the grog, can't handle it, and just get terribly violent.'

In the confident atmosphere of the white man's club, we confident whites handled more beer non-violently, and then still more. It was a friendly place. But when I stood up to stretch my legs and looked around a bit, no hospitality could blind me to the fact that Lae was a white man's suburb transplanted with fine trees, a startling profusion of flowers and a good deal of corrugated iron roofing.

Back on board *Chengtu*, I gave the ship's rail an affectionate slap. Hearing it, Sonny Generoso, on the foredeck, returned me a grin and the thumbs-up sign.

*   *   *

84

Things flew around my cabin. While I rescued the Gordon's gin bottle from the floor, books dived under the couch; drawers popped open. The deck was rocking like a seesaw. I tucked the bottle snugly into the blankets on my bunk and climbed with some difficulty to the bridge. I found Jim Bird holding onto the front rail with a puzzled expression.

'I've never seen this kind of weather here before,' he said. 'Never in twelve years.' I looked out on an angry greyness. Cascades of water pounded down the windows. A small, battered bird that seemed to want to land was snatched past us. We might have been off the Shetlands instead of a few hours east of Lae, passing the southern entrance to the Dampier Strait. The chart showed volcanoes and the 6000-foot Whiteman Range to port but the eye said they did not exist. Even the coast of New Britain was almost hidden by sheets of rain. A cement-grey sea broke over our bows, and the Filipino seamen struggled across the deck in oilskins, heads down in the spray like characters weathering a bad storm in Kipling's *Captains Courageous*.

In his radio room Robert Lau, too, was fighting the storm. Now and again he pounded out a lightning run of Morse dots and dashes but nothing much seemed to come of it. He shrugged at me, dimly muttering 'Gale' while, unasked, the machinery flung back gibberish. In rapid succession, plaintive chirps like the cries of newly hatched chicks, the drooling and burbling of a drunken idiot, angry bursts of what seemed like gunfire, and maddeningly insistent peeps as of some celestial traffic jam issued from the electrical apparatus stacked round the bulkheads. I thought Robert might start gibbering, too. I fled.

Across the Solomon Sea, the storm continued to rage. Thundering west through the darkness into the Gulf of Papua, it sank a passenger-freight barge called *Sir Garrick*, with thirteen people aboard, and drowned five of them, including the captain and his wife.

Eight

An important question in New Britain seemed to be whether Rabaul, its capital, would blow up or disappear under the sea before or after the year AD 2000. But that was something I only learned when I had been there two days.

In the unsociable way of container ships, *Chengtu* had sailed away the evening of the very day she'd arrived, wasting no time. Julian and Jim had barely managed a drink ashore because there had been a minor confusion on board: the Rabaul customs officers discovered a large cache of pornographic magazines in the Filipinos' quarters and seized them. While they were at it, they had confiscated books and two watches and a Sheaffer pen belonging to Patrick, the Chinese third engineer. They had even eyed Robert Lau's alarm clock. Harry, the young shipping man from Steamships, the China Navigation Company's agents in Rabaul, was going to have to negotiate with the customs people.

So, after sunset, *Chengtu* sailed away, leaving behind a cargo of cloth for sarongs (here called laplaps), canned duck, umbrellas, sewing machines and nylon fishing nets, and bearing away *bêches de mer* (sea cucumbers) for Hong Kong and cocoa for Singapore. Waving her goodbye, I found myself spotlit on the wharf like an actor on a stage by Jim Bird's searchlight; drawn away stern-first by an invisible tug, the *Chengtu* passed out of sight in the darkness of the bay.

Harry, the agent, drove me from the dock. He was a Polish Australian, he said. He liked Rabaul, and his wife was a local girl, a Tolai. 'It's become rather quiet here, actually. A whole lot of expats have moved out recently,' he said. 'The Burns Philp copra plantations are closing down, some of them, since the world price for copra crumbled away.'

'Copra is the industry?'

Harry the Pole looked at me through thick spectacles as if my ignorance worried him. 'It's always been plantations here. Coconuts and cocoa. All over PNG; and all over the Solomons; and Vanuatu, come to that. Vanuatu – that's what they call the New Hebrides.' Suddenly, he said, 'We'll make a detour. Just to show you a little bit ...' and steered the car into another world.

First, an empty avenue of beautiful trees, then a less kempt region of shrubs and bushes, and finally we drove into a low, dense forest of bananas. The banana trees screened off any glimpse of what might lie behind, and we turned into a small, shadowy region of thatched huts, smoking fires, an uneven earth floor and black-skinned people. Children ran out of dimly lit doorways and up to the car, which I saw they recognized.

'What's your name?' they shouted at me.

Harry got out and said, 'This is my wife's family's place,' and a handsome woman came out of the shadows and said to me, very quietly, 'Hallo.' A tall man who looked like her brother came up and shook my hand.

'Shall we go for a short drive?' Harry said to his wife.

'Oh, yes,' she said.

At the top of a hill of big trees, Harry turned off and stopped at a ramshackle bar with a billiard table in a three-walled wooden room open to the night. A number of fuzzy-headed men were drinking beer and playing snooker. Harry joined them; I watched and drank beer, and talked to Harry's wife, but without much purpose. I had hardly slept during the storm the night before, and soon I fell asleep in the car. Now and again I saw dark, bowed shapes against the weak light over the billiard table, and heard the click of the balls and the clash of beer cans, as if through the mists of a dream.

Next morning I wandered into the neat streets of Rabaul. They had the Teutonic exactness you would expect from a town that once was the capital of Kaiser Wilhelm Land; large white ladies from Hamburg and Düsseldorf had driven their horse-drawn gharries up Mango Street accompanied by stiff-necked men with cropped blond hair, high collars and white duck suits. The Germans had planted magnificent avenues of frangipani, too, and the streets still glowed as though they were not flowers but brilliant white candles. After the heavy Allied bombing that had destroyed most of Rabaul, the town had risen again, and in these days of independence and Australian residents I suppose it looks much as it did in the old colonial days.

Rabaul smiles. Among the one-storey shops of Mango and Kamakeke Streets, the smiles of its inhabitants match the white of the frangipani outside. 'Sorry to disturb you,' bushy-haired local girls said, inadvertently bumping into me in a doorway.

The hair of the New Britons in the streets amazed me. I had never seen anything like it. It is not the hair of the Caribbean. It is not what I had seen on West Indian heads in England, or on black American heads, or African ones. It was altogether fluffier and lighter in texture – it looked like thistledown – and it seemed to come in a variety of shades. Here, a head of midnight blue; there, one the colour of rust or lime. Sometimes, I saw hair that was apparently black but which, with the sun behind it, turned to a deep reddish-brown. And, most vivid of all, hair that was apparently an unabashed peroxide yellow, not far from the colour of a dizzy Hollywood blonde. *Was* it peroxide? *Was* it dyed? And the shapes were as carefully coiffed as the sculptured bushes in a rich man's park. Sometimes the fuzz ballooned up from its owner's head, framing it and crowning it; sometimes it looked like a giant puffball; sometimes like a guardsman's bearskin. On others – the most striking – it was exactly the shape of an atomic explosion, rising and expanding upwards and outwards like a mushroom cloud. The New British floated down the sidewalks, in and out of shops, their great clouds of spun sugar borne airily aloft, above broad, smiling mouths and big, inviting eyes, and the odd voices uttering the strange, half-familiar, almost-English sounds of pidgin. It was a new, rather grand spectacle. I found it hard not to stop and stare. I wanted to applaud.

Music issued from shop doorways and floated across Mango Street, and from one side of it or the other I heard a tight, rhythmic harmony of voices singing what sounded like cheerful Negro spirituals. I crossed over to the sign saying 'Rabaul Music', and inside the smiling, frizzy girl behind the counter told me the tape we were listening to was of the We Have This Hope Singers, a group from Port Moresby. She put on other similar local groups for my benefit: 'Guba Gaba Tona'; and a Papuan choir belted out 'Saved by His Grace' and 'I Must Tell Jesus' in fine spiritual style. Several customers joined in as they wandered about. Further up the street in a newspaper shop I bought that day's *Niugini Nius*, and on a shelf of religious books I saw the New Testament in pidgin – the *Nupela Testamen*.

In his office over the Steamships Company sales room, Harry the Pole handed me a booklet. 'You may find this handy,' he said. It was a simple guide to the local language, called *pisin* here, or to be more exact *Tok Pisin* (talk pidgin). Over a cup of Steamships tea, I flipped through it and read:

> Tok Pisin is a language in its own right. It is spoken by a million people in Papua New Guinea.... It is not broken English. It is not baby talk. It has rules and grammar. Pidgin is a language between language-groups which cannot speak each other's language. Typical would be the stevedores who load and unload the ships coming from dozens of countries into a harbour like Hong Kong. This is where the word pidgin originates. Pidgin is the Chinese approximation of the word 'business'. 'Business' = 'bisin' = 'pisin' = 'pidgin' (which only anglicises the spelling)....

Evidently pidgin is spoken in all the islands of New Guinea and in the Highlands of Papua. Since 1975, it has been the national language of independent Papua New Guinea.

Harry said: 'Start off with *Moning, Apinun*, and *Gut Nait*. That's easy. Remember the definite article is non-existent, but the indefinite article is *wanpela*. And if you want to say "This is my house", you say "*Haus bilong me*". See?'

He searched about again in the booklet. 'Look – *Dok i ron hariap tumas*. What's that say to you?'

'It says "Dog he run hurry up too much". Which I suppose means "The dog ran – or is running – too fast"?'

'Close. Actually, it's "The dog ran *very* fast". *Tumas* is "very", not "too much".'

It was fun to look through the vocabulary. At random I found: *sapos* meaning 'if'; *pikinini man* meaning 'son'; and *kalabusman* meaning 'prisoner'. *Namba wan dokta* meant not 'best doctor' but (more pompously) 'District Medical Officer'. I liked 'hill', which was *liklik maunten* (small mountain). And it was nice to find that 'to urinate' was *pispis*, and that 'penis' was simply *kok*.

When Harry introduced me to his assistant, a dark Papuan called Gimana Kila, he said, 'Gimana will take you on a tour of the Jap relics and the volcanoes.' He added, 'By the way, I've talked to John Taylor, the shipping manager of Burns Philp. They run most things in PNG – plantations, trading, shipping, all sorts. A small passenger vessel leaves for Kieta tomorrow evening, and it's got a tiny cabin. It may call at a port or two on the way – very small ones. Three days. Sounds good.'

It did sound good.

'We'll see John about it,' Harry said.

Rabaul's Simpson Harbour is a green-fringed horseshoe, with the peninsula of Gazelle like a hammer poised to close it. At the bay's entrance two rocky snouts stand up as if begging ships to bump into them. The Gazelle hammerhead was curiously knobbly, like the head of a man suffering from carbuncles, and close to you saw these knobs were volcanic cones overgrown with vegetation. There were open craters, too, like boiled eggs with their heads sliced off.

Behind the Gazelle peninsula, among a conflagration of flowery shrubs, I found my first Pacific island landscape. It was unforgettable.

We looked across the long, forested body of New Britain; a stormy ocean of trees, rolling waves of forest alternating with great troughs of palm, from which rose faint blue wisps of plantation fires signalling a few hidden clearings. Through my binoculars I could see enormous trees that put out long, smooth branches or shaggy, undulating ones from which screens of creepers fell to tether them to the forest floor. Flaring roots like the solid folds of grey-green togas buttressed their trunks, and on their slender, silver stems the tousled heads of coconut palms, neatly in line and gently stirred by breezes from the sea, gave an extraordinary illusion of movement, as if well-drilled waves of shock-headed tribesmen were advancing up the hillsides. Ridge after ridge the forest stretched away, green at first, then changing to deep blue that faded, paler and paler, and at last, on the farthermost ridges, disappeared into haze and rain.

Relics of the last war – it seemed to me unbelievably distant – lay half-visible in the luxuriant undergrowth. Gimana showed me rock caves that had sheltered Japanese naval barges from Allied bombers; their wheels and bodies were rusty now. We approached them up a muddy rivulet bed that led from the road through a coconut plantation, where in a clearing a small boy with an orange fuzz was playing with a yo-yo. High over the bay and the volcanoes was a great gun, a Japanese Big Bertha on a swivel, still pointing its metal snout at Rabaul and Simpson Harbour and Blanche Bay, like a forgotten sentinel watching for enemy ships that had long since been scrapped. No one had bothered to remove the Japanese pocket submarine that, like an Egyptian mummy case, crouched in a cave by the edge of the bay. The wreck of a huge floating crane still disfigured the view.

The Japanese in Rabaul had been heavily bombed and then left to rot. To get to General Yamamotu's Lilliputian bunker, his last refuge, I had to squeeze past a ruined tank and down a low stair – hot and damp and claustrophobic. Pre-First World War German wall charts anachronistically showed 'Humboldt Bay' and 'Berlin Road', and the mountains of New Britain were in 'Kaiser Wilhelm Land'. There were Japanese army radio parts and photographs of the bombed boulevards of Rabaul and iron carcases of cargo vessels destroyed in Simpson Harbour. Oppressed by the smell of damp and urine, the aura of forty-year-old decay, I turned to leave.

'Let's see the volcano experts on the Gazelle peninsula.'

'Okay,' Gimana said, relieved.

At the Observatory, a cool, modern hilltop complex of buildings with a good view, the senior government 'volcanologist', Dr Peter Löwenstein, sat me down with a report entitled *Recent Eruptive History of the Rabaul Volcanoes*, in which I read:

> Rabaul must be one of the most strikingly situated towns in the world. It has been built inside a still-active volcano.... The magnificent harbour resulted directly from successive large eruptions and the eventual collapse of one or more large volcanoes ... the harbour and the main port of the town is a volcanic caldera.

To this dramatic information Dr Löwenstein had more to add. The last eruption, it seemed, had been as recent as 1980, though rather mild. An old volcano behind Rabaul had sent up 'a cloud of ash and vapour, oh, several kilometres into the sky. The most recent *big* one went off in 1937. That one lasted four days. And at the end of the nightmare, a mass of land came up through the water, and stayed there.'

'Anyone hurt?'

'Five hundred people suffocated by ash and vapour.'

Imagine the horror of a whalelike mass rising through the surface of the bay.

'There was no warning?'

'Ample warning. Two days in which the earth shook and the dry land kept appearing, but quite gently. People had forgotten earlier eruptions. But then suddenly – whoosh! – up it went.'

There were five potentially active volcanoes in the immediate vicinity of Rabaul, Löwenstein said. It seemed a lot. 'Our calculations point to an eruption about the volume of the 1937 one before the year 2000.'

Lowenstein said the majority of opinion was against anything like the big bang of two thousand years ago, when the bottom dropped out of the land, the sea rushed in and the bay was formed. But a few experts gave it a ten-to-one chance.

I was aware of Gimana Kila shifting uneasily in his chair.

'The whole place might sink, the water rush in on all that very hot matter underground, and explode,' Löwenstein said. And then smiled. 'But I don't think it will happen.'

Now Gimana was prowling restlessly by the window. He looked as jumpy as a cat besieged by dogs. 'I suppose if you did,' I said, 'you wouldn't be here.'

'My predecessor was killed by a volcano out here,' Löwenstein replied. 'At Karkan Island off Madang.' I remembered the island

and its volcano, standing guard at the entrance to the little port.

Driving down the hill, Gimana moistened his dry lips and said, 'I may leave for Port Moresby soon, after what that man said about another volcano explosion.'

'Now, now, Gimana, Dr Löwenstein didn't say it would happen. Look, he lives here himself. Just keep an eye on him. If he does a bunk all of a sudden, then you might worry.'

In the Steamships office Harry admitted that he himself had quite often felt earthquakes. 'It's mildly exciting – your heart starts to pound a bit. Once, all the office workers of Rabaul dropped everything, vaulted over their desks like Olympic hurdlers and rushed out into the street. You did, too, didn't you, Gimana? Even left your shirt behind.'

The other black faces turned, smiling, to Gimana, lightly mocking the only Papuan in the room. Poor Gimana. I hoped he wouldn't start dreaming of a holocaust, of the population of Rabaul disappearing down a steaming red-hot hole in the earth. I hoped I wouldn't.

Nine

My notebook reads:

Amusing example of pidgin. On a shop door in Mango Street: *Go insite long ia* = 'Entrance'.

Harry the Pole says the mountain dwellers here liked very much to wear tea cosies as hats. Hundreds and thousands of tea cosies are imported; for a time no one could understand why they were ordered. Cases of ping-pong balls are shipped in, too. Harry says that modesty has driven many naked Highlanders to wear ping-pong balls on the ends of their penises – it's unseemly to leave them completely uncovered, and ping-pong balls are apparently much more comfortable than the traditional nutshell they once jammed on, and more easily replaced.

Harry has a nasty tropical sore on his foot. Sores like this are very common – in this unusual germ-laden atmosphere, he says, a small scratch can turn septic at once. I don't grasp why the germs are so rampant. Harry's simple and effective remedy: squeeze the juice of a frangipani leaf on the sore, and lightly bandage it.

I have run into a nice Englishman called Michael Tinne, a copra expert on temporary secondment in charge of Burns Philp's plantations in PNG: 'the lone Pom', he calls himself. From him I borrow a missionary's book of many years ago called (predictably) *Twenty Years Among the Primitive Papuans*. In it a Reverend William Bromilow displays his photographs of naked locals, and writes: 'Up to the time of marriage, the women are undisguisedly unmoral [*sic*], and afterwards the restraints are doubtfully observed. Among the men no moral code can be said to exist;

children are initiated to vice at a terribly early age.' Should be exciting scope for a missionary there. Another missionary wrote in 1897 that when he first arrived in Rabaul in 1870 he found 'all were naked, men, women, children'. Now, he said, 'all are clothed – not a single naked native is visible within the sphere of mission influence'. All dressed up within twenty-seven years.

Talking of clothes: Harry says to me, 'You'd better get yourself some shorts, Gavin.'

'Good God, no.'

Harry (astonished): 'You're going on wearing longs?'

Me: 'I certainly am. First, longs are a protection against insects. Second, my knees are too knobbly. And third, I don't want to look like yet another over-aged hockey player.' Like some of the yachtsmen in Lae, the Australian men I have seen in shops, in the hotel, all wear natty, tailored shorts, stockings and 'sensible' shoes. I add, to mollify him, 'Of course, it's all right for a young man. And your niftily tailored shorts are better than the absurd knee-length bell-bottomed things the British wear.'

I might have added that English accents must sound as bizarre to people here as some of the Australian voices in the bar of the Travel Lodge Hotel do to me. I note a few remarks at random: 'Oi rekin' the fade's not bed.... Yis, he sti'ed one yea-a end a hairf in Sidnee.... Yeah, he's got a mare-ster's degree.... Excuse oi, can oi use the phane?.... Thenks.'

John Taylor of Burns Philp's shipping department said, 'We've the *Burtide*, a nearly brand-new little ship, built in Singapore, sailing to Kieta on Bougainville Island tomorrow. Just right for you.' Perfect. But next day: 'Bad news, I'm afraid. The captain reports mechanical trouble. She's giving off black smoke. She'll be delayed at least three days.'

There was a nasty scene in the Travel Lodge Hotel that night. At dinner, a hideously drunken lout at a table of four Europeans kept bawling at the waiter, 'Come yer, friend!.... Hey you, you black bastard!' and similar insults. The Tolai waiter, understandably furious, finally and rightly refused to serve him. Other waiters who did so were similarly taunted and abused by this white monster with a bull neck and huge arms, a scene so noisy and disagreeable that no one in the restaurant could ignore it. Yet no one at the drunk's table tried to restrain him. Nor, despite the distracted comings and goings of the waiters, was there any sign of the manager who might have been expected to appear. The culprit was a giant of about forty-five and not less than 250 pounds, with yellow hair flopping over a face the colour of magenta with drink and anger. Habitual aggression had moulded his mouth into a bully's half-pout, half-sneer. The men at his table were frightened of him – that was clear. After the meal I looked for the manager. After all, despite the economic hold Australia has here, PNG is an independent country – a member of the United Nations and all that. In Singapore, or India, or any country I can think of the police would have collared this man double quick, very likely pending deportation.

The young manager told me with a helpless look, 'I've only been here a week.' He'd heard that complaints had been made in the past about this man to the head of his mission. 'He works in a Catholic Mission, you know.'

'A good advertisement for it,' I said. 'Why don't you bar him from your hotel?'

'Oh, well, Rabaul's a small place. I make it hard for him, he might make it hard for me.'

'It looked as if the waiters wanted to go to the police,' I said.

'They wanted to,' he agreed. 'But I advised them to wait until morning when they'd have cooled down a bit.'

'Why should they cool down? Doesn't this affect local attitudes to all of you foreigners?'

'I'm afraid it does. Because of this sort of thing, there are – well, nationalists – who resent us quite a lot. But, as I say – I've only been here a week. And it's a small place....'

When I told all this to Harry he said, yes, there were expatriates who went about insulting the local people. 'The people here resent these colonial attitudes, of course. They quietly note who behaves like that, and probably get their own back some time later, somehow.'

I said I hoped they did.

'Now that you've got a little time, you'd better see what a plantation is like,' Michael Tinne said. He was a large, breezy man, still youngish, despite years of experience of copra plantations in Africa and Central America. Because of the world's sudden relative lack of interest in copra, the dried pith of the coconut, he was closing some of Burns Philp's many plantations. For that reason, and because he was British, I had an idea he wouldn't be too popular in the region. But he didn't seem to worry. He drove me to the eastern tip of New Britain where a bungalow stood high over St George's Channel, looking out to sea under the branches of a huge frangipani tree. The blue, lumpy outline of New Ireland lay under cloud on the horizon.

A well-cut lawn plunged to a beach of black sand, and the sound of surf against the headland filtered up to us through a thick fringe of palms. Behind the house the copra forest began, sunless and glum. Ian Smith, the Australian manager, seemed as young as Tinne but he had lived alone on plantations here and there for twenty years; some far more remote than this one, he said. He poured Bloody Marys, and after a bit threw steaks onto a large metal sheet laid across two small piles of bricks. A fire composed entirely of coconut shells gave out an immense heat.

What sort of life was this, year after year on a plantation?

'Well,' he said, 'I can retire at fifty with a pension. I can save perhaps £10,000 a year out of my salary of £16,000. I've bought forty acres outside Melbourne.' He lived without air conditioning, doors and windows wide open; it was very hot and humid. Just standing still, I felt sweat raining off my face and soaking my shirt. I mopped away at it with the little towel I always carry in my belt in hot climates. Smith was a likeable man, happy in his environment; happy in shorts and walking barefoot – taking local conditions as they came. Mosquitoes? 'Don't worry me,' he said. Dengue fever? 'You sweat and shake like hell, you feel all your bones and muscles are on the rack. After that a fearful headache – oh, terrible!'

'What do you take for it?'

'There's no remedy. Just take an aspirin.'

Smith spoke highly of his 'boys', the plantation workers. One manager had been stabbed to death in the last ten years, he laughed, 'but he was sleeping with some boy's wife – even with lots and lots of boys' wives. So you see it wasn't racial.' He pointed a fork at his head. 'Once a worker hit me just here with a bush knife. It was heavy and sharp. Thirty stitches in that. But he was an epileptic, so you have to excuse him.'

Smith said the plantation people weren't vindictive. Still, tormented worms would turn.

'Like to hear a true story of the old days? Well, at my very first plantation, there was a guy called Henderson – a real tough of the old school of planters. Drank a big bottle of rum a day. He was my first boss, and on almost my first day he paraded a hundred and eighty boys with their bush knives and came along with the record book of their week's work. To the first one he said, "You're four bags short of copra. Now, drop that knife." The guy didn't move. "Drop it!" Still no movement. He went back to the bungalow for a couple of pick handles, and gave me one of them, saying, "Just back me up. See no bastard comes up on me from behind." Then he said again to the boy: "Drop that knife." And yet again no response.' Smith was handing out steaks. 'I didn't believe my eyes – he caught this guy with the knife a huge whack on the wrist with the pick haft – must have broken his wrist, I should think. And at once – wow! – a hundred and eighty men went wild with rage. They snapped branches off trees, snatched up stones, anything, in their fury to get at this hated man. They fell on him from all sides. I was ready to protect his back, but luckily they didn't come from there, and they weren't after me. Henderson's leg was gashed – twenty stitches. And he was hit on the skull by a bush knife. I heard it. It sounded like – well, a metallic resonance, like a knife hitting a stone. I'll never forget it. Thirty-four stitches he had later. But luckily he didn't pass out, and when the attackers thought they'd killed their master they ran off.'

'They must have been used to a lot of bullying from Henderson.'

'Yes, tough stuff was routine.'

We walked back to the house. Through the open window I could hear the surf and the continuous whistling of birds on the lawn. A large, knobbly crocodile skin covered much of the sitting room floor. He'd made some of the furniture himself, Smith said; it passed the time. He read, too; non-fiction mostly.

'It's the local humour I like,' Smith said. 'You can control the men through humour. Listen to this. Once I told a habitual sleeper on the job that if I ever caught him sleeping again, I'd pour petrol over him and then throw matches at him. He was scared by that, believing it. Well, we did find him fast asleep one night. So I told some boys to fill a bucket of water and throw it over him. Whoosh!' – Smith laughed – 'He woke up soused with liquid in the dark, and all he could see was me striking matches one after the other. Off he went like a madman – sprinting up the hillside through the trees, and away.'

He laughed again. I imagined that terrified, bushy-haired figure, lacerating his body against palm trunks and bushes, striving to escape immolation.

'Did he ever come back?' I asked.

'Of course – and this is where they are so good. Later on, he laughed like hell at the joke I'd played on him, and all the men laughed, too. It was a great joke between us all. That's nice, isn't it?' He paused. 'But I'll tell you this. In the old days there were managers who would have put real, flammable petrol in that bucket and *really* thrown those matches. Oh, yes. Boys were sometimes so badly treated they'd take off into the jungle and reappear half-starved, ragged, in a really bad way weeks later.'

I thought: a human torch wouldn't have much chance of returning, ·half-starved or otherwise. Thank God, Smith was a humane man. But what fear there had once been in the tangle of trees behind us; in the relentless ocean of green at which Gimana Kila and I had looked across from our viewpoint over Gazelle peninsula. As distinctly as the columns of trees and the bright birds on the lawn, I could see Henderson with his bottles of rum and his pick handles, and the furious magenta face in my hotel dining room the night before.

That night I went with Michael Tinne and John Taylor to the Retired Servicemen's Club, the regular hangout for expatriates from Down South – in their 'expat' accents it became 'Den Seth' – i.e. Australia. There I met Captain Stan, master of the local copra carrier. And again, I fell in with the extended, middle-aged hockey team, the burly, sunburnt men in the inevitable tailored shorts and calf-length stockings. Among them you couldn't have missed Captain Stan. He was, you might say, an anomaly. A short, skinny man of about forty, with lively features, big ears and an easy, lopsided smile, he was decidedly, in sailors' parlance, half seas over. He staggered with grog. He bobbed and weaved, crowed, hooted with alcohol.

Dashing at us with a wild cry of 'Ooops!' he skittishly ran his fingers up Michael Tinne's billowing shorts, causing Tinne to leap into the air as if a tarantula spider had run up his leg.

'Yoo-hoo! I'm the Coral Princess,' chortled Captain Stan. 'That's me! Yoo-hoo!' he yodelled, pirouetting up to the bar.

There was good-natured laughter. No one objected to such high jinks. The captain was obviously a popular member of the community, and a respected one, too.

'Bloody marvellous sailor, Captain Stan,' Tinne murmured, straightening his shorts.

'Totally reliable at sea,' John Taylor agreed, seriously. 'Ask anyone.'

'Y-i-i-i-h-e-e-e!' the captain yelled gleefully. 'Yoiks!' he added, lowering a provocative eyelid at a grinning Tolai barman.

His flirtatious fingers approached once more and Tinne, moving out of range like a veteran matador side-stepping a particularly clumsy bull, said in avuncular tones. 'Now, now. That's a good chap.' After a bit Tinne said to me, 'He really is a good man. You might be interested in visiting his ship.' The captain overheard this.

'Meet you on the wharf, ten o'clock,' he said with a merry wriggle. 'Arsk faw the Cor-al Princ-ess,' he added in a hi-falutin' English accent. 'Doncha-know, mah dear.'

Next morning I found Captain Stan on the quay. He was no longer pirouetting; evidently he only changed into the Sugar Plum Fairy after dark. It was hardly surprising that he looked as if he'd had a rough night, but he was cheerful, too. He had not forgotten the invitation to visit his ship. 'Come aboard,' he said, smiling. Up in his cabin, he strode across and abruptly pulled back the drawn curtains of his bunk, dramatically revealing a small black cat curled up on the pillow by a blond fuzzy head. Cat and head were asleep. Unabashed, Captain Stan seized a handful of the fuzz and shook it, crying, 'Up!' and with a small shriek, a muscular young Tolai scrambled out, skipped naked across the floor and vanished into the shower. 'Next thing, beer,' said Captain Stan in a matter-of-fact way, as though he had done no more than shoo the cat off the bunk. He handed me a cold can of Foster's lager from his little refrigerator, while sounds of spraying water issued from the bathroom.

We were joined by two Australians who chatted about the copra situation, the deplorable breakdown of *Burtide*, and the tragedy of the passenger barge, *Sir Garrick*, sunk by the recent gale in the Gulf of Papua. She was lost – but how? It was difficult to capsize a barge.

After a while and another round, this time of San Mig beer, Captain Stan shouted in the direction of the shower stall, 'All right, come out. Are you in there all day?' Abruptly wrenching back the shower curtains he revealed the Tolai, naked and wet, standing before a mirror clipping his pale yellow fuzz with a small pair of nail scissors.

'Oh!' the young man said, eyebrows theatrically raised, but without rancour.

'Oh, indeed,' the captain said, with only a touch of the previous night's skittishness. '*You* can clarify something. Your nice hair. Do you put peroxide on that hair, or is it natural?'

'All natural,' the Tolai said indignantly – adding with a careless smile, 'of course.' What nincompoops we were, he implied.

'But some people do put something on it, yes?' said Captain Stan. 'Not you, but *some* people?'

'Maybe *some* people.' Disdainfully intent now on the reflection of his butterscotch-hued muscles in the mirror, he showed an amused unconcern when Captain Stan took his left forearm and raised it. 'See,' Stan said to me as if he were lecturing an anatomy class. 'No one would dye their armpits blond, would they? And it's blond down there, too. There you are, then. That proves it. No dye.'

The youth was tall, even without his nine-inch yellow busby; his mouth was large with full lips, his well-modelled nose slightly down-ward-curving. He wore a necklace of shells. Now he walked carefully, almost regally, across the cabin, found his laplap on the bunk, wound it on, and sat quietly as the rest of us talked around him. He was not in the least embarrassed, nor was anyone else. Afer a while, another white man came into the cabin, British this time: a plantation engineer, he said, warmly shaking my hand. He removed an oily singlet and a crumpled pair of underpants from a chair and sat down. 'You must be from the Duke of York Islands,' he said in a friendly man-to-man way. No, the Tolai said, he came from a bay west of Gazelle peninsula.

'Oh, my geography – wrong again,' the engineer said, and they both laughed. Racial arrogance was not part of the mildly bohemian atmosphere of Stan's cabin.

On deck, sweating stevedores offloaded bags of copra into lorries on the little wharf; some were very black, others pale as golden syrup. Captain Stan strolled about wearing his wide pixie grin, showing bad teeth, exchanging jokes with his crewmen and the stevedores' foremen. He was obviously popular with everyone on the wharf, leave alone on the ship. 'Nice place, Rabaul,' he said. 'The best in PNG by a long way.' He told me he'd been in the islands eleven years.

It would have been pleasant to sail with an experienced island sailor like Captain Stan. But that afternoon John Taylor told me of the imminent sailing of another small vessel called the *Kazi*; she would take me to Kieta. She had a Filipino captain, Taylor said. I wandered down to the wharf again, and where Captain Stan's *Burtide* had been, instead was the *Kazi*. 'Captain?'

Several squatting men in torn sweatshirts opened betel-red mouths at me, waving hands towards the bridge: 'Up there.'

The *Kazi*'s awnings were low enough to make me stoop. Washing hung on a line; a radio was playing what sounded like 'Where My Caravan Has Rested' arranged by missionaries for a Tolai choir and guitars: a domestic atmosphere. I wouldn't have been surprised to see window boxes and chickens. The captain, a tall, nonchalant Filipino, put his head out of a doorway. 'Oh,' he said when I introduced myself. 'I've no cabins, you know. The contracted labourers sleep on the main deck, or below. Passengers take the deck at the stern. But, shit, that's not very good for you.'

'The after-deck is fine. Shall I bring a blanket? Food?'

'It's quite warm at night. If you can eat sardines and rice with the passengers....'

'That'll do,' I said.

'There *is* this small bunk....' Gesturing at me to follow, he ambled down to a cabin next to his which was as muggy as a greenhouse and smelt of unwashed armpits, feet and slept-in air. It had two bunks. Someone was sleeping on the top one, the other was strewn with dirty sheets and towels. I said I would prefer the deck, and he shrugged, 'Oh, well....'

My notebook records an optimistic mood: 'The captain says he expects to sail at 4 p.m. next day. Tonight I shall sleep well.'

But I did not sleep immediately. I opened Asterisk again and read:

> I don't think that even for a good screw I could stand this plantation life much longer. It's the nigger-driving that beats me. The mere fag of tramping about from dawn till dark I don't really mind.... No, it's the beastly slavery business that I cannot stand. I absolutely refuse to thrash the niggers or to trade. Trading simply means wholesale thieving, and I haven't sunk to thieving from a black man yet.... You remember I told you of the carpenter who had been with So-and-So? I heard the other day that he had been sacked for pulling out a revolver at dinner and letting fly at the Kanaka boy for not bringing the mustard quickly enough.

At least he was sacked. I put the book aside and closed my eyes. I suppose I should have dreamed of dark, furious men with birdlike faces pouring from a steaming ship's hold to tear me apart with their vultures' beaks and pour mustard over me while I struggled to fire an unloaded revolver into the black horde. But after a time I slept soundly without dreaming at all.

Ten

The *Kazi* puttered across the St George's Channel and swung round the inkdrop of New Ireland's southern tip and up the long, forested ridge of its eastern coast. We had left Rabaul after dark the evening before. I had watched the volcano shapes, the lights, the two rocky teeth that guard the entrance to Blanche Bay, all disappear; then sipped some gin, decided again against the airless cabin with the one empty bunk, removed the bunk's thin mattress and spread it on the deck outside, rolling my anorak into a pillow. I had been fortunate to find a space among the sprawling islanders, for the deck was cluttered with bodies. Now, as the morning light roused them, like furry moths from chrysalises, fuzzy heads emerged from the laplaps tightly wound like winding sheets to keep off the dew, and peered round, blinking. Something had bitten me; I scratched hard lumps under my shirt.

One stop was scheduled on the east coast of New Ireland before the *Kazi* turned about and steamed south to Kieta on the island of Bougainville. In heat untempered by the slightest breeze, hook-nosed Papuan Highlanders with faces like ebony masks at a ritual, their womenfolk with babies, and young, flat-nosed men from the islands, 'modern' in sawn-off denims, queued up to wash at a tap near the rail and then flopped down against coils of rope and sacks of vegetables and baskets made of woven banana or sago leaves that bulged with coconuts and pineapples. Through blackened teeth scarlet-stained mouths inaccurately spewed streams of betel juice over the ship's side where it stained the white paint like trickles of fresh blood.

I sidled across the limited deck space to the stern and watched the *Kazi*'s frothing wake. A slim young man with marmalade hair, mascaraed eyes and a blue and yellow laplap wrapped tightly round

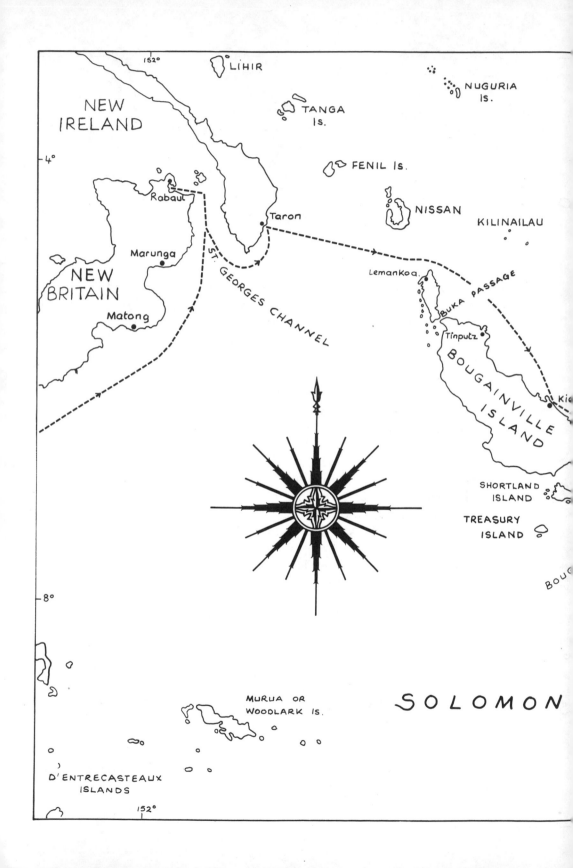

SOLOMON ISLANDS

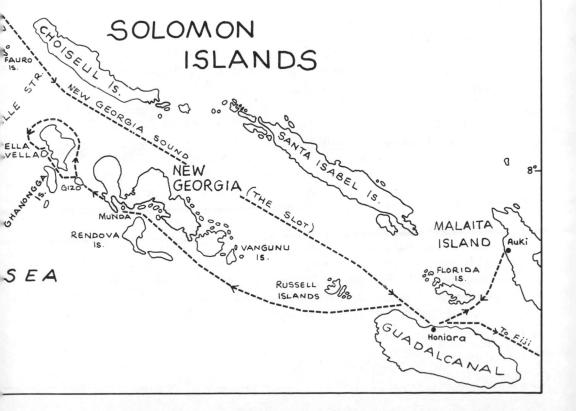

PACIFIC   OCEAN

NUKUMANU

TAUU

ONTONG
JAVA

SOLOMON
ISLANDS

CHOISEUL IS.

FAURO
IS.

NEW GEORGIA SOUND

'LLE STR.

ELLA
VELLA

SANTA ISABEL IS.

GHANONGGA
IS.

GIZO

NEW
GEORGIA

(THE SLOT)

MUNDA

RENDOVA
IS.

VANGUNU
IS.

MALAITA
ISLAND

AUKI

SEA

RUSSELL
ISLANDS

FLORIDA
IS.

To Fiji

Honiara

GUADALCANAL

his hips was twanging a tiny ukelele to an interested audience. He was watched with special intensity by a wizened Papuan Highlander through whose nostrils, bored through to accommodate some bone decoration, daylight disconcertingly showed like light through a tunnel. A group of men crouched down, frowning intently at a transistor radio blaring out brass band music, as though they suspected it of purveying a dangerous brand of alien magic.

A member of the crew with a Tolai face squatted by me for a chat. 'You travel,' he informed me, and then: 'What work?' When I told him I was a writer, he didn't understand, and when I mimed typewriting and said, 'Book,' he nodded his head, knowingly. 'Oh, yes. You write comics.'

He gave his name as John and showed concern about my comfort. 'You must sleep in cabin,' he said, anxiously. 'Not on the deck outside. You can sleep under chief engineer bunk. Better.' I had seen the chief engineer, a tubby Filipino, trotting about the deck in a flowered shirt flapping open to reveal a copper-coloured pot belly with a large convex navel embedded in it like the boss of a shield.

'Too hot in there, John.'

'Yes, too hot.'

At midday, sweating men appeared from the bowels of the ship lugging a great metal bowl containing a mass of sticky rice, and emptied six or seven tins of Australian mackerel onto it. They ladled the rice and fish onto metal plates which the passengers eagerly snatched, and at once they wolfed down the lumps of food in fistfuls and at amazing speed. In a flash the bowl was empty; no second helpings. Dutifully, the passengers took their plates to the railside tap and carefully washed them.

I wasn't in the least hungry. It was as much as I could do to force down a few biscuits I had bought in Rabaul. My mouth was too dry for them and I ducked down into the sultry near-darkness below decks to find the galley and perhaps a mug of tea. Any exact impression of what the galley was like is lost in a memory of pungent smells of fish and urine, of damp heat that drenched my body with sweat, of scuttling cockroaches, and of one or two dark-skinned men, half-hidden in steam, pouring hot water into a mug. I had a second vision, of a doorway, a large, murky portholed space and in it bare chests streaked with moisture, and anxious eyes. Fifty to a hundred men squatted: Papuans, with the ugly bird-mask faces and dwarfish aspect of the remote Highlands. These were the contracted labourers for the plant-ations of New Ireland and Bougainville. On deck I noticed some

decidedly African features – flat faces and thick lips – among the Highland beaks, and even one or two snub noses on men who strolled about with the easy sway of Africans and the same African double-jointed look of arms and wrists.

There were far more men on board than women, but four ladies in a busy circle near the rail made up for their lack of numbers with a great hubbub of jolly sound. They wore the loose blouses called *maris* with which the missionaries covered native nakedness in the name of civilization. They sat together, rocked by spasmodic explosions of laughter, sharing out little snacks wrapped in leaves. They fed their babies and scrubbed their children and their clothes, festooning the deck with acres of washing as colourful as flags at a naval review. They were indefatigable. When other activities waned, they produced large combs shaped like long wooden hands and attacked their children's wiry topknots, stabbing into the black or yellow tangles and flicking upward, snapping the knots in their depths.

On the wheelhouse chart, New Ireland looked appropriately like a shillelagh standing on its head. The chart showed Mount Bongmut, Schleinitz Mountains and Likiliki Bay. William Dampier, the English buccaneer, arriving here in 1670 on his ship the *Roebuck*, found the natives not particularly generous. They refused to part with anything more than a few coconuts, so Dampier's men helped themselves to pigs, wood and water, and sent back in exchange a canoe loaded with 2 Axes, 2 Hatchets, 6 Knives, 6 Looking-Glasses, a large Bunch of Beads, and 4 Glass-bottles', which seems a very fair exchange.

Off the east coast of New Ireland we stopped with a rattle of anchor chain. John came up to say that we would drop twenty passengers here. They would be ferried ashore to a small wharf just visible from the ship, but their departure was delayed by a mishap with the winch which would lower the ship's boat to take them. 'Shit,' said Captain Lim on the bridge wing. He looked tired and pale, and while the crew fumbled with the recalcitrant winch he told me he was much deprived of sleep because he had no deck officers on board. He was captain, first mate, second mate and third mate all in one; radio officer, too, he added. 'Maybe at night I sleep an hour; get up; sleep half an hour more; get up again.' He offered me a cup of cold water from his private refrigerator, and when we entered his cabin I saw it was almost entirely filled by a double bed – his wife, he said, had chosen to stay in Rabaul this trip. 'Help yourself. Also you want orange or an apple?' A video screen stood in one corner, and – oddly – a broken 'space wars' electronic game machine in the other. The air conditioner was also broken; at any rate it was not working. To get to the fridge, I had to step over a large rat trap against a wall. 'Oh, the rats are terrible,' Captain Lim said, throwing up his hands. I mentioned the cockroaches below. 'Ha!' Cockroaches! Rats are bigger.' He smiled in a resigned manner. I had taken him for a recluse. At Rabaul he had seemed cold and unfriendly, but now he began to tell me his grouses and I realized he was shy, unsure of his English rather than hostile. He told me his wages came to the equivalent of £1000 a month, 'less fourteen per cent tax'. It was not enough.

'Why not ask for more?' I suggested.

'If I ask for more, what do they say? They say, "Okay, finish your contract as you are, then we see". At contract's end they say, "Oh, if you aren't happy, go back to the Philippines."' All over the world the poor, despised Filipinos automatically brace themselves for this reply when, like so many Oriental Oliver Twists, they dare ask for more – more food, more money, more anything.

At last the winch was repaired. The departing passengers were helped into the boat, a light metal thing which swayed precariously away towards a ramshackle wharf on the shore where there was nothing like a town to be seen. Perhaps there was only a plantation there and the boat was feeding it more workers. That was likely, considering that the little boat's complement of passengers were mostly those parrot-nosed

Highlanders, clutching bags of plastic or woven sago leaves and cheap umbrellas, all plainly very scared of water. As well they might have been, since shortly after the *Kazi* had retrieved the returning boat and had got under way, there was a prolonged swirling in the sea. The captain called out to me: 'Sharks,' and John began pointing and waving like a maddened dervish, 'Shark! Shark! Ha-ha!'

As the headlands of New Ireland faded behind us and the light with them, I descended yet again to the murk below, this time to see how the plantation labourers were housed. Immediately sweat soaked my clothes and the smell of it mingled with the rancid stench of bodies in the gloom where the crush of men slept, or leaned against the bulkhead. An untuned television screen flickered and roared visual gibberish to these men of the hidden Papuan mountains who sat fascinated, or merely stupefied, by what they took, I suppose, to be a normal transmission. Who could tell what they thought they were watching – white magic of some sort. A voice in the semi-darkness said something, and a man less wizened than the others edged along the deck towards me. His stink reached me well before I felt his hand on my arm.

'Mister, how you like stop here? Too hot place.'

'Too hot. Plenty too hot, yes.'

It certainly was hot. It was lucky that the sea was flat calm. What would become of them down here if a storm began throwing us all about? I saw no air conditioning and it would be impossible to open a door or a porthole in rough weather.

'How you like stop down here? Eh, Mister?'

'No good,' I said, with the stink in my nose and the sweat in my eyes.

It had been a hundred times worse in the old days. In *Isles of Illusion* I read:

> An Australian went into the business of kidnapping niggers for work in Queensland. He enticed them on to the ship, and locked them in the hold. If a nigger got the chance he jumped overboard and swam for the shore. Then this beauty used to shoot, not to kill, but to maim so that the sharks'd get 'im. Oh, it was rare fun in those days.

Asterisk raised a horrid ghost. Probably no one today could force a Papuan to go to Bougainville, Queensland or anywhere else. It was most improbable that anyone today would jump overboard and 'swim to freedom', with or without the accompaniment of sharks. But

Asterisk's accounts of cruelty and mayhem are still appropriate reading. Plantations at any period of history are remote, and cheap labour is cheap labour....

The little *Kazi* pursued her plebeian way through sombre islands that had not changed in sixty or seventy years – and perhaps not much since Dampier stared at them from the deck of the *Roebuck*. The self-same shaggy profusion of trees, the identical silent dark green islands had appalled and excited the vagabond soul of Asterisk.

A black finger appeared on the horizon to starboard – Buka Island, the signpost to Bougainville – and in the early morning the *Kazi* approached Kieta. Unexpectedly, John brought me breakfast: a slice of currant bread, one fried egg. I had subsisted entirely on biscuits and mugs of tea, not out of sickness but due to the loss of appetite I associate with ships as others associate a raging appetite. 'From the captain,' John said, handing me the tin plate, and began hosing down the deck for our arrival, drenching the possessions of several protesting Papuans.

It was not going to be a joyful landfall. A black storm cloud like a crouching cat seemed to block our way to the little mousehole of a bay in which Kieta lies. I watched it, leaning on the ship's rail with the tubby Filipino chief engineer, his protruding navel resting against one of the metal uprights. The cloud was not his concern. He indicated, by tapping my arm and pointing, the growing crowd of sweating passengers that milled about near where the gangway would be lowered to the wharf.

'Filipinos would never travel like that.' He jerked a thumb in the direction of the hold. 'Every day you see thousands of Filipinos, poor people travelling by ship through the islands, third class, yes, but air conditioned, cheap, clean. No sweat. Here....' It was true. Filipinos suffered much, but among their own islands the shipboard accommodation I had seen was far better than this.

The cloud moved on towards the Solomon Islands and the *Kazi* moved into the bay. Kieta was in sight. A few buildings appeared on the shore, half-muffled by trees. I saw a compact little bay, its mouth stoppered by an island shaped exactly and uncannily like a monstrous green crocodile. A crocodile half-submerged, waiting for its prey, waiting for us. I felt no surprise when John sidled up and pointed to it. 'That is Puk-Puk or Crocodile Island.'

'I know,' I said, although I'd only known a second before he spoke.

'See the head and the long nose; and the tail.'

I could very easily see those features; uneasily, too. 'It looks very real.'

'Maybe it is – what is it? – a spirit. Maybe it will eat *Kazi*. And you and me as well – ha-ha!'

I didn't try to laugh with him at something that seemed too real to joke about. It was not only the waiting Puk-Puk and the great cloud that now reared an inky cobra hood over the south-eastern horizon that made me feel Bougainville was a place of ill omen. It was also the whole long, silent stretch of island coast that for hours had kept pace with us, as if malevolently and inquisitively watching our approach. It was the silent shelves of forest that heaved about like an erratic tidal wave – volcanic peaks pushed up here and there under the green blanket – that closed in at last on this insignificant little port as if preparing to bulldoze its few buildings into the bay and into the maw of that patient crocodile. I see Bougainville, as I write, as a sea and landscape in black and white; not a painting but an etching out of an old book of prints. It had a hostile, haunted look that inspired instant foreboding.

I gave John two tins of sardines, my remaining biscuits and an Air Niugini map. In return he gave me a grin and carried my heavy metal suitcase to the gangway, and later down it to the wharf. 'See you,' he said. On the dock wall, in big white letters, someone had painted *Kazi*'s name and her size, 400 tons. Next to that was a macabre reminder: one of her crew had painted '*Sir Garrick*, 150 tons' – the name of the passenger barge that had sunk the previous week. Seeing it was like finding in your pocket the visiting card of someone who had just died.

The Papuans left the ship in a black cascade to the jetty, a vociferous tumble of baskets and bundles. There they stood turning their angry bird faces here and there; helpless, waiting to be gathered up by a boss man from the plantation. Captain Lim chalked on a blackboard near the gangway, 'Sailing for Rabaul, Kimbe and Lae, today at 0900 hours. . . . Shore leave expires at 0800 hours.' He hung it on a nail over the heads of the disembarking passengers. It was half past six in the morning. Captain Lim didn't believe in hanging about. I waited for the agent's man to come to the ship. 'Shit,' Lim said. 'He won't be along before eight o'clock,' adding contemptuously, 'office hours.' When the agent's man, a shock-headed, blue-black Bougainvillean, finally appeared, his eyes blinking with anxiety, he said he hadn't expected the *Kazi* until tomorrow morning. No message; no telex. 'But I phoned,' the captain said, grinning with irritation. But Lim, long-suffering like all Filipinos, quickly composed himself. We shook hands. I carried my zip-bag down the gangway to where John stood with the metal suitcase. A sharp report – it could have been a pistol shot – sounded from the direction of Captain Lim's cabin. The rat trap had been sprung.

Eleven

My thoughts found an unexpected voice. John was standing by my bag, holding out his hand. He was saying, 'Kieta not good. Better watch out. Better not stay long time. Too much fighting.' He drew, in mime, a knife across his throat.

'Who, John?'

'Bad people work in timber yard down the road from Kieta Hotel. Too much beer. Fight.'

'I'll remember that. Goodbye, John.'

The agent's man drove me to the Kieta Hotel through the sticky heat. It was a three-storeyed, undistinguished building. It had a bungalow attachment with a receptionist's room, a television room, a low-ceilinged bar and then a simple dining room. On the reception office door a sign said, 'Sorry, no gat work.' I signed the register. Black, middle-aged ladies ironed shirts on the landings. A Tolai showed me to a room, and I stood under the shower for ten minutes sluicing away the sweat and grime of the *Kazi*. The small red fleabites were fading.

I telephoned an Australian plantation manager whose name Michael Tinne had given me – Tim Wilson; 'Tiny' Tim, Ian Smith had said. At the end of the telephone a voice said, 'Yis. Come up and stay if you like. I'll try and find a bloke to pick you up.' I thanked him.

I had a few hours. Best to make sure of the first possible onward passage. I only had to walk across the road to Burns Philp. Everything seemed to be across the road: the bank, the store, the post office. A large, fair, bespectacled man at the desk said, 'I'm John Fieldhouse,' and shook hands. 'Now let's see what we have.... The *Capitaine La Pérouse*, Sofrana Line, French.... Yes, in a week. Captain Luc is a young chap, very accommodating. I expect he'll take you to Honiara. If not ... there's the *Papuan Chief*. Umm. They don't take passengers. Very strict about it. Anyway, you've got a few days here.'

I returned to the Kieta Hotel, comforted. At noon I ordered a beer from the very black barman in the little bar. A notice on the door said, 'Minimum Dress – clean shirt, shorts with long socks and shoes. ... Or: tailored laplap and sandals. T-shirt and Thongs not permitted.' Thongs are rubber flipflops, comfortable for slopping about in.

An off-white New Zealander with olive-tinged half-moons under his eyes said, 'Kieta's no good,' echoing John, the seaman. Papuan labourers at the timber yard beat people up 'really badly', whites particularly. 'It's the grog,' he said. I must avoid the timber yard, I thought.

Tim Wilson's driver, a silent Bougainvillean, arrived in a rattling pickup. I heaved my metal suitcase into the back and we drove over tarmac for some time heading inland. Then we turned off onto a rutted dust road, bouncing about for some miles in relatively open bush. After that armies of trees swooped in and enveloped us like the dark soul of the island. It was a revelation. I knew a plantation was a sprawling, man-made, relatively disciplined forest. But this was different. The extent of the plantation – or perhaps it was two together – seemed infinite. A pall of gloom descended over the track, the pickup, the silent driver and me. The effect, mile after mile, was not only dark but unexpectedly chilling. There might have been an eclipse of the sun. The ragged heads of coconut trees blotted out the sky, imposing a sinister twilight. Rank after rank they hedged us in, uncountable, unmoving, silent regiments – no, divisions – so meticulously planted that from a right-angle or diagonal view of them hardly a single tree was out of line. As time and these trees went by, the impression grew that I had strayed into a fairy story by Grimm, that I was reviewing a ghastly parade in which all the soldiers were dead, the resurrected heroes of a long and disastrous war, an impression deepened by the husked coconut shells that lay singly or in small heaps here and there, under the trees or on the roadside, like severed heads.

'Haus Wilson' at Kirwina – Tim's home – was a long, well-built bungalow with a wide lawn, once the outpost's airstrip before a reasonable road came, Tim said, stretching two or three thousand yards to the sea.

There was a bay and there were reefs close by, and the wreck of a tiny coaster leaned its broken ribs on one of them, like a hopeless drunk. There were spreading frangipani trees on the lawn near the house, and the sides and back of it were tightly enclosed by the dense ranks of the coconut palms.

'Tiny' Tim was extra tall; he was also thin, a shaggy-looking thirty-something-year-old with short, unkempt, darkish hair. He had a long, bony face, a long, none-too-well-shaved jaw and the weathered look of a rancher in a film about the Australian outback, one who worked hard and liked his liquor. It was a good-natured face, and I found that he was indeed good-natured; and self-contained and self-confident without being in the least arrogant. How could he not be self-confident, marooned out here in this coconut forest with a ragtag army of imported labour from the half-discovered valleys of New Guinea. He wore shorts and a short-sleeved shirt; his long, strong, skinny legs disappeared into army-style boots which looked terribly heavy and cumbersome, but which I suppose were ideal in the mud and tree stumps of the plantation.

When we went in through the flyproof screen door from the verandah, the first thing I saw in the living room of Haus Wilson – the 'Haus' was a relic of the pre-1918 days when the plantations of Bougainville belonged to the Germans – was a prominent rectangular bar near the door. It dominated and welcomed. You had to step round it to enter the room, a considerable wooden-floored space well lit by numerous large windows. There was also a round dining table and an exotic bronze fan ('Won that in a tequila-drinking competition, ha!'). The room had no air conditioning, but it did have seven or eight armchairs and sofas, bookcases, a video and a hi-fi. It was a comfortable place.

On the walls hung mementoes and clues to an exiled, adventurous life. A rusty Japanese bayonet; photographs of birds and pin-ups; a polished brass shell case or two; empty Drambuie bottles; an ancient anchor and an even rustier axe; a punchbag; oddest of all, a convict's ball and chain. On the bar were a good few bottles, but Tim seemed to think I might find their number inadequate. 'Don't worry,' he said, 'we've got some more piss coming – or should I say grog?'

Hard rock, I swiftly discovered, was a relentless, omnipresent feature of plantation life. The mind-hammering bang-bang, thud-thud of it followed one around, as irritating as earache. I longed to switch it off. I would have preferred the silence of the thousands of trees, however much unease that might at times have produced. Not that silence was the alternative to pop music at Haus Wilson – the bungalow was usually full of some sort of sound. Various people lived in or near it. For a start there was Tim's Bougainvillean 'wife', a smiling young black

woman called Lizzie, and her small child, Maxie, as black as his mother – the plump apple of Tim's eye. Lizzie's face was pretty and strong, with big, glossy, responsive eyes that laughed much of the time.

'Uh, the – uh – relationships around this place are – uh – complex – ha!' Tim said in his self-deprecating, James Stewart way. He tacked the 'ha!' on to the end of almost every sentence he uttered – a strange verbal tic. 'You see, Maxie is Lizzie's son by the welder....'

'The welder?'

'Yis. See? That's the welder, out there. Welding the safety struts on the swimming pool chute.' I saw a young blue-black man by the small, prefabricated-style pool on the lawn. 'Now the welder – ha! – is married to Lizzie's sister, and she is having a baby by him, so what the bloody relationships will be all round here, God knows – ha! I mean when the kids grow up and go to the same school. Lizzie's and her sister's, all with the same father – ha!' He paused and added in a different, quieter tone of voice, 'Lizzie's pretty marvellous. I suppose Lizzie is a kind of saint – you know.' Suddenly embarrassed, he covered his mouth with a large hand, letting out a final 'ha!' before turning away.

Female laughter came from all parts of the house – sounds of struggles and then the giggling of girls seeped through its wooden walls, for Tim seemed to have at least three Bougainville girls around the place apart from the favourite for the last six years, Lizzie, the black beauty.

When a close friend of Tim's nicknamed 'Rommel' (though he looked nothing like him, being much younger, with a fair moustache to boot) came to join us in the house, he told me the story of a visit by Tim's mother to Haus Wilson.

'She was very upright. Forbidding. People stood up to talk to her.' He laughed. 'God knows what she thought of old Tim's friends who came round. I do know everyone called her Mrs Wilson from beginning to end. Actually, I asked her — I said, "What would you like us to call you? Mrs Wilson, or, you know, your own name?"'

'What did she say?'

'Well, she didn't quite answer that. Gazing round at Tim's kaffir girls, she said, "Well, I see there are four Mrs Wilsons here already."'

There was no doubt of Tim's love for Lizzie — and for Maxie. The living room of Haus Wilson had a sort of play area in which toys and cushions, coloured balls, koala bears and a teddy, a trumpet and a model bulldozer lay in confusion. Tim showed me a book of children's songs in pidgin. One song was called '*Wanpela Puk-puk wak-about isi*', a title which I took to refer to a happy crocodile living free. Another was a sad little ditty about a calf born without a tail. '*Mi laikim tel*,' the calf cried, pathetically — 'I want a tail' . . . but, alas, the poor beast ended in the stewpot instead — '*Kaf i mas go long sospan?*' '*Em. Yumi kaikai sori.*' ('Must the calf go into the pot?' 'Yes. You and I are going to eat him. Sorry about that.')

I soon got used to the way Tim's voice, too, seemed to echo from every room in turn. Perhaps it was something to do with acoustics. Anyway, he was seldom still, always clumping here and there in his heavy ammunition boots: into his office, to the telephone, to his bedroom, into the garden to see how the welder was getting on, back through the living room, out towards the back of the house for a word with Luke, the driver who had brought me from Kieta and who was also the accountant. Restlessness agitated Tim Wilson like a fever.

He read a little, though he preferred to watch a video film serial like James Michener's *Centennial*. He was a lover of Rolf Bolderwood's *Robbery Under Arms*, the novel of outlaws in the outback of nineteenth-century Australia. He was hooked, he said, on the manner of Captain Starlight's betrayal by the white bull that tags along with the herd of steers he has just hijacked.

'The real Captain Starlight,' he told me, 'was called Harry Redmond. I've seen his memorial at Corella Creek on Brunett Downs in the Northern Territories of Australia.' The life of the other best-known renegade, Ned Kelly, fascinated him. Tim's father owned huge tracts of north-western Australia, and he loved it there. He showed me photographs of his father's ranch, and of himself as clerk of the course at some Australian race meeting, his lean face mostly hidden in a wideawake hat that turned him into a real bush-whacker, every inch. Why did he leave? 'To be my own master.' He had had to learn this job in six months and how to speak pidgin as well. Indeed, he rattled off pidgin so fluently (interspersed with 'bastard', 'bloody', and 'ha!' and a good deal of chortling) that I could very seldom catch more than one word in ten or twelve; sometimes none at all. From 5.30 a.m., when the hammering of a gong sounded reveille for the workers in their barrack-like huts in the trees behind Haus Wilson – it was still dark at that hour – Tim was in sole command of a huge, remote and valuable estate; he was as responsible for every thing and human being on it as a liner's captain is responsible for the vessel, its passengers and crew. He was his own master all right.

I stayed a week there. When Tim was busy, I read more of *Isles of Illusion* – after all, I was actually *on* a plantation as remote in its way as anything in the New Hebrides. Asterisk told horrific stories of the old days.

Once there had been a deputation of white missionaries from Malakula to Vila, the capital of New Hebrides. 'They had a shocking story to tell and were so frightened that they had left their wives and children behind in the danger.... It appears that the natives had been getting truculent for some time. Last Sunday they made a descent upon a quite inoffensive English planter' – I looked up at Tim Wilson who at that moment was mending one of Maxie's toys – 'killed him, ate him, and then retired to the bush with six of his labourers, and ate them alive there.'

It was heartening to know that there are no cannibals on Bougainville Island. The Bougainville people are a quiet lot, Tim had said. Reading on, I found Asterisk's accounts of white savagery – like this one, for example, concerning 'recruiting' of island labour:

A trick played by a French captain. He arrived at an island where the natives are good strong men, but absolutely refused to go away and work. The captain told the chief he did not want recruits, but only thirty strong men to help him shift a large tank in his hold. The job would take about an hour and he would give them 2 shillings each for it. Thirty of the best braves in the village came and toiled away trying to shift the tank. Their efforts were not very successful owing to the fact that the tank had been carefully bolted to the ship's keel, and when, weary of the work, they came on deck, they found the anchor up and the ship well out at sea. The captain grogged them all, and as they could do nothing else they all signed on for three years. Their troubles didn't end there.

The niggers are supposed to be paid 10 shillings a month, but at the end of their three years they find that all their pay had been swallowed up in gaudy calico and tobacco, or else it had been stopped for refractory conduct. The poor nigger is so disgusted at having to go back to his home empty-handed, which would cause him to lose caste for meanness, that he signs on for another three years, and so on *ad infinitum*.

It was only in certain islands that the natives were prepared to go elsewhere to work ('Same here,' said Tim when I asked him. 'No native of Rabaul or of Bougainville works on a plantation.') In the old days, every planter kept a schooner and sailed round the most God-forsaken islands trying to get men to work for him. If they agreed they were signed on – they put a thumb mark on some scrap of paper – for a three-year stint in a plantation they had never seen, in a place they had never heard of. There were very strict laws and regulations governing the manner of recruiting. 'Needless to say,' Asterisk wrote home, 'these laws are set at defiance, openly by the French, secretly by the Britons.' At an hotel known as the 'Blood House' in Vila, Asterisk found a group of recruiters playing poker and drinking champagne ('Cliquot-demi-sec'). The stakes were

merely the recruited niggers who are ranged solemnly round the wall of the room and who change hands many times a night. All this in spite of the Anglo-French Convention of October 20th, 1906.... Fancy the excitement of a jackpot with four stalwart male niggers and two female (total value £92) in the pool. 'Years of labour' is a unit of currency here. For example, when I bought and resold my property there was a 7-ton cutter which I withheld and subsequently sold for twenty 'years of labour', i.e. five boys engaged for three years and five for one year or any other equivalent combination. In the open market a male Kanaka indentured for three years fetches £17. If you are a Frenchman it is cheap; because you keep him for nine or ten years, and then send him home without paying him. If you are an Englishman you are naturally more superficially honest. At the end of each three years you supply him with a new wife (generally your own cast-off), and then, when he insists upon going home, being tired of wives, you pay him in 'trade' at 10 times its cost price and throw in a Bible as a make-weight.

'"Pay your worker before his sweat dries up," says the Holy Prophet (Peace be upon Him)': I have seen that injunction in a Muslim newspaper in Pakistan. Apparently, it wouldn't have attracted much heed among the profiteering Christians of the South Seas. At Tim's, in 1982, the workers stumbled out into the plantation at first light, ate their *kaikai* (food – a bowl of rice) at noon, then worked from one to four o'clock. 'We pay them 28 Kina every two weeks,' Tim said in answer to my question: £46 a month. 'The government-approved wage.'

He took me to the coconut drying sheds behind the house, where the fires themselves were heated by coconut shells; the iron-roofed sheds stood on a driveway of shell chippings. Once dried, the half-shells were pushed down a chute to another room which echoed with the sound of hundreds of castanet players gone mad, as the workers banged them on the ground so that the loosened copra fell out like the lining of a helmet. In these sheds, the copra was bagged for shipment.

I stumbled with Tim over the dark uneven earth between the flawless avenues of coconut trees; gloomy avenues to which daylight never seemed quite to penetrate. Now and again we met a tractor pulling a wagon loaded with copra on which dwarfish workers crouched like black, brooding gargoyles. Most were bearded and dressed in nothing but ragged denim shorts, and their bush knives added menace to their ugliness. Yet some had jammed scarlet hibiscus flowers into their woolly locks and these, combined with their beaklike noses and wide, sensually lipped mouths, gave them a curiously ancient, pagan look. Among the trees, other sad self-exiles from the hidden, mist-filled valleys of Papua husked coconuts, bashing the fibrous outer skins two-handed against the pointed ends of bayonet-sharp metal shafts they had rammed straight up in the soft, damp earth; a dangerous business that could cost you a hand or at least a hideous wound as bad as a spear thrust through your palm. I asked Tim if he had a doctor on the estate.

'Well, there's Matthew, the supervisor – he knows quite a bit. And to get this job, I had to have some training. About district nurse level, I suppose, ha!'

Could he deliver a baby?

'I delivered Maxie. Round here, of course, there's two medicines, modern and local. The local midwife uses leaves to boil up for sterilized water, and she bites through the umbilical cord with her teeth.'

At each side of the tracks, between the trees straight as 'rides' in an English wood, I saw again the small heaps of nuts that had seemed, still seemed, like severed heads. Some were in fact cocoa pods (the much shorter cocoa trees were planted between the towering coconuts, making two plantations in one). These were the size of small melons, yellow, orange or green. Tim broke open a pod's softish outer covering, revealing inside the beans, sticky now with a white mucus-like substance, which would later be dried and become recognizably cocoa.

On the boundaries, the sullen forest waited – it really looked as if it was waiting to come back. Huge, wild trees stood like green King Kongs, straining, I felt, to regain the domination wrenched from them by saw and panga, and to disrupt for ever the unnatural symmetry of the humans' plantation.

Rommel was impervious to threatening atmospheres. A swashbuckling twenty-eight-year-old, he had already served in a mounted unit called Grey's Scouts which patrolled the borders of what was then Southern Rhodesia and hunted the guerrilla squads belonging to Mugabe, the man who later became Zimbabwe's first Prime Minister. Often the tables were turned and the guerrillas had hunted the Scouts. He had survived several ambushes. He had also been involved somehow, perhaps merely as a spectator, in a shoot-out in a bar in Salisbury in which a man was killed. Rommel drove me about when Tim was busy. He was a pleasant companion. As far as I am concerned, how exactly he came to Bougainville is a mystery to this day.

Rommel was joined at Haus Wilson by my namesake, the Tolai manager of a plantation two hours up the road, who was a protégé of Tim's. This Gavin was thick-set, bearded with a blondish fuzz, and heavy-featured; he had the thick nose and lips of New Britain (as opposed to the fine noses and mouths of the Bougainville people), and the chest, shoulders and arms of a boxer. Gavin was down here on a mission. A fellow Tolai, assistant manager at yet another plantation, a big one of 3800 acres, had fooled around, drunk, with someone else's girl. When his boss, an Australian, had remonstrated and ordered him to step outside, the Tolai pulled out a knife and stabbed him three times. The Australian was said to be in a serious condition in hospital. A local court had fined the Tolai 250 Kina (£200 – quite a lot, I thought). Gavin had come down with a kind of watching brief. Tolais stick together, Wilson told me. They had a sort of Mafia – well, a self-disciplinary freemasonry – which would chastise the erring Tolai in its own way if he had let the side down. But there was more to it than that. The plantation administrators were, I gathered, in a ferment of resentment. The fine was seen as trivial. 'If a fellow can get away with stabbing his boss, whatever next. . . .' Tim Wilson himself was disgusted: 'He could have won or lost that trivial sum in one night's gambling,' he said.

As a mere guest, I said nothing. But the incident struck me as a symptom of underlying unease in this odd and isolated world, where outnumbered whites could only preserve law and order – or even their lives – by force of character and the mystique of their whiteness.

Tim Wilson, like Asterisk, was a kind man behind a bush-whacking, outback appearance. He would never make a Henderson – it was inconceivable that he would kick or punch a worker. When I asked his opinion of the brutal world of Asterisk, he said, 'Beating workers isn't the least bit necessary. Doesn't work – ha! You have to try to understand them. They're frightened.... They're in a strange country.'

On the other hand, by all accounts the Papuans were no angels. Gavin, the Tolai manager, told me how he had been ambushed by his workers and had had to fight his way clear – I forget the cause of the affair. Papuans quite often got drunk, Gavin said, and then they ran wild – fighting, or even killing drunk. They attacked company stores, assaulted security guards with bush knives, sticks and stones – the guards ran for their lives – looted or destroyed thousands of Kina-worth of goods. Brought to court, their cases, Gavin said contemptuously, were too often dismissed by the magistrate (an Australian usually) for lack of evidence.

Gavin, I believe, took a tougher line than Tim. As he told it, his advice to managers was uncompromising. 'You must never – *never* – make friends with workers' – he was positive about that. 'Never admit mistakes. *You* are *never* wrong, remember. Never ever let them *think* they're on top, running you. It's the rule of the cuff and the kick.' To me he said, 'How else would you get these Highlanders to work? You've seen them on the *Kazi*.' I saw them again, the crouched, totem-faced men, the cruel hook noses and the deep, sharply watchful eyes. Of course, they were not simply a collection of murderers; they were anxious, bemused, baffled, lost, and quite often, no doubt, happy or at least satisfied. Nevertheless, their faces were like faces seen in a bad dream.

Gavin said, 'They brood about things.'

The Brooding Island: not a bad name for Bougainville.

Reading in my notebook, I find:

Scenes from Bougainville life. Merve King, the boss of the quarantine station down the jungle road. A hefty Australian, broad as a barrel: an Old Hand. Keeps white bull terriers and grows hibiscus plants, pale orange, dark red, even blue.

He says to Tim Wilson: 'Remember a mad bloke called the Screamin' Eagle. Skinny, reddish hair?'

'Yes. I used to go rootin' round Rabaul with 'im.' (Root, Tim explains, is Aussie for screw.)

'Well, there was a time when these Kanakas wanted to do 'im over. They put a whatsisname – a barricade – across the road and he came screamin' back in the Land Cruiser and just managed to pull up by this barricade. And the boys came out to do 'im over, y'see?'

'I get the picture,' Tim says.

'Anyway, the Screamin' Eagle just took off. Put his foot down and roared into the village and knocked down just about every Kanaka house in the place. Of course, his windscreen was smashed and that – he was chargin' right through the houses, knockin' down Kanakas and God knows what. They took down the barricade all right!'

The word Kanaka, though publicly taboo, surfaces between friends, I notice.

'Then another time, he was screamin' along and hit this narrow bridge down the road at sixty miles an hour. And there was a jeep on it already, with the Chinese trader in it. Well, the Screamin' Eagle didn't bother to stop or slow up – oh, no! He shot past it, full out – and by the grace of God the only damage was to take the door handles off. I tell you, Ah Wong –'

'Thought he was a gone goose – ha?'

'Too right. He was the whitest man on the island that day.'

A dance party was being held at a distant plantation. All the managers were invited and they drove their black girlfriends up there. Tim's Lizzie wore a costume with a yellow top and a yellow and orange laplap, beautiful colours against her glossy, night-black skin. Tim should find someone to paint her.

Up-country we stopped to pick up a planter, Colin, whose house I envied: attap roof, split bamboo floor, woven banana or sago leaf walls, raised on stilts. With nostalgia I thought of Borneo. This was the only plantation house I saw in Bougainville with a lot of books in it, from Gore Vidal to rare books on the birds of Papua. Colin was glad I noticed his books. In a nervous way he mentioned Maugham's *Narrow Corner*. I suggested that on the Malay archipelago Conrad was better – *Victory*, for example. Perhaps Colin, like Heyst in Conrad's story, had sought out an island in which to escape from the world. He was apologetic.

'You know, I have all these books. I brought them up from Down South. But I have to say, it's a long time since I read one of them. I used to. Now, there's no time somehow. I'm busy on the plantation, or in the office. In the afternoon I watch video or friends drop in for a beer or two. You get out of reading. No one does any reading here; not that I know of; not really. It's not only reading, y'see. Take my swimming pool. I hardly ever use it. Just never get round to it.'

The Brooding Island didn't only brood. It sucked up the human spirit, too.

Later, among all the shorts and beefy arms, the beer and tobacco fumes, I saw Colin dancing sedately, with great concentration and alone, a slow-motion performance like a ritual: a high knee action, an extending of the legs and pointing of the toes, and a flowing arm movement – elements of a Bacchante and Isadora Duncan. In such a smoke-filled tumult it was astonishing to see and, because of Colin's utter absorption, it was somehow moving, too.

Tim said, 'Poor Colin, the fire has certainly gone out of him. Even dancing without his tambourine.'

'Tambourine?'

'No one ever saw old Colin high-stepping it without his tambourine!'

Young white men were scrimmaging competitively round the eager, nubile black girls. At the bar an elderly man called Jock with cauliflower ears dispensed three-finger-deep shots of whisky and Bacardi. Every few minutes a tipsy Chinese fell heavily on the dance floor. Like a good actor, he could do it without hurting himself. Hauled to his feet, he collapsed giggling almost at once into the lap of one or other of the Australian wives, whose smiles became less real each time he did it. Someone said that now his wife had walked out on him he was going to pieces. . . . Oblivious of the increasing turbulence, a group of men played billiards at one end of the room as though they had the house to themselves.

The house was near a cliff. Wandering out for air across a patch of grass, I looked down at a bay curving far below it, cupping the dark glitter of the sea; a slip would have meant a sheer and fatal fall. Inland rose the dominating jungle ridges, made menacing by a low ceiling of black storm clouds, and the gloom of them drove me back to the happy uproar of the party where they could be forgotten in the pounding of pop music, the voices, the smoke, the clack of billiard balls, the sound of the Chinaman falling. And the grog – there was no shortage of that while Jock, the old bruiser, ladled it out.

No one stirred until noon next day. Then, in fragile health, Tim's little convoy headed back along the dust road to Kirwina. We stopped halfway, by a river pool. We were all suffering. We ate, sparingly, of tinned ham and chocolate cake, and drank, not hairs, but tufts of the dogs that had bitten us during the night, while the girls splashed in the pool and shampooed their fuzzy heads. Dragonflies rested in the sun on hot, smooth stones. 'Memories are made of this – ha!' Tim laughed, pouring Coca-Cola into his rum.

The river bed opened up a vista to the mountain ridge, heavily forested, ever frowning, discouraging visitors. 'Does anyone ever try climbing that?' I asked Tim. 'Any plantations there?'

He shook his head, following my gaze to the green dragon's back. 'A Jap plane or two, maybe. As we say Down South, it's so thick up in those mountains, a blue dog couldn't bark in it.'

Rommel had emptied the remains of a whisky bottle and was decanting a fresh one into his thermos, diluting it with water from the pool.

'Hey!' he yelled to Tim. 'Do you know why Australians suffer so much from *coitus interruptus*?'

'Oh, Christ, yeah! Because they can't wait to tell their mates about it – ha! Let's go, Rommel.'

We turned our backs on the mountains and in clouds of dust took the

afternoon trail back to Haus Wilson. Rommel drove as if he were still on horseback with Grey's Scouts, holding the top of the pickup's steering wheel in one hand like a fistful of reins and pouring whisky and water down his throat from the thermos with the other. Trees leaped by, and each sharp bend seemed almost too sharp. Rommel's foot kept the accelerator pinned to the floor. I began to come alive. Interesting, I thought, how swiftly perfect fear casts out boozer's gloom.

When one of his Australian friends, Scratch by name, asked Tim when he would marry Lizzie (he waited until Lizzie was out of hearing) Tim shuffled his feet and muttered, 'Oh, well... next year ... maybe.' And everyone present laughed.

'You've been saying that year after year,' Scratch's European wife said.

When little Dina, the Bougainville girl who had gone off for the night with curly-headed Bill, returned, she confided bashfully that she loved Bill, that he loved her and that he had said he would marry her.

'Will he, do you think?' I asked Tim.

He shook his head sadly. 'If you want a good time, you too might be tempted to say you wanted to marry the girl – ha! Anyone would.' It was too bad, he said, but what could one do? It was difficult – a black wife in Australia. And Bougainville girls are *very* black. On the other hand, a man had to have *some* fun, and there were no white girls out here. 'It isn't the place for 'em, d'you see?'

I did see, and I felt sorry for the local girls whose dream was to marry these white men they loved and whose babies they sometimes bore.

'It's very difficult, Gavin,' Tim said earnestly.

'Yes,' I said.

This wasn't the end of the topic. Before boarding the *Capitaine La Pérouse*, I had an enlightening conversation in the Kieta Hotel's bar with a huge, hunched sack of a white man who worked, he said in a harsh though friendly voice, far away in the jungle. His vast shoulders, battered face and big, calloused hands reminded me of Magwitch, the convict who leaps out at Pip in the graveyard in *Great Expectations*. At his side in the corner, a very black woman with a gap-toothed mouth staggered and giggled merrily; she was obviously enjoying her grog.

'The Missis,' Magwitch rasped, introducing her with a jerk of his thumb.

'Hello,' she said with a dainty little belch. A beer or two later he told me he was a bridge builder, up from Queensland. He liked it here. He might be stuck out in the back of beyond, but the wilds suited him, and he had managed to create the domesticated sort of life he needed. He confessed that, in any case, leaving the Missis might not be all that easy.

What would happen, I asked, if he said one day, 'Sorry, I'm off home – it's goodbye.'

'Oo, my Gawd. They'd cut off me head,' Magwitch said promptly, and he wasn't smiling.

'Do you have a formal marriage contract?'

'Well, no. But y'see, it's not quite like that. There's the jungle telegraph. And if the village people heard – and they would – that I'd planned to do a bunk, or was going with other women, they'd be after me like bloody lightnin' – with knives.'

The Missis put her head back and poured half a can of beer straight down her throat as one might pour disinfectant down a sink.

'With knives,' Magwitch repeated, eyeing her fondly. And with a slight narrowing of the eyelids he added, 'And the same thing if *she* goes off with other men. Oh, indeed.'

Magwitch was living rough, he said, in the south of the island, in a broken-down caravan with no air conditioning and no fans – he didn't care much about such things. Sometimes the villagers fought lively little wars around him and arrows whizzed about his ears.

'No harm meant to me, of course,' he added. 'Six-foot bows. Very accurate. They can shoot a parrot on the wing. I've seem 'em.'

It was pleasant to see these two human beings, one crumbling and off-white, the other a blowsy midnight-black, a sort of black Sarah Gamp, exchanging belches, guffaws and tender glances over beer after beer. Magwitch told me he was very proud that the Missis had learnt English – proper English, not pidgin – from missionaries, and the pride was evident from the tone in which he said it.

'Let me tell you – the other day it was raining, and know what she said? She said, "Rain, rain go away, come again another day." That's what she said. Pretty good, eh?'

Gratified, the Missis cackled happily, baring her infrequent teeth. A blob of froth on her cheek gave her a touching festive air.

'Three more beers,' I told the barman.

''Good goin',' said Magwitch appreciatively.

That, for me, was the last of Bougainville. Except, I suppose I should add, for a brief look at the World's Greatest Copper Mine in the hills above Kieta. To many people this hideous scar might be the most exciting thing on the island, but for me mines, however big, have minimal interest. They disfigure a landscape like an abscess on a person's neck. At this one the biggest earthmovers I had ever seen – seventy tons or more – trundled like robots from *Star Wars* up and down spiralling tracks of shale that descended, like rifling in a gun barrel, the sides of a crater hundreds of feet deep and as wide as an Olympic stadium. It was at once impressive and unutterably boring. I forgot it as soon as I left.

Twelve

The evening was dark and wild when the *Capitaine La Pérouse* left Kieta harbour. She seemed to sidle out, careful not to disturb the sleeping crocodile. Rather to my surprise, the giant Puk-Puk made no move, so perhaps John the seaman was wrong in thinking the island was an evil spirit. Looking back, I saw high in the sky the loom of the great copper mine, a blurred arc light over a black ridge skimmed by flying rags and tatters of cloud. And then I looked back no more.

Captain Luc Duflos, the ship's master, was a young, open-faced man in jeans and sandals. He took me below at once and gave me a stiff whisky, as a good host welcomes a guest – the only one, in this case. He asked me to bear in mind that quite often on the short passage to Honiara he would suddenly disappear up to the bridge, no matter whose watch it might be, and I wasn't to be put out by what might seem like eccentric behaviour. Our course was littered and bounded by islands, he explained in an easy, attractive manner, and they were by no means always well lit. 'Bad beaconage, how you say it?' he said in pleasantly accented English.

The *La Pérouse* was relatively old, spacious and comfortable. You could stride about her. Luc was fond of her, he said. She was formerly Dutch, 11,000 tons, built in 1960. Her owners, Sofrana Lines of Auckland, New Zealand, liked to employ Frenchmen of the South Sea islands, and if they are all like Luc Duflos I don't blame them. The ship had six cabins, but the company was not in favour of taking passengers any more as a general rule. Nor was Luc. Passengers were too much trouble and expense in this time of recession.

'You need stewards. Maybe a doctor. And companies think only of money – cargoes – these days.' For himself, he regretted that. 'These are bitter days,' said this friendly man who, it didn't take me long to guess, had no bitterness in him at all. Captain Luc was naturally hospitable. Despite the no-passenger rule, he gave people a lift now and again. It was up to him as master; his privilege, not a duty. 'Sometimes I take friends. I'm delighted to take you. But, you know....' He shook his head. 'I've had bad experiences.'

'Hippies? Drugs?'

'No. Simply.... Well, for example, a man came with us, a stranger, a New Zealander. I was hospitable. The stewards worked extra for him. He ate a lot, drank sufficiently. He was spoilt, you might say. At the destination, he just went away. Went ashore and vanished. Not a goodbye, not a handshake, no thanks. Nothing for the stewards.... It's not nice, that. Another man sat all day in the armchair on the bridge with his feet up.' I knew by now that on a freighter one was expected to behave as a guest in someone else's house.

Once we were well out to sea we resumed our whisky, and were joined in his cabin by an extraordinarily handsome woman – Luc's Tahitian wife. 'Marie-Louise,' he introduced her, and I shook her hand. 'I expect you will be seeing where she comes from. The island of Moorea, opposite Papeete. The most beautiful island in French Polynesia.' He laughed. 'And I don't say that just to please her.'

Marie-Louise Duflos was about the same age as her husband, and she had the high cheekbones, large, soft eyes and deep butterscotch skin of the eastern Pacific. She looked from one to the other of us, smiling. If Moorea is anything like as beautiful as Madame Duflos, I thought, it's certainly worth an effort to get there. She led a small boy by the hand. She had brought their two-year-old son on board for the voyage; he loved the sea so much, she said, and later I saw that the cabin next to mine had been turned into a nursery. Inside the half-open door a tiny gumboot and a toy train were visible on the floor.

Captain Luc was a big man, tall, moustached: sometimes he stroked, without thinking, a stomach that was unselfconsciously ample. A Norman, born in Mali in West Africa, he lived now in Noumea, New Caledonia. 'I wander,' he smiled.

Turning a corner on the spacious bridge deck next morning, I received a small shock. A furious white face met mine and a wild scream of horror drove me back against the bulkhead – 'Aaaaaawwwwwwwkkkkk!' A black sickle beak lunged at me, agape. Puffed up, in anger or fear, a cockatoo gripped the bars of its cage and regarded me with loathing. The beadlike eyes were encircled by tiny

folds of delicately wrinkled skin of a wonderful turquoise blue, like the expensive eye shadow of an ageing society beauty, perfect against the pure lotus-white feathers and the pale yellow brushstroke on his trembling crest. 'Good morning. Who are you?' I said. But the angry stare was silent and unrelenting.

I moved away to a grey prospect that once more belied my expectations of a blue Pacific. A single shard of sunlight fell across a long grey island to port, which the chart told me was called Choiseul. There were a good many killer whales around here, I'd been told; blue whales, too. We were now in the New Georgia Sound, otherwise known as The Slot because of its extended narrowness between mountainous islands and the way it led ships to Honiara, as a tram rail guides a tram to its terminals.

Luc joined me at the rail. I had noticed that the crew of *La Pérouse* bore little or no resemblance to the people of Bougainville. No atomic fuzz. Their heads were round like cannonballs and short-cropped like Cromwell's Puritans. They were formidably built; heavy and fleshy men like rugby front-row forwards. They looked surly, and vaguely menacing. I asked Captain Luc where they came from.

'From Vanuatu,' he replied – from what was, in Asterisk's time, the New Hebrides.

'They look an unfriendly lot,' I said.

'Oh, no, they're all right. Good people. They look frightening, yes, but, like Coco, they're quite harmless, really. You've met Coco, the cockatoo?'

I had, I said, and added that both Coco and the crew could have fooled me. These unsmiling men were descendants of the islanders who, as Asterisk had described, were regularly lured on board a ship at anchor by the offer of money for some meaningless task, and 'grogged up' by blackbirding ships' captains, so that they woke up miles out to sea with blinding hangovers, and were obliged, because there was no way to escape, to sign on for three years' hard labour in a plantation in Queensland. The *La Pérouse*'s crew looked as if they were waiting for a suitable moment to avenge all that. No, they were good men, Luc said – until they got at the beer. Then they became raging bulls. Quite uncontrollable. Incapable of resisting more and more booze, fighting like madmen. If you gave them even one can of beer, they couldn't stop themselves drinking their way through the entire stock. You just had to wait until they passed out. Not what you want from the crew of a ship, said Luc. It was the same thing anywhere in the Pacific islands. All islanders went berserk after a few beers. There were no exceptions.

I could understand why Luc Duflos was fond of the *Capitaine La Pérouse*. The ship had the stately, cosy, if rather fusty air of a seaside boarding house. Off-season, of course, because there were no other passengers, a fact which gave me all that unaccustomed room to move about in. To heighten the boarding house illusion, my cabin had a parquet floor, a large rectangular window, and reading lights over the double bed. I could even give the place a geographical fix. It conjured up Bude in Cornwall and Edwardian villas called Balmoral or Glendower that look out over the sea from garden walls enclosing monkey puzzle trees and red-hot poker plants, a setting in which I had spent certain summers of my extreme youth dreaming of voyages like this. The *Capitaine La Pérouse* had a homely saloon and a library with big windows looking over the foredeck. Areas of the deck were netted off for Luc's son to toddle about in. I suppose the baby and the cockatoo – unusual objects on cargo vessels – contributed considerably to my Cornish boarding house fantasy and to the affection for the ship I briefly shared with Captain Luc.

Sofrana names its ships after South Pacific explorers. Apart from the *Capitaine La Pérouse* they had a *Captain Cook* and a *Captain Tasman*.

'We had a *Kermadec*, too,' Luc said. 'And a *Bougainville*. But the *Kermadec* was sold, and the *Bougainville* had a terrible accident.'

'What happened?'

'Some spare parts in the engine room fell from a bulkhead on to a fuel line and the whole engine room went up in a blaze. Eventually the ship was a total loss. The crew got off in lifeboats, but one capsized and the captain and his wife and his three kids were all lost.'

'A freak tragedy.'

'Yes, a freak. Now no one feels like calling another ship *Bougainville*.'

'So there's no ship named after a great explorer. He has to make do with an island hardly anyone knows, and a flower that is known the world over.'

Luc said, 'Perhaps that's the best kind of memorial to have. A flower named after you. Everyone loves a flower.'

God knows who had provided the books in *La Pérouse*'s library. It was certainly an odd mixture, as if someone had walked into a secondhand bookshop, waved a careless hand, and said, 'Give me everything on those ten shelves.' I found Jack London's *De Zwerftecht van de Snark* (Dutch for *The Voyage of the Snark* which I had in my suitcase) and next to that *Dimsie Moves Up* by a Dorita F. Bruce. The works of Oscar Wilde were there, and the *Golden Hours of Kai Lung*. I found myself flipping through a novel called *Savoy Grill at 7.30*, by Stephen Lister, a very thirties novel full of tales of skulduggery in the big business world of London between the wars. Expressions like 'By God, you'll pay for this, you dirty swine!' cropped up regularly in its swift-moving pages, and gorgeous girls were incessantly entertained by the hero to cocktails at the Savoy and dinner at Maxim's (was there a Maxim's in London as well as in Paris in those days?). I enjoyed the incongruity of such high life aboard a ship moving down The Slot of Melanesia.

The French section of the library was really not French at all, although the titles were in French – *Carnage à Chicago, Cauchemar à New York, L'Enfer Hawaiien*, all by a certain Don Pendleton who, a publisher's note told me, was also the author of *Massacre à Beverly Hills, Violence à Vegas, Fusillade à San Francisco, Panique à Philadelphia*, and *Débâcle à Detroit*. Later, over a whisky, Captain Luc and I thought up a few more – *L'Horreur de Hoboken, Catastrophe à Kansas City, Meurtre à Martha's Vineyard*. We planned to settle down to write them in collaboration, and retire with a fortune.

The time posted on a wall of the dining room for the midday meal was 11.30, but to my relief Captain Luc, his wife, the chief officer – a silent Wallis Islander – and I ate together at noon after the other officers and crew had finished: tongue, cucumber salad, potatoes, cheese (strong and good), and a bottle of Côtes du Rhône. A poster advertising Sofrana Lines hung over us: a Tahitian beauty, standing naked to the waist in clear, shallow water. She was so close to the camera you could see the pores of her skin, and her breasts, like over-ripe paw-paws, seemed about to tumble out of the photograph and onto the table. 'Get to know the Pacific better!' the poster said.

Luc said, irritably, 'I'm going to put two Papuan masks up there instead.'

Luc and Marie-Louise would have liked to take a house in Vila rather than Noumea; it would have been convenient for his work, but there had been political troubles in Vanuatu. It had been difficult, after that, to know where exactly was best. There was New Zealand, of course, and Australia. 'But Australians and New Zealanders are really cow-boys,' Luc said, making a face.

Grey curtains of rain were falling outside the windows. Darker grey, a smudge of land crawled past in the distance.

'You'll find that French officials round the Pacific are often Corsi-cans,' Luc said over coffee. 'Corsicans travel all over the world, like the Scottish people.'

'Their names end in "i", you know,' said Marie-Louise.

'Even "j",' I said. And I told them about the old Corsican hotelier, Jean Ottavj, who became my friend in Saigon during my years in Vietnam between 1965 and 1973.

Ottavj (the name had some obscure Hungarian or Finnish derivation and was pronounced Ottavee) had arrived in Indo-China with the French Army in the early 1920s, already a sergeant after service in Syria. When the time for his discharge came, he decided to stay on – many Frenchmen chose to stay in this Asian paradise, particularly if they had the adventurous blood of Corsica in their veins – and, like so many, had felt the enchantment of the lively little women of Tonkin and Annam. He went into the hotel and restaurant business, starting as a waiter or a cook, presently climbing to higher things – his automatically good standing with Saigon's unofficial Corsican 'Mafia' must have helped. After the Second World War he took over an unpretentious but centrally situated hotel called the Royale which, with its wood panelling, wooden bar and red and white check dining room table-cloths, was more like a *relais* in some small Corsican town than a Saigon hotel. By this time Ottavj had a pretty, diminutive Vietnamese woman of great character; she had a good head for figures, he said. They were ideally suited: she sharp, quick, devoted; he soft-spoken, shrewd, unexcitable.

'He had developed a passion for opium,' I told Luc. 'He needed a good many pipes a day by the time I met him. She was far too Vietnamese to object to that.'

Luc shrugged as if to say, 'Of course.'

Ottavj was an amazing human spectacle. He was on the short side, frail, with papery skin. He brushed his hair straight back, flat on his skull, and his face was as creased as a relief map of the Central Highlands of South Vietnam. He had a long nose like a fleshy beak; his purple lips were thin by now and he pursed and unpursed them constantly like a man sampling mouthfuls of wine. His voice was a solemn, rather courtly murmur that matched an unflagging courtesy and dignity; and his eyes shone like black beads, full of life and humour. There was something in M. Ottavj's appearance that reminded me of a kindly Mr Punch.

To know Ottavj was to love him. Year after year, each time I put my foot across his threadbare doormat I felt I was coming home. The Royale! Oh, what a refuge! – from the hideous, exhausting world of the war; from the lumbering, cacophonous American presence that so smothered the small, quicksilver world of the Vietnamese. In another refuge, a little back-alley loft hidden up in a rickety wooden stairway, the war could be conjured out of existence as the birdlike attendant teased a dark, golden, hissing globe over a tiny flame, and the world outside became an obscene irrelevance. Here a few of Ottavj's elderly Vietnamese friends – doctors, teachers, lawyers – murmured, sighed and sighed, sucking up in long, steady, greedy inhalations the peace the sweet smoke gave them – temporary peace in a thirty-year-old war that might last who knew how long.

For years, at intervals, riots raged, baton charges surged outside the door of the Royale; tear gas eddied down the street. Time and again Jean Ottavj stood calmly surveying the aftermath of pandemonium. '*En somme, cher M. Yoong*' (in eight years of friendship I was always 'M. Yoong', never Gavin), he would say at last, pursing and unpursing his old, thin lips, '*Plus ça change....*' Old Ottavj's life could have been measured in the number of tear gas canisters he'd seen in the gutters of Saigon.

Ottajv was superstitious. He often talked to me of the sayings and doings of mysterious eighteenth-century dabblers in the occult like the Count of St Germain, and quoted unceasingly the predictions of 'Nostradamus *et compagnie*' (I never knew who made up 'the company'). One year, he told me across the dinner table in his little restaurant that '*selon Nostradamus, M. Yoong,*' the Mediterranean

135

would be a 'sea of flame' that summer. '*On va voir,*' he said, nodding his head with certainty. And the Egyptians and Syrians were soon at war with Israel. M. Ottavj shrugged almost imperceptibly; he was not surprised. '*C'était écrit,*' he explained, '*par les anciens.*' He believed unshakeably in Nostradamus and the Count of St Germain.

No one who met him will ever forget M. Ottavj. Rooms were hard to find, with all the soldiers and journalists crowding into Saigon, but he joyfully lowered his rates for people he liked. If they were short of cash they could stay for nothing. '*Plus tard, plus tard,*' he said, waving away the money. His restaurant was a delightful throwback to French Indo-China days; nowhere else had such elderly, gnomelike Vietnamese waiters, such dusty wall emblems of long-departed French Air Force squadrons, such friendly – though most respectable – Vietnamese bar-girls. As the war went on, and the Vietcong, closing round the capital, began spasmodically to shell the city's long, winding, vulnerable river outlet to the sea, food became scarce. Jean Ottavj continued to serve good, simple food: *soupe pistou* (the Corsican minestrone), clams, *cassoulets*, good omelettes, blood puddings, crisp French bread, cheeses, even *crêpes suzette*. After tense days out in the unpredictable provinces with baffled Americans and demoralized Vietnamese, to return to the Royale was not merely luxury – it was heaven.

'How was the wine?' Luc asked.

'The wine was both heaven *and* a miracle.'

Good wine had become harder and harder to get. Algerian wine was shipped out in tankers in bulk, and rammed into bottles in some obscure Saigon warehouse. What distinguished Ottavj's wine was the fact that the labels on the bottles, when they arrived on the table, announced not the year, but the day and the month of bottling. A label would say, for example, '23 February'. And Ottavj warned that some days were better than others. '*Oh, M. Yoong.*' His old, bony hand, tangled with veins and blotched with grave marks, gripped my wrist. '*Je vous conseille . . . le dix mai – non! Jamais le dix mai!*' I suppose certain shipments had gone 'off' in a ship or a warehouse. Ottavj made it sound as if he had personally removed a dead rat from that day's cask.

Luc roared with laughter. 'Oh, yes. Or let it mature a week or so. "It'll be ready to drink by 3 p.m. on 1 June."'

As the Americans began to pull out, friends of M. Ottavj asked him what plans he had made. Wouldn't it be better to retire to Corsica? The Communists would surely confiscate his hotel; they might give him a very hard time.

I don't believe there was much real debate in Ottavj's mind. He was seventy. He hadn't been 'home' for years. He had his Vietnamese 'wife' to think of; she would not be happy in France. Besides, he himself had lost all his close relatives. Above all, there was the necessity for good and sufficient opium. France was not like easy-going Asia. It was difficult. Even Nostradamus, he told me, had nothing much to give him in the way of advice. His situation might become tragic....

'Is he still there?' Luc asked. 'Getting on with the Communists?'

'No,' I said.

Before they came, Ottavj celebrated his seventieth birthday in fine, hilarious fashion with a party at his own restaurant for which he brought out good wine he had hoarded for years. A short while later, the French Consul pinned the Order of the Legion of Honour on the lapel of his well-brushed, shining blue suit and kissed the pale, bony cheek, while old Ottavj, forcing his rheumatic bones to attention, pursed and unpursed his lips and water swam in his red-rimmed eyes. Fifty years in Indo-China! Ottavj and his friends celebrated again in his restaurant with a few bottles of hoarded champagne, and innumerable bottles of red wine labelled with a bewildering variety of days and months, and a good outpouring of calvados to end up with. I was sad because I missed this party, but I wrote to him, and he wrote back, sending a photograph of the event and a pair of Parker pens, with a note: *'L'objet n'est rien! Ce qui compte après tout, c'est le gueste* [sic], *l'idée, l'intention qui constitue l'ensemble du souvenir quand une pensée ineffable n'est pas capable d'exprîmer toute la psychologie qui l'enveloppe ou qui l'invoute. Jean Ottavj.'*

Then, before the final collapse of South Vietnam, before the horrendous panic at the American Embassy and the entry of the Communists into Saigon – in his own hotel, in his own time, Jean Ottavj died of heart failure.

'That was *my* Corsican,' I said to Luc. 'He made me believe one can meet saints anywhere.'

'A great old man.'

'Yes, he was,' I said.

There was a pause.

'Well, now,' Luc smiled and raised the bottle. 'I don't know the day or the month of this wine. Even the year is dubious. But have another glass anyway. To Corsica!'

*   *   *

Honiara. At six in the morning I came up to the bridge, having quickly splashed cold water over my head. A low coastline under an overcast sky, a few native fishing skiffs; two or three rusty motor vessels, one very battered indeed. 'That's your next adventure!' Captain Luc laughed, pointing to it. 'That's yours.'

'Just so long as it moves and points east.'

'Welcome to Honiara' was stencilled in huge black letters on a long corrugated iron shed on the wharf, and other sheds were enlivened with the painted silhouettes of crocodiles, serpents, a canoe. A hooting, giggling crowd of stevedores with the familiar busby hair arrangements rushed through the dock gate and on to the wharf, shouting up at us, 'Good morning to you!' A good sign, I thought.

'Have you an air ticket onwards?' an immigration officer asked me when we were alongside and tied up, flicking a finger at my passport in the saloon. A new question, but Captain Luc said, 'That's something you'll be asked right through the Pacific – "Where's your return ticket? Where's your onward ticket?" Modern travelling! No adventuring allowed! Everyone must be the same, have an air ticket, copy everyone else. That's it, eh?'

Luckily, the Sofrana Line's agent, a pleasant, bearded young German, came to my rescue and said he would sponsor me. I said a warm farewell to Captain Luc Duflos and Marie-Louise and told them I would miss their floating *pension*. 'Drop me a line to Noumea.' There was a possibility we might all meet again in Tahiti – if Luc could get leave, and if I could get there at all. 'Go and see old Gauguin in the Marquesas Islands. His grave,' Luc advised me. I would do my best, I said.

Thirteen

'It's as if they were wading through wet sand,' I said. 'Mentally, I mean. And I don't mean they're stupid.'

It was disconcerting. The Solomon Islands seemed to exist in a different timescale from Asia. Time seemed to pass more slowly here. In the Mendana Hotel, down the road from the wharf at Honiara, the receptionists and waiters, though pleasant and smiling under their fuzzes, reacted to questions or requests like men and women in a dream. Sometimes there was a pause before they answered; sometimes they just smiled and wandered slowly and airily away. The air might have been drugged.

Gerry Stenzel, who had gone surety for me with the immigration officer, had driven me to the Mendana, and next day came round to see me. He agreed.

'Everybody notices this,' he said. 'Everything really is slow. You will become slow. I have. It gets to you. I've been here two years and I've noticed newcomers trying to act as they have in other places: in quicktime. They seem unreal, even to me. They move at quite a different speed from people here. I can't help laughing. They look like, well – '

'Clockwork mice?'

'Ha! Yes, exactly, and they can't keep up that speed for long. Like a man in deep water trying to fight the waves, they learn that to float is the only way to avoid exhaustion.' It was really a nice way to live, floating, he said, as long as everyone else was floating, too.

We were sitting in his bungalow office with the sign of Tradco Shipping on the door. 'Islanders are very self-sufficient. If you speak too sharply to a lazy man in his office, he'll just get up, wander out into the street. And he'll keep wandering to the bus stop, and take a bus to his village. Why should he care? The village has everything. He'll be looked after. He really doesn't need money at all. Anyway, there are times when he'd rather forego money than work. It's very usual, this kind of thing, in the Pacific. You'll see.'

I am impatient by temperament, despite my years in Asia. Yet I could see how this easy-going place had its attractions, particularly if, like me, you lacked any pressing reason to hurry life along. Stenzel seemed to have adapted cheerfully. And later, when I met other foreigners who lived and worked here, they swore by the place and its people – and defended their life in bottom gear with enthusiasm.

The Mendana Hotel was named after the Spanish explorer Don Alfonso Mendana, the first European to set eyes on the Solomons, which he named in the expectation – false, as it turned out – of great caches of gold on these shores. My guidebook told me that the Mendana visit turned into an appalling tale of cannibalism and massacre, from the moment when some succulent part of a boy, tastefully garnished with taro roots, was presented to Mendana for his dinner by the islanders, until their villages were razed and they themselves put to the sword by the Spaniards. It was the first gory instalment of that grim saga – the Fatal Impact of white men on the South Seas.

Here, I was back in the world of gold or black atomic hairdos and honey skins, and the excited exclamations and falsetto giggles with which all Melanesians enliven their conversations. Honiara, the Solomons' capital, is also the main town and port of Guadalcanal Island, a name I knew very well but only from an American war film. It is a modest-sized place. Running past the hotel and the Tradco office and supermarket is a single main street, on which, in one direction, are the law courts and government buildings, and in the other, banks, a few stores, Air Nuigini's office, the office of Solair (the inter-island line of propeller-driven hopabout planes), a Chinese restaurant and a trio of tiny offices belonging to the local shipping firms that carry cargo and passengers through the islands. A shabby cinema was showing a new version of *Dillinger*. Honiara port was hardly more than one long wharf, several long warehouses and a few Nissen huts smartened up into offices.

With Gerry I discussed the all-important matter of my onward journey. My next port of call, we both agreed, should be Suva in Fiji, about 1600 miles away across open sea according to my measurements with a pencil on my map. However, there was, said Gerry, one serious problem. The big cargo vessels that might take me travelled, almost without exception, from east to west, not the way I was going, west to east. It had to do with currents and obscurely technical things like the way the planet turns. The old explorers had come that way, and more recently, yachtsmen did so, too.

Tradco were also agents for the Bank Line of Great Britain, whose big cargo ships were regular visitors. Lord Inverforth, the Bank Line's chairman and owner, accompanied by several Bank Line bigwigs from London and Australia, and their man in this island area, Captain John Mackenzie, a veteran sailor who based himself at Lae, were arriving on a brief visit in a week's time. A marvellous character was John Mackenzie, Gerry said. It would be worth my while to meet him and ask his advice about what to do next. But I could see from the board over Gerry's head that the next Bank Line ship, *Clydeside*, was coming *from* Samoa and Fiji, not going there. Meanwhile, what about local ships, I asked. What about those motor vessels lying in the harbour? Admittedly, some of them looked a bit dilapidated – but did none of them go to Suva?

Gerry laughed. 'Well, if you want that sort of thing – '

'Anything. The soonest possible, although I would like to look at the Solomons, too.'

'Don't worry. I think you'll get time for that before we find you a ship.' The vessels I had seen from *La Pérouse*, he said, were mostly inter-island craft. There was one, it was true, he said – the *Ann*, a bit of an old rust-bucket belonging to an Australian called Roy Clemens.... He picked up the telephone. 'Oh, Roy....'

Clemens, I soon gathered, was willing to be helpful, but the *Ann* was not due to go anywhere as far afield as Suva just yet. Perhaps she had a cargo for San Cristobel Island, the next one of the Solomons to the east of Guadalcanal. I forget the reason. But if I would keep in touch, Clemens said.... I certainly would, Gerry told him.

So there was time to explore a bit.

Gerry said, 'I've a suggestion. Spend the next day or two with me here. Then take a boat to that island to the east. Malaita. A very big island, and an interesting one. It takes seven or eight hours to get there. Stay there a day or two, then come back and we'll see what's moving east.'

That afternoon we drove along a long, flat coastline, treeless and rather dull. Inland a dark mass of foliage rose into Guadalcanal's central spine of mountains, but by the sea the road trailed wanly through the soaring stems of coconut plantations. Here, the interest for me was not in the landscape, but in what lay half buried under it. It was forty years since American marines repulsed, then decimated, the Japanese in the Second World War holocaust that the Solomons became. In the appropriately named Iron Bottom Sound, facing my hotel terrace, lies who knows what tonnage of sunken scrap metal that was once the most modern component of the American and Japanese battle fleets. Along the coast road to the west there was a garden museum of that terrible time. In it, twisted chunks of Japanese Zero and American planes I couldn't identify had been arranged like modern sculptures in an exhibition, side by side. It was a weird metallic cemetery; the dead machines were their own headstones. Some of the planes had been dredged up from the seabed; yet, after thirty or forty years under the Sound, the metal in their crumpled wings and broken cockpits gleamed like new, almost like silver. They made things well in those days: of stainless steel. One cockpit had survived its crash intact and, hoisting myself up to look into it, I half expected to find a pilot's torso and a goggled head bowed over the joystick. I saw only instrument dials and a tangle of wires like worms. Beside these planes, there were anti-aircraft guns and machine guns and bayonets; and rows of helmets laid out, like two lines of country dancers. American this side, Japanese that, among the hibiscus in the short-cut grass. You could see the bullet or shrapnel holes in the helmets.

To reach the main battlefield we drove past the airport and turned down muddy tracks. After a time Gerry stopped the car and led the way on foot in the shade of a coconut forest through the damp afternoon heat.

'The Americans invaded the island here, took the airfield and then had to defend it for six months,' Gerry said. 'The Japs threw everything at them. Then they broke. A slaughter.' It was wilder here: no gardens. We stepped over rusty barbed wire, and scuffed through ugly tough grass and creepers that dragged at our ankles like the fingers of dead soldiers. It was twilight under the trees, and very still.

We were in the battlefield now. In the grass there were swampy shell holes, half filled with black mud, half dug out again. 'Look.' Gerry stopped and poked at the earth with a rusty bush knife. I saw that the creepers and mud partly covered dozens of Japanese military water bottles, fragments of rotting boots – studded heels, uppers with metal laceholes – and whole boots, too. And boots with no toes and heels whose owners had lost half a foot when those boots took their last step in the minefield. Mess tins, rice cooking pots of the Imperial Japanese Army, more flaking bayonets, more skull-like helmets. . . .

Sweat ran down my face. In the fading rays of the setting sun, hundreds of small white and yellow butterflies tumbled about us like spirits of the mutilated dead. Green parrots screeched among the palms. The Japanese had crawled through the trees, calling to the Americans, 'Marine, you die.' The black mud underfoot gave out a nasty, dank smell and I imagined decaying human bodies. At any moment I felt I might see a skeletal foot in a putrefying boot, or a skull in a punctured helmet.

Searching, in awe, we moved closer to the contested airstrip – Henderson Field – and Bloody Ridge, another major American defence line, a curiously lumpy upheaving of the land, now green with grass like an old Roman encampment. Then, it must have been a bald, ruined expanse of shell-filled mud.

A heroic American, Colonel Merritt Edson, and his men had thrown the Japanese *banzai* attackers back from another zigzag outcrop now called Edson's Ridge. And between here and the sea – not far – is where the material refuse of battle mostly lay – the shells of trucks, jeeps and armoured cars, a tank or two: steel corpses. Ammunition, mortar bombs and shells lay where they had been carefully stacked forty years before – pyramids of explosives that looked (and may have been) still too dangerous to touch. Sudden birds' cries, our legs swishing through tall grass on the jungle's edge, and the soft sound of sea creeping up the beach – that was all there was to hear now. And in the stillness, I shuddered at the thought of peering too closely into concrete bunkers

whose mouths gaped through the creepers, harbouring God knows what neglected phantoms. They were as lonely as lost Inca tombs in the remoteness of a South American rain forest.

Gerry told me that human remains were still being found here. 'We've found a lot of Japanese teeth here. Some of them gold and silver.' He thought fifty Americans were still missing, unaccounted for after all the others had been shipped home for burial so long ago. Only a week before a bulldozer driver, a local man, had dug up a skeleton in a valley near here. 'It had US Army medical tags. The driver pinched all its teeth, but the police got some of them back, and sent them to the United States authorities in Hawaii. They think they may be able to identify him – a guy 5 feet 8 inches tall and with big hands.'

There are numerous Japanese still unaccounted for, too. The Japanese Government is convinced that several soldiers of the Imperial Army who fled into the densest jungle in 1943 are still hiding there, unaware that the war ended forty years ago.

'It's touching,' Gerry said. 'The Ministry of Health in Tokyo sent two expeditions to entice them out – well, whoever may be there. They dropped leaflets on the jungle – in Japanese, of course. They brought loudspeakers, too, and waded about in the bush broadcasting messages that said, "Come out, come out! It's all over."'

'Anyone come out?'

'Well, no one as yet. But the Japanese haven't given up hope. One of the expeditions is still around. They've even put up mailboxes in out-of-the-way places, which these lost soldiers could use if they wanted to communicate with Tokyo. Of course, any left-over soldier would be getting a bit aged now.'

'Any actual evidence that they are there?'

'The locals say they've found odd footprints quite different from their own. And one day in the jungle people saw a hairy man, in rags, eating a banana. He ran away, but they swear he looked Japanese. Who knows?'

At the Japanese war memorial, white, concrete, overlooking Honiara, I found a strange sight. At its foot a group of Japanese squatted or knelt in prayer. A wavering, unearthly chanting rose like incense from a small tape recorder over the bowed heads of nut-brown old men in singlets and wide khaki shorts and elderly women in smart picture hats and pleated skirts. One old man wore a kind of commando knife in his belt; I supposed it was part of his old uniform, and that the men were survivors of the war, or that some of them and the women were mourning relatives of the owners of the rusting helmets and scattered teeth. The plain fell away to the Sound where the Japanese and American battle fleets once pounded one another to scrap. The plain was green and humpy and oddly scattered with dead trees whose bare white trunks stuck up like skeletal fingers. The landscape looked unreal, as if all its spirits had fled.

In the Honiara Yacht Club, a modest-sized place, tanned young men, mostly Australian, dressed in shorts, ankle socks and heavy boots, lounged about in wicker chairs; these were managers in from the copra plantations. Others, older and better dressed in white shirts and slacks or tailored shorts, had brought their wives. The general drink was Castlemaine X X X X ('Four X') beer.

The club, perched on a strip of beach on the edge of Iron Bottom Sound between the hotel and the port, was half traditional, half modern; iron beams and wood supported a very high coconut weave roof arching over tables and chairs, a small film screen and a bar. You could almost step from the club into the water.

'A word of warning. Don't drink here with the islanders,' said a German called Fritz Markworth, introduced to me by Gerry as the owner of two or three inter-island trading vessels; an Old Hand. His accent had overtones of Queensland. 'I like them,' he told me. 'But after two beers, three, there'll be an argument about race' – he pronounced it rice. 'They will start it and it's pointless to argue. They won't listen.'

'The Samoans are the most vicious in grog,' another man said. 'Everybody says that.'

Gerry was talking shipping 'shop' to somebody else. 'Polish Lines have the concession to ship the copra from the Solomons by undercutting the freight rates. But the Bank Line – British – gets all the general cargo: coconut oil, timber, canned fish, cocoa. Bank Line does well. It's old and reliable.'

Cheerful waiters topped with black fuzz moved about with trays. One wore a T-shirt with a cryptic messsage: 'Solomons, where are you, yourself?' it asked.

Darkness fell. More beer came, round after round. People began to talk of the Solomons' Government practice of cutting down trees indiscriminately and not replanting – or of ministers allowing unscrupulous foreigners to pay them for the privilege of doing so.

'Fiddling about with nature,' Markworth said. 'I used to have a couple of boats on the Rhine. Well, you know they had a fine idea to straighten' – striten, he said – 'the Rhine, to smooth out some curves. And they did. And the river ran straight towards the sea. But something unfortunate occurred. Some towns and villages downstream had been used to getting plenty of fresh water for washing and so. Now the river was straight, no more water. Why? Well, the river water now was flowing very fast down between its bank and the speed somehow was draining water from its sides much faster. No one had thought of that.' He waved his glass at us. 'No one had thought about nature.' Throughout the world, greedy governments were allowing greedy foreign timber contractors to decimate their forests. You could never replace a rain forest and its fauna died with it. It was happening all over Asia, they said.

'With the exception of India,' I put in. In the Andamans, in the Bay of Bengal, I had walked through forests so selectively trimmed that it was hard to tell where the missing trees had been. The Indian Government deserves the ecological equivalent of the Nobel Prize for that.

I went to Auki the next morning. In my notebook I read:

Auki, Malaita. What Jack London in his book, *The Cruise of the Snark*, called 'the savage coast of Malaita' is invisible. It's still dark at 0500 when I step off the little motor vessel from Honiara. A single street of stores, little more than painted sheds, slopes gently up from the jetty. I had been advised to stay at the Auki Lodge. Two friendly policemen on the wharf direct me 'up the street' and one of them walks with me, flashing his torch over the frequent puddles and along a wet, grassy lane as far as a bungalow with a lit verandah. A large toad crouches on a step pretending to be a stone. No other sign of life. The front door is closed. I find a chair and wait on the verandah, watching the first slow rays of dawn begin to touch the cassia trees on the lawn, slowly tinting their dew-drenched blossoms with gold and the delicately splayed leaves of the flame trees with a fringe of silver. The silent birth of a new island day; with sun-up, a white-necked kingfisher swoops past me to perch in the trees, uttering a harsh, monotonous squeak like someone rhythmically squeezing a teddy bear. The silence is broken. I hear human beings stirring within the bungalow; soon the door opens.

The Auki Lodge is small and cosy and owned by two well-to-do Baptist Malaitans, David and Ethel, both of them built like middle-aged sumo wrestlers. I have it from Gerry that David is the grandson of a chief and an elder of the South Seas Evangelical Church, and, bulky, almost stately, he looks it. 'You should see the Langa Langa Lagoon,' they say, when I have registered. 'And the artificial islands.'

After breakfast I walked down to the wharf and the market, past the little police station and Chinese stores with shelves piled with umbrellas, corned beef tins, Johnson's baby powder, cans of pilchards and Ma Ling roasted goose, Lux soap, soy sauce and Creamy Custard biscuits, ladies' 'frilly undies' and much else.

In the open market, sixty or seventy tuna fish lay in the sun on coconut fronds, and a boy with almost white hair waved branches over them to keep off the flies. He had a Union Jack patch on the pocket of his open shirt. Mullet were laid out, too, and eels, and a yellow and black striped fish that looked too beautiful to eat. At a vegetable stall, a man said, '*Wata cabis*,' pointing to bundles of cress. '*Bitalnat, kokonat from garten*' – meaning 'from a plantation, not wild'. There were bamboo stems filled, as ice-cream fills a cornet, with taro mixed with milk – 'Not *bulamacao*', the stall-owner said, 'but *kokonat*. Custom milk.' *Bulamacao* meant 'cow', I knew. Decades ago, some white man landed the first bull and the first cow in the Solomons, and said, 'See – a bull and a cow!' But the islanders thought he referred to each animal by that term, so '*bulamacao*' entered the local pidgin. 'Custom' means 'traditional'. All this I learnt from a pamphlet I had bought in Honiara called *Pijin Bilong Yumi* (Our Pidgin).

Among the rows of betel nut and sweet potatoes and bananas a large, fat young man, with a T-shirt splitting over his pot belly, shouted at me, 'G'mornin'. I'm Andrew from the Gilbert Islands. And you?' An old man with a tattooed face came up, shook our hands and said something. 'Ah-ha! That's nice,' Andew explained in a foghorn voice. 'He said to us "Bless You". That's nice.' Andrew walked with me round the market. He was a well-driller, visiting a sister married to a man in the post office here.

'Auki is very quiet and good,' he bawled at me. 'In the Gilbert Islands always drinking trouble, fighting.' He seemed drunk himself, despite the early hour, and I was mildly alarmed. He swayed away towards a man loading wood into a ramshackle cart. 'Ha, John!' he roared. 'When'll I get the ten dollars you owe me? Eh?' The man laughed and so did other men standing around. Andrew, I was relieved to see, laughed too. 'You want a fight? Hey, wanta fight?' He rolled about the street shouting with glee and the whole street laughed with him.

Auki is a tiny place at the head of the large Langa Langa lagoon, the limits of which are clearly marked by a thin, white line of waves breaking over coral, and by outcrops of the coral itself, which although a beautiful turquoise underwater reveals ugly blocks of jagged lava above it. From the canoe which Andrew arranged to take me down the length of the lagoon I saw floating coconuts like dozens of severed heads – appropriately, for Malaita is an island of former headhunters. Men in ragged shorts fished from small, village-made dugouts.

A line of man-made islands runs the length of the lagoon, created by the patient piling of coral block on coral block, and then the piling of earth on top of that. These artificial islands are topped by coconut palms and hamlets of sago-thatched houses, and ride offshore like men-of-war in battle line. By putting the seawater 'moat' between themselves and the envious head-chopping warrior tribes from the interior of the island, the 'saltwater' dwellers on the coast had escaped an age-old persecution. There is something oddly silent about these beachless excrescences. And a strange absence of birds, except for the black, piratical frigate birds that lazed about the taller trees.

At the far end of the lagoon, I asked the canoeman, 'Can we land?'

'With permission.'

We were allowed to land by a plump, short man of about forty-five, wearing shorts but no shirt or shoes, whose curly hair, beard and moustache were more mauve than black. 'I show you,' he said. His name, he added, was Peter. He led me through the small wooden house around which fishing nets were hung up to dry. Then he showed me many graves, some half smothered by undergrowth. 'That grave is four days old,' he said, pointing to a few melancholy stones with faded paper flowers strewn about like refuse. Later, coming to a hut, he said, 'This is taboo house, not for tourists. Here no girl can go in, only men.' It was his house, he said. 'And here I keep skulls of the aunties, father and grand-grandfathers. My family skulls.'

'They bring good luck?'

'Sometimes. Sometimes they give lucky. But the missionaries come to spoil things, saying to me, "You under mission now; do not listen to spirits, don't talk to them." But I *should* talk to them, because in my custom I ask the spirits to help me. I *should* ask them. Sometimes they give lucky.'

'I'm sure you should ask them,' I said.

At a raised 'bed' of stones, Peter stopped. 'That's where we put chief's body. We put chief's body on those stones. Rain come and cover him until body's rotten.' I thought: The smell – but he anticipates me. 'We put plants on the body so smell them through all the village. When all flesh is gone, we put the skull in a small basket and take it to water and wash it and keep it to show. Then bury the bones. When new chief dies we bring new body to the stones for rotting.' I stooped to peer into thick bush. The empty sockets of skulls looking back at me, half hidden in the shadows, had a wide-eyed look, seeming to ask a question – a question that expected a funny answer, because the jaws were already grinning. Shifting light gave them a kind of false life. Uncomfortable. Nearby, in a shaggy-roofed house, women were singing old songs; the sound was as soothing as the sound of lagoon water lapping the coral.

We wandered on: more houses, taro and yam gardens over a plank bridge – 'taboo for women' – big banyan trees. Boys trailed fishing lines. I saw Peter's log dugout which he had bought with the traditional money of Malaita – strings of threaded shells. 'Buy wife, too, with shell money.'

It strikes me as I write this that, for some reason, many of the lively younger people were away, perhaps at school. So, despite a number of infants and small boys, a few smiling women and old men, and the courteous welcome that Peter of the mauve hair gave me, the atmosphere was a joyless one. Of course the talk of skulls and rotting corpses, and the isolation one felt here, had depressed me. Life and death seemed disconcertingly mingled. In fact, these artificial islands were a bit too much like floating cemeteries to be comfortable. But the care of the skulls and spirits was not based on the sadness of irretrievable loss. Surely, the point of it was that the lamented dead ones *lived on* through the skulls? I half remembered something about all this in Arthur Grimble's book, *A Pattern of Islands*, and later I looked it up.

The seen and the unseen made but one world for them [the Gilbert Islanders, in this case]. The belief was that the more recently departed could and did return.... They wanted to see what their descendants were doing. The skulls were preserved ... for them to re-enter as they liked. If skulls at least were not kept, their ghosts would come and scream reproach by night with the voice of crickets from the palm-leaves.

Yet there was love as well as fear in the ancient cult of the ancestor, and often love predominated. I liked the story Grimble told of the old man whom he found blowing tobacco smoke between the jaws of a skull. The old man explained he was 'loving the skull' because his grandfather – who was inside it at that moment – had been very good to him when he was alive. He had chosen tobacco as his offering of love because, as far as he knew, there was 'no supply of that luxury in the ancestral paradise'.

At the Auki Lodge that night I discovered on the verandah an American professor of biology with two young assistants from New York. They were collecting Malaitan bats, they said, or hoped to – they had had difficulties on that score with the Government. Officials in Honiara feared that their collecting would seriously deplete the local bat population. Was that likely, I asked.

'Hardly,' the professor laughed. 'We may take away, oh, two hundred skins and stomach contents for analysis. And a number of parasitic fleas.' He introduced himself – Goodwin was his name, from Colgate University, New York. He estimated there would be twenty-three species of bat on Malaita, each species consisting of several million individuals. 'We're talking of several billion bats here. In caves. In trees. All sizes.'

As we talked on the verandah, stabbed by a maddening swarm of mosquitoes, creatures like large birds flapped slowly overhead, black and ponderous against the evening sky. Owls? Vultures? 'My God. Fruit bats,' said one of the two young men.

From a sackful of squeaking, moving things he took something that looked like a flying mouse, and held it up by the tips of its black, membraned wings, stretched like very thin leather. It wriggled and tried to bite his gloved hands.

'How will you kill these bats?' I asked him. I half imagined the two younger men rabbit-punching them on the backs of their diminutive necks.

'Oh, they'll die in the sacks,' the professor said. 'The temperature will do that for 'em.'

When I ventured a remark about the vampire bats of Europe, the professor feigned indignation. 'I must tell you,' he said, 'that no vampires exist in Europe — not even in Transylvania. Of course, vampires do exist in South America. They like to suck your toes when you sleep. Their teeth are so sharp that they won't even wake you.'

'Fruit bats?'

'Fruit bats eat fruit,' the professor said, severely. 'Not humans.'

As I left the garden to search the shops for a mosquito killer, fruit bats as big as brown owls flew heavily past, aiming for a nice sheltered place in which to hang upside down and sleep. Whatever the professor said, they looked like the Dracula family returning from an evening's blood tasting.

I took to bed with me the guidebook to Solomons pidgin, and made a note, as I had in Rabaul, of phrases that especially pleased me. An expression I found particularly appealing was *Tingting bilong me*, meaning 'I think'.

Slip, of course, was 'sleep'. I slept.

The jungle-covered mountains and ravines towered up over the corrugated iron rooftops of little Auki, where boys, with hair so palely yellow that they looked like little old men, fished from the pier. Malaita looked like a huge shark on the map. 'No white man,' Jack London wrote, 'was sure of Malaita crews in a tight place'; and the Solomons, he found, were full of tight places. A Captain Jansen, with whom he sailed, advised London and company: 'You'd better bring your revolvers along and a couple of rifles,' adding, 'I've got five rifles aboard, though the one Mauser is without ammunition.' The bushmen, apparently, were armed with Snider rifles – the generic term for any old rifle. They also had 'tomahawks': in fact, the European master of a local vessel had been 'chopped to pieces with tomahawks' quite recently. 'Murder,' London wrote melodramatically, 'stalked abroad in the land,' and the air 'seemed filled with poison'.

I wondered if all this was not a bit of an exaggeration, a literary aid to London's he-man image. I felt nothing here of the menace I had felt growling at me on the shores of Bougainville. In Auki, I knew from a friend I had consulted in Hong Kong, resided a man called John Freeman who was the district magistrate, and might know something of Malaitans and their fairly recent history.

Philip Smiley, my friend in Hong Kong, had been Freeman's predecessor in the job, and had had several years' experience of Malaitans in the 1970s. He had given me a travel book, *Bride in the Solomons*, written by an American, Osa Johnson, about a visit she and her photographer husband had made here after the First World War. Philip's own close acquaintance with Malaitan affairs was reflected in the inscription he scribbled on the title page: 'To Gavin, en route to

Malaita, from one who had many brides there (albeit ephemeral ones)'.

I found Freeman in a four-roomed office with louvred windows in a low-ceilinged bungalow. Portraits of Queen Elizabeth and the Duke of Edinburgh (the independent Solomons remained in the British Commonwealth) stared down at his desk from a wall, and hopeful Malaitans with urgent petitions stared at him through a window from a bench under a coconut thatch roof.

Freeman was a good-natured young man with a black beard, a wide mouth with a good many healthy-looking teeth, and a skin browned by the Solomon sun. He had, he said, come here willingly but by chance. From Cambridge University he had tried to join the Foreign Office, but having failed the interview he had decided to settle for the law, and found himself in Birmingham. There, one of those strange things you read about happening to someone else actually happened to him. He saw an advertisement: 'Magistrate Needed in Solomon Islands'. He applied at once. He would do two years here and return to practise law in England. 'Two years is enough – or that's what I think now. I deal with living people and that's what I like.'

Freeman lived with his wife, Alison, in a tiny house on a hill overlooking palm trees. It looked as if it might slide down the hill in the next good rainstorm.

'Sorry we can't put you up.' The spare room was occupied, he explained apologetically, by two parakeets named Joyce and Francis, 'after the Chief Justice in Honiara', and in the kitchen a possum looked at us from a wooden box with a wire-netting door. 'We were offered him in the market,' Alison Freeman said. 'For *kaikai* – for food.' The possum's eyes were ungrateful buttons in a woolly overcoat.

The Freemans had few luxuries. The Government couldn't afford even to give them a jeep, although Freeman was expected – and wanted – to know as much about his sprawling district as possible. He had to borrow one before he and Alison could visit a favourite place on his day off: a cool, clear river pool where they could swim like Adam and Eve in the Garden of Eden under beautiful trees, festooned with creepers.

The Malaitans, in John Freeman's opinion, were very Irish: charming, hardworking, tradition-minded. They cared more about land ownership than things like sex or violence, although there was often violence about land ownership.

'I think one of the nicest things is walking down to the courthouse every morning to see all the prisoners I've sentenced sitting around, with great long bush knives, saying to me, "Oh, good morning. Hello!".'

John Freeman walked with me to the courthouse, a long brick building with large, paneless windows. A few benches stretched from wall to wall. A magistrate's bench and a handsome, hand-carved magistrate's chair under a painted wooden royal coat of arms were lit by strips of neon. In the doorway someone had left a squashed can of lager.

Malaita was rather a moral place in Freeman's opinion. 'Jolly strict.' He showed me one sort of deposition he'd had to deal with: an incest case – there weren't too many of them. The defendant had been tucked up with his wife and daughter, Surara, and his other children, and, well, his statement went on:

Me sleep long house bilong me, withem wife bilong me, daughter bilong me, Surara and olketa small piccaninee more. Time me lookem calico [clothes] *Surara, him come out and him no wear underpant. From time me lookem this one, me start to think wrong long hemi, when me kasi holem* [catch hold] *and me fackem now.*

But, his statement continued, his wife was roused by this untoward activity –. '*Time me go ahead for fackem, missis bilong me hem wake up and hemi tok long me*' – and now he was in trouble.

I forget what punishment Freeman handed out.

What was referred to in court as 'night trespass' but was more popularly known as 'creepin'' – young men attempting by stealth to deflower sleeping maidens (a common misdemeanour) – was punishable by six months in jail or a $200 fine. That was a much heavier penalty than the two months' prison (or $40 fine) you'd get for 'spreading panic by making magic', or casting spells to induce impotence in a rival, and so on.

Superstitions had to be learnt. Kingfishers, for example, bring rain. Fireflies are spirits of the dead. It's a good sign if a butterfly wishes to enter your house. Thunderstorms are good, too; they mean visitors are on their way.

We talked of Jack London, and Freeman said Malaitans were certainly quite savage until the twenties and thirties. 'Headhunters, certainly.'

'You're never worried?' He and his wife were quite unprotected, alone here.

'Oh, no. But there are some quite wild places here still.'

Back in his battered, friendly little house, eating avocados and cold roast beef, his wife said, 'You've heard about Malaita's famous murder, of course? One of John's predecessors was murdered.'

'No,' I said.

'You haven't?' She sounded amazed. 'A district officer of Malaita, in the 1920s. Name of Bell.'

'No. Sorry.'

Freeman said, 'Yes, I'm surprised you haven't heard of Bell.'

But then I remembered that I had read about Bell in *Bride in the Solomons*. And from what Freeman related and a re-reading of Osa Johnson's book, the story of the Solomons' most famous massacre came together.

William Robert Bell was fifty-one years old when, in 1927, he fell dead across his desk with a broken skull. He had been a district officer in Malaita for twelve years. In his younger days he had fought in South Africa in the Boer War where, inexplicably, after having been tried for cowardice, he was awarded a medal for valour. His photographs, taken at the time he came to Malaita, show him to have been the prototype of almost any white hunter from the *Boy's Own Paper*: large, big-boned, 'eyes blue as steel' (someone said), his jaw 'strongly-set'. He was a dedicated man and a solitary one, so he was not easy to live with. Or so some visitors said. Mr and Mrs Johnson from America, an intrepid, newly wed pair of travellers out for adventure and offbeat photographs, stayed with him in Malaita in 1917, and though they came with an introduction from the Governor they got a discouraging reception. Mr Bell seemed 'more pleased to receive his week's mail than to see us,' Mrs Johnson admitted. He was 'extremely cool and formal', and Osa Johnson winced as he shook her hand, and saw that 'he was going to be no man to cross'. But, she asked herself a trifle guiltily, was *she* partly to blame? Was he upset by her loud checked gingham dress and enormous straw hat after so much healthy native semi-nudity around him? Was it possible that he resented the pet cockatoos that perched on each of her shoulders wherever she went? He stared at them, then – '"There will be tea, if you like," said Mr Bell abruptly. And sat down to his mail.'

Still, he did put them up in his house, and even played them his beloved Gilbert and Sullivan on the gramophone after dinner. And then Osa Johnson boldly brought out her ukelele and sang her Pacific medley: 'Honolulu Tomboy', 'Aloha', and 'Sweet Little Maori Girl'. Bell also took the Johnsons on treks through the island and its waters, always by canoe or on foot (he had no motor transport),

155

even though the island was evidently a dangerous place.

Bell talked to them calmly, without bragging, of his first 'brush' with a headhunting chief: an ambush. 'Arrows flew,' he said, 'from every side. But we fired into the bush and stopped the attack. Next day, the chief sent a messenger with a warning that Mr Bell should stay away unless he wanted to leave his head.' Bell sent word that if he heard any more such nonsense he'd wipe out the entire tribe, but that if the chief wanted peace he should let him know. In a few days a messenger returned from the chief with a basket containing a bloody head of a Malaitan. It was a peace offering. 'We're on very friendly terms now,' Bell told the Johnsons with satisfaction. Evidently he was almost fanatically devoted to Malaita and to his job. But he had no illusions that he was universally loved, or that his life was not in constant danger. When Osa Johnson strayed away into an area taboo to women, after having been warned not to, he exploded in fury.

'You bloody little fool.' His hand trembled and he struggled to control his lips. 'Do you know that hundreds, probably thousands of people have been murdered within sight of where you are sitting at this moment? And that I spend every hour here at my peril? I have expected the house to be rushed any night and have had special guards posted. Why, this place reeks with murder and headcutting. And I wouldn't be surprised if they have my head one day!'

Mr Johnson turned 'white with this unpleasantness'. He stammered out that he and his wife would leave at once: a local schooner had turned up whose master, an Englishman, they had met in Guadalcanal. 'Capital!' snapped Bell; and he strode off to the drill ground.

The master of the schooner to which the Johnsons fled, Creswell by name, was a different type of Old Hand (he reminded Osa of a handsome British colonel she'd met in Sydney), but his message was much the same as Bell's. He had drawn up a personal code of do's and don't's for expatriates in the Solomons. Through years of local trading he had come to know the islands as well as he knew his old island bosun, whose name was Satan and who wore bone ornaments in his fuzz, shell earrings, and a large bone ring through his nose. ('How did he manage to eat with such a piece hanging over his mouth?' Osa Johnson wondered.)

'However peculiar the Malaitans may look to you,' Creswell advised (as he might well do today, if he were living), 'treat them as though they were very wise and entitled to every respect. Don't be cocky; these people think they are actually *better* than you are. Remember, lassitude, drink, the climate can do for the whites in ten years.' Now came a piece of timely practical advice. 'Don't turn your back on them, or let them surround you. Don't touch spears and arrows. They may have poisoned tips and are sure death. Don't pick flowers until you know which ones are taboo.' Creswell added, for Osa Johnson's benefit, that this must be pretty discouraging, 'but I don't want your head with those blonde pigtails, to hang in some Solomons headhouse'. His advice to visiting boatmen was succinct: 'Keep your stern to shore and within good running distance.'

Creswell moved about the islands filling his boat with copra in exchange for cases of tobacco, which the chiefs found irresistible. One old man wanted to trade two women for a full *bokkus tobacu.* Creswell knew how to parry that. '*Mi no wantum two-pela more mary* [woman], chief,' he said, genially. '*Wanpela mary bilong me, he trouble too much.*' The old chief grunted understandingly.

Creswell was amazingly prescient. He obviously was no mere old renegade island salt. He had visions of the future, realistic and humane. Of the Malaitans, he had this to say to Mrs Johnson: 'They aren't much different from the rest of us. Some day, the idealists, like Mr Bell, will calm them down and show them they can get along better with each other by peace than by war, and by reasoning better than by magic and superstition. The only remaining difference between them and us will be colour.' These were hardly the sentiments Asterisk was hearing at that very time from the mouths of his 'Orstryliun' acquaintances on the not-too-distant plantations of the New Hebrides.

However, they were decidedly the sentiments of the dedicated Mr Bell, as he progressed down the lagoons in his 'war-canoe', twenty feet long, its sides inlaid with mother of pearl and cowrie shells, its twenty paddlers moving and grunting in rhythm; or as he sweated up the steep, slippery jungle paths, freezing, with his gun raised, at any sudden sound that might be the swift and only warning of an ambush. Bell was no mere nigger hater. This was his theory:

'These house-boys,' he said, pointing to the Malaitans working with him, 'they're right out of the bush. They've learned to be clean and obedient. They have plenty of talent and capacity. I've always believed that our civilization is only skin-deep. Give me a hundred boys from England and put them into this jungle on their own or with the natives, and they will survive; but with the same standards as the natives. Take a hundred of *these* boys and put them through good schools at home and you will have fine English clerks, shopkeepers, and scholars. At least that is my opinion – and I am making it work, so far.'

He made it work in the rough, unbending fashion of the time. A photograph shows Bell sitting beefily on his verandah in an old swivel chair with a lace cloth over a table on which are two ponderous-looking law books. Three native constables stand alertly to attention, in knee-length cotton kilts but otherwise naked, their chests muscular, their fuzz-hair shooting up fiercely, their bright eyes on the camera. They flank another Malaitan, similarly kilted, muscled and camera-conscious but in handcuffs. The caption says: 'Mr Bell holding court. The shackled native was found guilty of murder, taken to his village, and executed.'

The purpose of Bell's last and fatal tour, in 1927, was to collect taxes, gather in unlicensed firearms – the 'Sniders' – and initiate a programme of village sanitation. But the tour was more than that. It had the special significance of a display of government power in a recalcitrant district. The paying of taxes had aroused a great deal of anger in the bush and, when it was heard that Bell himself was coming, a man named Basiana began to confront him with force. When Bell had last come, in 1926, there had been a fierce demonstration with tribesmen shaking their spears and dancing round the tax house. But they had paid. This time it was different.

Disembarking from their boat, Bell and a cadet called Lillies seated themselves in the open, side by side at two tables at which the tax monies were to be paid. They were flanked only by two constables and a clerk. And now Bell did something extraordinary. He ordered his escort of armed constables to fall out and to wait huddled inside the tax house behind him – this despite the fact that, as Philip Smiley pointed out to me, Bell had been warned by local chiefs that an attack had been planned. (Smiley added that in those days such an attack could be expected at almost any time in one of the wildest parts of the Solomon Islands.) Bell's extraordinary action has been put down by some people to downright stupidity, by others to suicidal bravery, and by still others to a romantic but overblown trust in his own charisma. At any rate, he disregarded one of Creswell's rules for basic security: 'Don't let them surround you.'

When the tribes arrived, Bell told them brusquely to lay down their weapons, and then to form into two lines, to pay their taxes at his and Lillies' tables. This they began to do, and the line of queuing tribesmen stretched from the tables to the rear of the tax house where the policemen were, but after about twenty people had paid Basiana picked up his gun – which he had laid down twelve feet away – broke through the queue and struck Bell on the top of the head as he bent over the table. Bell died instantly. Poor Lillies, the clerk, and twelve constables (they had had no time to raise their rifles before the leaf walls of the tax house were broken down) were speared and chopped to death before more than a single shot could be fired. Two constables, badly wounded, managed to bolt into the jungle and swim out to the government ship. The massacre itself was all over in a few minutes. The culprits fled. Soon Bell and Lillies were buried on a nearby island by a government landing party.

The aftermath was tragi-comedy. Within two weeks, a punitive expedition was on its way to Malaita. A force of thirty local expatriate volunteers had been enrolled as special constables: most of them planters, some minor government officials and foremen. Few of them were young. They were shipped to Malaita not long after the arrival from Sydney of an Australian warship, HMS *Adelaide*, which lobbed a few shells into the bush to keep native heads down. Innocent heads probably, because neither the warship nor the special force of over-age and overweight planters proved capable of efficient retribution for the death of William Bell. The planters blundered about panting and wheezing in the bush (they quickly became known as the 'Breathless Army'), downing case after case of whisky – although apologists for this consumption claimed that whisky kept malaria at bay – and making so much noise shouting to each other that the guilty tribesmen had plenty of time to hide. The innocent, who thought they had no need to hide, suffered for their naïvety. People not involved in the attack on Bell were meant to wear a headband of red calico, but the 'Breathless Army' paid little attention to sartorial detail, shooting the wrong people and destroying gardens and several coastal villages quite uninvolved in the massacre. Luckily, despite the formidable consumption of whisky, many volunteers soon went down with malaria; weak leadership and lack of success led to serious quarrelling, and the 'Breathless Army' (about which no doubt Asterisk would have had some ribald things to say) was disbanded in ignominy.

A later, effective, punitive expedition consisted of real Solomon Island policemen, some of whose relatives had been among those killed in the massacre. They were ruthless. In an assessment for an Honiara newspaper on the fiftieth anniversary of the tragedy, Philip Smiley wrote that the number of men, women and children killed indiscriminately will never be known, but 198 people were arrested. They included the ringleader, Basiana, who walked to the coast and gave himself up to avoid further bloodshed. He and five others were tried and hanged.

That was sixty years ago. In those days, district officers had cabinets built into their walls to house racks of rifles and revolvers in holsters, all clean and shining. Now, John and Alison Freeman slept in their little ramshackle house without so much as a popgun between them. Since 1978 there had been a Solomon Islander in the President's office in Honiara, an island Prime Minister and an island Parliament. Only in the judiciary are Britons to be found. That is why the Chief Justice of the Solomons is Francis Daley, an Englishman of long experience in the Islands, with a parakeet in Auki named after him. Before I left the Solomons he invited me to his seaside house in Guadalcanal, and over dinner his affection for the Islanders and their traditions became movingly clear. He had served in Malaita, and in his experience the tribesmen called Kwaio, whose grandparents had killed Bell, were as independent in spirit as they have ever been.

'I get on with them,' he said. 'My Kwaio is quite good.' From his verandah we looked out across the Sound towards Auki and the Langa Langa lagoon which lay invisible and far away but which the darkness seemed to bring very close. The walls of the room behind us were tapestried with the books Daley and his wife Joyce collected – not a rifle cabinet in sight. Mosquitoes evidently colonized the trees in the garden; we slapped them off our arms and the back of our necks.

'They have a will of their own, though, you know,' Daley said. 'Imagine I visit them. The chief and I sit chatting; we get on well; we laugh. All very friendly. Then I happen to let drop that the police patrol will be here, passing through, tomorrow. The chief smiles. "Oh, yes, of course. Let them come." But that talk is just for my benefit. Next day when the police actually do come without me, the Kwaio won't let them pass. It's a question of pride.'

I seemed to be hearing the voice of a gentler Bell.

I said, 'How can they stop them?'

'Well, the Kwaio live two thousand feet up a very steep and narrow place. You have to scrabble your way up for three hours – but you can slide down on your bottom in thirty minutes, if you're not very careful. The Kwaio could stop you simply by lobbing stones down on you. And they might.'

'So what do you do?'

'I have to go back there with the policemen. If I go the Kwaio will let them through — because of *me* being there. And I used to go with the police to get the government presence up there. It's something I think needs to be done, although,' he smiled, 'I suppose I care about that more than the Government itself does.'

'I imagine you could get your men up there by helicopter?'

Daley laughed. 'Well, we haven't got one. Anyway, we won't use force. We wouldn't risk damaging their taboos — their ancestral skulls and so on. The Government wouldn't sanction anything like that. Quite rightly.'

My neck and arms were burning with needle pricks. High insect whines filled the air. I squashed a mosquito on my wrist, and Francis Daley leaned forward to give our ankles a squirt of insect repellent.

'Tinkering with the skulls — ' he continued, shaking his head.

Mrs Daley said, 'The ancestors could get back at you.'

'Give you a hell of a run of bad luck,' Daley agreed.

He went into the house and came back with a book. 'I was just reminded: D.H. Lawrence. His poem 'The Mosquito' is his best, I think, don't you? At least it's got some humour. He's not all that full of humour, is he?'

When do you start your tricks,
Monsieur?

I heard a woman call you the Winged Victory
In sluggish Venice.
You turn your head towards your tail, and smile...

I behold you stand
For a second enspasmed in oblivion,
Obscenely ecstasied
Sucking live blood,
My blood.

Away with a paean of derision,
You winged blood-drop.

Fireflies danced in the warm darkness under the trees. Spirits of the sea, I said to them soundlessly, I am glad to see you happy. The mosquitoes — 'you winged blood-drops' — could go to hell.

Fifteen

In the sweet by-and-by, we shall meet on the
bee-oot-iful shore.

The day I left Auki to return to Honiara was a rainy Sunday. Rivers of
water flowed past a small, open-sided church near the Auki Lodge; the
sound of singing drifted after me as I walked to the jetty. '... On the
bee-oot-iful shore', I sang with them. 'We shall me-ee-et....'

On a bench under a shop's awning across the flooded road from the
Golden Dragon Bar, two Malaitan men were sitting staring at the
puddles. Drenched, I joined them, sat down and poured the water out
of my shoes. They looked from the puddles to me, and said, 'Hi!' One
was middle-aged and very fat; the other, nearer me, was quite young
and a uniform tawny colour from the top of his frizzy hair to his naked
feet, like the Lion in *The Wizard of Oz*. He wore knee-length jeans and
a shirt open down the front but his face, chest, arms and legs were all
lion-coloured. Three horizontal lines tattooed on each cheek had the
effect of whiskers. I expected him to open his mouth and roar. A knitted
tam o'shanter sat on top of his yellow fuzz – a hideous thing of pink,
magenta and yellow, with a purple pom-pom the size of a cricket ball.

'You goin' to church?' He didn't even growl. His voice was a soft
drawl, low enough to be barely audible.

'No, I'm going to Honiara. And you?'

'I have my own church,' he murmured with the faintest of smiles.
'Colson's Witnesses.'

'Oh,' I said. 'I see.'

'I'm Colson,' he said, plucking at the curly hair over his ears. He
pointed to the outrageous tam o'shanter. 'Irish Colson,' he said, and he
and his friend giggled quietly. 'Where you goin' in Honiara?' Colson
asked.

I would try to take a ship to Fiji, if there was one going there. If not, I said, I fancied the western islands for a few days. That visibly interested Colson. He, too, was heading for Honiara. From there he would go by boat to a timber camp at Viru, he told me – the purple pom-pom nodding agreement with everything he said – that lay on the way to the western islands. He would be there the day after tomorrow. He would try – he didn't sound very happy about it – for a job there.

'But I may not like Honiara,' he whispered. '*They* may not like me. So suppose I come with you? I am very quiet man. I can cook. I can be bodyguard, exceptin' I have no gun.'

'Will I need a guard, Colson?'

'If you do, I am your bodyguard.'

'Thanks for the offer.'

''S'all right,' said Colson.

I thought quickly. I wanted to meet Solomon Islanders. Colson was a Solomon Islander and spoke English. 'I might be passing by your timber camp in three days' time,' I said. If I wasn't off to Fiji instead....

'I'll be waitin' on the wharf at Viru,' Colson said, immediately. 'In three days I join you on the boat, the *Yu Mi Nao*?'

'If I'm *on* the *Yu Mi Nao*.'

'I show you west Solomon Islands.' The pom-pom nodded encouragingly. 'I am very-good Colson. You'll see.'

'In that hat, very-good Colson, I can't miss you at the wharf, at any rate.'

Colson released a little shriek of joy – 'Ha-heee!' – whipped off his tam o'shanter and began furiously teasing out long strands from his yellow frizzy mane; I came to recognize this nervous habit of his. It was a perfectly acceptable one. Other islanders, I had noticed, were vigorous nose pickers. 'In three da-ays. Yeah!' His tattooed whiskers positively bristled.

In Honiara I pursued my efforts to find a passage to Fiji. Kind Gerry Stenzel managed to call Tarawa, the main port of the Gilbert Islands, about twelve hundred miles north-east of the Solomons. The master of a ship due to arrive in Honiara soon would agree, he thought, to take me there. He wanted to find out if an Australian ship he'd heard of would carry me from Tarawa to Fiji. My hopes were dashed. From Tarawa the answer came: no – the ship's owners in Australia wouldn't consider a passenger they didn't know personally. What then...? 'Well,

a Sofrana Lines vessel is due here in two weeks. And there is always the old *Ann*. She might be ready some time soon, to go ... well, somewhere,' he laughed.

Hanging around the yacht club and the hotel wouldn't do.

'I'll go to the western Solomons,' I said. 'Just a few days.'

'Might as well,' Gerry said. 'Not too long, please. You never know what will happen with the *Ann*. And Roy Clemens, her owner, won't hang about for you.'

And so, twenty-four hours later, the cargo-passenger boat *Yu Mi Nao*, en route to the tiny western island of Gizo, pulled alongside the wharf at Viru with me on board.

It was a night stop. The little ship's searchlight illuminated a patch of jungle, coconut trees, the toy-sized wharf. People stood waiting for us, holding parasols. Canoe shapes, half seen, drifted round us. Our gangway, once down, was the centre of a laughing mob of wild young men who charged up the ramp as medieval soldiers would storm a castle's drawbridge, and rushed in a beeline for the snack bar. It was an operation that had been perfected by much practice. In no time, like successful looters, they had carried ashore with triumphant shouts virtually every loaf of wrapped bread. Bread seemed worth its weight in gold here.

I might have been in the Congo, or in Borneo. The floodlit clearing, the sago-thatched huts, the little wharf looked like a film sequence out of Joseph Conrad's *An Outcast of the Islands*. Where was Almayer? I

remembered Conrad's description of a sweating white man in shabby drill trousers and singlet, a man with a harassed, Dutch-Eurasian countenance, round and flat, with a curl of black hair over the forehead and a heavy, pained glance. I pricked my ears for a voice with a bitter tone grumbling, 'I have a pretty story to tell you. . . .' But I was the only white man there that night.

I leaned over the rail and searched the shouting ruck for a tam o'shanter with a purple pom-pom. I didn't expect to find it – but there it was. Colson strolled on board with what I suspect was a deliberate show of nonchalance – and drawled with his slow, leonine smile, 'You goin' to Gizo? Not Fiji? I can come with you?' I would have to leave him in Gizo when I returned to Honiara, I told him. Now, I would give him his fare to Gizo.

'That's fine,' he said. He had an overnight bag in his hand, otherwise he was the same. 'With you I see places I never seen. Places in my own country.'

'It'll be brief,' I warned him. And he repeated, 'That's fine,' in his low, almost inaudible voice.

Now I looked at him again in the indirect light of the ship's searchlight. He really had a lion's face. Yellowish hair on his tawny cheeks under the yellow fuzz that swept up and out, like a mane; a short nose, a good, wide mouth with hints of hair at the corners; a sleepy lion's green-broad eyes; the three parallel lines of tattoo shooting out from the corners of his mouth across his cheeks. He pointed to them: 'Pussy cat tattoo.' His chest and arms were oddly blotched as acid blotches a lacquered table top; and there were other tattoos – on his biceps and forearms: anchors, a cross and a swastika (a Buddhist swastika, not Hitler's). Out of his hair a long stalk of grass stuck from one side and a red pencil from the other. Soon we wandered off to get two cups of tea from the snackbar which by now was quiet, and as utterly stripped of bread as a plant's leaves are stripped by locusts. Colson walked with a slow, controlled, swaying motion, swinging his broad shoulders as if to some rhythm in his head.

'Poor, poor, beautiful me-e-e-e,' I heard him singing, falsetto, as he went. It was a popular number on the Solomon Islands radio hit parade.

Here my notebook reads:

At dawn, Gizo. A number of stops during the night, all more or less similar – a wharf, sheds, shouting people. Each time the tannoy annouces: 'You come here on board buy wanpela nice ticket,' signing off the announcement with 'End no more.' At the stop before Gizo, I note things being disembarked: one kitten in a box – a .22 rifle – two huge cases like coffins marked for the Commissioner of Police – one old dartboard – a case of lime cordial – a case of Bell's whisky – a kettle – one outboard motor – a case of Foster's lager – a variety of battered suitcases.

Near Gizo, reefs ugly brown above the surface – the waters are full of them; the ship zigzags through this deadly maze of coral following a pathway of markers to avoid them, but the captain, in shorts, sandals, dragon-stencilled shirt, gazes about him through dark glasses without concern, his mouth smiling, betel-stained. Jolly, bright underwear waves like bunting on a line behind him.

'Kennedy Island,' he says pointing, and I see very nearby a tiny island with a rim of sandy beach, apparently only a few dozen paces across, with tall palms thrusting up from it like hatpins in a vivid green pincushion. At first, I can't understand the significance of the name, but it was here that the PT boat containing the future President of the United States was rammed and sunk by a Japanese warship, and John F. Kennedy was washed up onto the white sand. Its real name is Pudding Island, Colson says. It is exactly like everyone's idea of a shipwrecked mariner's desert island. I look for an emaciated man in rags waving an oar with a tattered shirt tied to it, signalling distress.

Colson's English is good. He was at a secondary school with Australian teachers – missionaries. He had worked briefly with a fly-by-night Australian who went broke operating a peanut canning factory in Honiara and disappeared Down South. Colson scrounged two years' work in a Lever Brothers plantation. 'Then I met you,' he says. 'Lucky Colson.'

'When I leave you,' I ask, 'what will you do?'

'Go to Auki to see Honey-May – my girlfriend.'

'And marry her?'

He shakes his head, 'No, only ask her.... Oh, I don't know.' He laughs in his secret fashion, hardly opening his lips.

At the Gizo Hotel. I sit in the bar with Colson, drinking beer. Soon, we are joined by two white men; both are tanned a deep copper. Old Hands. One says: 'Remember, I have some knowledge.... Never count on what islanders say.' He looks tough and sixty-something. Years ago, he tells me, he was in the shadowy business spoken of as 'voluntary recruitment of labour' – he uses this phrase with a wry twist of his thin lips; in the Bad Old Days it was often a thin euphemism for blackbirding. He has the wrinkled eyes of a hunter in the tropics. 'Then I shot crocs for a bit.' After that he'd bought a boat and gone in for island trading. Now, he keeps a waterfront store on another island. 'Drop in,' he says.

Next morning, a bit of luck.

A boat lay alongside the little wharf that the *Yu Mi Nao* had brought us to – a small motor vessel with a government flag and the name *Lanalau* on her stern. Several very black men on her deck (Colson looked pale by comparison) called a cheery 'Mornin''. They were setting off at any minute, they said, with a government doctor on a two-day routine visit to Simbo Island, the smallest outpost of land in those waters. 'Come on,' they said.

'Like to go?' I asked Colson.

'I follow *you*,' he replied, quietly.
'We're off, then.'

The next two days were filled by quick dashes ashore against a background of calm, glassy seas, or vicious torrents of rain that always seemed to envelop the little vessel, like the blinding sprays of a car-washing machine, whenever the captain began to edge her through the worst of the reefs.

Colson was immediately useful. I gave him money, and he ran off ('For me, cheaper!') and bought rice, coffee, corned beef, tuna fish and canned Japanese roast goose. He thoughtfully added to this, on his own initiative, a twenty-four-can case of beer. He and I shared a twin-berth cabin about the size of a large shoebox, but then the vessel as a whole was tiny. Her bearded captain was as black as his crew, which was explained when he told me he had been trained by the Royal Navy instructors in the days when the Solomons were British. Of the crew I remember Caspar, young and round-faced; Rawnesley from Santa Cruz, the 'Far East' of the Solomons, with filed teeth; big George, the engineer, who came from Malaita; and small Jesio who strolled about with a mug in his hand, announcing, '*Me tingting laik drinim Milo*,' a reference to a health drink popular in the Pacific.

The government district medical officer turned out to be a small, slender, middle-aged man with a fringe of beard and a lively, talkative manner. He was delighted to have us with him, he said. He was going to inspect some village clinics. He laughed a lot – sudden falsetto outbursts of laughter expressing exuberant life. Indeed, the little vessel echoed with the crew's own expression of exuberant life – hoots, whistles, cries and shrieks as if exotic birds had escaped from an aviary and come to roost on the bridge, in the tiny galley, the cabins. Solomon Islanders were an exhilarating experience in themselves.

Our ports of call were ragged clearings in jungle that came down to the shore. Inside the sheltering lagoons, mop-headed palms and the beautiful flowering trees of Melanesia screened the village huts, schools and clinics from the sea. Small, dun-coloured herons flapped about the brown lumps of coral on the shore. Women and boys in canoes trailed fishing lines.

Time after time the ebullient little doctor, Balthazar, was ferried to land by a couple of crewmen in a metal dinghy. He was well known here. People waved at him from the bush, and crowded round. A boy with an open gash on his forehead ran up to him, the slogan on his shirt saying: '*Iu mi evriwan brata*.'

'Hello, brother,' the doctor said, and led him to the little clinic with a corrugated iron roof. Grassy paths led us through avenues of coconut palms. Skins here were midnight black and men and women wore hibiscus flowers in their fuzz and cowrie shell necklaces. They stared and smiled at me as if I were Gulliver.

At some stops we offloaded iron roofing and planks of wood.

The *Lanalau* refused to start again after one call, and Balthazar peered over the stern and cried out in alarm, 'Ah! We're buggered up, is it? Oh!' But we soon started again, and he threw up his hands, giggling, 'Oh! What a relief,' while the crew drummed on the wheelhouse roof to celebrate our small deliverance.

I had told Colson to share our rice and tinned food with the crew. Colson was pleased by this demonstration of democratic feeling. But he went further. Unasked – and after dark – he distributed most of the beer, too. The crew became red-eyed and giggly. Luckily we soon pulled into a creek for the night, and then the crew's tipsy shouts and hoots reverberated harmlessly round the ring of huts and thick bush that circled the jetty. Villagers came aboard, and soon Caspar rolled up to announce, indistinctly, that, 'All girl here wan' good time.' Hiccupping, he led his friends ashore towards lantern light in a hut from which sounds of ribald laughter and excited voices drifted down to the water.

Women's voices predominated, and I sat in a deckchair under the stars with a book, hardly expecting to see the crew again that night. But after a short time they returned, pursued by angry female voices. Colson was back first – 'Too many people drunk,' he said sheepishly. 'Too much noise. Girls say no.' He wavered off to our cabin singing in falsetto – 'Poor, poor beautiful me....' Subdued, the crew sat about, smoking, talking, giggling, their high birdcalls intermingling with the more infernal noise of pop music from a transistor radio.

Next day I followed Balthazar ashore to a village that lay like the unreal creation of a film company or a romantic novelist, up a path green and slippery with night dew between the dark, thick foliage of mango trees. An old chief, speaking English in weak but spirited tones, met us, and when the doctor was inspecting the tiny clinic (its cupboards were full of medicine) he told me his four hundred people sold copra, nothing else. Fish? No. Why? No need. Bushnut trees dangled their white, flowery concertinas, the mangoes provided shade. There were big wooden houses here among flame trees, which the old man called fire trees. Laughter and shrieks came from inside them. A young man with 'Star Wars' on his singlet held my elbow when I looked like slipping on the ground and I asked his name.

'Smith,' he surprisingly said.

'You work?'

He said he did not.

'Go to school?'

No, he emphatically conveyed with a brusque shake of his fuzz. He stopped at home, he said.

'Sometime he make house of sago,' the chief explained. 'Sometime garden work. Sometime fish.' Smith nodded confirmation.

'It's a good life or a bad life?'

'Oh, a good life,' Smith and the chief answered together in matter-of-fact tones. Smith took my hand and led me to the riches of their luxuriant world. Mangoes, oranges, limes, bushnuts, yams, taro. Chickens ran alongside us expectantly.

Looking down to our little boat, we could see the water churned up in white spurts as if someone was spraying it with a heavy machine gun. Fish. Smith of 'Star Wars' said, 'This time is time bilong smallpela bonito.' Bonito, yes; but out here any time I imagine is the season for fish, big or small. What more did they want?

No wonder that, as Gerry Stenzel had said, disgruntled office workers in Honiara, reproved by the employers too sharply for their liking, simply walked out of the door – and kept on walking until they reached their villages. Their villages had everything they needed. Well, practically everything. The old chief went on to say that, of course, they had to buy kerosene, corrugated iron for roofing, and canned tuna fish from the market. Tinned fish? Living fish leaped in the sea beside them. They needed canned tuna as much as they needed Australian beer.

The old chief and his people live in a place some people in Asia or Europe would call paradise. They even had medical attention – here was Balthazar to prove it. But that evening, from his deckchair, the little doctor murmured, 'Primitive life, eh?' nodding towards the coastline where the trees stirred under a theatrically bright moon. His tone was disparaging. Evidently he wanted to see cement and tin roofing, housing estates, heaven knows what else.

'There are primitive places and primitive people in America and Europe. Ugly, violent, crude, loud, hollow.'

'Primitive. Too much custom,' he said, meaning tradition.

'Well, keep the good custom, throw away the bad. Be proud of good custom. It belongs in the Solomon Islands.'

A silence fell between us. Then Balthazar said, 'Keep what good things?'

'Take laplaps. Laplaps are useful, cheap, comfortable, pretty. You have been told to throw laplaps away and wear trousers. Who told you? Australian trouser manufacturers?'

Balthazar whooped with laughter.

'Or the missionaries? Does God wear jeans, Balthazar?'

'Whoo-oo! Haa-eee!' he hooted, joyfully slapping the sides of the deckchair.

'Another thing – ' I pressed on – 'take those cheap sago-thatch roofs. They keep out rain and heat. Why import expensive corrugated iron? Isn't iron very hot?'

'Very hot,' Balthazar giggled.

'So, why not save money with cheap, cool sago roofs?'

'Good idea! Good idea!' Balthazar cried, fanning away mosquitoes with his hand. 'Custom belongs to us. You're right.' But whether he really thought I was right I shall never know. Balthazar was a gentleman of infinite tact and courtesy.

*   *   *

The *Lanalau*'s course south of the islands took her into the exposed water of the five-hundred-mile-wide Solomon Sea, and here she plunged and corkscrewed horribly. Rain fell in relentless grey curtains with the sinister hissing of a thousand cobras. With the naked, anxious eye the many reefs I could see on the chart were masked by the rain and waves. Reefs become strips of turquoise neon under the sun, but sunshine had vanished.

We plunged abruptly, right or left. Peter, the captain, knew them all – the gaps in the reefs – by instinct, he assured me. Sometimes he stuck his head out of the wheelhouse to peer through the lashing rain at a shoreline that seemed to play a game of nerve-racking hide and seek with us. The merest glimpse of a tall tree perhaps, or a makeshift beacon, would have helped, but whether he saw me or not, he remained unruffled; a fine island seaman. I suppose we heaved and bounced over coral that could have ripped the *Lanalau*'s bottom out in a trice, and I was glad this was not some chrome-covered rich man's floating gin palace from Sydney, chancing its luck. And there was another comfort: dolphins rushed along with us. Playful, muddy brown under the surface, slate black when they arched over it – up and over and down in twos and threes – they slid smoothly back into the trenches of the waves, leaving an impression of old friends too briefly seen. I felt that whatever happened they would pick me up and carry me to shore.

And this outside shore was wild and rocky. When the dinghy was lowered, its outboard motor had to struggle against breakers, and villagers ran down to lay out coloured cloths to mark hidden rocks. Balthazar, who had to scramble ashore and back, was a brave man.

Later, Colson washed his hair: a long operation, involving much water and soap. After a superficial drying with a towel he pruned it, pulling the crinkly strands out straight and carefully snipping their ends off. Then, he sprayed it all over with insect repellent, explaining, 'Sometimes insects go in.'

Later still, I heard his murmur from the bunk above, 'I'd never see all this but for you. So many places today and yesterday, because I'm with you.' Like a spider, his hand dangled in the dark near my face. 'Shake my hand,' he said, and I did so. The sweet smell of insect killer filled the cabin, and the soft snick-snick of Colson combing his nice clean fuzz lulled me to sleep.

Next morning, the *Lanalau* rounded the southern point of Vella Lavella Island. At the sight of the vivid green speck of Kennedy Island, and beyond it the waterfront of Gizo, the crew began to chant and drum with their palms on the side of the wheelhouse, as if they were a war canoe charging an enemy, but these sounds meant joy for a safe homecoming. I said goodbye to Captain Peter, Rawnesley, Jesio and the rest.

Balthazar said, 'Come and live on my island.' He giggled. 'Under a custom sago roof. Not expensive Australian tin.'

'Wait for me,' I said.

I was flying to Honiara next morning on the little inter-island twin-engined Solair plane, and before that I had to say goodbye to Colson, too. When morning came he was a sad sight. He paced about my hotel room, moaning to himself and looked so forlorn and abandoned that I put my arm round him and tried to reassure him about the jobs he would find. But, of course, he knew more about the lack of jobs than I did. But at least I did not leave him utterly alone in this distant part of the Solomons. The islanders, Colson had already explained, had evolved an admirable social safety net called the *wantauk* system. A *wantauk* is a fellow islander who speaks your dialect (the word is pidgin for 'one-talk', a man who shares your language). A man exiled for reasons of work or travel could expect the automatic help and hospitality of anyone from his island, even of a stranger. (If this system existed in Britain, a Scotsman meeting a fellow Scot resident in, say, Wales, could greet him as his *wantauk*.) Now, I was relieved to hear Colson say, he had discovered from the *Lanalau*'s crew that a Malaitan in Gizo came from a village near his own. The man was a policeman. Colson had never met him, but this, he said, didn't matter.

'How many days can you stay with your *wantauk*, Colson?'

'That's up to me. I maybe stay one week, two weeks, then I go.'

Even with the unstinted hospitality of Arab tribes, he would have been expected to move on after three days. I waited with interest to see what would happen.

As Colson had predicted, the policeman instantly accepted his duties as a *wantauk*. He was setting off to work when we met him, but that didn't matter in the least. He smiled and shook hands, listened to Colson's explanation and request to stay, and promptly said, 'Here are the keys of my house,' handing them over as though Colson was a blood brother who had been away in Honiara for a week. 'Food is in the refrigerator. Cook what you like. Make yourself at home. I'll be back this evening.' I was astonished, and had to force myself to remember that he had never set eyes on Colson before that morning. The *wantauk* system balanced the lack of generalized hospitality.

Nevertheless, Colson was still despondent. He shuffled his feet under the trees near the water, removed his tam o'shanter, and twisted it in his hands, moodily crooning, 'Poor, poor beautiful me,' and regarding me woefully. In the last minutes before the motor boat came to ferry me to Gizo's little airstrip, he muttered, 'I'm a poor lost guy,' in such pitiable tones that I put my arm around him again. Even his tattooed 'whiskers' seemed to droop.

I said, uneasily, 'What will become of you, Colson?'

He scuffed his bare feet in the dust. 'I'll look for work. Maybe find some work here. Some plantation here ... very difficult.'

'Write and let me know what happens,' I said. 'Promise?' When he had promised (he bumped my shoulder with his head in an awkward, affectionate gesture as he did so), I gave him some money to be going on with, and a long shell necklace I had bought as a reserve 'store' of local custom currency. He stood waving after me until the motor boat was almost at the island airstrip.

His letter caught me up a month or two later, and its tone was happier than I had expected it to be. He had found work in a forestry camp near Gizo. 'Dearest G. Young, my work is everything always in good condition. Except, poor, poor beautiful me! Getting all hot and scratched by wood branches. Penniless, hopeless, all alone in the world. I am longing to talk to you again. You must come back.' It was written in a remarkably fluent hand the missionaries had taught him, and it was signed, 'Your everlasting friend, Irish Colson (The Lost Guy).'

Sixteen

The little room smelt vaguely of oil, ageing files and urine. The owner of the *Ann*, Roy Clemens, unshaven, friendly, stood in shorts shuffling some customs forms at a small untidy table in the hole-in-the-wall office facing the harbour. I had walked past it twice; it was easy to miss. He said in a pleasant way, 'Five days to Suva with luck – sixteen hundred miles or so at ten knots if you have good weather. You should just about fit into the second officer's cabin. It's about six foot by four. A bit stuffy perhaps.' I wanted to get to Suva by sea, so I wasn't complaining. We were to sail that evening, Roy said.

A large-boned impassive islander – but not, I judged by his lack of fuzz, from the Solomons – was standing by the table; he said to Clemens, 'Hawaii weather station broadcasts a depression over New Caledonia. Could be bad weather.' Clemens introduced me: this was the *Ann*'s captain, a native of the Ellice Islands north of Fiji, which with independence had taken the name of Tuvalu. Ellice Islanders, like their neighbours the Gilbertese, are fine sailors, everyone agrees, but they can be heavy drinkers, too, and formidable brawlers.

'Call me John,' the captain said pleasantly in a low, unassertive voice that reminded me of Colson. He had a boxer's face, calm eyes, short hair, very long arms, and a hand large enough to overwhelm my own when he shook it.

'No grog on the *Ann*, I'm afraid,' Clemens said as though he were a mind reader; a vision of drunken brawls in the middle of the cyclone seven hundred miles out from Honiara had indeed momentarily arisen to appal my mind. 'Not my ruling. The crew are all Seventh Day Adventists or something. Teetotallers, anyway.' I was glad to hear it. 'Still, I expect you can arrange ... er, for yourself,' Clemens added with a wink. As for food, the captain now put in, I should buy some canned stuff and a bag of rice.

'Oh, and the other chap,' Roy Clemens added. 'He can bunk down over the steering gear. There's an awning over it.'

The other chap? Yes, Clemens explained, there was an Englishman, James Barclay by name, who had recently arrived here from Fiji in a yacht, the *Camping Loo* – odd name; she was lying off the yacht club just now. Her owner and his navigator, also Britons, were waiting for a spare engine part to arrive from Australia before sailing westwards to Bali, but Barclay couldn't wait and wanted to return to Suva the cheap way, by sea. 'He'll be good company for you,' Clemens said pleasantly, adding: 'I hope.'

I hoped so, too. I don't much like travelling with Europeans; I travel partly to get away from them. I soon met James Barclay, a stocky, bearded young man with an Etonian accent and a friendly manner, drinking beer in Honiara's little yacht club. I knew after a few minutes of small talk that we would get on – and this despite the fact that among his first words were, 'Of course, you know that ham radio operators are talking about a very, very low depression in our path to Suva? That could mean we're just about certain to run into a rather bad cyclone.'

'Surely they won't sail if that's the case?'

'Oh-ho, don't be too sure. They're a pretty foolhardy lot in these parts.' That didn't sound too good. Never mind. I packed my metal suitcase and took it to the *Ann*. Then I went off to do some shopping. A bottle of gin first – if we were going to go down in a cyclone, I might as well go down happy. Then rice, tins of Ox and Palm corned beef, sardines, pilchards, Kraft cheese, sweet biscuits, a tin opener, a plastic plate and mug. It seemed a lot for five days, but supposing bad weather or engine failure turned five days into fifteen?

A fight had broken out in the street near the hotel. A bad melee: ten or twelve infuriated men were beating each other with clubs, and hurling huge stones that could have cracked open a skull. One man, holding his opponent by the fuzz, was beating his head on the asphalt. To avoid this, I plunged into a bookshop and emerged when peace was restored with an Agatha Christie novel, a Ngaio Marsh mystery, and James Joyce's *Ulysses*.

A New Zealand warship was in and its sailors had bought some unusual T-shirts. On one I read:

If it's safe —
  Dump it in Tokyo
  Test it in Paris
  Store it in Washington
  But ...
  Keep My Pacific Nuclear-Free.

Wouldn't the ship's officers judge that bad for discipline? Earlier that day I had seen a Solomon Islander wearing a T-shirt that said: '*Nuclear hem save killim iumi evriwan*' — a sign of what Gerry had said was growing irritation, from Tahiti to the Solomons, with the French nuclear tests in Polynesia.

It was a miserable departure. As darkness came, rain fell on Honiara like a curse. I pulled my anorak on over my *Chengtu* T-shirt and met James Barclay at the yacht club, drenched by the few minutes' walk from the hotel. All we had to do was wait for a member of the crew of the *Ann* to come and tell us when the captain intended to sail.

We drank farewell beers with Gerry Stenzel and Fritz Markworth, and James's two mates from the *Camping Loo*, glimmering just offshore. The club was filling up in preparation for the weekly film show — this time *Young Winston*. Neither the subsequent cries of battling men and sound of exploding shells on a small screen suspended from the rafters, nor the beer did much to distract my thoughts from the sixteen hundred miles of exposed Pacific that lay ahead.

'Ship sail soon,' a voice said out of the tempest.

'Send a cable from Suva.' Gerry shook my hand. 'Just so we're sure you've actually arrived.'

'Not the reassuring words I need at this moment, Gerry.'

I heard James's former shipmates mocking him with warnings about the cyclone ahead. Then, stumbling miserably through enormous puddles, we made our sopping way to the port.

The *Ann* lay passively enduring the deluge alongside a short pier. Last-minute loading cluttered her small foredeck with tackle and wires and hatch covers. Roy Clemens stood on the jetty with a couple of cronies. A dinghy was being winched from the ship to the shore; I hoped there were others still aboard, and Clemens called out with a laugh, 'There's a brand new inflatable life raft in the stern. Don't worry.' Once again he seemed to have read my mind.

'The third officer's name is George,' he added. 'I should find his cabin right away, if I was you.'

I ducked through a low doorway under the bridge – the *Ann* was Japanese-built, I could see that. A squat, smiling Solomon Islander stood by a cabin door. 'I'm George,' he said. 'This my cabin and you take it, please.'

'Thank you, George,' I said. 'Where will *you* sleep?'

He said amicably, 'I sleep with friends.'

My metal suitcase almost filled the cabin. Six feet by four, Roy Clemens had said. For someone my height it seemed even smaller, but I found I could make myself quite comfortable by resting one foot on a shelf near the door and the other on the bulkhead at the foot of the bunk. I might have hung a foot out of the small porthole, but it was too near the water level. A tiny wall fan beat away against the clammy thickness of the air. 'Forget Me Not, Darling' was embroidered on George's pillowcase. I hoped my sweat wouldn't ruin it.

At 10 p.m. there was much shouting, and the *Ann* shuddered into life. Above the metallic pump-pump-pump of her engines Roy Clemens called 'Good luck', and we moved slowly into the sodden darkness of The Slot. It seemed a long time since I had sailed down it from Kieta with Captain Luc on the *La Pérouse*, but now it would lead us out into the hazards of the greatest of all the world's oceans.

I poured a mouthful of gin into its bottle top, drank it, and lay down on George's bunk. I felt like Alice after she had tried the bottle labelled 'Drink me' and become a giant in the house of Bill the Lizard.

The next morning my embroidered pillowcase was wet and yellowing with sweat. The rain had stopped. Stooping to avoid bumping my head on alleyways and lintels, I found James Barclay sitting in sunshine on the forehatch. He said he had tried to sleep under a crude awning on the hatch top, but the rain had been too much for him and he had slithered aft to the flat wood platform over the steering gear. Here he had found the captain's huge muscular bulk sprawled half-naked and asleep, oblivious to the hideous racket the gear made. Forced below, he cautiously settled down on the minuscule dining room table in the crew's quarters. Ignoring the intermittent snores and farts of sleeping sailors in the shadowy bunks around him, he passed the night, sleeping an hour here and there. It had been difficult, he said, to avoid being rolled onto the deck by every movement of the ship.

Rust-bucket was the word for the *Ann*. She was only fifteen years old, Roy Clemens had said, but she looked more. She'd had a new bottom since a grounding in Japan a year or two ago, John the captain said, but that operation had done nothing for her looks. Her narrow, stubby funnel seemed to have been sprayed by small arms fire from close range. A painted mermaid posed on it, flourishing impressive breasts with vivid green nipples and a purple fishtail. The same bilious purple covered rust patches all over the ship's superstructure, like dabs of iodine on a mauled leg.

Yes, rust-bucket was the word. What would Julian Gomersall and Jim Bird have said? All the same, I had a feeling that the *Ann*'s appearance wasn't of the smallest importance; it was her engines that mattered. To be caught in a cyclone with engine failure.... But I wasn't going to think of anything like that.

My notes at this point actually show a new optimism.

After the gloom and rain, the shambles of yesterday's departure, I'm glad to be here. (Will I be saying this all the way to Suva?) Malaita 'runs out' to port; St Cristobel to starboard. We need chairs! There's nowhere to sit except on the two hatches or the steering gear platform, and they are often occupied by sprawling members of the crew.

We have nine men aboard, apart from John the captain. They are all islanders, but not in the least alike. After George, we met the chief engineer, who came up on deck to supervise an abortive attempt to catch fish – there doesn't seem to be much fresh food aboard. The chief is also called George, to James and me simply 'The Dwarf', because he is one of the shortest men we have ever encountered. Stout, bearded, and forever puffing on a long, thin pipe with a thimble-size bowl, he gazes imperiously about him, dignity personified. As the *Ann* putters through an agitated area of sea in which bonito leap like minnows in a village pond, the Dwarf takes charge of fishing operations, shouting, 'Slow down' in Napoleonic tones to John on the bridge. Our two fishing lines quiver taut over the stern rail as the bonito take hold, the Dwarf snaps orders, the crew shout back, but we lose the fish.

Breakfast – on the steering gear housing – is instant coffee, bread, jam, butter, brought up to us (and Shem, first officer) by

Richard, a lolloping deckhand from the Santa Cruz group. Richard is of alarming aspect, nineteen years old, he says, with fair fuzz on his head and light hair on his bare chest. Huge buttocks, protruding like a shelf, put a permanent strain on his blue and white laplap. But it's his mouth that startles. A very wide mouth, cavernous nostrils and forward-thrusting teeth as big as organ keys – the unsettling image, in fact, of the appalling wooden masks on sale to tourists in Honiara. Nevertheless, poor Richard seems extremely amiable. 'Learn English from Christian father,' he lisps. And he tells me, 'I am Jehovah.' He means a Jehovah's Witness, but Richard, too, is re-christened; for us he has become for ever 'Jehovah'.

Shem, the mate, like the chief, is tubby, unbearded and very black. After breakfast, he sits on the steering gear housing, silent, frowning and threading fish hooks, and sways about alarmingly much of the time, as if drunk – which he can't be because he is a Seventh Day Adventist. The rest are Anglicans, I think, including Reginald, a greaser who is strangely clean for a greaser, and who moons about like a bewildered phantom everywhere but in the engine room. Reginald's long, mournful face is as expressionless as a watertight door. His attention focuses exclusively round his shiny metal pipe which he jams in his mouth unsmoked (pipes seem *de rigueur* on the *Ann* – only John the captain and Jehovah don't smoke or chew tobacco). Seated on deck, Reginald stares at the sea. 'Like one?' – I hand him a biscuit. His eyes turn to me like grey pebbles. He slowly takes the biscuit – looks at it closely, tries to bite into it, fails, breaks its, eats the smaller bits. When I mention his trance-like condition to Captain John, he says enigmatically, 'Oh, he's got his pipe.'

Under my yellowing pillow I found a book. Called *Health and Happiness*, it was published by Inspiration Books, Phoenix, Arizona. It was an Adventist publication, which is mysterious because George was an Anglican, or so he said. The book was full of instructions for good conduct. About dress, for example:

The Bible teaches modesty in dress. 'In manner also, that women adorn themselves modest apparel' (I Tim. 2:9). This forbids display in dress, gaudy colors, profuse ornamentation. device designed to attract attention to the wearee is to excite admiration, is excluded from the modest apparel which God's word enjoins. . . .

Another serious evil is the wearing of skirts so that their weight must be sustained by the hips. This heavy weight, pressing up on the internal organs, drags them downward, and causes weakness in the stomach.

For some time, I tried to grasp the physiological sense of that passage, but failed. Other passages spoke of everyone's 'sacred duty' to cook 'healthful' food: 'Cheese is wholly unfit for food.' The book had no time for drinkers – 'A steamer is run aground and passengers and crew find a watery grave. When the matter is investigated' – this was stated as an inevitable rule of life at sea – 'it is found that someone at an important post was under the influence of drink.' These words were underlined in red pencil. A stamp on the title page said the book belonged to 'Kopin Adventist School'. Never mind: the book had nothing to say against stealing.

The rain hammered down, raising steam from the surface of the sea. The second morning, James looked all in. 'The captain gave me a *choice* of places to sleep last night. The minuscule floor of the wheelhouse, the sodden deck over the stern, or the crew's food-encrusted dining table again. I didn't fancy the wheelhouse with Jehovah breaking wind there at the wheel, picking his nose and flicking it all over me, so I took to the table again.' He looked bleary, like a tramp after a hard night on the Thames Embankment.

'James, I hope you're going to get used to this.' I was feeling thoroughly guilty now about my comparatively luxurious cabin. Should I offer to lend it to him every other night?

'Oh, yes, I'll get used to it. It was just the noise last night – ! Jehovah came down later, crashed into the galley door and banged about, gulping handfuls of rice and tuna, slamming the fridge door, and pouring water down his throat like a sanitary inspector pouring disinfectant down a drain.'

'Poor Jehovah. Poor you.'

'Do you know, when he switched the light on in the galley, there was a bloody great rustling as an army of feeding cockroaches dashed into dark corners to hide.'

I sneaked into the galley myself to have a look at it when the cook wasn't around. I found no army of cockroaches, only half a dozen or so grazing in the sink, who looked up uneasily and waved their antennae at me. I had time for a glimpse of the contents of the fridge – two filthy fruit juice cartons, some mouldy bread, a half-eaten tin of butter, half a coconut, and a good deal of grime – before the mighty bulk of the cook suddenly and silently filled the doorway. He stared at me with his knife in his fist; I muttered something placatory and slipped past him, feeling like a schoolboy caught in an orchard. I hurried to my cabin and returned with an armful of tinned food and rice in a paper bag. Laying it all before the cook, as if I were a terrified devotee assuaging a sulky god, 'Please take what you want,' I said, with a weak smile. He accepted the offering with a grunt but no more, and slowly stacked the tins on a shelf; while his back was turned I left him again. After the Dwarf and Jehovah, I mentally added a new name – the Cannibal Cook.

Bathing on the *Ann* was done in a bare room with a pump and a plastic bucket encrusted with heaven knows what. I pumped water into the bowl and sluiced it over my head, while my feet slid around on the tilting floor. The doorknob rattled unceasingly as members of the crew tried to get in to take their turn – to give them their due, they loved washing. My thoughts turned to school bathrooms I had known, and foot fungus. The toilet required skill. It seemed essential not to sit on the discoloured, violin-shaped lavatory bowl fixed low in the rust and dirt of a bulkhead. You tried to straddle the rim of the bowl without touching it, like a jockey standing in his stirrups, but it took a champion jockey's strength in the thighs to maintain this half crouch for more than five minutes at a time, particularly when the deck was corkscrewing under you like a temperamental racehorse. Sometimes I just squatted there in agony, paralysed by cramp. I am sure these few days of exercise put an inch on my thigh muscles, even though I learnt to take some of my weight off them by clinging to the heavy pump-handle with which the toilet was flushed. It was not a place to loiter in and read a book. I paused only long enough to scatter quantities of Harpic – even on myself – and fled from the tiny, smelly sweatbox like a bow-legged submariner leaving an escape hatch, exhaling with a whoosh the breath I had held while inside it until I felt my lungs would burst.

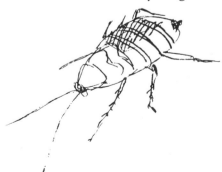

Among these seagoing, churchgoing teetotallers James and I were properly circumspect about our drinking. When the mood for a tot was on us, we retired discreetly behind the dingy curtain of my tiny cabin – it was far too hot to shut the door – to sit sweating side by side on the bunk over pegs of my gin or his whisky out of plastic mugs.

James had been at Eton and had come out to the Pacific for the adventure, I think. He had done quite a lot of adventuring already, and it was experience that had made him more nervous than I was of the rumours in Honiara of the cyclone ahead. He had spent ten weeks in a rust-bucket not unlike the *Ann*, puttering about Pacific islands at one to five knots, a slave to the whim of storms and half-cock engines.

'Why do you do it, James, if you fear and dislike the sea?'

'Well, I don't know,' he said – and I, who fear the sea without disliking it, could understand.

He had travelled a good deal in pursuit of what he called 'The Old Buffers of the Islands' – retired Europeans who still cling, like elderly crustaceans, to the edge of the Pacific lagoons rather as the survivors of the British Raj cling to their bungalows in Simla or Hyderabad. To his surprise, he had found many of them rather dull – 'as boring as old men in a golf club'. They seemed to have spent all those decades between house, office and club never meeting anyone or hearing anything of interest, or not remembering if they had. They hadn't had much to do with the natives either. Nevertheless, he might write a series of articles on them some time, if he found enough material.

It was not a sense of adventure that had brought James aboard the *Ann*, but the need to get to Suva to claim a hefty refund on a ticket from an airline that might be going broke. In any case he was an admirable companion, easy-going and humorous, and to my relief he bore no grudge for my occupation of George's cabin. He did, however, suffer from a permanent itch to read the ship's barometer. Having done so that first morning, humour left his face. 'It's fallen to a thousand,' he told me gloomily. Anything below a thousand millibars, I knew, meant trouble ahead – very likely a typhoon, or cyclone as they were called in the Pacific.

I looked nervously at the sea. The swell looked harmless enough at present, and the sky was an amiable blue, lightly scattered with clouds. John the captain was unconcerned. 'It should be a good voyage,' he said in his calm voice. The *Ann* was a tiny little thing, but in a cyclone a small ship can sometimes be better than a large one – a big, long ship could find herself suspended by a wave fore and aft and then her midships, unsupported, would go – snap! Of course, it would be very uncomfortable and dangerous for the *Ann* to run into a cyclone. (Quite an understatement, I thought.) Uncomfortable – oh, yes.... About the falling barometer, he replied, 'To me it still says a thousand and four. If it had fallen more, we would be feeling a strong, bad wind, y'know. And we'd see a line of cloud over there' – he pointed to the north-eastern horizon. That sounded reassuring.

But James was not in the mood for reassurance. 'This awning won't last long in a 175-mile-an-hour wind,' he said in graveyard tones, jerking a thumb at the plastic covering over the stern.

'I believe you're trying to worry me, James.'

Ulawa Island in the Santa Cruz group was our last call before the long hop to Fiji. We had to come in for official 'clearance' before leaving the Solomons for good, and anchored some way off a tiny wharf in a horseshoe bay. A customs man in shirt and trousers and a uniformed policeman stood watching us from the shore, surrounded by a small group of men and women.

I found Jehovah at my elbow. 'Ooh, boss,' he said, lasciviously darting his tongue around his great lips and pointing at the women. 'Let me spy for lady.' He swivelled my glasses wildly about, before focusing on two girls. 'Ooooh, look, look, I see lady,' he cried, exploding into wild laughter, and began frenetically to pick his nose with the fervent concentration of a pauper delving for buried treasure. It was an hour before our business with customs was complete. We left as white lightning flickered on the rain around us, and seagulls came to inspect us like vultures sizing up a dying sheep.

We moved into the wider ocean.

Jehovah was at regular, screaming verbal odds with Daniel, another deckhand, a Seventh Day Adventist like Shem. From time to time shrieks of glee and falsetto cries of anger, delight or pain – who knew? – arose from the crew's cramped and airless quarters, causing the Dwarf to deepen his habitual frown, take his pipe from his bearded lips and look vengeful.

These disturbances reached unusual crescendos when either Jehovah or Daniel had to shake a leg to take his turn on watch. I found Jehovah glumly nursing a bruised cheek. 'What's the matter, Richard?'

'Daniel he killim me.'

'But why he hit you?'

'I pull him penis,' Jehovah unsmilingly replied.

On another occasion, James said he had jumped off the crew's dining table in panic, woken by howls so inhuman that he feared a mutiny had occurred, or that the Cannibal Cook had run amok. But there was no blood. Only Jehovah – who had decided once again to wake Daniel for duty by roughly seizing his genitals. Daniel had been serenely dreaming, flat on his back, snoring and defenceless, in nothing but a pair of moth-holed purple briefs, and the screams were appalling, James reported. That seemed a very serious escalation of the conflict. There appeared to be growing reason to suppose that before long Jehovah would kill Daniel, or vice versa. But George, the genial third mate, reassured us: it was all in good fun, he said. 'It's love,' he shrugged, indifferently.

Despite the running battles I got along well enough with Jehovah *and* Daniel. Jehovah was glad to wash my shirt and towel, and I gave him tinned sardines in return. His relations with James were less amicable. Early on in the voyage he mistakenly thought that James had laughed at him – he had happened to pass near us as James made a laughing reference he wrongly thought was an insult. He had turned on James, a mask of fury, pointed to the mug in James's hand, and shouted, 'You drunk! *Drunk!*' After that, whenever he was obliged to share the forehatch with him, James was likely to wake up to find himself edged onto the deck by the battering ram of Jehovah's outsize buttocks. James took this with complete equanimity, only remarking, 'Jehovah's last name is Matangi. That means "strong wind",' adding, 'appropriately enough.'

Squalls multiplied over the North Fiji Basin. As if mellowed by the visit to his home village, the Dwarf, who had showed a distant contempt for his two white passengers, now showed pity. When the awning proved utterly inadequate in the rain, and the great downpours engulfed us on deck, he invited us to sit in his two-windowed cabin under the bridge. It was the *Ann*'s best cabin, modest but larger and lighter than the captain's – for another thing, it contained the only chairs on the ship. His kindness came with a warning. We should expect bad weather two days out of Santa Cruz, he said, puffing darkly at his thimble-bowled pipe. It was usually bad there, he said. This led James to tell us about the storms on his only other rust-bucket voyage.

'What did you do?'

'I took to my cabin,' James said, 'in terror.'

'As bad as that?'

'Well, Christmas and New Year had just passed and the Polynesian crew celebrated on the ship's grog, and just went wild.' The Dwarf removed the pipe from his bearded lips to purse them in disapproval.

'And you didn't join them?' I asked.

'Good God, no! I locked myself in and listened to the uproar raging up and down outside.'

With a quick movement, the Dwarf smashed a cockroach on the bulkhead with his sandal.

'Well,' James went on, 'just then the tail of a cyclone caught us good and proper. Big seas, breaking right over the old ship; a lot of rolling and pounding. One result – we had ten extra weeks at sea – ten. Phew!'

'And the crew in the cyclone?'

'They just went on raging up and down. I suppose the booze made them impervious to everything.

'Odd thing,' James went on, 'before the cyclone a big bird, a booby, flew up from nowhere and perched on the winch forward. It must have been very tired, because a member of the crew just walked up and banged it on the head with a piece of rubber piping.'

'You killed it?'

'We cooked it.'

Here the chief emitted a bark of unbelief or, possibly, of contempt.

'Very nasty, too,' James said.

'To kill a booby or an albatross is almost a criminal act,' I said severely.

'Is it?'

'James, you've heard of the Ancient Mariner? Terrible things happen if you kill an albatross.'

'No wonder the company went broke soon after.'

All three of us laughed now, watching raindrops like bullets bouncing off the Pacific.

'Boobies,' the chief engineer murmured to the smoking thimble of his pipe. I decided to assume the remark was not addressed to us.

On this noisy shipful of mission boys a passage in Asterisk's *Isles of Illusion* came to mind *à propos* religion. Asterisk had decided to catechize his kitchen help, a 'cheery ruffian' and a mission-bred Christian. He did so thus:

> 'Time you altogether dead-finish, Nirawa, where you go stop?'
> 'Me no savvy, master. Missie [missionary] he speak body belong me go in ground, wind belong me go up-tree [on high, aloft, etc.]. Me think he

speak altogether gammon too much. Me think time me fellow dead-finish me stop altogether same pig.'

Jehovah happened to prance up to me on deck as I was examining a copy of St Mark's Gospel I had bought in the Christian Bookshop in Honiara. In pidgin, this was entitled *Gud Nuis Bulong Jisas Krais – Mak Hem I Raetem*, and it began, '*Hem nao Gud Nius bulong Jisas Krais, Pikinini bulong God.*' John the Baptist eating locusts and wild honey became: '*Kaikai bulong hem, girshopa an wael hani.*' In pidgin, for the appearance of Jesus before Pilate you read: '*Nao olketa soldia i tekem Jisas i go insaet long haos bulong gavna Paelet*'; and for the crucifixion: '*Olketa i nilam Jisas long Kros.*'

'Ha, you reading Holy Bible, master?' Jehovah said. He was munching a mouthful of biscuits, and crumbs shot out between his great organ-stop teeth like soft shrapnel.

'Yes, Richard,' I said. 'You are a Jehovah's Witness, aren't you? A pious man. Are there many in the Solomons?'

'Oooh – many. Many Seventh Day Adventists, too.'

He seemed vague about details of faith. 'Adventists no eating meat and no eating fruits,' he said indifferently. 'Jehovah's Witnesses eating meats and fruits.'

Jehovah's thick, wide lips opened and closed on an unceasing stream of utterance, often nothing more than abrupt, birdlike squawks – 'eeh! eeh!' When not in use his jaw hung open like an unlatched trap door. Now, leaning his ample buttocks on the ship's rail, he was in danger of toppling backwards into the sea.

'Hey, Richard,' I said. 'You fall in the sea, you drown. See this – *"Jisas hem i wok abaot antap long wata"*. You can't walk on water, Richard – can you?' I asked, and he staggered away, giggling.

James had never stopped checking the barometer. It eased gradually down – it was at a thousand millibars again now. Long, slow, swells began lazily to lift and lower the *Ann*, almost to lull her with loving care – but this cradling movement, John the captain explained calmly, signified a distant but rapidly approaching menace. The languid swells were caused by some severe disturbance of the ocean many miles away. Soon James ran down to where I sat sweating on the forehatch, trying to catch a little breeze, and spluttered out more upsetting news still. The hourly radio weather reports from Hawaii were warning of not one cyclone, but two. The first was the one we had heard of in Honiara, gathering its strength south of us near New Caledonia, and expected to move north. Hawaii's latest discovery was lurking somewhere near the Gilbert Islands, apparently deciding to swing south. We stood a very good chance of being caught like a very small nut in an elemental nutcracker halfway between the Santa Cruz group and Fiji, a very large area of ocean devoid of the smallest piece of land.

James and I anxiously examined every horizon for the telltale cloud formations that would herald the approach of our doom from north or south. It was odd, I thought, that the immediate prospect could be so outwardly placid and yet so implicitly menacing. The *Ann* gently rose and fell on the long, languid, soothing swells on an ocean so sleek it might have been smoothed out by the sheer weight of the thick heat. Nothing could have been farther from a landlubber's idea of the prelude to a storm. Yet I found the stillness and the relentless undulation of the water deeply disturbing. Something huge and threatening seemed to be moving under that suave surface. . . . It recalled a recurring nightmare I had had since childhood – a dream of a gigantic whale, as big as the *Queen Elizabeth*, rising slowly out of the sea like a wet slate hillside from the waves and then – horror! – leaping like a salmon. Imagine the tidal wave when it fell back into the sea.

Luckily there were comforting distractions. Flying fish a foot long skimmed the water as if playing private games of ducks and drakes, quite unaffected by the malevolent aspect of wind or sea. Comforting, too, were Jehovah's falsetto cries from the stern of 'Fees! Fees!' and the sight of Reginald the Cannibal Cook or George rushing to the lines and hauling in tuna, yellow-finned and yellow-spined, measuring two and a half feet from nose to tail, good to eat. The fish flapped and writhed on the battered deck, then lay staring at us with big, dead eyes before the cook chopped them up with swift, brutal strokes of his knife, and Jehovah, giggling excitedly, sluiced the blood and innards over the side.

All over the *Ann*, washing hung out to dry like makeshift bunting that, despite all elemental threats, lent her the air of some down-at-heel, back-street reveller tipsily celebrating a royal jubilee. Blue shorts, white singlets, green and yellow towels and laplaps of all colours hung slackly in the still air on the deck, in the alleyways, around the engine well, even over the porthole cover in the chief engineer's cabin.

Whenever the grim cook – the massive Cannibal Cook – came on deck, he emerged into the light like a hungry but suspicious badger emerging from its sett in search of prey. He trimmed his moustache on deck, nipping off each tough hair with a pair of scissors almost a foot long, and peering at his dark upper lip in a thin sliver of broken mirror. The severed hairs lay at his feet like short lengths of black wire. His usual expression was a ferocious one, but if he had really been as ferocious as he looked someone would have been obliged to lock him up; in fact he was shy. His scowl broke into a most sweet smile when he spotted my binoculars. Seizing them in his huge hands, and clapping them to his reddened eyeballs, he swept them over the empty sea until they focused quite by chance on a flying fish, and then his pleasure was a delight to see. He pumped my hand saying, 'Ha-ha! Yah!' and showed me every tooth in his head. 'Good!' We were friends from that moment, and to cement the friendship he brought me an extra sardine and extra half-handful of rice at noon.

Of course, Jehovah had taken against James, but no one else showed hostility of any kind. John the captain was amused by him and said: 'Your friend is nervous.'

'So am I,' I said.

'Well, see, the low depression six hundred miles south could move east or south-east or south-west. If it moves north towards us, we can always change course.' We would make Suva in three more days, he estimated – that would make it a week in all. Usually reserved, he was sometimes in a chatty mood. His master's certificate came from

Singapore, he said, and I was glad to hear it because Singapore is not one of those places where incompetent officers can buy, for a few hundred dollars, permission to steer ships around the world like drunken truck drivers.

James waved to me from the fo'c'sle, sweat band round a forehead scarlet with sunburn. His nose, white with anti-burn cream, stood out like an alp in a forest fire. He clutched a yellow, sweat-soaked paperback called *Trucks*, a novel, its blurb announced, about evils in the transport business. 'One thousand millibars on the barometer,' he said with grim relish. 'It was just below that yesterday evening.'

'Well, we're holding our own, then.'

'Well, yes . . . but remember one thousand and ten is a healthy norm,' James said. 'And – let me tell you about the captain's last experience in these parts; he's just been coming clean about it.'

I leaned against a rusty winch and prepared to be harrowed.

'He was master of another old rust-bucket, called the *Pluto*, I think, and just about where we are now, when he discovered that nine bolts in the hull were either loose or entirely missing. The bloody ship was coming apart, and already leaking badly. The pumps weren't working either, so the Singapore-Chinese crew – a no-nonsense lot, Singaporeans, aren't they? – struggled to improvise a pump, God knows how. Well, this was not a howling success – not in the crew's eyes, anyway. Water kept coming in. It looked bad. So . . . they mutinied. Went in an angry bunch to the wheelhouse and told the captain, "Go back at once to the Santa Cruz Group – the nearest land." Quite bravely, he refused point blank, and insisted on going to Port Vila in New Caledonia. They made it, but once there the Singaporeans promptly leaped off and disappeared into the blue!'

'Did he go after them?'

'He didn't bother. He hired a new crew locally – a whole lot of Jehovahs, I suppose – then he blundered blindly up to Tarawa and – what do you think? – ran the ship aground on a reef. I'd say he's a bit of a chancer.'

'James, will you stop trying to make my flesh creep? He's got a master's certificate from Singapore. He must know more or less what's what.' I hoped I was right.

'Oh sorry.'

But James, I knew now, throve on drama.

Meanwhile the *Ann* laboured bravely on, panting like an old and dutiful dog up humps of water as smooth as the Sussex Downs. The northern horizon filled with bruise-coloured clouds; they dispersed; the southern sky darkened in its turn. Rain storms came and went. Then, at last, thirty-six hours later and quite suddenly, all my anxiety ebbed away. The powerful swells had grown gradually weaker and fewer. James tumbled down from the bridge, sweating and grinning: 'The barometer says one thousand and four!'

'Saved!' I cried, like a character in a boys' adventure story. Evidently both cyclones had missed us; as if in collusion, they had changed their minds about pincering in on us and gone to terrorize someone else. My relief was tremendous. I have little doubt that in a cyclone we would have gone down without a trace. I had imagined the *Ann*'s bows dipping into an extra large swell like a diving submarine; Jehovah, cockroaches, the Dwarf's Y-fronts and all.

The captain peeped into his 'toy' radar screen, his forehead on the rubber eyepiece, as if it were a 'What the Butler Saw' machine on a seaside pier. 'Not far now.' Bligh Water lay ahead of us. Is this where Fletcher Christian set the captain of the *Bounty* adrift?

Circling inquisitively, the first friendly terns appeared. The crew wanted their photographs taken and they posed expectantly on the forehatch like schoolboys at the end of term. A strange school. Reginald and the Cannibal Cook squatted grimly in front, disdaining to smile. Shem, John the captain, the Dwarf behind them, inscrutable; in the back row, Daniel thrusting out his chest to bring into focus the tattooed eagle diving on the mermaid; and Jehovah, his mouth gaping, a chicken feather in his hair like a cockade, a can of pilchards in one hand, and the first finger of the other beginning to work its way up a flaring nostril. The Cannibal Cook held his great knife like a sceptre – his orb was a can of corned beef. Both Reginald and the Dwarf flourished their thimble-bowled, long-stemmed pipes. When the group broke up, Jehovah sprang to the rail, turned his great bottom towards us, hauled up the front of his laplap, and began to pee untidily into the sea. This infuriated Daniel who, with a roar of disgust, real or feigned, rushed at Jehovah in his unusually vulnerable state, beat him away from the rail and chased him, stumbling and shrieking, his legs tangled in his laplap, towards the stern. Is this really love, as George said – or sheer raw hate, as it appears? 'It's just a way of killing boredom, if you ask me,' James said.

The green mountains of Viti Levu – the largest Fijian island, with Suva on its south-eastern coast – came to meet us through an afternoon mist. We entered an area of reefs and a bay with a semicircle of white buildings. We stopped. Presently, from behind the bulk of a big Mobil tanker, the *Satucket*, a launch emerged and circled our way. 'Health,' John said. I had expected bossy, energetic young men with brown skins and bushy hair, but the trio of health department officers who came aboard consisted of a very tall, elderly Indian in a long-sleeved white shirt and baggy grey trousers, an only slightly less tall Fijian lady – her head supported the highest and widest fuzz I had ever seen – and a shorter, stout man who might have been part Fijian and part European. Courteously they said to us, 'Welcome to Fiji,' and glided about the *Ann*, murmuring apologies whenever they sprayed insecticide. They soon left as genteelly as they had come, waving and smiling from their launch. We waved back. It was a pleasant landfall.

We were alongside; no delay. 'Fill in this form. That's all.' An immigration man put a month's visa in my passport. Someone else gave me a 'Miscellaneous Gate Pass' in the name of 'Mr Gavin and Barclay'. I went below for the last time to lug my metal suitcase up on deck. George was there.

'George, I've made a damp, sweaty mess of your bunk. I'm sorry and grateful.' I saw he had already replaced my 'Forget Me Not, Darling' pillowcase with a fresh one embroidered with 'My Dreams Follow Where You Go.'

'You were welcome,' he said, smiling in a most open way, and 'I won't take that,' when he saw money in my hand. I gave the remaining cans of food to the Cannibal Cook, who just smiled silently and touched the haft of his knife to his forehead in a rough salute. Jehovah and Daniel were at work on the forward hatch – at peace for once. I called to them and they waved back. Of Shem and Reginald there was no sign.

'Thank you,' I said to John the captain, 'for avoiding the cyclones.' And to the impassive Dwarf, 'Thank you for keeping up the revs.'

When I suggested a meal ashore John said, 'Well, we should be loading tonight for Funafuti in Tuvalu. Let's see.' I followed James over the rusty rail and from the quay glanced back to the *Ann*'s mermaid flaunting her green nipples from the funnel. I had a last glimpse of Jehovah, too, his mouth hanging open, a finger probing a nostril. With his other hand he waved again.

I saw in the *Fiji Times* a day later that the *Ann* had not hung about; she had swiftly taken on biscuits and general cargo and rolled away north-east, past the Yasawa Group, Bligh Water and the Great Sea Reef to Tuvalu. She'd allowed poor Jehovah no time to 'spy for lady' in Suva. Over a long glass of white rum and pineapple on the terrace of the Grand Pacific Hotel, I imagined my pillowcase where George would have pegged it like a brave banner on the *Ann*'s washing line, white as a gull once more, flapping its lovelorn entreaty to each indifferent wave that passed.

Seventeen

Suva. Here they were around me, these brown giants, six foot or more, big-handed, saying, 'Good morning' on the sidewalks, smiling with strong teeth. Colson had been a fair-sized man; these Fijians were half as large again. Pint glasses could disappear in these fists and, judging from the laughter, high shouts and sound of breaking glass in some Suva bars, many were doing so.

James and I parted in Suva. Tonga had recently been hit by a particularly bad cyclone and he wanted to see the damage, which was said to be incalculable. If in Honiara I had felt a little apprehensive at the prospect of a white man's company on the *Ann* it had been totally unjustified. He had been a good companion; we had got on very well in that strange, restrictive little world. A cutting from the *Fiji Times* sent on by James reached me later, in Samoa, with the following news:

BERNIE BREAKS YACHT IN TWO

A 42-ft yacht bought in Fiji about six months ago, was broken in two and sunk off Honiara in the Solomons when Cyclone Bernie struck the islands late last week. According to reports from Honiara, none of the crew aboard the yacht *Camping Loo* were injured although nothing was salvaged from the wreck.

The ketch was skippered by an Englishman. It was reported to have broken its anchor chain in the yacht basin off the Mendana Hotel, and broken in two on the rocks, leaving only broken wood washed up on the beach....

So our good luck had been the *Camping Loo*'s matchwood. It looked as if Cyclone Bernie had been misinformed; searching for James, it had destroyed the vessel he had just left. Later still, when I was back in England, James wrote again from the Solomons. He had rediscovered the *Ann* – and found that there had been one significant crew change. 'Yes,' he said in his letter, 'you've guessed. No more Jehovah. The captain mysteriously mentioned that Jehovah would be better off as a married man on Santa Cruz. His behaviour had become so arbitrary that he had been put ashore at some obscure port.' He added, 'I was surprised to find a blonde German girl emerging from the captain's cabin. He explained that she was married to an Ellice Islander and was on her way to Funafuti. Well, well. Tut, tut.'

As soon as I was ashore and settled in my hotel, I began as usual to think about an onward ship. My next stop was Western Samoa. I longed to see the island Robert Louis Stevenson had chosen; the sultry place of his death on 3 December 1894; the path up which devoted chiefs had carried him to his grave on the hilltop overlooking the bay of Apia.

I visited a few shipping offices, including Burns Philp, of course – a name as ubiquitous in the South Seas as Gray Mackenzie is in the Middle East, or as John Swire or Jardine Mathieson are in south-east Asia. But there was nothing doing. Not just then at any rate. It was in the offices of Carpenters Shipping that I found salvation this time. A friendly, thick-set man with dark hair rose from behind a desk in a moderate-sized office to take my hand and pass me his card:

Fritz Falkner
Master Mariner
Area Manager Central
Shipping and Transport.

Captain Falkner was a traveller himself; he understood at once what I wanted and why, and without delay he decided to help me.

From him I learnt to my great delight that a small Tongan ship – the *Tasi*, 1300 tons – was due in Suva within a few days and would be proceeding to the port of Apia. 'New Zealand owner. Smallish company. I should think they'd take you. I'll ask their head office, if you like. No trouble.' Tongan ship! To Samoa? What more could I want?

With that next step half assured (Captain Falkner had an optimistic look about him as he sat down to write out the request for a berth from the owners), I turned to the question of the next move but one. (To

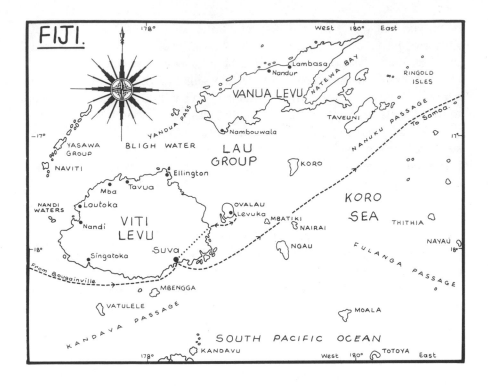

anyone who might think I was being over-anxious, I can only say that by
now I was fully aware that, on top of the ordinary problem of getting
aboard cargo vessels, I had doomed myself to the role of a swimmer
battling adverse currents. By moving against the prevailing east-to-west
flow of ships across the South Pacific, I had made things very hard for
myself.) Nevertheless, a perusal of the shipping pages of the *Fiji Times*
revealed, among the schedules of the Kyowa Line, the Columbus Line
and New Zealand United Express service, something that looked very
convenient indeed. The Bali Hai service, an advertisement told me, plied
between Kobe in Japan and the South Pacific islands, and I saw the name
of a Swire vessel, the *Pacific Islander*, which had become familiar to me
from the conversations of Julian Gomersall and Jim Bird on the *Chengtu*.
She would be in Apia in a couple of weeks en route to Tahiti.

'Bali Hai Service – You'll Find It, Where the Sky Meets the Sea,' the
notice said, and I saw that Burns Philp were its agents in Suva. I hurried
to their office in the small centre of the town and, as at Carpenters,
found friendliness and a promise. A tall shipping manager in glasses
said he would ask permission by telex from Tim Bridgeman's China

Navigation Company office in Hong Kong for me to take a lift from Apia to Papeete. I didn't believe the kind men at Swires would refuse me. I left Burns Philp ecstatic: from Fiji to Tahiti my way seemed secure. And Tahiti – I checked it on my Bartholomew's map of the Pacific – lay roughly halfway across the ocean. I was getting on!

What could I see of Fiji? I had seen the bay of Suva, a wide, misty piece of water within the reef, enclosed oddly as if by a pair of dislocated arms, and a strange outcrop of rock like a comb on a rooster's head. I walked about Suva town – a well-kept place of pleasant old and the usual nondescript modern buildings, low, green with trees and parks. I had been smiled at, I had seen soldiers wearing the famous jagged-hemmed kilts.

From a book of Fijian history I knew that indented Indian labourers, brought by ship from Madras and Calcutta by the British in the later years of the nineteenth century – coolie labour for sugar and cotton fields – had subsequently multiplied until they formed more than half the population of the Fijian Islands. Energetic, they now dominated the economy, and this had alarmed the Fijians. In the *Fiji Times* an election campaign was reported in which Fijian nationalists were talking about 'restoring Fiji to the Fijians'. The then Indian Prime Minister, Indira Gandhi, on a recent visit to Suva, had warned the Fijian Indian community, 'Your ideas must be totally identified with your country, Fiji,' which seemed to be the most sensible thing she could have said. If the opposition party won the election, the newspaper editorials prophesied that Indian ambassadors would soon represent Fiji abroad. Intimations of racial friction hung over a group of islands that, to judge by their looks, should have been a fairly close approximation to paradise.

The *Fiji Times* advertised itself as 'The First Newspaper Published in the World Today', because Suva is just west of the international date line where the new day begins. I read it in a chair under palm trees on the front terrace of the Grand Pacific Hotel, a majestic pile whose colonial outline, pillared and tall-windowed, stood on the bay, visible from every ship coming in or leaving through the reef. Built rather on the lines of the Raffles Hotel in Singapore, it had the same cell-block configuration with landings that ran round a deep, rectangular court. But it was a disappointment. Though you entered under a stately porch and climbed broad steps, the effect was hopelessly marred inside by a central court cheapened into a 'video-lounge'. The sound of soap opera actors, police sirens, film music and amplified pop filled this dignified building, a monument worth cherishing but in dire need of a sympathetic hand.

Fiji is outside the frontiers of Australian hegemony, but Suva is very evidently a tour port. A big cruise ship was in, the *Oriana*. Fritz Falkner had said, 'Fiji is the biggest tourist centre in this part of the Pacific. Duty-free shops. Cruise ships with Australians and New Zealanders, mostly.'

In Cummings Street, the duty-free market, the *Oriana*'s passengers surged in and out of shops like soldiers clearing houses in a street-fighting operation. 'In here, Glenda – *bargains*!' – the penetrating accent of Down South issued from Abdul Razak's Camera and Radio Emporium, where a young Indian with a small gold ring in his ear lobe inexpertly showed off a Pentax's semi-automatic function; failing, growing flippant at first, then irritable with the customers.

James Barclay had given me the name of a friend in Suva, a British lawyer who had spent some years in Fiji and, though still relatively young, worked in the office of the Chief Justice as – I think, though it seems an unlikely title – Sheriff of Fiji. I soon introduced myself to Michael Scott, a voluble, intelligent man with a lively humour and a desire to help. I wanted to consult him on the best way to pass my few days in Fiji, and he invited me to his small house, a modern bungalow surrounded by gardens and trees.

He spread out a map of the scattered islands of Fiji. 'Well, here you are – in the old Cannibal Islands, as ancient mariners called them. There's plenty to see. Yachts and a marina outside Suva. A big pleasure resort in the west of this island, Viti Levu – modern hotels, swimming pools, scuba diving, all that jazz.... No, I didn't think you'd want that sort of thing.' His finger moved northwards across Bligh Water. 'You could see the other big island, Vanua Levu. Or there are those eastern islands scattered about over the Koro Sea towards Tonga – the Lau Group. There are small inter-island ships, of course.'

A few moments later, he said, 'Oh, I know. There's Levuka. That might be your place. A whaling station of the early 1800s that became the old, rough capital of Fiji for a bit, until King Cakobau, a genu-ine cannibal warrior turned Christian gentleman, ceded the islands to Queen Victoria, and even sent her his bloodstained warclub to show he'd given up that sort of thing. Lots of stories of pirates and cannibals, and slaving and all that. Picturesque spot, pretty well unchanged. Not far. Take a bus.' It sounded like good advice. I bought R.A. Derrick's

A History of Fiji and a copy of a special edition of the *Fiji Times* which reproduced articles from the mid-1800s up to today (I love old newspapers) and, a few hours later, took a bus to Levuka on the island of Ovalu.

Of course, there was a bus *and* a boat. Both were full of Fijians guzzling food as if it were their last nourishment on earth. Ices, soda pop, milk, currant buns, wrapped loaves – the bus floor was soon covered in crumbs. An Indian collected fares, and now and then the Fijian driver stopped the vehicle, hooted once or twice and waited for men to appear bearing enamel bowls of *kava*, the local grog. 'Ivi, *ivi*,' a woman said, smiling up at me, and held up in a leaf envelope what looked like a cube of potato. That was not the only offering. A child gave me a sweet and a young man offered me his newspaper. In the Solomons, I couldn't remember anyone offering me anything much.

A man began massaging his chest under his shirt, smearing on a pungent balsam, groaning horribly as he did so and filling the bus with a gingery smell that grew almost overpowering as the self-massage continued all the way – an hour or so – to the ferry head. The smell persisted on the smart little launch, with brass fittings in her wheel-house, which bounced us across the narrow strait to Ovalu. The friendly woman handed out more *ivi*. The groaning man finished his massage and lay full length on a padded bench, covering his head with his hands as we roared through blue water shallow with reefs and round the corner of the mollusc-shaped island. Soon, we turned down its green eastern shores to Levuka. A wharf appeared, jutting into the sheltered Koro Sea, and then the white-boarded warehouses of the Fiji Port Authority, and a low stretch of buildings that retained the frontier town appearance Michael Scott had promised.

With relief, I saw only a few trawlers moored in the huddle off the northern end of the town and another – I saw her Japanese name through my glasses – heading past us out to sea. Levuka hardly looked big enough to be called a town. I could imagine friends contemptuously telling me that Levuka is a 'dump'. But I am a dump man. And for the moment this dump particularly interested me because I had just learnt from *A History of Fiji* that when the white men first erupted into this isolated, innocent South Seas world they turned Levuka into a place as wild as the wildest frontier township in the bad old American West.

Eighteen

I carried my small bag along Beach Street, away from the wharf and the trawlers, past low, wood-framed offices and shops with verandahs. Tall trees rose behind them, soaring up a sudden precipitous cliff. I passed Burns Philp (South Sea) Co. Ltd, which had an office here; outside a mission school a girl called out, 'Come on, Emma. Choir pract-ees.' I passed the Pacific Fishing Co., Choy's Building, the Marist Church of the Sacred Heart, facing the sea at the foot of shaggy cliffs. I looked in at its wooden walls and saw over its simple altar a large Fijian warclub under the wooden cross. A notice said, 'The Pioneer Total Abstinence Association – Central Director, Pioneer Association, Upper Sherrard Street, Dublin'. From a clocktower the machinery tick-tocked, deep and heavy, like Poe's tell tale heart. Fijian men in sulus and Indian women in saris idled about the narrow street. One or two guided me up a lane to an hotel half hidden among trees. A middle-aged and impassive Eurasian woman gave me the key to a small first-floor room. 'Dinner at 6.30,' she said. 'The girl must go home outside the town, so she'll leave food in your room, if you want it later.'

'Perhaps some sandwiches, then.'

A youngish Indian came down the stairs, shirtless; his beard straggled down his neck to meet the wool of his chest. 'Is there, by any means,' he addressed the woman, 'a pressing facility in the hotel?'

'No,' the woman promptly said.

'Give me an iron, I'll do it.' His hair was brushed forward over his eyebrows, straight and thick like black thatch.

The woman looked with distaste at his matted bosom. 'No iron,' she muttered with finality, and left us.

He turned to me. 'I didn't see you coming over on the plane.'

He sounded suspicious. I was on the boat, I told him.

'I sat under a great big hail of rain,' he said accusingly, his wet, red lips pouting through his beard. 'It poured down through the roof of the plane. Just onto my head. A shower of water. Onto my head.' Before I could ask him what he meant, he turned and stumped frowning up the stairs with his unpressed trousers over his arm like a mutinous valet. Rain in an aeroplane? 'I'm in insurance,' he called back defiantly

I sat in a dim lounge over a cup of tea with *A History of Fiji* on my knees. In 1849 the white population of native Levuka was a mere fourteen or fifteen. But the settlement grew as more British and Americans sought its sheltered harbour and cool breezes, and by 1870 its population was six hundred, mostly British. Up to then it had been a rough-and-ready foothold on a cannibal island – a mere straggle of weatherboard and corrugated iron stores, grog shops, hotels, dwellings and huts. The beach was 'unsavoury', horses, cattle and pigs roamed Beach Street and, with no sanitation, the place smelt, according to a Dr Messer of HMS *Pearl*, like some filthy Turkish village. Behind the buildings, behind the mountain that hemmed it in, lived wild and aggressive tribes who raided the settlement at frequent intervals.

The first European navigator had arrived off Fiji in the year 1774, in the no-nonsense shape of Captain James Cook. Cook merely brushed the islands, however – he left nails, a knife and a few medals (what would the Fijians have made of those?) on a small island in the Lau Group, Vatoa, which he called Turtle Island. From there, he sailed west to the North Hebrides. Lieutenant William Bligh RN had been with Cook, and fifteen years later he was in the same region again as master of HM armed vessel *Bounty*, gathering young breadfruit trees for transplanting in the West Indies. The famous mutiny of 28 April 1789 took place off the Tongan island of Tofua, south-east of Fiji, and Bligh, with eighteen loyal officers and men, was set adrift in the ship's boat, twenty-three feet long, with some bread, water and cutlasses but no firearms.

Bligh turned his boat's bows towards the Fiji Islands – he had heard of them from the natives in Tonga – but the particular Fijians he ran into were not friendly and pursued him in swift, thirty-foot double war canoes, the finest canoes in the Pacific. Was Bligh aware that every local chief launched his war canoes, according to immemorial ritual, over the bleeding bodies of his enemies? Had they been caught, there is no doubt that Mr Fletcher Christian's castaways would have been dispatched by Fijian warclubs – or perhaps served as slipways for new canoes before being cooked and eaten. (The hearts and tongues, I read over my cup of

Lipton's tea, were reserved for the chiefs; children carried off the hands; the heads were buried.) By a stroke of luck, a favourable wind enabled Bligh to escape through the reefs and islands north of Viti Levu, across what is now called Bligh Water, and into the deep ocean to the west. If he had not, news of the mutiny on the *Bounty* might never have reached England, and Christian and every one of his fellow mutineers might have lived out their lives in uninterrupted serenity (as it was, only ten were tried for mutiny, and three executed). Certainly Bligh would never have made his extraordinary voyage in that open boat across three thousand six hundred miles of sea to Timor in the Dutch East Indies. Equally certainly he would not subsequently have become Governor of New South Wales.

Even in extremis among the reefs of Fiji, Bligh calmly took sightings on the islands around him, and his charts were used by later Europeans. These soon arrived, drawn by reports of two valuable local products – sandalwood and *bêches de mer*. Both were much prized in China: sandalwood was made into joss sticks; *bêches de mer* (from the Portuguese *bicho do mar*), eight-inch, slimy, sausage-shaped sea cucumbers very common in the Pacific, were smoke-cured in Fiji for the Chinese, who supposed them to possess unusually potent medical properties. For these products, European and American whalers bartered the teeth of the Cachalot or sperm whale, elephant tusks from India, and ray stings from Tonga to tip the Fijians' spears. One chief released a boat's crew on payment of fifty whale teeth, four axes, two plates, some fish hooks and cloth. The bona fide traders were soon equalled, if not outnumbered, by arrivals of a much more sinister nature: escaped convicts, deserters, marooned sailors, the derelict scourings – in the words of the *History* on my knee – of the ports of the Old World. Between them, traders and scallywags brought two gifts to the Sandalwood Coast which Fijians could well have done without. The first was a spectacular range of European diseases: measles, whooping cough, syphilis, influenza, smallpox, dysentery. The second was firearms.

The Fijian chiefs, constantly at war among themselves, took to firearms with the utmost enthusiasm. They were desperate to procure them – their possession established their owner's power over a weaponless, merely club-bearing chief in next to no time. Soon, all the most important chiefs had firearms, and because they barely under-stood how to fire them they employed down-and-out white men to shoot and maintain them. The chiefs spoke of their tame white riff-raff as proud owners talk of pedigree pets. Runaway sailors, convicts from wrecked Australia-bound transports and other 'low whites' found themselves personages of importance and standing in various cannibal courts throughout the islands.

Mutineers, murder, cannibalism, shipwreck! One ruffian in particular attracted my attention in this extraordinary story – a man named Charles Savage, a Conradian figure if ever there was one outside the pages of *An Outcast of the Islands* –

The thought was oddly interrupted. A tall Oriental with a sad, long face came in. Japanese?

He seemed about to pass me by, then he cautiously approached. 'Hello. You are staying long?'

'Only a day or two,' I said. 'And you?'

'Oh, I am here already two weeks. One month more. I work for fishing company. Japan.' He looked pathetically lugubrious. 'What you read?'

'History. About Levuka. Very interesting.'

'History?' He looked at me as if he had discovered a madman. 'No history here. No nothing.'

'You don't like it, then?'

'Oh....' His gaze wandered about the furniture as if he had left something here and was looking for it. 'Oh ... ha!' Again his narrow eyes stared at me in dismay, and he shrugged his thin shoulders. 'It ... is ... not easy.'

'Lonely, I suppose.'

'Very lonely,' he nodded desperately – and even before I could offer him a cup of tea he left me without another word. Presently I heard his solemn footfalls on the wooden floor of his room overhead. A serious case of homesickness. There was a Japanese fish-canning factory here – Japanese and Koreans have fishing rights and canning agreements in many places in the Pacific. It was difficult to think of many people more different from Japanese than Fijians. And now Levuka had nothing to offer a visitor but its history.

I took up my book and strolled out through the trees, down the lane towards the sea, and into Beach Street. Levuka Central Store ('the shop of fancy wear'), shops 'licensed to sell patent medicines', Rachhod's Liquor Department. Every second store had sold alcohol in the early nineteenth century – 'gunbarrel' rum and moonshine whisky, mostly. The beach itself was unsavoury no more, but little Beach Street still had a distinctly Wild West look. It might repel a Japanese visitor, but it was easy to conjure up Charles Savage here.

This Charles Savage was an interesting prototype of the cruder Fijian-European rascals of his age, and I retell here the story I found in Mr Derrick's book.

In May 1808, at Tonga, two ragged sailors, John Husk and Charles Savage, begged Captain E.H. Corey of the American brig *Eliza* to take them aboard, claiming to be the sole survivors of the massacred crew of another ship, the *Port au Prince*. The captain obliged, but shortly the *Eliza* was run onto the Mocea Reef near Levuka, the crew managing to save from her forty thousand Spanish dollars and a quantity of muskets, powder and cutlasses which they rowed ashore in the ship's longboat. Here Fijians were waiting for them, quite uninterested in the dollars – they preferred coloured trinkets. They stripped the sailors of their clothes, providing them with bark loincloths instead, and were perfectly friendly. Captain Corey and four of his crew were allowed to sail away in the longboat with six thousand dollars. But the Fijians took a fancy to Charlie Savage, who spoke quite good Fijian and Tongan after eighteen months in Tonga; they adopted him, and carried him off to the nearby island of Bau. As tame white man to Naulivou, the chief of that time, he set about rehearsing the eager warriors of Bau in the use of the strange firesticks called muskets – with terrible success. Before long he obliged the chief by leading an attack on a village called Kasavu. An eye witness described the massacre: 'Savage stood on his canoe in the middle of the river, less than a pistol-shot from the reed fence of the fortification, and fired on the inhabitants, who had no means of defending themselves' – except, he went on, by crouching down, terrified, behind the piled corpses of their friends and relatives. Soon, the 'village stream ran red'. The Bauans were overcome with gratitude, and Savage organized many more such attacks. There was at first pathetically little opposition. In one village he shot the defenders down as they stood gazing at the sky; they thought the noise of the muskets was thunder.

As Derrick says, Savage and his like, with their muskets (and later cannon) led Fiji into an era of bloodshed and civil war inconceivable in the days of club and spear. Savage became something of a god; depending who you were, you spoke of him with the utmost reverence or with infinite horror. After a while he was joined by other renegades, some of them his shipmates from the *Eliza*, runaways from sandalwood ships – all with muskets and a handful of dollars. This army of ruthless scallywags assured the supremacy of Naulivou. But eventually their numbers were much reduced by drink and homicidal jealousies. Even the Bauans they served were finally disgusted with their barnyard morals, and once, when an opportunity occurred at a feast, they swiftly clubbed several of them to death where they sat. (The question of whose morals were worse was not generally agreed. Savage shot Fijians whom he found eating human flesh, yet he thought nothing of cold-blooded murder, and he took to polygamy 'like a rooster in a henhouse'.)

The unholy reign of 'King Charlie' lasted for about five years, spent in alternating periods of beachcombing idleness and bloody campaigning. Then he decided to visit the Sandalwood Coast to work the boats of a Calcutta ship, the *Hunter*, and he took with him a few of his mercenaries from Bau. (Derrick's list shows what a mixed bunch they were: two Chinamen of the *Eliza*, an ex-convict from New South Wales; William Parker, an American deserter; a seaman discharged from the *Hunter* a year before; Michael Maccabe and Joseph Atkins, both discharged from another vessel; Martin Bushart, a German; a Lascar; a Tahitian; and a Tongan carpenter.) At the same time, Naulivou sent two large canoes with 230 men and two other chiefs from Bau to bring back Savage and his men once the work was completed. Unfortunately for all concerned, Captain Robson of the *Hunter* had fallen into dispute with some local Wailean tribesmen and felt obliged to destroy their canoes before landing his men.

Charlie Savage, the other foreigners and two or three score men from Bau went ashore, climbed a hill, burnt some houses on it – and found themselves ambushed by Waileans waiting for them in the forest. What could even 'King Charlie' do? After hours under siege, he became impatient and decided to trust to his knowledge of Fijians to haggle his way out. With one of the Chinamen, he descended the slope. He bargained with the Waileans. But he overestimated his negotiating ability – and his mystique. When the bargaining faltered, the Waileans clubbed the Chinaman to death. Presently – when those still cowering on the rock refused to come down – the Waileans seized Charlie Savage and held him head down in a pool until he drowned. Then they cut him up, and cooked him before his comrades' eyes, for their encouragement. In a final Wailean gesture of hate and triumph, they made his bones into sail needles. Of his companions, only three escaped to the *Hunter*.

The characters of the noble and humane Captain James Cook and the murderous rascal, Savage, were of course quite dissimilar. Yet reading of Savage's end recalled the haunting eye witness account by Captain James King of Cook's death in Hawaii (like Magellan he was

cut down in an almost accidental skirmish at the water's edge), and of the chief's apologetic, tearful return two days later of Cook's bones to the grieving officers of the *Resolution*.

> We found in it [a wrapping of fine cloth and a cloak of black and white feathers] the hands of Captain Cook entire, which were well known from a remarkable scar on one of them, that divided the thumb from the forefinger, the whole length of the metacarpal bone; the skull, but with the scalp separated from it, and the bones that form the face wanting; the scalp, with the hair upon it cut short, and the ears adhering to it; the bones of both arms...; the thighs and leg-bones joined together, but without feet. The lower jaw and feet had been seized by different Chiefs....

I liked the sequel. When King asked them whether they had eaten some of his captain's flesh, 'They immediately shewed as much horror at the idea as any European would have done; and asked, very naturally, if that was the custom amongst us?'

As for the odious Savage, surely it is impossible not to see in his terrible death a projection of the repulsive end of Conrad's Kurtz in his domain by the dark currents of the Congo – 'The horror! The horror!' Less profound, maybe, in his vileness than the fictitious Kurtz, Savage, after all, actually lived.

I stood in Levuka, this forlorn old town, hearing the put-putting of Japanese fishing vessels off the beach, and let images of Charlie Savage's wicked time flood into my mind, like stills from a film. Tall, bushy-headed warriors, raging through the trees; a white man standing in a canoe, musket to his shoulder, gleefully picking off villagers staring skyward; dark figures against a fire stooping over the fragments of a human body; a child happily jiggling the fingers of a severed hand; and the evil white man drowned, cut up and eaten before his comrades' eyes....

'The horror! The horror!'

*   *   *

Opposite Burns Philp an old building belonging to another venerable Pacific trading company, Morris Hedstrom, had become a museum. Its old walls displayed fine mid-nineteenth-century engravings of massive ocean-going druas or double canoes of Ovalu – heavy, swift and ninety feet long, crewed by two hundred armed warriors whose aim was to ram other canoes and slaughter the swimming enemy. By contrast, in a billiard hall nearby, peaceful conduct was the purpose of the rules displayed on the wall:

No smoking while playing
No swearing
Do not bang cue on floor or table
No making noise
Do not stop black or coloured balls
Wear shirt or singlet while you play
Strictly no drunkenness

'You like playing?' A short, friendly Indian stood at my elbow.
'I'm interested in your rules.'
'Oh – we have too much trouble. Sometimes terrible drinking. People stop the balls and start shouting they've won. Then a fighting starts. People from the villages.' He shook his head. 'Grog.'

I liked the atmosphere of little Levuka – that spectral presence of the nerveless explorers, the mutinous sailors, grog-hardened traders and ragged beachcombers of long ago. I thought: Past and Present overlap here all right, and I saw the town and its bay as an old etching, like the prints in the Morris Hedstrom museum.

Further along the road, a little outside the town, under palm trees by the sea, I came upon the monument commemorating the cession of Fiji to Great Britain on 10 October 1874, at the request of King Cakobau. That afternoon, after a morning's postponement because of driving rain and threatening clouds, the Deed of Cession was signed here in the presence of Sir Hercules Robinson, the British representative, and the Fijian chiefs, all of whom had been gathered up from their islands by HMS Pearl, acting as a sort of school bus. At one island, the two local chiefs were engrossed in a private war and oblivious of the historic moment; they had to be impatiently separated, but at last they, too, heard the announcement of King Cakobau, the grand old cannibal turned Christian. According to the *Fiji Times* of Wednesday, 14 October 1874:

> Before ceding his country to Her Majesty the Queen ... the King gives her his old and favourite war-club, the former, and, until lately the only known, law of Fiji. In abandoning club law, and adopting the forms and principles of civilised societies, he laid by his old weapon.... Many of his people died and passed away under the old law; but hundreds of thousands still survive to enjoy the newer and better state of things.... He sends his love to Her Majesty....

It was a happy time. After the cession ceremony, the rough men of Levuka took on the officers and men of HMS *Pearl* and her consort ship HMS *Dido* at cricket – a triumph, as it turned out, for Levuka, for the scores were: Levuka 109, *Pearl* and *Dido* 15 (top scorer: Martin, c. Groom, b. Brodziak, 7) and 83. 'There was goodly array of the fair sex on the ground, and the splendid band of the *Pearl* greatly added to the enjoyment of the day.' Mr H. Norris, owner of the Little Wonder Store in the Lane of Totoga, nearby down the coast, begged to announce 'to their friends the public that although they have been silent now for some time they have only been

Hushed in grim repose awaiting – ANNEXATION!'

Mr Norris now promised monthly mail steamer deliveries of provisions guaranteed 'NEW AND FRESH'! Already the Royal Mail ship *Cyphrenes* was at Levuka port with Norris-bound supplies ranging from apples to two-pound tins of rump steak; while down the road Otty Cudlip was preparing to auction wines, spirits, bedroom furniture, beer, engines, atmospheric lamps, and 'one of Alcock's Best Billiard Tables (Complete)', at the Criterion Hotel.

Two days later, another billiard table (not necessarily an Alcock) was raffled in the old Levuka Hotel and won by a Mr Huon of HMS *Dido* – the sailors sailed away to Sydney with one trophy at least – and an amateur dramatic show 'fully merited the liberal patronage accorded – once one had made due allowances in favour of places like Levuka where professional theatrical talent is entirely absent'.

When I returned to Suva, I sought out Michael Scott. Over drinks in the Grand Pacific, he asked if I realized that one reason for the British Government's agreement to cession was the flourishing traffic in plantation labourers? A ship's captain could earn a pound sterling for every fuzzy Melanesian head snatched from the Solomons and the New Hebrides and dumped in Levuka for work in Fiji's plantations. Melanesians, smaller and more vigorous, worked better.

These thoughts about blackbirding took me back to Asterisk and to Colson. Perhaps one or two of Colson's forebears had left their bones in far-off Levuka. I fetched my history of Fiji and *Isles of Illusion* for Michael to see.

'Look at this,' Michael put a finger on a footnote in the history. 'The London *Times* in reporting a hurricane that occurred in December 1879 said: "The *Stanley* of Queensland, 113 tons, caught the full force of the gale. She had 150 islanders on board for Fiji, who were kept under battened hatches for thirty hours at a time. Fifty subsequently died, and one committed suicide on being discharged from Levuka hospital." Pretty typical.'

At least Jehovah's fierce ancestors would have avoided such a fate. Blackbirders learnt that to land in the Santa Cruz group in the Solomons, Jehovah's home which I had visited briefly in the *Ann*, was to court death at the hands of frenzied warriors, and they steered well away from it. For some savage reason, the Santa Crucians had always been scornfully indifferent to – or were roused to martial fury by – rough Queenslanders trying to woo them with glamorous bribes – 'knives, tomahawks, cheap print, calico, turkey-red twill, small coloured beads, twist tobacco, short clay pipes, jew's harps, mirrors, fish-hooks, washing blue (for face paint), and scrap iron'.

What the British consul in Levuka discovered about the blackbirding brig *Carl* of Melbourne helped to save the harassed islanders from more of the white man's impact.

The Crew had collected about eighty labourers by the usual methods of upsetting canoes or dropping pig-iron through them; and [one night] a disturbance broke out in the *Carl*'s hold ... the kidnapped men breaking up the bunks and using the pieces as spears, to fight among themselves. The crew fired through the bulkheads but so far from quelling the riot the shooting only increased the frenzy and terror of the men confined below. The crew themselves seem to have panicked, for they continued firing for eight hours. At daylight the hatches were opened to expose a shambles. Of the kidnapped men, five came out unaided, twenty-five were wounded, and over fifty were dead. To make matters worse, dead and badly wounded were thrown overboard together; and all evidence of the affray was removed in order to avoid awkward questions should the ship fall in with a warship — which, indeed, happened shortly afterwards.

'I think you'll find that incident helped convince the Government in Westminster to accept Cakobau's offer,' Michael said.

Captain Fritz Falkner of Carpenters Shipping warned me to be ready to leave: the *Tasi* would arrive at 0700 or thereabouts the day after tomorrow. She would sail to Samoa the next day. I had no difficulty in filling in the time. The *Fiji Times* advertised a rugby football match; just the game for Fijians with their great height and big bones. Today, they had a match against Sydney — a first-class side, the paper said. Where had I heard that the Fijians played in bare feet?

I sat in a good seat in a crowded stadium, on the edge of a perfect sea. Behind banked rows of fuzzy heads, the crisp white sails of yachts moved infinitely slowly beyond the surf and the reefs. It was an extraordinary scene: the sea; the striped parasols of the spectators; the swirling, speeding brown and white players, every one with boots on. The Fijian supporters whistled and yelled 'Off side' in high good humour. The heat was intense; the rising score remained even. Senivalati Laulau — was he six or seven feet tall? — scored one of the swiftest tries I have ever seen. Two other giants in his team were called Vilikesa Vatuwaliwali and Josefa Korovulavula and looked as formidable as their names. Take away his gun, and they could have laid a murderous ruffian like Charlie Savage dead at their feet in no time.

To my surprise, Michael Scott informed me that a message had reached him for me: the Prime Minister of Fiji would be pleased to see me briefly next morning in his office. It was a wonder he could spare the time with an election campaign in progress. The meeting had been arranged by a Mr Don Diment of the Department of Information, who had heard from Michael that I was in Suva and interested in Fiji. It was a gesture which I would certainly not refuse.

I found the Prime Minister in his modern office not far from the hotel. Like most Fijians I had seen, Ratu Sir Kamisese Kapaiwai Tuimacilia Mara, who was in his fifties, was as tall and broad as the rugby players I had watched the afternoon before — or the chiefs of old

Fiji depicted in engravings, advancing into battle twirling warclubs. But the resemblance ended with his size. Ratu Mara looked anything but warlike in an open shirt which he wore over a fawn-coloured kilt and sandals. His hair was white and curly and he wore glasses. His expression was benign. He walked to a chair and I noticed he had a limp.

He said, 'I got that playing rugby football at Wadham College, Oxford. I think a South African player did it.' He laughed. 'Not on purpose, of course.'

He looked scholarly and at the same time aristocratic.

'Fiji is an aristocracy,' he presently said. 'Did you know that? And did you know that Fijians wept when the Union Jack came down in October 1970?'

I hadn't known. I was used, in Africa and Asia, to patronizing tales, not of tears at the sight of the sinking Union Jack, but of some 'liberation struggle' (real or invented) to account for 'freedom' from colonial bondage. Here, in 1874, Cakobau had asked his friend Queen Victoria to annex the islands, and ninety-six years later Queen Elizabeth had handed them back to the Fijians. It seemed a civilized way of doing things. No one had wanted to be seen to have scored off someone else. It was a consolation to hear that. But the Prime Minister was making another and more painful point.

'People here used to call the UK the "home country",' he said. 'We valued and trusted the values of the British.' I noticed the past tense. 'Now, we're losing a friend – a friend who no longer wants to be our friend.'

'I'm not sure I understand.'

'It's now become virtually impossible to send our young people to Britain. The British have made it too expensive. The British Government won't help our students with subsidies any more – the fees are impossible, unless you're a millionaire from Hong Kong. And,' he smiled, 'Australia and New Zealand are not the same.' He shook his handsome head.

'You know, we have Fijian troops in Lebanon and Sinai with the United Nations. It helps our young people get some discipline and training.'

Later, Don Diment showed me a report on a Fijian corporal who had won a Military Medal – a British award for gallantry.

At Wadi Jilu in South Lebanon, a Fiji Battalion post came under intense small arms, automatic and grenade fire from Lebanese National Movement men.... Savu hit in the leg ... refused to leave his post or have Medical Officer come to his aid.... Post surrounded.... Returned fire.... Terrorists give up. Corporal Savu displayed the highest sense of duty and personal bravery.

'Two thousand young people have been rotated through the Lebanon,' Ratu Mara said. 'They have matured very quickly there. You see, here' – he shook his head again – 'we have young ones here with ... problems.'

'Problems?'

'Dissatisfied. Unemployment. Drinking beer. We need jobs. Our university is churning out graduates, but unfortunately with no jobs our young people are emigrating to the United States, Canada and Australia.' He had just mentioned one universal problem of far-off, delectable places. Who these days, with a degree in electronics and business management in his pocket, would stay on a beautiful Pacific island dependent on tourism, copra and fishing? Armies of the world's young would go off, if they could, to where the flashy money is – to the suburbs of Los Angeles and Philadelphia, to where the 'upwardly mobile' people live. They would soon succumb to the Johnnie Carson Show, group psychiatry and God knows what else, and within a generation – perhaps less – they would have thrown away their mother language. And then they would no longer be Fijians....

'Once upon a time – it was a darker time, no doubt, in some ways, but not in all – the missionaries told us, "Don't do that. That's wrong. You'll never get to heaven that way." But, you see, we now know that some of the things the missionaries wanted banned were fine for our way of living.'

'Clothes –' I started to say.

'How ridiculous it is, this sickly world! The missionaires said, "Put on these clothes!" Now, it's the Europeans who come back as tourists half naked, topless.'

Tourists: the third Fatal Impact, I thought.

'We need tourists, of course. But we had two hundred thousand last year. We could double that figure, no doubt.'

'And will you?'

'Some people want to. But what would happen to us – we are only six hundred and fifty thousand Fijians. Hotel after hotel.... Would we all have to become waiters and cooks and disco operators?'

He had often, he said, pointed to Honolulu as a dire example of how vulnerable Pacific cultures can be swamped. 'Do we all want to become like Hawaii?' he had asked other South Pacific island leaders at a conference, and they had shuddered, shaking their heads.

Another South Sea preoccupation was the nuclear one. 'I told President Mitterand of France: "As long as you explode nuclear devices in the Pacific, no one here will want to have relations with you." Mitterand said, "Well, if you want a nuclear-free Pacific, stop the United States and the Soviet Union."'

I thought of the T-shirt motto I had seen in Honiara: '*Nuclear hem save killim iumi evriwan.*'

Shouts floated in through the open window: 'Fiji for the Fijians.' The Prime Minister smiled. 'Oh, Enoch Powell is those people's patron saint.' I understood just enough of Fiji's politics to know that Ratu Mara's ruling party was mostly Fijian, and that the main opposition party was largely Fijian-Indian. The 'Fiji for the Fijians' faction, shouting outside, was a tiny minority group. 'They say the Indians, who are just about a majority of our population now, are taking us over,' Ratu Mara said. 'But it's nonsense. Those people shouting are silly extremists. Nothing to worry about.'

At the gate a tall, dark soldier stood guard in a scarlet tunic and a kilt with a jagged hem. Perhaps he had been shot at by Arabs or Israelis in the murder grounds of Lebanon. What an irony that the once cannibal Fijians are now a respected part of an international force formed to restrain some of the most savage killers of our time – even if they do stop short of eating each other – who dwell in a region known as the 'cradle of western civilization'. A block away, on a large green school field, boys with fuzzy heads played football with Fijian boys who had the delicate features of India. Already the 'Fiji for Fijians' meeting was dispersing in small, laughing groups. The 'extremists' did not look very menacing. Strolling in the golden light passers-by said 'Good morning'.

Fiji seemed to have done well. After all, it was not much more than a hundred years since Cakobau had signed over these cannibal islands to Sir Hercules Robinson in Levuka, on that memorable day when lucky Mr Huon of HMS *Dido* won a billiard table in the celebration raffle.

It remained to say goodbye to Fritz Falkner of Carpenters Shipping, who had arranged my onward passage so switfly. He would be sending his man, John Wong, to the dockside when the *Tasi* sailed.

I exchanged addresses with Michael Scott, the obliging Sheriff of Fiji, and then there was little left to do but leave. I took one last look at the neat white capital, Suva. Beery Fijian voices and laughter came from the bar of the Central Hotel. On a bank wall a tourist poster said: 'Fiji ... The way the world should be'. A good slogan. Had Charlie Savage and the blackbirders, guffawing horribly, said the very same thing?

The *Tasi* lay alongside the wharf. A Soviet vessel – a trawler, a survey ship? – sprouting sinister antennae, nuzzled her from behind. On the *Tasi*'s deck, John Wong waved to me. A Tongan deckhand as big as a native hut lifted my metal suitcase onto his shoulder. I went aboard.

Nineteen

Jellyfish floated ghostly-white in the green, sunlit water below the reefs. On a path of reflected light too bright to look at the *Tasi* swung eastwards, past the turmoil of surf, past a rusty wreck tilted on a lump of coral like a cockeyed hat. The ridged mountains of Fiji began their steady retreat. When, after an hour or two, the sun had set into strips of dark blue cloud, the effect was as if a great bonfire had been lit behind the headlands of Viti Levu. It was an elementally dramatic departure.

So elementally dramatic, indeed, was the entire brief passage of the *Tasi* from Suva to Apia. I shall always recall it with a special affection. Later I read the words of R.L.S.: 'The first sunrise, the first South Sea island, are memories apart and touch a virginity of sense.' Samoa was, in a storybook way, my first South Sea island, and memory sets my approach to it apart. Partly because the fat, white little ship had a wonderfully comforting, matronly air about her, partly because her mountainous Tongan captain and his giant sailors were as good-hearted as any I have ever met – and partly because to be sailing from Fiji to Western Samoa in a Tongan ship seemed to me to be an idyllic state of affairs.

'*Tasi*, Nuku'alofa, Tonga' was written on the vessel's stern, but I could read her origins from a plaque: 'Kaldnes Mek. Verksted, 1966, Tonsberg, Norge' – so she was another Scandinavian vessel among the many to find their way to the South Seas. Bags of taro were stacked on her deck, marked: 'For Tonga. Cyclone relief from the American Embassy, Suva'.

Fijians are tall and big-boned – every Fijian I had seen seemed to be built to play American or rugby football – but Tongans, if the *Tasi*'s captain and crew were anything to go by, are big in a different way: big all round, verging on corpulent. In his way the captain reminded me of a very genial Japanese sumo wrestler.

'We will be happy to take you,' he said, beaming. 'Everyone here will be happy with you! They like to talk.' He wore a 'Hawaiian' shirt of delicate sea-blues and sea-greens, pinks and yellows, over a long, light blue kilt: a many-splendoured Buddha with close-cropped white hair and eyes that, when he smiled, were pinched up Mongol-fashion by his billowing cheeks.

The second officer, Etuate Lemoto – I read his name from the crew list – had moved in with the third mate so that I could use his cabin, and this worried me until he said, 'Oh, never mind. I'm okay. Pleasure,' with such a cheerful expression that I slept almost without guilt for having stolen his bunk. While the *Tasi* moved across the Koro Sea, aimed for Nanuku Passage through the eastern reefs, leaving Bligh Water, Ovalu Island and old Levuka behind us, choirs of Tongans brought me the first words of Tongan I had heard: the sort of sound an Arabian dove would make, a rather guttural cooing. Tongan music from radios in the saloon or on the bridge was an almost permanent feature of life on the *Tasi*: electric guitars and soft, singing voices, languid or lively, filled the ship. A lot of the music had a religious ring. I remembered the hymns in the streets of Rabaul. Tongans are very religious people, the captain explained: half of them Catholic, half of them Methodists.

As he had said, Tongans like to talk. He was no exception. At our first meal of fried eggs, spaghetti, sliced tomatoes, toast and tea I learnt that he was himself related to the Tongan royal family, and a number of other things.

'You won't be able to say my name,' he laughed. 'It is Polonga Tau'alupe. So, I have written it out for you.' He handed me a small, oblong piece of paper with his name and address on it: such-and-such a town, Tonga Tapu Islands, South-West Pacific Ocean. He talked of his mother – how she had killed a giant octopus that had grabbed a girl and was holding her anchored to a reef while the tide came in. His mother had told the screaming girl to keep still, felt about for the middle of the octopus – the captain felt about his own ample tummy with a forefinger – and stabbed it with a spear 'all the way in'; here he jabbed an imaginary spear into a gap in his shirt where a button had given way to reveal billowing flesh. The stricken octopus had released the girl and had died quite soon, but it was a monster, so big, so heavy that no one could pull it into the boat; they'd had to tow it home. 'So big,' the captain shook his head in disbelief at the very memory of it. 'So big. Oh, jeez. You remember Queen Salote, perhaps,' he said. 'The mother of our King.'

'I saw her riding in a coach at the coronation of Queen Elizabeth,' I replied. No one who saw her would forget the hugely regal figure of Queen Salote, six foot if she was an inch, bravely smiling and waving to the crowds from her open carriage, utterly undaunted by the cascading rain that must have reminded her of a Pacific typhoon. That day Queen Salote had been the best loved foreigner in London. She had put Tonga on the map for several million Britons. If a last-minute miracle had dictated a double coronation of Queen Elizabeth and Queen Salote, applauding British mobs would have borne her joyfully to Westminster Abbey.

'I sailed with Queen Salote round the islands of Tonga,' Captain Tau'alupe said, greatly pleased by what I had told him. 'Then we tied up at Nuku'alofa, our capital and port, where to do so was forbidden from one hour before sunset and one hour after sunrise. Silly regulations. "Okay," the Prime Minister told me. "Stay alongside all night." But the police chief came down furious – saying "What! Go out of here and anchor! Outside! Not alongside!" ' The captain beamed. 'But, going a mile out to anchor is expensive. So I said, "I cannot move unless the agent tells me." So the police chief goes to Queen Salote. And *she* says, "You have to ask the PM about dis. I have nothing to do wid ships' movements." So he goes to the PM and the PM says, "Oh, dis ship has a very big freezer and I need dis freezer for my own use in dis night." It was very hot, you see.'

The captain crammed toast into his mouth and came near to choking with laughter. 'So, the police chief – dis is true, mind! – went back to Queen Salote and told her about dis freezer. "Well," said Queen Salote. "It is true, the PM is a very big and fat man. It is hard for him to breathe in hot weather like dis. I am sure he needs the things from de freezer, like ice and so and so. He may die without them. If he dies, you...." And she just look at him. So we stay alongside. Queen Salote was a very sensible lady.'

Later the third officer said, 'When I was in primary school, I'd heard of this captain.'

'He's famous in Tonga?'

'Oh, yes. He comes from the same island as the King.'

After dark, the captain joined me on the bridge wing. Four-square in sandals and an ankle-length kilt, he was like – although I need hardly say there was nothing effeminate about him – one of those hearty, good-natured ladies who play bowls in English seaside resorts, or a very trustworthy nanny.

'I want to see the ship through these islands,' he said. 'Fiji captains have put at least ten ships on the reefs here.' He grinned. 'Fiji people never did sail far in the old times. Tongans are more used to that. Samoans, too. And Gilbertese, yes.'

Just then the third officer bounded up with extraordinary news. An Australian radio station had just reported that a big British fleet had left Portsmouth for the South Atlantic. It was heading for the Falklands: a powerful task force with two aircraft carriers, troops – marines and Gurkhas – even the *QE II* had been called up.

I was stunned. Absorbed in my own wanderings, I had missed what I only caught up with much later – the growing political and naval drama that started with the invasion of the Falkland Islands by the Argentines. I suddenly realized I had heard no world news since leaving Hong Kong – at least nothing had registered in my mind as out of the way. Nor had I felt any sense of loss. On the contrary, I felt this world was what mattered. Everything else was unreal. Now, as we moved under the bright eye of the planet Mars towards the international date line, Britain was about to go into battle against Argentina.

Captain Tau'alupe had followed the crisis from the beginning, and he had made up his mind about its rights and wrongs. 'I hope de British will shoot dese people out of de islands,' he said fiercely. 'What are they doing, de Argentines, invading and occupying de islands? Dese days, de correct thing is to talk about all dat, peacefully. In a *civilized* way!

'I'd like to be de commander of a battleship,' he said, quite angrily. 'Then I'd go to dat war.'

'Take the *Tasi*. As a hospital ship.'

'Ha! As a target ship, more likely. Too slow and wide.'

Suddenly I couldn't help thinking: if there are naval battles near Argentina and the Falklands, how on earth will I manage to find a ship to take me round the Horn? Apart from shells and missiles there might be mines. I might be blocked there for weeks – in the Chilean midwinter, too; I had worked that out. Of course, there was time enough for the crisis to develop and fade away. It might be all over by the time I arrived there. I wouldn't let it worry me now. But still.... A cloud as big as a man's hand settled on my mental horizon from now on.

Dinner on the *Tasi* demanded stamina – it matched in weight the men who sat down to it: a chillied stew, mashed potatoes and breadfruit, three chunks of it to each man. How they could eat so much of it, God knows. I find breadfruit quite edible but dull and uncomfortably filling. The stew was heavy, too, and I gulped mouthfuls of black tea to wash down the chunks of unchewable meat like logs over a shallow waterfall. It was a miracle that I avoided falling dead of asphyxia at the captain's ample feet. Recovering in my cabin, I mopped my face, took deep gulps of warm air and finally composed myself to open the *Vailima Letters*. I found Mr Stevenson finishing *The Wrecker* and commenting on it:

> ... a good yarn on the whole ... a long tough yarn with some pictures of the manner of today in the greater world – not the shoddy sham world of cities, clubs and colleges, but the world where men still live a man's life.... As for wars and rumours of wars, you must surely know enough of me to be aware that I like that also a thousand times better than decrepit peace in Middlesex? I do not quite like politics ... to sue and sneak to keep a crowd together – never....

The increasing nearness of Western Samoa began to affect me palpably. Despite an open porthole, I felt a film of sweat on my back and chest. Though the night air on the bridge was cool and fresh, below by day it was uncomfortably stuffy. 'Samoa is hotter than Tonga,' Etuate Lemoto said in explanation. 'Apia is only 14 degrees south of the equator. Nuku'alofa is 21 degrees south.'

Samoan heat ('It suits me and all our family, others it does not suit at all. It is either gold or poison.') had not slowed up Stevenson's literary production. In the letters, I found him (after only a month's writing) fifteen chapters into *David Balfour* (later to become *Catriona*), and complaining, 'What makes me sick is to think of Scott turning out *Guy Mannering* in three weeks! ... Heavens what thews and sinews!' Even so – and this was the year before his fatal cerebral haemorrhage – R. L. S., thin and sickly, could go five hard hours in the saddle and come home, sopping wet, like a schoolboy, 'with such a lightness of spirits, and such a brightness of eye, as you could have lit a candle at!' It was as much as I could do to keep up my note-taking – although this was more to do with the agitating excitement of the approach to Samoa – and Vailima – than with the soggy heat.

From these notes I read:

We sight some volcanic islands to starboard – the Niua Fo'ou

Islands. We are approaching two important points, according to Etuate Lemoto: 'First, we pass my island – very remote, halfway between Tonga and Samoa, called Niuataputapu. You can't pronounce it. We should pass it without seeing it – too far. Second, we pass the international date line. We cannot see that, too.' The international date line is due to make a change to my life this evening: because I am eastward-bound I gain an extra day. We shall put our clocks on one hour. Then we shall put them *back* a whole day, and we'll have two Wednesdays. I look forward to comparing my first Wednesday with my second! (I have often thought of crossing the line the other way – i.e. *losing* a day of my life. Later, a policeman would say to me *à propos* some nameless crime, 'And what were you doing on Wednesday, 7 April?' And me, I would be able to reply, 'Nothing at all, officer. For me that date simply did not exist.' (At that point, I suppose, I would be arrested for contempt.)

I expect some mark on the surface of the sea. The captain: 'What I cannot understand is why the IDL is not straight. Tonga should be to the east of the line, but a zigzag leaves it in the west.' No one on the *Tasi* knows why.

Once more, I notice that the *Tasi* is a floating music box, as full of music as the island in *The Tempest* was full of noises. Just now I heard 'Abide with Me', beautifully sung, with whistled accompaniment from the third officer. Radio Tonga's news bulletins are heralded by a furious, warlike pounding of drums – particularly appropriate and dramatic when it is the prelude to the latest report of the southward advance of the British task force....

Good Captain Polonga Tau'alupe was a great one for making young officers learn their stars and use their sextants. He got them onto the bridge wing and waved his wrestler's arms as if conducting the music of the heavens. Never depend on satellites and giros and radar, he said: they can all go wrong. The most important thing on a ship is the magnetic compass. He showed me the Southern Cross, which I had failed to recognize so far. It was not spectacular like, say, the Great Bear. It was like a very simple, and so beautiful, necklace – an unpretentious, diamond-shaped, four-star group with two pendant tail stars. Once I had seen it, I knew I should never mistake it again.

'My mother took me sailing in de islands of Tonga,' he said, 'and she would suddenly stop and say to me – "Ha! Do you smell dat? What is it?" I'd say, "Oh, what smell is dat?" And she'd say, "Stop. Breathe it in. What do you smell now?"'

'And did you really smell anything?' I asked.

'Ooh, yes. A smell like smoke. "Ah," my mother said, "that means we'll have rain. Very heavy rain is coming this evening." And – wheeeee! – very, very heavy rain came down dat very evening. Jeez.'

'Is that superstition?'

The captain was scornful. 'Superstition, no-oo-oo. My father says, "Listen to me, you know if leaves fall in de water, and lie dere and die, dere is a special smell? Do you know dat?" And he tells me dat means a terrific wind comes later on. No superstition. Fact.' He turned his nose to the wind, and seemed to be sniffing out a storm then and there. 'I teach all my young officers. To *smell* de weather. To *feel* de wind. To *see* de water.'

He looked at me and nodded in time to his words. 'Smell. Feel. See.'

*   *   *

The third officer came cantering down to us as I was drinking breakfast tea with the captain. 'There's whales,' he cried from the saloon door (pronouncing it 'whal-es'), 'if you want to see.' Whales or whalers? Whales. I shot a mugful of hot tea across the table in my rush to the companionway. Puffs of white spray shot up over the perfect blue of the water. Then a black back or two heaved up; then another; then three black, low islands, rising and falling a hundred yards away. My first whales – I hope not my last. I was surprised they hadn't heard our engines and taken fright. These days Jap and Russian whalers infest the Pacific. No wonder whales are dying out if they won't run from such relentless but noisy predators. I felt quite irritated with these heedless mammals.

The Tongans are proud of their whalelike size in a way I found touching. 'Have you been to Indonesia?' Captain Tau'alupe asked, and went on: 'One day a Norwegian captain told me, "In Macassar, Indonesia port, always must give customs men cigarettes. They come on board, six or seven officers, and will not clear the ship unless you give carton, one to each man." I say, "Oh? We see." So we go into Macassar. The customs officers come aboard.'

He laughed – a good joke was coming. 'I say to them, "Okay, here is de crew list and de stores list." "Captain," dey say, "you have cigarettes?" I take out cigarettes and give one packet to every officer. "Oh!" dey say – "but, captain, one carton each, please. We are heavy smokers." I say, "If you do not like de packets, I throw dem over de side. Then you clear de ship."'

'You're a brave man,' I said, thinking how dangerous seven furious Indonesians grinding their teeth could be.

'Tongans *are* brave,' he agreed with a smile. 'And dese officers *are* surprised. So I explain. "Look," I say. "We are Tongans. We are not Filipinos."' How indignant Sonny-Sebastiano-Sonngen III of the *Chengtu* would have been to hear that, I thought. '"And we are not Europeans with many stores." "Oh? Oh?" they say, like dat. I say, "No, we are like you, except we are very *big* and you are very *small*. One Tongan," I say, "can pick up twenty Indonesians."'

I said I knew something of the people of Celebes round Macassar; they were fiery-tempered. That was putting it mildly, in fact. What on earth...?

'Well, dey cleared de ship,' the captain said, indifferently. 'Very quick. And den dey say, "Your men should go ashore two-by-two, or three-by-three. Our young men will sometimes take on foreign seamen ashore – sometimes with knives. Yes, with knives."'

'I hope you took their advice,' I said, 'to be careful.'

'Oh – our men went ashore all de time one-by-one. Not afraid.' He made a ballooning motion with his arms. 'So big. Tongans are not afraid to go ashore one-by-one.' Well, it was true it would take an exceedingly long, sharp knife to penetrate a Tongan to any depth. But Tongans did have a serious Achilles heel, the captain admitted. Alcohol. He allowed no beer aboard his ships. 'If they have one beer, they cannot stop.' He tut-tutted sadly, telling me of the Fijian women and children he'd seen waiting outside bars in Suva on pay nights for their man to spend all his money on beer.

The second evening's sunset was as fine as the first – no, finer. I had put down the *Vailima Letters* and gone onto the bridge wing. One memory from the Pacific that is embedded in my mind for ever is what I saw then – a massive bank of cloud that had reared up over us: towers of cloud, swelling mountains of orange, pink and silver on the western horizon. How can you estimate the size of clouds like these? We were dwarfed utterly. The sun's rays shot out of the immense, solid-looking continent of vapour in great glowing shafts of light. Stevenson (I found the letter later) put his finger on it: 'O what aweful scenery, from a ship's deck, in the tropics! People talk about the Alps, but the clouds of the trade winds are alone in sublimity.' He talked of a cloudtop flamed in sunlight enlightening all the world. 'It must have been much higher than Mount Everest. . . . A thing to worship.' As I watched, a member of the crew came up, scraped some chicken bones from a plate over the side, looked up and said to me, 'What an art, eh?' referring to the miracle above us.

Presently, the sky was doubly worthy of worship. Darkness was gathering fast. Behind us, the sun had sunk below the horizon yet still threw splashes of fire across the very tips of the cloud banks, and now the near-full moon rose, scattering its quite different light, giving the sea a queer, pink, flat look, like gently undulating swathes of Oriental brocade.

In the midst of these unearthly lights of sunset and moonrise on sky and sea, the *Tasi* crossed the date line from one Wednesday to another. How can I forget that evening? How could Tongans ever *not* have worshipped the god of such sunsets and such moons? Now, indeed, several Tongans came up from below to point at the glory overhead, laughing and chattering among themselves. And slowly, the character of the beauty changed. Deep darkness succeeded the sun. The Southern Cross, Jupiter and Mars threw their own reflections in the water, and the rising moon, so harshly bright I could not look at it directly, hung like the glittering disc of a kite, its reflection wavering on the ocean like a fluttering tail of pure silver. I made my way to the *Tasi*'s bows. Everything was white. I put out a hand and saw the hand of a leper. White moonlight seemed to have covered the winches, the anchor chain, coils of rope, the ship's mast and rail with a layer of snow. Fragments of silver glinted on the waves, and for a moment I thought the sea was full of the natural phosphorous blobs that bejewel the shallow night-time seas of Java and Borneo; but it was the moon's broken reflection winking on small, abrupt upheavals of water.

I lived an idyll that night and the following dawn as the *Tasi* approached the two islands of Western Samoa. What more could I have desired, with that sky above us and then, slowly and darkly rising from the water, the dim shapes of those so-long-imagined Samoan mountains. We should reach the little port of Apia at about dawn, the captain said – the best time to reach anywhere. 'I hope dere is no ship sitting in de wharf at Apia. Den we can go straight in.'

Any thought of the British task force in the Atlantic had vanished from my mind, banished by my reading more of R.L.S.

On the Mountain, Apia, Samoa, November 2nd, 1890

My dear Colvin,
   This is a hard and interesting and beautiful life that we lead now. Our place is in a deep cleft of Vaea Mountain, some six hundred feet above the sea, embowered in forest, which is our rangling enemy, and which we combat with axes and dollars. . . .

I sprang up, restless, and wandered down to the saloon. An obliging steward gave me ice from a fridge quite empty except for a strange smell and two small dishes of butter. Over a whisky or two, I looked up Somerset Maugham's story *The Pool*: 'He liked Apia straggling along the edge of the lagoon, with its stores and bungalows, and its native village....' Then I slept, on the brink of fulfilling one more dream; as excited as a child on Christmas morning.

At 2.40 a.m. we could see the dark hump of Savaii Island to port, the sleeping turtle of Samoan legend. A light flashed on the pinprick islet of Apolima. The sea was calm, the stars still hard and bright; the Southern Cross was lying on its side now, with its tail horizontally behind it like a flying silver arrow. But when I next came up on deck, at 0600, the lights of Apia were advancing low on the water; the stars had become faint and watery, and the moon, palely orange, was sinking to extinction. Over the eastern silhouette of Upolu Island towered indigo domes of cloud, and strips of gold, fiery orange and blue shot up like the trails of unimaginable rockets. The Tongans once more came up on deck to watch the celestial fireworks as if they were aweful portents. Perhaps poor, suffering 'Lou' Stevenson, arriving here, had taken one such Samoan sky as a heavenly sign that this would be his last resting place. Perhaps the world would end with 'something to worship', like this.

We stopped outside the white waves along the reef. Captain Tau'alupe peered through the early morning haze. He looked more hugely nanny-like than ever in his kilt and a white shirt with scarlet hibiscus flowers on it, holding a mug of tea. Almost at once a voice on the radio said, 'All right, you can come in.' We moved slowly through the turbulent line of waves that enfolded the lagoon.

A woolly ridge, before it a hill (was that Mount Vaea?). A scattering of low, colonial-style buildings; white church towers; several large, spreading trees; a wharf. Now the sun was up, sending a warm wash of light across the little horseshoe bay. We slid gently alongside the wharf, not a bump, not a scrape. The ropes snaked down.

Captain Tau'alupe took my hand at the head of the gangway. 'Come to Tonga,' he said. 'You have my address. Christmas time it is very amusing. Lots of choirs in de streets and brass bands.' A jolly Tongan brass band was playing at that moment on the *Tasi*'s radio – the last few bars of 'Rule Britannia' and then 'Sussex by the Sea'.

And when you go to Sussex –
Whoever you may be –
You may tell them all that we stand or fall
For Sussex-by-the-Sea!

Twenty

A land
In which it seemed always afternoon.

Alfred, Lord Tennyson: 'The Lotos-Eaters'

Henry Betham, the shipping manager of Burns Philp in Apia, said, 'The *Pacific Islander*. Oh, yes. She's due in here in a week or so. Let's see — she's got a Japanese captain now.'

The *Pacific Islander* was the Swire container ship I had looked up in Suva. I hoped she would get me to Tahiti. Was there a new policy at Swire's China Navigation Company to employ Japanese officers — something to do with placating Nippon? It seemed unlikely.

'I don't think that can be right,' I said.

Henry, a large friendly man, checked his files again. 'No, sorry. It's Captain Carter now. It *was* Captain Ralph Kennet.'

'I know Ralph Kennet.' A couple of years before I had sailed with him from Manila to Hong Kong on another Swire vessel, the *Hupeh*.

Betham smiled. 'Well, you've got a week or so before Captain Carter gets here.' Time enough to pay my respects to R.L.S. and see something of Samoa, too.

I walked up the few steps into a two-storey white wooden building that seemed the perfect entrance to a Samoan hotel, and found a large Samoan lady behind a counter.

'Aggie Grey?' I asked, and she shook with throaty laughter as if she had never heard anything so funny.

'Not Aggie. I'm Annie,' she said. 'Call me Big Annie, dear.' She had a room for me — 'Of course, dear' — in the garden.

Aggie Grey's Hotel stood a few hundred yards from the wharf, ideally situated with a wide view over the little bay of Apia — a famous hotel, Michael Scott had told me, owned by a handsome South Seas 'personality'. Some people thought Aggie Grey was the original of the character James Michener called Bloody Mary in the Rodgers and

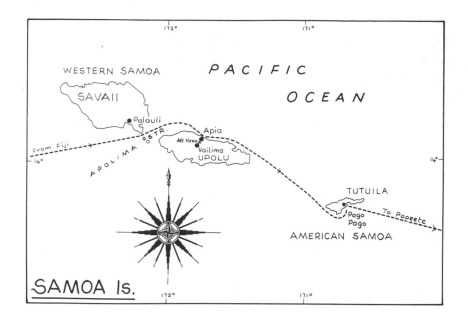

Hammerstein musical *South Pacific*. It seemed she was in New Zealand. Her son, Alan, and his wife were in charge.

There was a book about Aggie Grey on sale in the lobby and I took a copy to my room. It told the story, the blurb said, of 'how Aggie rose to fame from selling hamburgers at her rollicking waterfront club to owning a mighty tourist complex in the South Seas'.

A mighty tourist complex? When I took a stroll I found a pleasant tangled garden and thatched-roofed guest rooms: no mighty tourist complex at all. In an open-sided bar a few tourists quietly sat over beer, and presently the sound of singing led me to a beehive-shaped thatched building where a group of young men and women in lava-lavas were rehearsing native dances, stamping and chanting with flowers in their hair.

My first Samoans were quite different from the Solomon Islanders or Fijians—no one here had a busby like Colson's, or a Papuan gargoyle face. These Polynesians had straight hair, black or dark brown, skins that were fair and faces that were almost Malaysian.

Somerset Maugham, Stevenson and Rupert Brooke had all extolled the glory of the Samoans, sometimes in such extravagant terms that one suspected poetic exaggeration. 'God's best, his sweetest work,' Stevenson had written. And now, watching these unself-conscious dancers, I knew there had been no exaggeration at all.

Aggie Grey's Hotel commanded one end of Apia's horseshoe bay, while Burns Philp's emporium and office, with Henry Betham in it, stood at the other end. In between were stores, a church or two with off-white towers, a bank, and a modest complex of wooden verandahs which, a sign said, housed government offices, including the office of the Prime Minister. There can hardly be a more self-effacing Prime Minister's office in the world. Modern Apia, it was evident, had mercifully escaped the ravages of 'progressive' architects, and was still a small town. I had no difficulty in imagining the little trading station Stevenson saw in 1889 when he disembarked from his schooner, the *Equator*, and took his first brisk exploratory ramble, looking, one of Apia's merchants said later, 'like a lascar out of employment'. The emaciated writer and his family – possibly because his stepson, Lloyd Osborne, chose to wear earrings and dark glasses and carry a ukelele – were taken by the chief Anglican missionary for a troupe of scallywag vaudevillians from San Francisco. Who else, he wondered, could they be?

Stevenson's house at Vailima was still standing and his grave was now a place of pilgrimage, so it took an effort to remember that when he came here no one in this Pacific backwater had heard of Robert Louis Stevenson. Who among the German, American and British traders and plantation managers had opened any book other than a ledger or a shipping timetable? Anyway, it was the Samoans who gave him the name Tusitala, the Teller of Tales. Now he was a tourist attraction. Exploring beyond the centre of the town, I found a looming block of masonry built in the sixties or seventies with a sign which said it was the Tusitala Hotel, and its bar stocked Vailima beer.

In Aggie Grey's breakfast room next morning the young Samoan dancers of the day before had become smiling servants, but there were few customers. A Samoan and his jolly wife (between them they must have weighed a ton) bolted papayas and eggs and bacon and beamed around them. A sallow young white man in stained shorts blocked conversation from a pallid girl with two unvarying replies – 'No way' or 'Not likely' – while he gave an American student hints on how to travel round Samoa cadging off the natives. 'Just leave quick when they begin to look less hospitable,' he said with a snigger.

I consulted Big Annie, bought a map and a Samoan dictionary, hired a car from a European garage and headed east in it along the shore.

After two or three miles I pulled up by the roadside with a thumping heart. Of course, I had expected the magnificent, violent blue of the Pacific, beaches of pure white sand and graceful colonnades of tow-headed palm trees – all that was a common natural combination in the South Seas. Yet here it was only part of a much greater beauty.

Beehive houses, somnolent under their sunbaked thatch and raised on platforms of stones, appeared to float in a sea of brilliant foliage, their mat walls rolled up now to catch the sea breeze so that whole families were visible, sitting cross-legged, chatting and smoking, or gazing silently across the lagoon at the white tumble of foam on the reefs. Barefoot men, elegant from waist to calf in bright-coloured lava-lavas that no Paris fashion designer could improve on, and women with parasols and flower-patterned skirts, strolled on the road's edge with the upright yet languorous grace that only people who walk barefoot can achieve. Village after roadside village basked serenely in the sunlight behind glistening screens of breadfruit, papaya and banana trees, frangipani, hibiscus and hedges of flowers whose names I do not know. On my map I read their soft, lilting names – Lauli'i, Salelesi, Vailele, Lufilufi. I moved on. Soon, a bumpy red-dust track swung inland, and I slowly climbed into a different world of scrub and upland trees. Villages and resplendent flowers disappeared, the sea was only visible in snatches from sharp turns along the way, and wisps of mist like an old man's beard rose from slopes of green mountains that looked two thousand feet high.

I had bumped along for perhaps an hour when I saw a house by the track. There had already been a few houses along the way, but they had been set well back, half hidden in the bush. This particular shaggy little roof lay near the road from which an apron of coral chips and flowering bushes ran up to it. A chestnut horse was hobbled by the doorposts. Behind the thatch, blue smoke rose from an open fire. I had slowed down and somebody waved. I stopped and got out of the car and a teenage girl in a lava-lava with a flower in her hair ran out of the house towards me, framed by the flowers and clouds of tiny blue butterflies.

'*Talofa*,' she said, smiling, and then unexpectedly in English, 'Will you have some food?' Her large eyes tilted up from a small, slightly flattened nose. 'My name is Emma,' she added as two women, one of them grey-haired, the other old enough to be Emma's mother, ducked out of the house, followed by a boy of eleven or twelve. A larger boy, perhaps seventeen, evidently Emma's brother, came towards the car from the bushes. 'This,' Emma patted the smaller of the two boys on the head, 'is Isaia. This is Manino.' She pointed to her mother.

The bigger boy patted his own bare chest. 'Fili,' he said. Within a minute I had been conscripted into Tolu's boisterous family.

The simplicity of the house on the empty track and Emma's wave among the flowers were the reasons for my coming to Tolu's house and my 'adoption' into his family. Not that I knew Tolu at that moment. Now I was answering five excited voices at once. 'Where are you going?'

'Just to the end of the island,' I said.

'We show you. Come!'

I hardly had time to get the doors open before Emma, Fili and Isaia dived into the car.

I had wanted to meet Samoans – well, here they were.

The eastern beaches of Samoa are everybody's dream of the *Blue Lagoon*. The one my new friends preferred looked across its inevitable reef to a green pimple in the sea, a miniature Treasure Island, it seemed, where with Captain Flint's map and a bucket and spade you could find pieces of eight in a dead man's chest. Instead, I sat quietly with Emma on sand like caster sugar while the boys splashed and screamed in turquoise water so curiously bright it looked as if it was lit artificially from below. On the way, we had discovered a family friend, Amosa, clinging halfway up an eighty-foot palm tree; his athletic descent in response to Fili's call was so immediate that he might have been waiting to join us all his life. He and Fili were in the water in a flash of limbs.

'Fili ... ooo!'

'Amo-o-o-sa!'

Their shouts were like seabirds soaring from the lagoon or Ben Gunn's demented yodelling from the island opposite. While they played I talked of prosaic things to Emma. 'You go to school?'

Yes, she went to Lufilufi school, she said. And she was nineteen years old.

'You have a boyfriend in Lufilufi?'

'Oh, yes.' She smiled, not at all minding the question.

'You marry soon?'

She laughed. 'Oh, no.' She preferred to go to New Zealand, find work there and send money home.

230

'Why not work here?' Perhaps teaching English. Her English was quite good enough.

'Oh....'

Opposite us, the frigate-sized outcrop of Treasure Island waved its topknot of palms. Terns sideslipped in the breeze on wings that flashed like fragments of white porcelain.

'I like to see New Zealand,' said Emma. 'Then I can send money to my father. For his plantation.

Tolu, the head of my new family, came home just before sunset and was astonished to see me. He was of medium height, stocky, with a fair paunch and a navel like the boss on a bronze breastplate. He carried a bush knife in his large and calloused hands; he had been working in his gardens, he said. The bones of his face showed that it had once been square, but a strong jaw had now become heavy and round. For about two inches above the waist of his lava-lava his skin seemed to be covered with terrible bruises, but on a closer look I saw that the 'bruises' were an elaborate tattoo encircling his body like a corset. He was pleased at my interest and drew up the hem of his lava-lava to show me how the tattoo extended round his thighs and down to his knees. The complicated dark blue patterns were densely, and no doubt painfully, pricked into his skin.

Tolu was proud of his tattoo: it conveyed noble status. '*Matei*,' he explained, pointing to himself: 'Chief.' The *South Pacific Handbook* had told me that Samoan society is based on its ten thousand chiefs, the guardians of the *fa'a Samoa*, the Samoan way of life, who elect the forty-five-member National Assembly of Chiefs in Apia. Chiefs control local affairs through the islands' village councils. Tattooing was part of *fa'a Samoa* but unfortunately it was dying out, Tolu said. I asked Fili why he was not tattooed, offering to pay for one for him, but he made a face and shook his head.

'Fili scared,' said Emma to tease him. 'Hurt too much.'

It was not easy to explain to them exactly what I was up to, but with the help of my Samoan dictionary and Emma I managed at last to convey what had brought me here and how soon I had to leave, indicating sea by holding a forearm and hand parallel to the ground and undulating it. In return I learnt that Tolu, though not rich (the little house told me that), owned land down the long, steep hillside out of sight of his original village by the sea. He and Fili worked a plantation of three thousand taro plants, yams, papayas, sugar, bananas and a good many coconut palms. They had cows, too, and chickens, a dog and the one chestnut horse, which was the family's sole means of transport. Nobody in Western Samoa starved: nearly all Samoans owned a 'plantation' of some size, even if some owned it indirectly through their membership of an extended family. But they had to work it. You could not let plantations go.

We sat cross-legged on woven mats, leaning against the pillars supporting the lozenge-shaped roof of sugar leaves and palm fronds. The walls consisted of adjustable panels made from woven coconut leaves, that were hoisted up and down like homespun Venetian blinds. The panels were rolled up when it was fine, so everyone and everything in the house was visible to passers-by. Not that there was much to see: a few large trunks; a plain wooden dresser full of cups, teapots and metal dishes; a deep wooden chest stuffed with schoolbooks, the family Bible, assorted clothes. Newly washed lava-lavas hung over poles in the ceiling. Meals were cooked under a separate roof behind the main house. Most dishes, I noticed, were wrapped in leaves and baked on hot stones.

After dark, when dinner was ready, Manino, with Emma and two smaller daughters, Ruta and Ala, brought in bowls of baked fish and taro spread with coconut cream and laid them on banana leaf 'plates'. Tolu murmured a prayer in Samoan, while Fili and Amosa made faces at me – I took this to mean we were now all friends together – and then we dug into the food with our fingers. The taro – a fibrous root vegetable about the size of a pineapple and the Samoan equivalent of bread – was cut into round slices as chewable as a rich fruitcake but with a dull, neutral taste; it was better dipped into coconut cream and sucked like a lollipop. Tolu sucked each fishbone, too, loudly and with great care, before spitting it into his hand. Any food that spilled onto the mat-covered floor was cleaned up by two furtive cats that cleverly dodged slaps from Fili and ignored Isaia's whispers of 'Pussi, pussi.'

A humid heat lingered long after the sun had gone down in a blaze behind the forest and the last fruit bats had flapped heavily home. Flying insects were the problem. Throughout the meal they did their best to disrupt us. Smack! Smack! The family slapped arms, legs and bare torsos as swarms of indefatigable mosquitoes sniped at us like highly trained hit-and-run guerrillas. Struggling with fishbones, I could see these 'winged blood-drops' placidly grazing on my vulnerable arms and feet and feel needlelike bites on my neck and forehead. They crawled boldly into one's ears. It was difficult to eat and just as hard to relax later; the teasing, remorseless whine continued long after the dishes had been cleared away and even after the side walls of the house had been lowered for the night. Fili covered my feet with a spare lava-lava and Isaia squatted down by me and began flapping a leaf-shaped woven fan round my ears, but I wondered how I was going to sleep. Stevenson hardly mentions the mosquitoes at Vailima, yet they must have been a nightmare for a writer with no insecticide and little or no window netting. Had he forgotten this little bit of hell in paradise? With the moon, a cool breeze came like a blessing and Tolu yawned, evidently a signal for Fili and Amosa to drag up mattresses and pillows. 'You sleep here,' Fili said, patting a mattress by his own. This was luxury. I had expected to sleep on the bare mat. More than that, there were to be some anti-mosquito measures: Amosa unfurled three huge nets over the mattresses and soon, at long last, the infernal whining died away and I saw some possibility of sleep. I heard the muffled shifting of springs: Isaia had begged to be allowed to guard the car and had curled up in the back seat. Then Amosa went home, murmuring '*Tofa*.'

''*Fa*, Amosa.'

When Tolu lowered the flame in the pressure lamp, the mosquito nets seemed to swell in the dark and fill the little house like three white phantoms. In the silence, like a hundred sewing machines, the cicada chorus began in the undergrowth outside. The chestnut horse, tethered to a banana tree, blew now and again and stamped a hoof. A dog barked on the hillside.

'Gavin stay one week,' Emma called in the darkness.

'Gavin stay one year,' Fili said.

'Gavin stay,' Tolu gruffly told his family, cutting the talking short.

I watched moonlight seeping through the wall blinds and listened to the night. The breeze rapped the bamboos; a nightjar chuckled behind the house.

'I stay,' I said, giving in to the Samoan night. To them all.

Twenty one

The early morning was as cool and fresh as if Samoa had been created that very sunrise. Dew gleamed on each banana leaf, on every blade of grass, on every hibiscus blossom and gardenia. The smoke of Manino's fire hung motionless round her kitchen like a blue horizontal screen, giving out the smell of roasting cocoa beans. I had roused Isaia from the car by tickling his feet, and he held a bowl of water as I cleaned my teeth hear a clump of sugarcane. Fili hacked firewood and soon Amosa strolled up, his nose deep in the petals of a gardenia.

'*Talofa*, Gavin.'

'*Talofa*, Amosa.'

With Fili and Amosa, I pushed through thick bush to a deep, stony cleft where water ran so cold that the first plunge took my breath away. The two Samoans, apparently unaffected, splashed and laughed, warmed by a halo of sun. Stevenson had written of such scenes. In his time, not so very long ago, war drums had sounded on this very hillside, and warriors had raced home through these trees from battles, waving the heads of their enemies and crying excitedly to their chiefs, 'I have taken a man!' It was easy to imagine those days of severed heads in this hidden, untouched place where the great trees, scores of years old, trailed feathery creepers like hairy arms. Amosa and Fili conversed in high-pitched cries like bird calls, and their singing was falsetto, too. On our way back to Tolu and with the house in sight, I was suddenly alone – they had taken off like a brace of excited snipe, racing through a field of waist-high taro plants, zigzagging through the upturned, heart-shaped leaves which swayed out of their path like an army of green, flat-faced extra-terrestrial beings taken by surprise. Amosa, with his gardenia in his hand, his yellow lava-lava, his brown limbs and his streaming hair, might easily have been some wood demon spirit of the place celebrating another fine day.

Samoan superstition peoples the island with spirits. Belief in ghosts runs in the blood, and where a people speak of ghosts the phantoms tend to respond. Known in Samoa as *aitus*, they dwell in every tree and stream, as *jinns* live in the hills and groves of Arabia. According to local tradition Apia is a sort of spirits' transit camp, a seaside springboard from which they launch themselves into *Pulotu*, the Other World. Stevenson wrote that he had an *aitu* for a neighbour at Vailima – 'It is a lady, *Aitu fafine*: she lives in the mountainside; her presence is heralded by the sound of a gust of wind, a sound very common in the high woods; when she catches you, I do not know what happens; but in practice she is avoided, so I suppose she does more than pass the time of day.'

Little Isaia shared Amosa's puckish quality. He frisked about in as sprightly a way as any child I have ever met.

I tapped his nose very gently with my finger. 'You...are...an...*aitu*!'

'*Aitu!*' – delighted, Isaia ran hysterically around Tolu's banana patch, scattering the chickens.

'*Aitu!*' Emma screamed.

I saw Manino laughing behind her cooking pots, and Tolu, too, called, 'Isaia is *aitu*.'

Across the commotion, Amosa smiled his wood demon's smile at me over his gardenia and closed one slanting, green eye in what might have been a conspiratorial wink.

Whack! A huge, middle-aged *matei* in a black and yellow lava-lava swung his three-sided bat at the ball hurled directly at his stomach and smacked it over the copra trees towards the sea. Gathering up their lava-lavas, three fielders rushed headlong to retrieve it from a tangle of morning glories. The most headlong of them, I saw, was Tolu.

His village was playing cricket against a neighbouring village.

Whack! The next ball soared inland and for a long time a number of boys feverishly searched the undergrowth. Ten minutes went by ... fifteen. No one showed impatience. You could tell from the crowds of onlookers that *kirikiti*'s importance to Samoans easily transcended long hold-ups like this. The hold-ups, I soon saw, were frequent because Samoan cricket is a more straightforward game than its British model. You cannot be out leg before wicket because no one wears pads and so fancy play becomes physically dangerous. No one can be bothered to block a ball, and because batsmen are warriors at play, blocking is not very highly considered. Manhood demands a virile swing of the bat – of the warclub, really – and Samoans usually hit the ball. Nine times out of ten it flies high over the short jungle boundaries – it is made of light rubber – and the long search begins. To be out, you must be caught or bowled.

There are frequent casualties. Tolu had explained that the suppurating sore I had noticed on his leg was a cricket injury. Chasing a ball from pitch to beach he had stumbled into coral, a dangerous thing to be cut by because it leaves poisoned gashes. But worse wounds than that can be sustained in Samoan cricket. Teams of twenty or twenty-five hot-blooded players have been known to turn village rivalry into real war, and now and again when that happens a bad sportsman, or umpire, is sometimes chased and clubbed to death.

On this occasion propriety reigned. Sportsmanlike handclaps rose from groups of figures smoking in the shade of breadfruit trees, and spectators perched like bright birds halfway up the trunks of coconut palms cheered and called encouragement to the batsmen who one after the other strode fiercely to the wicket, clutching their bats like semi-naked warriors advancing to lop off a few heads.

Amosa and Fili were not playing at warriors or sportsmen. They sat in long grass singing in falsetto to a small guitar. 'We go,' said Fili when it was quite dark.

Soon clouds hid the rising moon and spits of rain splashed the windscreen. The headlights wavered along the long, steep forest track, illuminating boys carrying baskets of coconuts, women holding umbrellas over small children, half naked men on dripping horses. The wet, bare calves, shoulders, chests made shining patterns of brown and gold. After a while there were no more human beings and then suddenly the lane opened out. The grey tower of a church and thatched houses loomed as unreal as an exotic film set. There were figures on the roadside, shaking fists, waving. Young men were shouting, running frantically from the deep shadow of trees and bushes. They looked demented. Had there been a terrible accident?

I began to slow down. The last thing I expected was that Fili and Amosa would go berserk. But I felt Fili pummelling my shoulders from the back seat, and heard Amosa beside me yelling – 'Go, go, go! Stop no! Stop – no!'

Figures gibbered and gesticulated.

'Go to home!' Fili shouted. 'Bad, bad!'

Battered and half deafened, I accelerated recklessly, wrenching the car away from what looked like a mob of madmen throwing themselves at our headlights. I shall never know how I did not run down at least two of them. Was it a hold-up? Wild, indecipherable words were lost in the night. I remember close-up, split-second images of open, twisted mouths, flying hair, furious eyes at the window. Worse – dark, solid objects flew across my vision towards the by now swiftly moving car.

'Fili – what ...?' I swerved to miss the trunk of a perfume tree.

'Go, go!' Fili was breathless with passion.

After a minute I slowed down. 'Now then,' I said, and now it was explained.

'Very bad boys and girls. Come from New Zealand. Too much beer, too much –' Fili mimed a man smoking and his finger drew circles round his temple. Drugs.

'*Kkhhhh! Kkkhhhh!*' Amosa's exclamation conveyed the strongest disgust. It was an odd, harsh sound, half gargle, half growl, like a file against a knot of wood.

So that was it. We had run into a coven of boozy and very violent Samoan layabouts – typical, according to Fili and Amosa, of most young emigrants to New Zealand. There they had acquired a taste for liquor, drugs and fighting. Girls as well as boys. Lost souls. A serious menace to an innocent, church-going population. As a Methodist, Fili said sententiously, he thoroughly disapproved of alcohol. It made

238

Samoans behave like animals. Those solid flying objects had been bottles. For drunken fun, they would have damaged the car, and beaten us up. Kkkhhh!

'What about the police?'

Fili said, impatiently, 'Police only in Apia.'

'Girls very bad,' Amosa said. 'Drink beer then make –' Gestures told me what they did.

'With you, Amosa?'

'No, no! Me-tho-dist!' he cried righteously.

Fili interrupted. 'Amosa like *fu-fu* with girl.'

'*Fu-fu?*'

More vivid gestures assailed my eyes in the rear view mirror. *Fu-fu* evidently meant what used to be known as heavy petting.

'Fili like *moetotolo*,' Amosa said in one-upmanlike tones.

'*Moeto* – ?' I dodged a troop of piglets that charged across the track behind a sow big enough to have overturned the car. But the panic was over. Fili and Amosa soon settled down again and we drove home to the sound of falsetto Samoan singing. The mosquitoes were as bad as ever, but Manino had cooked green pigeons and spotted crabs for dinner.

The Methodist minister, a Samoan in his mid-thirties who had spent some years in Australia, was Tolu's friend and neighbour. His bunga-low and church stood by the track a few hundred yards away.

'*Moetotolo* – so you've heard of that.' The minister seemed amused. '"Night-creeping", in other words. Very common in Samoa.'

His wife gave a polite little laugh over her teacups.

The aim of *moetotolo* was for a young man to steal a girl's virginity as she slept in her parents' house. I had seen how a Samoan family slept side by side, sharing mats and mosquito nets, and I found it difficult to imagine how on earth Amosa, say, could deflower poor Emma and against her will without raising the household within half a minute. What contortions would do the trick? Surely it was impossible. And the boy would be courting serious physical harm – if the girl's father and brothers woke up, they might beat him to death.

'Of course,' the minister said, seriously, 'it is a *manual* deflowering. Not a ... full-scale ...'

'And the object?' I asked. 'Just the thrill?'

Tolu said, the minister translating, 'The only motive is to force the girl to marry him. From shame.... You see, if the boy steals her virginity,' the minister went on, 'he shames her deeply. Shame is a strong element in a girl's make-up, so he will threaten to tell the village unless she agrees to marry him.'

The minister's handsome wife lay now on her stomach on a mat on the floor, her arms and chin resting on a bolster. She said, 'It happened near here only the other day.'

The minister said, 'Yes. This boy comes creeping in the night to the girl sleeping among her family. He makes *moetotolo*. But he is clumsy. The girl jumps up and shouts to her father. The father wakes up and this boy is all tangled up in the mosquito net. The boy runs too late. The father catches him and beats him very badly. Then the father complains to the *mateis'* village council and they fine the father of the boy – pigs, a hundred taros, some fine woven mats: a heavy fine in these parts.'

The minister's Bible lay on a chair and, to see what Samoan looked like, I turned to the first words of all: '*Na faia e le Atua ma le lalolagi i le amataga . . .*' ('In the beginning God created the world . . .'). The Gospels here were according to Mataio, Mareko, Luka and Ioane. Amosa, I discovered, was Samoan for Moses.

'Drink,' said the minister. 'Drugs. That's the serious problem. Growing fast, I'm afraid. *Kava*, the traditional root drink we make here, that's all right – that calms you and sends you to sleep; nobody fights on *kava*. But the grog that comes from Apia or Pago-Pago in American Samoa – whisky, gin, vodka – and the drugs brought in by hippies and tourists – marijuana, cocaine, heroin from Auckland or Sydney – that's another matter. The chiefs here ban liquor in their villages but, all the same, young Samoan men and women who learnt to drink in New Zealand do it secretly in the bush at night, as you saw. In New Zealand they learn to reject *fa'a Samoa* – the Samoan way of life. That's what it amounts to.' He smiled. 'I don't mind telling you, I was a whisky and drugs man myself when I was studying in Australia. Oh yes, I was. Of course, that's all over now. But it shows I know what I'm talking about.'

Outside, Samoan matrons, demure in white blouses and ankle-length skirts, were coming down the path, leading their children to the minister's Bible class.

'What is happening to the essence and charm of Samoan traditional culture? We cherish it so much – oh, so much. Why should our people be forced to change by Western progress?'

The minister himself was a good example of Samoan charm and vitality. But a few days previously I had driven to visit a different sort of pastor on the south coast who had recently married Tolu's sister – an old man, a Congregationalist with a tight, lipless mouth. The pastor had held an evening prayer meeting in his low, barnlike house by the sea. About ten rows of his parishioners squatted before him under the corrugated iron roof in the dim oil light, listening to interminable prayers and verses of the Bible intoned in a dry voice that seemed quite devoid of compassion – or even of life. The mosquitoes there had made the night unbearable, and in the morning their bites had puffed up my eyes like a boxer's. At breakfast he had eyed his plump wife as she tucked into her taro and murmured sourly, 'Greed is *not* one of the virtues.'

'We are not accustomed to visitors like you. We used to get many visitors!' the old man said before I left to return to Tolu's. 'Americans. Not so many now.'

'Why not now?'

He gave me a hard glance. 'I always asked them for their passports when they wanted to stay. Well, the Prime Minister had warned us that foreigners, Americans mostly, were bringing drugs into Samoa.'

'How did they take that? You asking them for their passports, I mean.'

He cackled with satisfaction. 'They'd go away and not come back. Not many come now.'

Would he ask me for my passport? I waited but he didn't.

Instead, he leaned towards me. 'Tell me, Mr Gavin – if modern development means the dehumanization of societies, what is the use of it? No one starves here. These islands – their plantations – could support five or six times the present population. Instead, young people neglect their plantations. They drift to towns, buy beer, see imported X-rated movies, lounge about – go, I suppose one might say, to hell. We Samoans have a paradise here. Do you agree?'

'Yes, I do,' I said. He might not be one of the most lovable citizens of this paradise, but I agreed with him that it was one. Many Samoans, I thought, must be haunted by the image of Apia destroyed by concrete and neon, every thatched house showing re-runs of *Dallas*.

To Tolu's neighbour, the young minister, I said now, 'Stick to *fa'a Samoa* like grim death.'

Animated women followed by little girls with white bows in their hair were coming in. There was much laughter and spirited chat.

He nodded. 'Travel doesn't always just broaden the mind, does it?' He got up and began to greet his ebullient parishioners. Over his shoulder he called, 'As far as we are concerned, it can destroy it, too.'

241

Twenty-two

After a few days with Tolu I drove to Apia. The excursion ended dramatically. My notebook records:

Two unprepossessing Samoans thumb lift. They wear jeans and T-shirts, their hair is wild, their chins stubbly, their eyes red. One has two missing front teeth. Will I take them to Apia? 'All right, get in.' After five minutes on the road, one of them says abruptly, 'Turn off here. We'll go to such-and-such-a-village.'

Dutifully, I turn off. We drive for some time on a road that climbs into the bush; there is no sign of a village or even a house. It is disturbing. Am I being hijacked? I have an uneasy feeling that they are communicating with each other secretly, with winks and glances.

I say, 'Well, where is the village?'

They talk in Samoan together.

The one with missing teeth gives a sickly snigger – 'Oh, we'll go to Apia instead.' No explanation.

Odd – and sinister. I turn the car with relief. At Apia market they get out. A shaggy head pokes through the window. 'Will you take us back in half an hour?' Vodka wafts about me. I tell them I am staying the night in Apia.

'Oh,' and they shrug and walk off.

But that was not the end. The same evening, in Aggie Grey's bar, a waiter says a friend of mine is outside. A friend?

'Says he your *best* friend.'

It was one of the two hitchhikers, swaying, his eyes blood-red. He looked terrible, clearly drugged but reeking of liquor too. He also looked violent. The two middle-aged Samoan businessmen I had been with in the bar came out and talked soothingly to him. Money, he said, or a drink. We gave him money and luckily he staggered away into the night. One of the businessmen said, 'Never give a lift to such people. Did you see? On his forearm he has a tattoo – "Deported from New Zealand".'

'Don't say the New Zealand Government tattoos deportees!' It seemed barbaric.

'Oh, he probably tattooed it himself. Some of these Samoan druggies are proud to have been deported from, or even jailed in, New Zealand. They think it gives them status among Samoans here who haven't been abroad. Did you know Auckland has a bigger Samoan population than any city in the world? Very many unemployed.'

His friend said, 'Drunkenness, muggings, killings, too.'

'Yes, a lot of that.'

In the morning, the singing, dancing waiters and waitresses were rehearsing in the same beehive house. I watch them, hypnotized again by so much beauty and enthusiasm. The songs were conducted by the wife of Aggie Grey's son Alan, and later she gave me the words of one of the songs, translated (very roughly) from Samoan:

Samoan teenagers ready to go abroad,
Remember Samoa's name and be safe and free.
So many problems come up over there
And a Samoan is blamed for causing the lot.

Thirty days is your permit to stay in New Zealand,
Yet towards the end you overstayed,
Hiding and sneaking so joyfully.
When you are caught, you know it's deportation.
Why not be more careful and stay honest?

You come back so pale and white.
You've gained nothing, and you're just a fiery barrel of trouble.
Forget all about these motor cars and that la di da English.
Time is precious. Do something useful. Get to work on a banana
    plantation.

So people are so worried about the emigration problem it has even been put to music. I told them I hoped the song would go to the top of the Samoan charts. It is there already, they said, smiling. I wondered: if these boys and girls go to New Zealand, how great is the chance that they, too, will become denimed derelicts?

The sight of a Catholic mission down the road from Aggie Grey's stirred a happy, if flippant, memory. Clipped, unmistakable tones sang wickedly in my head:

> The natives greeted them kindly and invited them to dine
> On yams and clams and human hams and vintage coconut wine,
> The taste of which was filthy, but the after-effects divine....

Pace Noël Coward's Uncle Harry, there had been severed heads in Samoa but no edible human hams. Still, the local *kava* I had tried with Tolu's friends, though bitter, had a pleasant calming effect.

> They didn't brandish knives at him, they were really awfully sweet,
> They made concerted dives at him and offered him things to eat,
> But when they threw their wives at him he had to admit defeat.
> Uncle Harry's not a missionary now – he's on the island –
> But he's certainly not a missionary now.

I had never met a South Seas missionary and I need hardly say that the venerable Catholic priest I called on was quite unlike poor lapsed Uncle Harry. He was good to talk to because he loved Samoa, speaking the language, knowing the islands as he knew his Bible. He was a humorous Irishman, had been here many years. Indeed, he was not really a missionary at all. Catholics had long ago given up chasing converts. Why convert the converted? By now, he said, Samoans are ninety per cent Christian, so what was the point in Christian proselytizing? That would be to steal from friends – the Methodists, Congregationalists, Seventh Day Adventists, the Assembly of God people, and all the rest. Samoans had not been pagan for a hundred years or more. 'Samoa is founded on God', after all, is the national motto. 'We are not against lava-lavas,' he said, 'or tattooing or *kava* ceremonies, or singing or dancing. Let me put our attitude like this: we are not against the Samoan way of life – on the contrary we, so to speak, baptise the *fa'a Samoa*. D'ye see? ... Only the Mormons are recruiting,' he continued sadly. 'Strenuously recruiting, I'd say.' They seemed to him to go about like the United States Marine Corps, spending enormous sums on advertising – literally millions, perhaps billions, of dollars – across the world. I forget now if it was this quiet Catholic or Tolu's Methodist neighbour who gave it as his opinion that the Mormons were sometimes not above bribing chiefs to join them. If you could net a chief you could land the whole family. Of course, this may have been sour grapes.

The old Irishman didn't look sour. He said, 'They are buying land all over. They are building modern, American churches imported from Utah. They are building a multi-million-dollar temple here in Apia. You see, the Mormon Church is a great worldwide business, into mines, shipping, supermarkets.' He made it sound a bit like Goldfinger, General Motors and Billy Graham rolled into one.

I went to have a look at the great temple.

The Mormon headquarters in Apia certainly looked as if it meant big business. In this sleepy town, on this sleepy green island it was quite shockingly incongruous, though it would probably attract little notice in Hawaii. Its complex of neat, air-conditioned buildings reminded me of a newly built American Army headquarters in Vietnam. Americans with short hair, in crisp white shirts, walked briskly in and out of doors marked 'Education Department' and 'Real Estate Department'. Shining pickup trucks with 'Love One Another' stickers on them stood in parking bays. It was all 'go'. I half expected to see a helicopter pad, a PX store and people exchanging military salutes.

The Irishman had been right about the new temple. It was not finished but you could see there was going to be nothing cheap about it. It resembled a combined nuclear fallout shelter, concert hall and ultra-modern city crematorium, and it was designed to be noticed. Its soaring spire would certainly attract the awe of Samoans of one sort or another.

In a cool office an American woman sat behind a rectangular name plaque on her desk and said: 'Sure, the temple is very costly. It's made of very costly material, mostly in white and gold. Three million dollars' worth, I understand. You could check that out from our Dale Cook from Utah. He's in charge of construction.'

I gave Dale Cook a miss, but saw instead the man in charge of the Mormons in Samoa, President Carl Harris, a slim, confident, fortyish man in a white, short-sleeved shirt and a striped tie. He kindly offered me a cup of coffee in his office.

'We have a duty,' he said when I asked about missionaries and proselytizing in Samoa, 'to take the Gospel to the four corners of the earth, just as our Scriptures tell us to. When we read John in

Revelations saying that he saw an angel in the midst of heaven carrying the everlasting gospel – we take this as applying to the present time. The Mormons have 183 missions around the world now, and we have a duty.'

Outside President Harris's office, Samoan youths and girls stood about in an orderly fashion in short-sleeved white shirts and black ties that gave them the goody-goody air of senior prefects at an exclusive school.

They wore identity badges, too – the boys were 'Elders', the girls 'Sisters' – like members of a convention or a military mess. None of them wore flowers in their hair. I had already seen young Samoans with ties and shirts in the streets of Apia self-consciously walking in pairs. It would be unfair to describe them as zombies, but they didn't seem quite real either. They were nothing like Tolu or Fili or Amosa. Carl Harris explained this.

'We like them to walk in pairs of the *same* sex – because our Scriptures say it's better that way. A boy or girl alone might feel discouraged, but two can buoy one another up.'

He smiled ruefully, shaking his head. 'Sometimes Samoans act very young. They believe in eat, drink, be merry – and then some. That's their trouble.'

He shrugged. 'So we must be strict. No dating with the opposite sex. Rigorous study. More and more proselytizing. And, of course, self-discipline: we ask them to refrain from rugby, cricket, swimming. And there's to be no dancing, naturally.'

Questions about *fu-fu* and *moetotolo* withered under Mr Harris's steady Dr Arnold of Rugby gaze. I asked myself a question. What was the point in turning lively young Samoans into self-satisfied, buttoned-down youths from Utah?

On the wall, rows of photographs with names under them ('Elder This' and 'Sister That') stared down with the blank look you see in all passport pictures. These were the Samoan converts, now 'on mission'. President Harris saw my interest in them and said, 'Those hundred and seventy boys and girls on the wall are working in Western and American Samoa today. We have about thirty-six thousand in the two Samoas now.' A number to boast about in a population of a hundred and ninety thousand, already mostly Christian for decades. 'Of course, some have been called outside Samoa. To Los Angeles, Guam and New Zealand. And, of course, to our Mormon University in Hawaii.'

I stared at him, wondering whether separating Samoans from their islands and their *fa'a Samoa* was what God really wanted for 'His

246

sweetest work'. The other churches on the island did not think so.

I thanked President Harris and went out into the sun, passing the boys and girls standing about outside in ties and shirts and badges, and drove back to Aggie Grey's. It was nice to see Mount Vaea's green hump in the sun and the shine on the bay. Nice, too, to be greeted at the hotel by Big Annie and one of the waiters I'd seen dancing and singing in the garden. I knew he wasn't a Mormon; he wasn't wearing a tie. He was probably a Methodist. Whatever he was, he was a real Samoan. I gave him a big smile.

I had to check on my next ship.

The *Pacific Islander* would be on time, Henry Betham said when we consulted his telex messages at Burns Philp. So I prepared to return to Tolu's for my farewells to Samoa. I bought large bags of rice, sugar and tea, corned beef, baked beans, biscuits – all the things Manino had asked for.

It was raining when I reached the house. Great silver drops ran down the flanks of the horse tethered on the coral chips at the door. Fili was chopping taro, his hair dripping, his sopping lava-lava clinging to his thighs – lopping the stalks off the fat, edible roots with his long bush knife and tossing them into a coconut-frond basket like a Samoan warrior of a hundred years ago, tossing enemy heads before his chief. He greeted me with an arm thrown about my neck, shouting '*Talofa!*', and I went in to meet Tolu and the others with a wet smear of dark brown earth down one cheek.

There was to be a feast. Manino had made a dish called *pusilami*, a delicious, yogurty, spinachy mess of coconut cream, onion and salt wrapped and baked among hot stones in taro, banana and breadfruit leaves.

Soon, Amosa brought in a piglet in a woven basket. He and Fili laid the squealing brute on its back, placed a stout but slender pole across its throat and stood with both feet and their whole weight on the pole, one at each end. The pig choked to death, taking its time.

Not that I waited. Unable to watch this public murder, I drove Manino and Isaia to the lagoon where they scoured the shore for red-lacquered crabs with yellow bellies and large spots the colour of dried blood on their backs, smaller white-bellied crabs, sea slugs, cockles (*pee-pee*), and the speckled cowries whose shells, with their varnished look and jagged mouths, are in Europe usually decorations on a mantelshelf. (I found their contents hard and rubbery, impossible to chew without making your jaw ache.)

It had stopped raining as we drove back from the sea. Pink and blue strips of sunset sky lit the horizon. The black wings of solitary flying foxes flapped home overhead. Muscular young men like the bareback cavaliers of a medieval army rode down the track, or led horses straddled with loads of coconuts.

'*Tofa*, Isaia!' they called.

' '*Fa*, Ioane!'

' '*Fa!* '*Fa!*'

The voices came and went in the dark now. The pressure lamps glowed in homes along the way, turning them into friendly dolls' houses.

Tolu's prayer tonight was a long one.

'*Le Atua ua matou faafetai ...*' (Emma wrote it out for me later). '*Fesoa saoni mai i la matou mafutaga ma Gavin ... Amene.*' 'O God, we thank you for your love ... and help us to strengthen our fellowship with Gavin. Guide him safely to his country. This is our prayer. In Jesus' name.' There was much more, and while Tolu's deep voice rumbled on I looked surreptitiously at the others. The women buried their heads in their hands – the old woman bent double on her mat in an attitude of devotional abandon. Fili and Amosa made hideous faces. Then the meal came. Along with the shellfish and the poor piglet, now baked in hot stones, we ate mullet and pieces of a fat white squid caught by Tolu.

Afterwards it was present-time. I had bought a good Seiko watch for

Fili, a smaller one for Manino and a tiny digital watch for Isaia which reduced him to tears. I gave Tolu my rubber-sealed torch, but I had three Parker pens for him, too. I had a beautiful lava-lava each for Emma and the old woman, two fine lava-lavas for Amosa, and a large bag of sweets for the little ones, Ruta and Ala. In return, the old lady presented me with a fine mat she had woven and hemmed with scarlet feathers; Isaia gave me a basket; Emma a prayerbook with an inscription in ink – 'This Belongs To You, Gavin, Please Do Not Forget Me, Love Always, Emma Tolu.'

Fili was holding out an amazing piece of local art: an upturned half-coconut shell on tiny pillars, a decorative circle of cowrie shells: a model of a Samoan chief's assembly hall. How could I pack that? A letter went with it. 'To My Dearest Friend, This is my *meaalofa* [present] to you my best friend. Don't forget me, because I didn't forget you my best friend … I love always for you, G. Young.' Amosa knelt to hang a necklace of cowrie shells round my neck, and, on behalf of the family, Tolu took from a wooden chest a heavy Bible in Samoan, 'For you,' he said.

Later, I lay under the mosquito net, listening for the last time to the rain thrumming on the thatched roof and the wind clattering the bamboos like a witch doctor making music on old bones. The wind reminded me of something Stevenson had said: 'I have always feared the sound of wind beyond everything. In my hell, it would always blow a gale.' But this was no gale. The night was soft and peaceful.

Something scuttled across my neck, settled there, moved slowly on my shoulder … a tarantula – the Speckled Band? A hot iron seemed to touch my skin, and I leaped up, shouting – 'Hey, Fili! Snake!' That roused the house. Tolu searched the mattress with the torch I'd just given him, while my neck and shoulder burned like fire. Between us we found it in the end, looking down at us from the mosquito netting – a centipede, the biggest I have ever seen, three inches long. '*Atualoa*,' Emma said when it lay crushed by Tolu's foot. It was a pretty name for a centipede. 'It came to kiss goodbye.'

They laughed when I said I hoped the *atualoa* wasn't an important *aitu* in disguise.

I drove to Apia early next morning. I was in a good mood for a funeral, though the car looked fit for a wedding. Isaia and Ruta had collected hibiscus and gardenia blossoms and strewn them on the bonnet and decorated the dashboard with frangipani flowers. Emma had tied a flowering creeper a yard long to the radio aerial so that it would stream behind us when I moved off. And Amosa arrived with a flower in his ear and a bush lime as a nosegay. The car smelled like a florist's and sounded like a music parlour – Fili and Amosa sang all the way to Apia and always in falsetto. Tolu, Manino, Emma and Isaia followed us in a bus with a load of Tolu's copra. It was too messy for the car, he said.

At Aggie Grey's Fili peered at my books. 'This book? Mormon?' He held up the hotel copy of *The Book of Mormon*, in which a former occupant of the room had scribbled: 'All complete bullshit stories for small children.' From the frontispiece the Mormons' Prophet, Joseph Smith in a buff coat, looked at us with a pleasant, innocuous face. Next Amosa dug my old metal flask of whisky out of my bag.

'Medicine,' I said. 'Not for you. For me.'

'*Bad!*' he retorted, undeceived. '*Kkkhhhh!*'

They scrutinized my maps, examined my clothes, tasted my tooth-paste. They might have been detectives investigating a prime murder suspect.

'All right, I'm guilty,' I said. 'Come on, we go.' But it took a little longer.

The room was suddenly flooded with evangelism – the Revival Time Choir from American Samoa singing a song entitled 'Eternal Life'. Amosa was carefully combing his long hair with my comb. 'Sing along as Brother MacClellan leads us,' said a radio voice as sludgy as cold molasses, but Fili was struggling into my *Chengtu* T-shirt. I switched off the radio abruptly and wrenched the T-shirt from Fili's back. Then we went to join the others at the market. At last I was going to pay my respects to R.L.S.

Twentythree

When work is over Louis sat down to rest, and sighed for a cigarette ...
At that moment Sosimo [his valet] appeared with the tobacco. '*Quel e le
potu*,' said Lou gratefully, 'How great is the wisdom,' and was deeply
touched by the quick reply, 'How great is the love!'

Mrs Stevenson: Letters from Samoa

The pass from the Prime Minister's Department was made out to me
alone, so Tolu and his family agreed to loll about under the great trees
at the foot of Mount Vaea while I looked round the house. I could see
that since Vailima had become the guest house of Samoa's head of state
it had been expanded; it was rather wider than the house Stevenson
built in 1892 with the wood he had expensively shipped from San
Francisco. Yet the original was still there, too. It was beautifully
situated among the great trees, its porch half buried in flowering
creepers. It was empty now; seldom used. A pale, white-haired, white-
clothed figure met me on the verandah steps. 'Miki Lalogi,' it whispered
its name, smiling. This was the cook and guardian I had been told to
expect – half-Samoan, half-German, born here. Quite old and very
friendly, he was pleased to have a visitor.

I recognized the airy verandah from old photographs in R.L.S.'s
Letters: its white, wooden ceiling fourteen feet high, its great width. I
had the two books of Stevenson letters with me – Louis' and his
mother's – and I showed Miki Lalogi the photographs they had taken
here and what old Mrs Stevenson had written on this house:

> ... the pleasant hours we spend grouped on the verandah whither we
> always betake ourselves after meals; lounging on easy chairs or squatting
> on mats, according to taste. The verandah is twelve foot wide, and as it
> goes round three sides of the house, we can always be sure of shade: I
> wish I could add of breeze also, but that is not so easily to be contrived.

He nodded his old white head and pointed at a sepia photograph of the
verandah. 'It is the same,' he said. We could not contrive a breeze today

any more than the Stevensons had. Even at nine o'clock in the morning it was warming up. Soon it would be uncomfortable. In the Great Hall there was nothing but a long table now. You had to imagine the oil lamps, the *chaises longues*, the kneeling ceramic or wooden buddhas guarding the wide staircase – and Louis Stevenson himself, long-legged, skeletal, moustachioed, nervously pacing up and down the waxed floor. And old Mrs S., looking like a thin Queen Victoria, sipping brandy and soda and nibbling ship's biscuits, scattering the crumbs, talking to Fanny, Lou's wife, who sat sombrely watching her restless husband and smoking. Where we stood now, Lou had read aloud chapters of *The Wreckers* and *Weir of Hermiston*.

On the stairs I felt sweat prickling my forehead. No wonder R.L.S. worked best at sunrise. In his bedroom, now a library, there was a framed poem by Rabindranath Tagore on one wall:

Our voyage is done
We bow to Thee, our Captain ...

Bookcases held hundred-year-old Tauchnitz editions, published in Leipzig. *Zanoni* and *Kenelm Chillingly* by Sir Edward Bulwer Lytton, Conan Doyle's *The Stark Munro Letters*, and Wilkie Collins' *No Name* and *Hide and Seek* – how many people living have read those novels? Who has heard of Rider Haggard's *Jess*, his *The Witch's Head* or his *Joan Haste*? Across two shelves were ranged the complete works of R.L.S. himself, in the Heinemann Vailima edition of 1922, and an 1898 copy of *St Ives*.

The room was quite airless, and smelled of must and dust. A dying fly lay on its back, filling the silence with its buzzing. 'There is one novelty that ought to prove a comfort,' said Mrs Stevenson again from the pages in my hand. 'The doors and windows are closed in with wire gauze, so that it is insect-proof, and I can sleep without a mosquito-net. Moreover, I hope that horrid creature, the mason bee, won't be able to get into my books and spoil them.' There were no mason bees in evidence, and no wire gauze either.

The study had a sketch by Belle Strong of R.L.S. reading to his wife, from which we were distracted by an extraordinary sound from the front lawn. A most peculiar brass band was trying its best to strike up 'Colonel Bogey', but total disarray prevented struggling tubas, sousaphones and trombones from matching key for key, failing even to match oompah for oompah, and half the bandsmen were collapsed in

helpless laughter on the grass, rolling about among their shiny, dented instruments. One or two wore uniform jackets of an unidentifiable (and unmatching) order. Most had bare torsos, though a very few had ragged shirts. A saxophonist, flat on his back, convulsed in hysterics, looked like a pirate in green headscarf and purple lava-lava. My ghostly guide, Miki, giggled. 'Apia police band,' he whispered. 'Practice.'

From the anarchy on the lawn I could look straight up at Mount Vaea, which seemed only touching distance away. Stevenson had leaned from this louvred window the morning of the day he died, aged forty-four, of a cerebral haemorrhage; he had gazed up at the mountain almost as if he had a premonition of death. His gardener, Lafaele, standing where the big drum banged now, had seen him and waved, and Stevenson had called '*Talofa!*'

I could see a semicircular gleam of ocean above and beyond the garden plants of Vailima – flamboyants, gardenias, avocados, mangoes, lemons and oranges, padanus, roses and cassias. Before the garden there had been a jungle track, up which the Stevensons' two packhorses, Donald and Edinburgh, had brought the first stores from Apia. Often the woods of Mount Vaea had been full of war drums. One of R.L.S.'s letters said, 'A man brought in a head in great glory; they washed the black [war] paint off, and behold! it was his brother. When I last heard he was sitting in his house, with the head upon his lap, and weeping.' Another letter told of warriors who 'brought in eleven heads, and to great horror and consternation ... one proved to be a girl – a Maid of the village.... It had been returned, wrapped in the most costly silk handkerchief, and with an apologetic embassy.'

Yet, in this room, despite war drums, battle cries and maidens' heads, he had dictated stories of the cold, mist-bound north. Looking out at the drumless woods of Vaea, I thought: The early missionaries did at least bring peace, yet Stevenson was not against small 'hedge-wars'. They made the blood course; kept men on their toes. Men died, no doubt, but the race, purged and regenerated by battle, survived.

'Give me five minutes, Miki ... to browse.'

I riffled the pages, stopping where I had made a pencil mark. Here, Stevenson was about to negotiate a truce between battling Samoans: 'I must ride barefoot.... Twenty miles ride, ten of the miles in drenching rain, seven of them fasting in a morning chill, and six stricken hours

political discussion by an interpreter; to say nothing of sleeping in a native house, at which many of our excellent literati would look askance of itself.' The energy of a semi-invalid. His wife Fanny said, 'Sometimes he looks like an old man, and then, at a moment's notice, he's a pretty brown boy.' And here was an ordinary day:

> Wake at the first peep of day, come gradually to, and had a turn on the verandah before 5.55, at 6 breakfast; 6.10, to work ... till 10.30; 11, luncheon. Make music furiously [on the flageolet] till about 2.... Work again till 4: fool from 4 to half-past, 4.30, bath; 5, dinner; smoke, chat on verandah, then hand of cards, and at last 8 come up to my room with a pint of beer and hard biscuit: turn in.

It was on the verandah that the end had come. Mrs Stevenson wrote:

> My beloved son was suddenly called home last evening. At six o'clock he was well, hungry for dinner, and helping Fanny to make a Mayonnaise sauce; when suddenly he put both hands to his head and said, 'Oh, what a pain!' and then added, 'Do I look strange?' Fanny said no, not wishing to alarm him, and helped him into the hall, where she put him into the nearest easy chair. She called for us to come, but he was unconscious before I reached his side.... At ten minute past 8 p.m. all was over....

The police band had shambled away down the drive. Two gardeners in red and yellow lava-lavas were cutting back the creeper by the verandah. There was a great whistling of birds.

> We brought a bed into the hall, and he was lifted on to it.
> When all was over his boys gathered about him, and the chiefs of Tanugamanono (the nearest village) arrived with fine mats which they laid over the bed, bowing and saying, '*Talofa, Tusitala*'; and then, after kissing him and sitting a while in silence, they bowed again, and saying, '*Tofa, Tusitala*', and went out.

It was hot already. Miki nodded his snowy head towards the back of the house and poured me iced water in the head of state's kitchen, where R.L.S.'s cook, Talolo, had prepared Scottish food — stewed beef and potatoes, and soda scones — as well as baked bananas, and pineapple in claret. I took Miki's pale hand in both of mine and thanked him. 'Pleasant to have a visitor who knows the Tusitala,' the reedy voice said. 'Come again.'

I found Tolu and the others sprawling patiently under the trees, and we set off to climb the mountain in an atmosphere like wet gauze.

My notes at this point are disfigured by drops of sweat:

A hard climb. Mount Vaea stands 700 feet above Vailima, and we take the 'fast', straight-up track. How on earth did old Mrs Stevenson manage to follow Louis' coffin – borne by chiefs – to the top? If she could, I can. Underfoot, the track is muddy and covered with sodden leaves. Even Tolu, who has not seen Mount Vaea before but should be fit with farming and cricket, sweats heavily. 'The hill is very angry,' he says, meaning 'high'. It is all very well for the young – Fili, Amosa and Isaia hitch up their lava-lavas and disappear into the trees like woodcock. Their cries make the wood seem as if it's full of taunting *aitus*.

Manino and Emma keep with me. Manino's stomach is upset, but she insists on coming. I have given her Lomotil. She plods gamely upwards, giving me a warm smile now and then. Thirty minutes' steep, slippery climb. I feel crippled. My legs need to rest. Luckily there is a bench halfway up. Two young Samoans, running down, call in English a cheerful 'Good morning.' Up and up. And at last at the top. Unexpected Samoan music – a group of Samoan boys and girls are playing guitars under the trees. We sit and listen and cool off. Manino, smiling all the time, fans herself with a red and white handkerchief. The Lomotil seems to have done the trick. Isaia appropriates my binoculars. The crest of Mount Vaea is a wide, open space sloping towards the bay, hanging over Vailima. The tomb is white and rectangular, shaded by trees. R.L.S. lying in the earth here would only have to lift his head to see the ocean.

Fili's fingers run casually over the bronze lettering on the plaque: '1850 Robert Louis Stevenson 1894'. Amosa lightly polishes the raised letters of R.L.S.'s own *Requiem*:

Here he lies where he longed to be;
Home is the sailor, home from the sea,
And the hunter home from the hill.

It is not love of Tusitala, of course. It is just a feeling they have....

On a second plaque a quotation in Samoan from 'Ruta I, 16–17'. When I look it up in English it reads:

And Ruth said, Entreat me not to leave thee, or to return from following after thee; for whither thou goest, I will go; and where thou lodgest, I will lodge; thy people shall be my people and thy God, my God: where thou diest, will I die, and there will I be buried: the Lord do so to me, and more also if aught but death part thee and me.

Beneath the words, a dying wreath of peonies. Red-bodied dragon-flies dart like inquisitive spirits. The peace is exquisite. Manino begins to comb out her hair, letting it fall thick and black to her waist. Isaia is in a tree, his *aitu*'s cheek resting on a branch.

'See.' Tolu is pointing. Below us, through dark ancient trees a bright green lawn, the blue of Vailima's sunlit roof. East, rising land and forest; a mountaintop lost in cloud; the silver wriggle of a river. South, the ocean; and the glittering pond of the harbour, with three small ships at anchor within the white curve of surf. The faint sigh of waves on the reef.

An old man comes quietly out of the trees, grey and very grizzled, carrying a bush knife and a basket full of cut shrubs. To me, he says, 'The leaves I have make the patient be healed.' In clear English, holding up a leaf. To the view, he says, 'Such beautiful sights.'

He chats in Samoan with Tolu and Fili, turns again to me.

257

'Where — may I ask you — is your home situated? Oh! So near to home of the Tusitala. The same country! And you come all this way....' He waved a hand. 'These friends say you are a writer, sir.'

I smile and point to the almost empty hilltop we stand on. 'Do you think there's space for me here?'

'Oh, plenty. Certainly, space.' He smiles back, pointing down to Vailima. 'I live near the pastor's house in Vailima, sir. I have several books by Mr Robert Louis Stevenson in my house. Come and see.' He waves, drifting away.

It is hot. And silent. The singers have gone. Fili sleeps. Amosa sits cross-legged in the shade, slowly blinking enigmatic eyes, like a cat. Tolu stares at the sea. Manino pulls petals off a flower. Emma is combing Isaia's hair. For half an hour, except for a murmur or two, we are all silent. But it is getting *too* hot. 'Shall we go?' We begin the descent. Tolu, Manino, Emma and I descend sedately. Fili, Amosa and Isaia fly ahead as usual, and again the mountain-side echoes like an aviary with their cries. In this damp heat I am glad to reach the falls in the valley where you cross over to the 'Road of Loving Hearts' the Samoans had built for Stevenson. He had admired these great forest trees. He heard the waterfall in that

valley, the 'wonderful fine glen' at the bottom of the mountain. The house for him was 'a place for angels'.

I was leaving Samoa, old and new.

Had I only known the Tolu family for the inside of a week? We said our goodbyes near the Apia market. Tolu's smile was solemn when he shook hands. 'Thank you,' he said. Manino, blinking, said, '*Tofa*,' and Emma, 'Come next year.'

Taking her hand, I said, 'Try to be here then, Emma. Stay in Samoa and teach.'

To Amosa: '*Tofa*, wood demon.'

His green-brown slanting eyes smiled. '*Tofa*, Gavin.'

'Come next year,' Fili said.

It was difficult to get Isaia to leave the car. He had slept in it every night and now it was his, he thought, as much as mine. I led him out by the hand and brushed his tears away and kissed his forehead.

'*Tofa, aitu.*' I tapped his nose to make him smile. Then I ducked into the car and drove off, waving from the window without looking back. The flowers Ruta and Isaia had scattered on the dashboard were beginning to wilt by now, and I let them lie when I left the car at Aggie Grey's. I noticed something on the back seat. It was Amosa's bush lime. For a moment or two I sniffed its delicate perfume. Then I slipped it into my pocket as a souvenir.

Twenty four

'So travel doesn't always broaden the mind, eh?' Captain Tony Carter said. We were standing on the bridge wing of the China Navigation Company's container ship *Pacific Islander*, watching the receding shore of Western Samoa.

'In the case of some Samoans, it seems it may destroy it,' I said. The blue roofs of Vailima were visible on the left slope of Mount Vaea. I felt as if I had left something there I would have to go back for.

'And were those missionaries the first you'd ever met?'

'Almost.' I said. 'The first was a young Methodist in a sampan, halfway up the Chindwin River. In Burma. Quite remote. I was travelling illegally to the Chinese–Indian border to write about guerrilla war in the jungle there. No one was sure it existed.'

'And did it?'

'Oh, it existed all right. But thanks to that missionary I nearly missed it. You see, I was pretending to be a missionary myself – they were the only foreigners allowed up that way.'

I saw again the overloaded sampan and the great meandering, muddy river, and my chicken coop of a cabin on the hot metal deck. The sampan made slow progress. It went aground on every second sandbank, and we had to wait for the crew to pole us off. I hadn't actually told anyone I was a missionary, but I suppose the two Bibles I carried rather ostentatiously amounted to a disguise. I expected trouble as soon as I saw the white man in sarong and sandals on the bamboo jetty, waiting to come aboard and share the chicken coop. He had a stack of Bibles tied up with string. There was trouble, too. He took one look at me, my Bibles and my whisky bottle, and said he was going to denounce me to the local police. Interlopers like me should be made to suffer.

The Burmese police officers squatting outside the coop, tirelessly playing cards and smoking, were on their way to upriver posts; their specific object was to trap unauthorized foreigners like me. One call and I would have faced a Rangoon jail for ... well, indefinitely.

'He took a righteous view, did he, this missionary bloke?' asked Tony Carter.

'Not as it turned out. You see, he'd got an idea I really was a missionary – a Seventh Day Adventist come to poach his Burmese converts. When I told him I was a journalist travelling *sub rosa*, he became as friendly as anything. Even forgave me my whisky.'

Carter laughed.

'His name was Edwards, and he came from Reading. I sometimes wonder what became of him.'

The *Pacific Islander* had left Apia for Pago-Pago and Papeete on the afternoon of my visit to Mount Vaea. There had been no problems. Tim Bridgeman in Hong Kong had telexed the company's permission for me to board her, subject to her master's agreement, and Tony Carter, I soon realized, was another of the China Navigation Company's friendly officers. There was a bonus, too: Steve Komorowski, the second officer, was an acquaintance from the *Hupeh* of two years before. I had told him to read Joseph Conrad: their names were similar.

Then there was Miss Yip, the radio officer.

Miss Yip Pui Fun was no relation at all to Angel Yip who had helped me to Shanghai. This Miss Yip was small, trim and wore her hair pulled back tautly over her ears – and she was afraid of men. Chris Macdonald, the mate, said with a wicked grin, 'She has fixed a very strong bolt on her door. She takes it with her from ship to ship. So if you're thinking....'

Miss Yip, I thought, was an appropriate person to meet at this stage of the voyage, if she had any puritanical affinity with Somerset Maugham's Mrs Davidson, the intolerant, hypocritical missionary's insufferable wife in the short story *Rain*. Maugham was a shrewd setter of scenes. American Samoa is famous for its rainfall. We were now within a very short distance of the tiny port of Pago-Pago (pronounced Pango-Pango), where Maugham's character, Sadie Thompson, the hooker from San Francisco, ran into the appalling Mr Davidson.

Mrs Davidson had 'served' in Hawaii, and the Samoan lava-lava scandalized her as 'a very indecent costume'. How, she demanded in high-pitched tones, could you expect people to be moral when they wore nothing but a strip of red cotton round their loins? 'In our islands,' she proclaimed proudly, 'we practically eradicated the lava-lava. And the inhabitants of these islands will never be thoroughly Christianized till every boy of more than ten years is made to wear a pair of trousers.'

My first meeting with Miss Yip was not encouraging. To my polite 'Good evening' she returned no answer at all.

In no time we were at the entrance to Pago-Pago – a horseshoe with an extremely narrow southern opening onto a long curve of beach with, behind it, a soaring, spectacular ruff of mountain and forest.

'Tricky entrance,' I said to Tony Carter.

'If you want to see a really narrow gap in a reef, wait until Papeete.'

'You push the buoys apart there,' Chris Macdonald added.

This was nothing like little Apia. Through my binoculars I saw a big modern hotel, bungalows that belonged in Los Angeles, large American limousines, and a lot of baseball caps and jeans. A hefty white rich man's fishing launch, prickly with antennae, roared out of the harbour as we came up to the wharf, and cable cars moved dizzily between two peaks on either side of the harbour abyss. Evidently, Pago-Pago had changed a lot more since 1920 than Apia or Suva. 'No town,' Maugham wrote of it then. 'Merely a group of official buildings, a store or two....' Sadie Thompson had called it 'a poor imitation of a burg'. But the Second World War had come and gone since Maugham, and the harbour had passed through a stage of being a great naval and Marine Corps base. The base had gone too, but Pago-Pago, though materially impoverished by its loss, had never reverted to the damp, sleepy place Maugham saw.

'Samoans here,' said Captain Carter, 'refer to "The Mainland". Guess what that means to them?'

'Tell me.'

'America. Can you believe it?'

'Not easily.'

Pago-Pago had not forgotten Somerset Maugham. The big modern hotel I had seen was called the Rainmaker, and it had a Sadie Thompson Bar. I wanted to see if it was on the site of Maugham's hotel, so I took Miss Yip there. I thought she might be lonely in the locked cabin by herself.

'I like to come,' she said, rather to my surprise.

'Are you worried on the ship with so many men?' I asked her.

'Filipinos frighten me,' she said. 'But this ship is quite okay. Because the crewmen are very old. Only the laundryman is twenty-five; the rest are not below forty.' The over-forties were past it in her estimation. No wonder she felt safe with me.

In fact, the Sadie Thompson Bar was the height of propriety. Appropriately, it was full of cheerful American sailors from a visiting warship, as well-behaved as the Broadway chorus of *South Pacific*. No one sang 'There is Nothing Like a Dame', but a jukebox jingled. At the bar with a phoney Samoan thatched roof, Miss Yip accepted a fruit cocktail – passion fruit, mango, milk, soda, grenadine. I kept her company with a *mai tai*: hefty jolts of three different rums mixed with fruit juice in a glass like a birdbath. Around us sailors called high-spiritedly for more Budweiser. 'Have a Happy Day' a bar sign said. Outside the plateglass windows the rain poured down. Old Maugham would have liked that. As for Miss Yip Pui Fun, she looked calmly around her, smiled, and accepted a second fruit cocktail. I liked her. Apart from anything else, she did somehow remind me of Angel Yip. When Pui Fun offered me a sweet I felt as if I had been awarded a good conduct medal.

Iniquity, according to the *Pacific Islander*'s good-natured third officer, Graham Harris, was to be found at a dive called the Pago Bar. 'A cross between the Butterfly Bar in the Bangkok docks and a flophouse in Singapore's Bugis Street of, well, twenty years ago,' he promised. 'Good chance of a punch-up to boot. The Korean trawlermen go there, mostly,' he said. 'They spend three months at sea non-stop, then come back here with all that stinking fish. You can imagine what *they* get up to.'

'But not you, of course,' Chris Macdonald said sarcastically.

'I'm getting married in six months. You can have those Samoan hags. I'd rather screw a tin of corned beef.'

'I believe you would an' all.'

The Korean trawlers lay all around; a fleet of battered rust-buckets, built for nothing but very rough work. Larger, more modern vessels were visible alongside the Star-Kist fish canning factory across the harbour. Several of the trawlers were strung about with lines on which diminutive Oriental underwear hung out like bunting. A Korean in a singlet and shorts was trying to manhandle a squealing pig up the gangway of No. 73 – the *Kwang Myong*. When darkness fell, the lights of the fish cannery shone across the water sharp and bright. It worked all through the night to keep American Samoa running.

'No beer taken outside' a sign said when we pushed through the door of the Pago Bar and into the fog of heat and smoke beyond. Koreans were thick on the ground by the time of night Chris, Graham, Steve and I got there, leaving Tony Carter on board singing to himself over a beer. A mirrored globe over a postage-stamp-sized dance floor scattered fragments of light over the tatters of leftover Christmas decorations on the ceiling. In the gloom I saw big male Samoan shapes in dark glasses, bearded and drunk, and women with bottoms like upholstered railway buffers. Most of the Koreans had long hair, and came in two sorts: James Bond's Oddjobs, with the look of killers who had volunteered for special homicide duty; or jolly Oriental dolls, red-faced with beer and only wanting a good time. Perhaps the Samoan hostesses were too big for some of them – they might have feared being crushed to death – because a few preferred to dance with each other. Soon, unbelievably, the atmosphere thickened even more. Vast dancing Samoan shapes wallowed through it like hippos in a mudhole. Beer came, was drunk, was reordered. I saw Komorowski swaying about with a woman as old as Boadicea's aunt. 'Oh, darling, to me be tree-ooo ...' a pretty girl was singing on the tiny dais with a ragged trio of guitarists behind her. In the murk a bottle smashed on the floor and there was a sudden swirl of male figures beyond the bandstand. An elderly American sat down in Komorowski's place.

'They don't have to have it so loud,' he bawled into the gloom. 'Jeesus Christ!' He had a shining bald dome, and W.C. Fields' nose so pitted by heavy drinking that mice might have nibbled at it. 'They've no savvy. That's it,' he declared mournfully. 'No comprehenso.' He held up a fist and shook it at me. 'Don't say I said it.' 'I won't,' I promised.

Komorowski jigged by again, held fast this time in the arms of Whistler's granny in black face. Even in this dungeon-like obscurity, the sweat gleamed on his brow like quicksilver. On my other side, a long-haired Korean – a jolly type, not a volunteer killer – was trying to entice Graham onto the dance floor: '*Tak-shee, tak-shee*,' he was imploring – or that's what it sounded like. Graham looked at me, making signs like a man drowning.

The Korean muttered again, '*Tak-shee, tak-shee.*'

I said, 'Have a little dance with him, Graham.'

'Go on, Graham,' Chris said, encouragingly.

'I'm getting married in six months, for God's sake.' But the Korean was speaking urgently now. '*Tak-shee, tak-shee – tak-shee!*'

'Get a move on, Graham, or he may turn nasty. He's been at sea three months, remember.'

'Here – put this whisky down for courage.'

Graham took the drink, but his face still wore an expression of desperation. 'You're just a couple of bloody sadists, throwing a young boy like me, that's about to be married, into the arms – '

'*Tak-shee, tak-shee! Bok!*'

'Graham!'

'Oh, blimey. All right. The things I do....'

He and the Korean dived together into the struggling mass, and the music – a Pacific version of 'Embraceable You' now – closed over them like animated treacle.

The old American said, 'No savvy, as far as the eye can see. Take a drink?'

I thanked him: 'A scotch, please.'

A double came. The American was a drilling expert, he said; he drilled for anything – water, oil, gold – you name it.

Graham waltzed uneasily by, holding the smiling Korean almost daintily at arm's length. They might have been dancing ring-a-ring-o'-roses in slow motion.

The American said, 'Jee-sus Christ. You don't have to sleep alone in this place.' A smiling woman like Babar the Elephant came up to our table. 'Nice, but no comprehenso,' the American said, waving her away. 'No savvy. That's their trouble. But don't say I said so.' He ordered six more beers for the three of us.

'How old am I?' he demanded when they came.

'Sixty-two,' I said.

'Thanks very much.' He was gratified. 'I'm seventy-five. I'll buy you a drink.'

'A large scotch,' I said.

Time passed.

Graham Harris's sweaty face went by yet again. By now his shirt clung to his back as if he'd been out in a rain storm. The Korean's left hand sat on his shoulder like a tarantula.

'Yoo-hoo!' somebody yelled at him. Perhaps it was Chris – or me.

Almost immediately, as if summoned by a war cry, two Koreans were standing in front of me, bowing their heads up and down like birds drinking.

'That's a kow-tow,' the American said. 'They're kow-towing you. It's the custom. *These* guys have plenty of savvy. Better be polite and give 'em a kow-tow back.'

But the kow-tow didn't save me. It turned into something between a Highland reel and a galloping version of Auld Lang Syne as the three of us bumped and crashed around the dance floor like dodgem cars at a fairground. I was luckier than Graham. The music soon changed to rock 'n roll. The Samoans went wild, and the Koreans scuttled off the floor like terrified mice at an elephant round-up.

'No punch-ups?' Tony Carter said next day. 'That's odd. I expect you'd have liked a punch-up. You should have been with us New Year's Eve in Nuku'alofa with the Tongans. We had a good 'un there. The radio officer had to get back to the ship by walking along the top of a reef up to his waist in water!'

Pago-Pago had a sort of village green now and some attractive colonial-style wooden houses.

The tiny, dismal hotel in which poor Sadie Thompson had been bullied and then raped by Mr Davidson had actually existed – 'a frame house of two storeys, with broad verandahs on both floors and a roof of corrugated iron. . . . On the ground floor, the owner (a half-cast named Horn) had a store where he sold canned goods and cottons.' I found a 'Sadie Thompson's Mart' in what was said to be the same building. It was a two-storey wooden structure, at any rate. I bought some plum-coloured cotton cloth there, half listening for some echo of Sadie's famous cry of contempt – 'You men! You filthy, dirty pigs! You're all the same, all of you. Pigs! Pigs!' And I took a turn down the long sweep of beach where kind Dr Macphail had seen, lying half in the water and half out, a dreadful object, Davidson's body . . . 'the throat cut from ear to ear, and in the right hand still the razor with which the deed was done'.

There was no one here now. Only the smell of fish from the canning factory, and dark clouds gathering overhead. As I reached the asphalted road to walk back to the ship, it began to rain.

Twenty five

We lay off Tahiti – in sight of what Maugham had called 'the unimaginable beauty of the island that is named Moorea'. Its mountains floated mistily in a perfect sea. Maugham had not exaggerated.

The radio was giving out dismal news. I was suddenly made aware again of the Falklands situation. Now what had happened? The Royal Marines had re-taken South Georgia; an Argentine submarine had been attacked by British helicopters and badly damaged. A British naval blockade was in force round the southern extremities of Argentina – precisely where I was headed. This called for some thought. Tony Carter and Chris Macdonald huddled with me over a chart. There was Tahiti, a turquoise spider at the centre of a web of black lines that meant regular sea routes.

'Where do you want to go after Papeete?' Tony asked. 'Chile? Are you sure? Nothing regular seems to go there, does it?' True enough, nothing did.

'There's a regular line up to Panama, though,' Chris said encouragingly.

'Or all the way up to San Francisco.'

I found no encouragement in that. I was determined to see Cape Horn, British blockade or no British blockade. And I had one gleam of potential comfort: there was time for the war to fade away. After Tahiti I still would have half the width of the Pacific Ocean to cross.

Tony said, 'Leave it to a very, very shrewd and helpful man in Tahiti. Our agent – Raphael Tixier.'

'I'll have to.' Graham and Steve came up and suggested a drink and after that I felt a little better. At least Cook, Melville, Gauguin were just ahead. I wasn't going to let General Galtieri or Mrs Thatcher give me

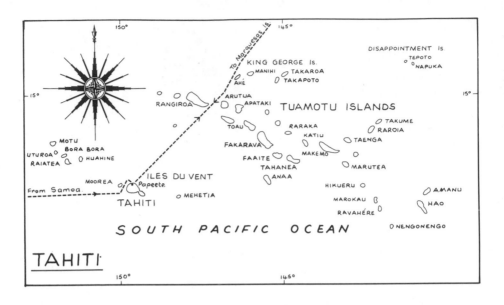

TAHITI

grey hairs yet. I would pray to Raphael Tixier. He was only twenty miles away.

The entrance to the harbour of Papeete was as narrow as Chris Macdonald had said. The curved volcanic ridges were creased like stiff, crumpled paper. A UTA jet took off with a roar over the lagoon. A small warship lay between the *Pacific Islander* and the beautiful silhouette of Moorea. The blue in the French tricolor matched the blue of the water.

In his office Raphael Tixier said, 'Anything we can do, just say,' and my spirits rose. For a start, he was the part-owner of a vessel plying to the Marquesas and back. 'The owner's cabin is yours,' he said, smiling. Jim Hostetler, his American assistant, had hope of a passage to South America. A new line was sending a ship, the *African Star*, quite soon. She would go to Valparaiso, the port of Chile, after one stop in Ecuador and another in Peru.

'It looks as if you're in luck,' Jim said, and we went to have a farewell drink aboard the *Pacific Islander*.

A furtive figure put a ratlike head round Tony's cabin door and hissed 'Capitaine?'

A man came in who might have been on a starvation diet for a week.

His blond hair was *en brosse*, his trembling hands were calloused and he had sores on his legs. A Victorian writer would have described his eyes as haunted. He might have been twenty-five or thirty-five. In accented English he said he was an Austrian deserter from the French Foreign Legion base in Tahiti.

'Good Lord,' said Carter.

The man wanted to escape. He had done seven months in the Legion, he said, and could take no more. He had been two weeks on the run. It didn't look as if he could take much more of that either.

'Sit down,' Carter told him kindly, and pushed a can of beer towards him.

There were five of them on the run, French and German, the man said, lapping the beer – they were dodging the cops round Papeete.

I wondered why he had not waited. It seemed idiotic to desert in Tahiti, an island in the middle of the Pacific. Why not wait for Europe?

'Where d'you sleep at night?' Carter asked.

'In a garden, sometimes. Sometimes with a Tahitian girlfriend. The Legion hates men who escape.' He stretched a hand towards Carter. 'Please take me. I do any work. Any kind. No matter how hard, how dirty.'

Over his second beer, and very gently and patiently, Tony told him about crew lists, the seamen's unions, the terrible penalties for harbouring wanted men. 'I have a Chinese crew – you see? They wouldn't like it either.'

He would get at least a year's hard labour in a military prison, the Austrian said lugubriously. He had no papers; none of any kind. He was bound, he told us, to be caught.

'I am truly sorry,' Carter said with real compassion.

It was harrowing but hopeless, and the Austrian didn't insist. It was evidently not the first time he had begged captains to help him escape from the biggest mistake of his life. And when he knew it was hopeless, he began to relax. His hands stopped shaking, he drank his beer, and he sat back and smiled with evident interest at photographs Carter showed him of a recent holiday in Gstaad, nodding his head as if he were looking at photographs of some lost paradise. '*Wunderbar, wunderbar,*' he murmured.

Docile, he shook hands before going back to his bolthole. I pointed through the window. 'Try a yacht,' I suggested. 'Find a couple of American hippies about to sail. They might like to take you just for the adventure.' I had no idea how he would manage at the other end without papers, wherever they dropped him, but it would get him off the island. He nodded, and went down the gangway.

Later, when the *Pacific Islander* had sailed, I met a legionnaire called Luigi ('Or Louis, if you prefer') in a bar called the Jasmine and heard his view of the Austrian's chances. The legionnaires stood up at the bar. They tilted their white kepis to the back of their heads and leaned across to kiss the Polynesian bar-girls. I was sitting at a table with a cup of coffee when two of them joined me by chance.

Luigi was not young – in his late thirties, perhaps; Salvador, his *copain*, was not much younger, small, thin, taciturn. We shook hands, and after introductions I told them about the deserter. Luigi said he'd heard there were three or four at large. Everyone heard about escapees. They'd be captured, of course, he shrugged. It was clear he had no sympathy for them. I was surprised. I had thought that all legionnaires, like prisoners of war and convicts, dreamed of a Great Escape and made heroes of those who got away. That showed how little I knew of the Legion's *esprit de corps*, Luigi said.

'A deserter has broken his word. He is not to be trusted. You said, try an American yacht. Even if he is lucky, that *mec*, and makes it to San Francisco, as you say, and tries to publish his story there – *eh b'en, quoi donc?* – will anyone buy it? Won't the *flics* just ship him back?'

'It's an old story,' I said, 'that Legion escape.'

'*Oui*, it's an old story anyway,' Luigi agreed. 'And to desert in *Tahiti*! The young guy is crazy. The Legion offered him a regular life – in exchange for what? For one thing. For loyalty. Now he's broken his word. Now no one can respect him.'

I don't know why the idea of honourable obligation to the Legion surprised me. I suppose *Beau Geste* had created an impression of press-ganged desperadoes in uniform, whose loyalty was exclusive to themselves; men without a country or a code, except the code the Legion imposed through its brutal drill sergeants. I had forgotten that legionnaires were not press-ganged. They had volunteered. They owed something.

Luigi had a hard, dignified face. It could have belonged to a Mafia hit man or a head waiter in a swanky Italian restaurant. His father and brothers, he said, were of Italian origin, miners in eastern France. He himself was saving up to retire to Brittany, beside the sea. Tahiti? It was too *enfermé*. Claustrophobic. Of course, there were some nice-looking women. Fickle enough. Take silent Salvador, for example. He had a beautiful Tahitian woman; had had her for a few years. Now, unfortunately, she was beginning to play around, not looking after his baby son. 'The neighbours are always telling him that she's out. And the baby's left alone,' Luigi said. 'That's not good. So Salvador slapped her around a bit yesterday. He'll send the baby's allowance money to her parents in future.'

Salvador heard all this and managed a smile.

'Oh, he's *très colérique* sometimes, is Salvador. Spanish. He has a small old car,' Luigi said sadly. 'He drinks and then drives. One day he'll smash himself up.' He had wanted to go straight, and for that he needed papers. 'Yes,' laughed Luigi, 'he joined the Legion for the papers. Well, the Legion gave him the papers. And now at last he knows who he is – eh? Don't you?'

'At last,' murmured Salvador. They were his first words.

'Hey, you,' Luigi called to a passing waiter. 'You dance beautifully. *Comme une belle dame*. Please bring three beers here when you get tired.' The waiter shrugged disdainfully.

'See there,' Luigi pointed behind the bar. 'That's a disco that has everything. *Travélos*.' Transvestites. 'People go *pour tirer un coup, eh? Pour faire la pipe*.' For screwing; for oral sex.

'*Pour moi, les gonzesses*, the good-time girls.' The waiter came with the beer. '*Tu es fait pour les fêtes, chéri*,' Luigi told him, winking at me.

We had dinner together in the end: raw fish, calf's head sauté, red wine. For a legionnaire Luigi was a revelation. He talked of books. '*La Condition Humaine*, yes, good – *pas un mot, eh!*' But the writer he really liked was Pearl S. Buck. '*The Good Earth*, ah, *ça*....!'

I had no desire at all to hang about the streets and tourist hotels of Papeete. It was not unpleasant, but it just wasn't interesting. It belonged to France – after all Tahiti is in French Polynesia – and it was the least 'Pacific' place I had seen so far. With its palm trees, its Corniche, its cafes, its yacht harbour, it was like a French Mediterranean town with a naval base tacked on. The beauty that makes Papeete 'Pacific' and memorable belongs to Moorea, the island with the fingerlike mountains across the blue bay. An island like that could only be in the Pacific Ocean.

Of course, writers had been bewailing the demise of old, traditional Tahiti for well over a hundred years. Alan Moorehead wrote in *The Fatal Impact* that, at the time of Cook's arrival in 1769, 'they [the Tahitians] were probably happier than they were ever to be again', and by 1830

New England whaling ships called at Tahiti regularly, with the usual calamitous results. The rape of the Pacific had followed the same pattern here as elsewhere. A surgeon on a whaler told people back home that the nightly brawls and riots in Papeete would have disgraced the most profligate purlieus of London. That was only sixty years after Cook. 'In the slovenly and haggard and diseased inhabitants of the port, it was vain to attempt to recognise the prepossessing figure of the Tahitian as pictured by Cook.' By 1830 a listless aimlessness had overtaken natives ravaged by tuberculosis, smallpox, dysentery and venereal disease. Even European food was a menace – it decayed the fine Tahitian teeth.

By the time Paul Gauguin arrived in 1891, Papeete was a place dominated by officious second-rate French *petits fonctionnaires* – all the competent ones seem to have gone to North Africa or Senegal. 'When you reach Tahiti, the travellers who are going back, get off the ship. The new arrivals must be inspected; the Governor is there (the top-hat is indescribable) and all the riff-raff . . . but very graciously, they ask, "Have you any money?"'

The Tahitian chambermaid at the Tahiti Hotel saw my book of Gauguin's writings, painting and sketches lying on a side table.

'*C'est M. Gauguin, le peintre?*'

I opened the book and showed her colour photographs of modern Tahiti, somehow expecting her to admire those most. But no – she gazed for a long while at the reproduction of a Gauguin painting of two women.

'*Oh, elles étaient jolies, les femmes de cette époque,*' she cried. 'She is the *maman* of the other. Or the sister.'

She liked the wood carving of the Tahitian moon goddess, Hina, and the earth spirit, Fatu.

'Hina and Fatu!' she repeated. 'Hina and Fatu!'

There had been many stone carvings of gods and ancestors in the Marquesas Islands; Stevenson had seen them. Herman Melville's valley of Typee was on the island of Nuku Hiva. Paul Gauguin's tomb was on a hillside on Hiva Oa; in the Marquesas – that was where I wanted to be now.

Twenty six

Off to Typee!

A young Chinese in Tixier's office had made out my ticket for the Marquesas Islands, and Raphael Tixier went with me to the harbour to watch the ship sail. The *Taporo* was not large; she had a red and white hull, a French flag on her stern, and a yellow funnel with two thin blue horizontal rings. She had two hatches forward and two large ventilators like bat's ears. Her captain was a short, moderately dark-skinned man with a gravelly voice and a hand which shook mine powerfully. 'Captain Alphonse,' he said, without smiling.

The cabin Raphael Tixier had given me was under the bridge across a stairway from the captain. Relatively large and smelling not unpleasantly of varnish, it had a window to each of its bulkheads and so was extremely light. There were a number of tables and chairs. Just right, I thought, and '*De luxe*,' I said to Tixier. Compared to the *Ann*, she was *de luxe*. And in a small vessel you were that much nearer to the surface of the sea; you could feel part of it. I preferred her to relative monsters like the *Chengtu* and the *Pacific Islander*.

'Jim has sent a telex to the owners of the *African Star* in Sydney. We should have an answer by the time you get back.'

So that was taken care of – as far as it could be.

Tixier waved from the shore. The *Taporo* began to move to the entrance of the lagoon.

Now I could imagine I was Herman Melville in the whaler *Dolly*, turning my face towards a group of longed-for islands.

'Hurra, my lads! It's a settled thing; next week we shape our course to the Marquesas!' The Marquesas! What strange visions of outlandish things

273

does the very name spirit up! Naked houris – cannibal banquets – groves of coconuts – coral reefs – tattooed chiefs – and bamboo temples; sunny valleys planted with breadfruit trees – carved canoes dancing on the flashing blue waters – savage woodlands guarded by horrible idols....

Coconuts, coral reefs, valleys of breadfruit trees, carved canoes – these I could say I had already seen something of since abandoning the South China Sea. I had even, come to think of it, been befriended by a tattooed chief. I hoped – if it was too late for naked houris and ravening cannibals – for at least one or two horrible idols. I had no plans, though, to jump ship.

Dolly was the fictional name Melville gave to the whaler from which he and Toby Greene deserted in the Marquesas. In reality, he had signed aboard the *Acushnet*, under Captain Valentine Peace Jr, at Fairhaven on 3 January 1841 – becoming one of the crew, he said, of 'twenty-five dastardly and mean-spirited wretches'. Eighteen months later, the *Acushnet* arrived at the Marquesas Islands with only salt horse and sea biscuit left to eat. Eighteen months! – but this was not unduly long. The progress from New England to the Pacific sperm whale grounds included the rounding of Cape Horn and calls at ports in Chile or Peru for provisions. 'The longevity of Cape Horn whaling voyages,' Melville wrote, 'is proverbial, frequently extending over a period of four or five years....' I liked his story of the whaler *Perseverance* which, after many years' absence, was given up for lost. At last she was glimpsed somewhere in the vicinity of the ends of the earth, her crew composed by now of venerable Greenwich Pensioner-looking old salts, who just managed to hobble about her deck. Herman Melville and Toby Greene had had no intention of ending up as grey-heads, dastardly or not, on the *Acushnet*.

I found Captain Alphonse on the bridge in nothing but a pair of white shorts. As soon as we were out at sea, '*Une bière?*' Good. A crewman appeared with four bottles of Heineken. The biggest man I had seen so far in Polynesia, from the point of view of sheer girth, came in from the wing and introduced himself: the chief engineer, Aroma Huri. Beside him Stan Laurel's Oliver Hardy would have looked like the undersized fish you throw back.

We headed NNE, through the Tuamotu Archipelago, making for the Palliser Islands, King George Island, Disappointment Island. Low lines of palms appeared from time to time in the distance, grew moderately and faded rapidly. No wooded hills, no volcanic shapes here. This is the region of atolls – erratic rings of coral barely higher than the surface of the ocean, on which the tousled heads of coconut palms soar up like petrified distress rockets over waterlogged ships.

The officers and crew of the *Taporo* were far from resembling Melville's 'dastardly and mean-spirited wretches'. Gruff Captain Alphonse turned out to be a most friendly man. I taught him some English – although he knew some to start with. He looked round my small collection of books, picking up *Typee* while I poured him a whisky. When I explained about Melville's visit to Nuku Hiva in 1842, the warriors, the bamboo houses, the description of the people, he nodded.

'No *vrais Marquises* people any more. They are *mélangés* with Europeans. Or maybe there are a few old ones!' He laughed. 'Listen. Never involve yourself with *une marquisienne*. Take my word. Never. I've known these islands for – *ouf*! – many, many years – *tu me crois?* Can't be trusted. Talk, talk, talk – bla, bla, bla! Behind your back.' He made an unmistakable gesture. 'And *this*, whenever you're away. *Toof-toof*!' – the gestures multiplied – 'with *everyone*!' He downed the whisky with a flourish. 'Avoid the *marquisiennes*. . . . *Attention!* I should know.'

Had I any books on French, he wanted to know. Only a life of Gauguin.

'Why do people pay so much for his paintings?' the captain sighed, giving me a second local opinion on the man whose grave I longed to see. 'I don't like them. Not at all. The drawings – so ugly.' He pointed to a sketch of a breadfruit tree and said, 'Capitaine Bligh was here to buy this. They built a double canoe, the traditional Tahitian kind, in the Marquises, just for the film *The Bounty* [he pronounced it 'Boonty']. Le Capitaine Bligh! The film was not too good.'

'Marlon Brando has an hotel on an atoll, is that right?'

'He keeps well hidden. Tourists go to his hotel, but it's very expensive. Of course, I've never been there.'

'Papeete is expensive.'

'That's because Tahiti is run by the Mafias.'

'Mafias! French? Tahitian?'

'Both. Half and half.' He explained that *kava*, for instance, was forbidden here because the beer importers were against it. 'Big potatoes, cabbages, other things that grow easily on some islands here, have been "suppressed" by men who have an interest in importing. The *entrepreneurs*.'

Kava forbidden? It was legal all over Samoa, Fiji and Tonga, I told him, and was universally considered a much less harmful drink than the Europeans' alcohol.

The captain said in astonishment, 'What? *Kava* legal?'

'Why not? It is an honourable drink. The Samoans use it ceremonially at important functions. It doesn't make people fight as alcohol does.'

Alphonse called in a loud voice to the chef, 'Hey, Capitaine Cook! *Venez ici!*' He winked at me. 'Capitaine Bligh *vous parle!*' And the chef remained Capitaine Cook from that moment.

We ate marinated fish, tomatoes and onions with tabasco sauce, then meat and potatoes mixed with rice. Five of us filled the little mess. Captain Alphonse; the mate, Eric Maamaatua; the supercargo, Michel Tiareura, a grey, helpful man; the gargantuan chief engineer, Aroma Huri; and myself. At noon we squeezed into Eric's cabin and drank beer or whisky. Then we drank Fontel, *vin de table supérieur*, from plastic bottles. It went down well with marinated fish. 'At sea, no Tahitian is fighting when he drinks. Never. But ashore....' Michel's stomach heaved with mirth. '*Oh, la, la!*' But the officers left the booze alone at dinnertime, because they all shared the night watches and would not take risks with reefs in the darkness.

There were other forms of life in the tiny mess. Cockroaches clung to its walls, looking like decorative studs until they moved. When, on the second midday at sea, a cockroach plopped from the ceiling onto my plate, Captain Alphonse yelled, 'Capitaine Cook! Give the place a spray with the American stuff.' But that evening the cockroaches were quite unaffected; they even seemed to have acquired a somewhat self-satisfied air. Whatever 'the American stuff' was, it must have contained vitamins.

276

Cockroaches were ubiquitous on the *Taporo*: there again it was like the *Ann*. Going to the galley to fill a glass with cold drinking water, I discovered pots and pans with herds of 'cockies' browsing on them. I could feel them at night on my blankets. Fortunately I don't worry about cockroaches. Snakes, leeches and scorpions – I care about them. Once I was almost driven to distraction in a hotel at Meknes in Morocco by bed bugs so big that, roaming about in my pillow stuffing, they sounded like elephants in dense pampas grass.

To contain the rats that Captain Alphonse admitted were virtually ineradicable in the cargo area, there were two purposeful-looking cats aboard. They were small now, but they knew their job, the captain said. 'You wait, they should get bigger every day.' The cats had oddly splayed toes. In the moderate swell they prowled about sticking their funny flat feet out to each side – like true sailors crossing a bucking deck.

My notes:

'*Les Iles du Roi Georges*,' the chief officer, Eric Maamaatua, says, pointing. From the wheelhouse, King George is just visible. We roll a good deal, but it has a soothing quality about it. In the bows, a sailor is playing a guitar and someone is singing a tangy Pacific island song.

Three scruffy, unshaven French youths lie on the deck. A thin, bearded Frenchman is a technical teacher at a new government school at Nuka Hiva. His wife comes from there. A youngish, heavy lady in a loose, cool dress, she never seems to smile or speak. Her expression shares the hopelessness of the nude girl in Gauguin's painting *Nevermore*. He's been out here ten years. He dislikes Papeete intensely: '*Pourri, pourri* – ruined.'

How much longer would he stay?

'*Ouf* – difficult to say.'

Next day, before our landfall at Hiva Oa, the French teacher says he will introduce me to an engineer friend in Atuona, the main 'town'. He explains his poor wife is terrified of a rough sea like the one they had going to Papeete. Reverting to his remark, '*Papeete, pourri*,' he explains that too many no-good Frenchmen are coming here, getting footholds in various fields. 'Oh, lots of

things. There've been people selling electric blankets to the Tahitians on islands without electricity. That sort of thing.'

What about the ban on *kava*?

'Ha – that's the *curé*'s ban – he's a powerful force.'

I note that people – French, at that – talk to me about the
powers of Church and State in modern Tahiti in the scornful tones
that Gauguin used about it in 1900.

Approach to Hiva Oa. 8.45 p.m. Captain on the bridge in
singlet and shorts. A sky full of shooting stars. A great range of
cliffs: moonlight strikes down on sharp, knifelike outlines of rock.
A star falls like a cigarette end and goes out in mid-flight.

We head for a narrow opening in the inky masses ahead. Hiva
Oa is the long, high outline, black with blacker shadows, that
Alvaro Mendana – the first European here – saw when he came
from Peru in 1595, naming the island group after his wife, the
Marquesa de Mandonca. He left two hundred dead 'Marquesans'
and three large crosses to commemorate his passing.

Waves break on tall black shoulders of rock – white shapes
leaping up like dogs to welcome their master home. Captain
Alphonse checks the radar. We are entering a tight little bay. A
shimmering circlet of lights is visible at the foot of the soaring
screen of blackness that is slowly enfolding us, and above which
the Great Bear is standing on its head.

Then, a breeze and – very distinctly – the smell of flowers and
vegetation.

'*Ah, oui,*' Captain Alphonse waves a hand. 'The *noa-noa* – the
parfum. The flowery valley.'

He whistles sharply. The anchor is let go. We are surrounded by
silence, and the perfumed air of Atuona.

Once upon a time, the whaling fleets anchored here and carried off a
complement of women for their next voyage. Now it is yachtsmen,
mostly from America and Canada. Here, unlike in Western Samoa and
the Solomons, the damage has long been done. In the 1840s, the
Handbook tells me, the population of the Marquesas was twenty
thousand; now it is two thousand.

Ashore next day, I experienced nothing of the harassment R.L.S.
received from the 'ruffianly fellows' from a whaling boat, who
surrounded him 'with harsh laughter and rude looks', reminding him of

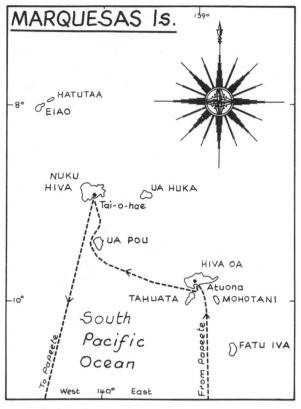

MARQUESAS Is. 139°

HATUTAA
-8° EIAO

NUKU HIVA   UA HUKA
Tai-o-hae
UA POU

HIVA OA
Atuona
TAHUATA   MOHOTANI
-10°

South Pacific Ocean

To Papeete
From Papeete

FATU IVA

West 140° East

the inhabitants of 'the slums of some great city'. It was peaceful and orderly now. The village (Atuona can only be called that) straggled up the valley along a few narrow, asphalted lanes. There was a modern school; a *gendarmerie* post at a junction; everywhere flowers. In a central store, in the Café de la Paix, a few 'yachties' stood chatting and drinking beer or soft drinks from cans under an advertisement for a *Bal à la Maison des Jeunes – repas sur place (avec pâtisserie).*'

'How ya doin'?'

'Pretty good. How are you guys?'

They were re-meeting after sailing from Hawaii or San Francisco. They were the World Outside, just as much as a memorial in the lane that read: '*Mort pour la France. 1914–1918: Soldat Naspuo A. Puu Fafiau. 1939–1944: Soldat Tehaamo Tohiau.*'

I plodded up a lane towards the house of the teacher's friend – he had drawn me a sketch map – past a post office, a bank, the *gendarmerie* and the *Maison des Jeunes* into a dense valley which sloped gradually upwards through the trees and foliage in which I could hear an invisible stream running over rocks. Here nondescript bungalows with iron roofing crouched among fruit trees and plants with flowers like white stars, or scarlet bells, or mauve firecrackers, and little things of yellow and blue that looked suitable for any British hedgerow. Added to that, there was the *noa-noa* – the extraordinary perfume of the valley – even stronger here than it had been the night before. Occasionally jeeps passed up or down the lane, their drivers occasionally sunburned white men, presumably French.

I found the French teacher's friend in one of these bungalows. He had a striking name – Jésus L'Evêque – and obviously liked visits. His wife was in Papeete, I think. He was not perturbed by the absence of his friend the teacher, whom I had left wrestling with some video equipment on board. He had been a plumber in Paris; now he ran a job-training school, he said, when we both had beer in our hands. An experiment. The idea was to keep the local youth occupied, but, more than that, to teach them rudimentary techniques of construction, engineering and so forth. To make young Marquesans proud of their traditions – the tradition of house building, for example.

'There are no Marquesan houses left,' he said. 'I want to get my pupils to build one – you know, bamboo, wood, leaf thatching. Just to show them how it was done. And I want them to learn all the old, beautiful, forgotten designs for *tapa*, the bark cloth.'

In *Oviri*, his *Writings of a Savage*, Gauguin had written:

> We don't seem to suspect in Europe that there exists, among the Marquesans, a very advanced decorative art.... Today even for gold you can no longer find any of those beautiful objects in bone, rock, iron-wood which they used to make.... There is not the prettiest official's wife who would not exclaim at the sight of it, 'It's horrible! It's savagery!'

'The Tahitians today don't give a damn. They want video, Papeete, Paris. We try to get the young Tahitians to copy the old delicate *tapa* patterns. But it takes a foreigner to tell them.'

He brought me a book of strong, simple *tapa* patterns, saying, 'See. A German made that book. Take the valleys of the Marquesas,' he went on, 'they were kingdoms, fiefdoms. The old civilization – if you'll excuse the expression – was in these valleys.' He shook his head. 'No Tahitian or Marquesan is interested in all that. *We*, foreigners, know more about the corners and valleys and bays. They don't give a damn for culture, for their past in any form. It's video, Papeete, Paris.'

It made depressing hearing. Who, I thought, made them aspire to Western-style material wealth? We foreigners. Who undermines the will to independence? The French, and elsewhere the Americans. Of course, the real Marquesans had been destroyed ages ago. Still, I had to confirm the ban on lava-lavas and *kava*. Could there exist such an impertinent interference with other people's culture?

Apparently, yes. L'Evêque said at once, with a laugh, 'The bishop here forbids the pareo – that's the local word for lava-lava. Absolutely. A girl was turned away from school the other day for wearing a dress that only came up to her collarbones and only fell to her calves. The principal said – and she was supported, of course, by the *curé* – that she must cover her shoulders. Yes! Can you imagine? And no pareos for *anyone*. As for *kava* – forbidden. Completely.' He looked at me, still laughing. 'Madness, you say? Oh, yes, I agree.'

L'Evêque broke off here and put some fruit on the table. 'My wife produces pineapples, avocados, paw-paws, mangoes, limes.... Polynesians are lazy. They grow just enough for themselves. They're not commercial. That's why the French and Chinese are able to import far too many things.' He shook his head. 'They take the commission. The Government takes the tax. And the cost of living soars.... The Tahitians don't like us French at all really.' He reflected on this for a moment, then continued, 'They'd much prefer the Americans. Did you know that?'

'The Americans have more money.'

'That's it. They see the yachts and the dollars coming in. People in Bora Bora, one of the islands nearer Tahiti, had an American base dumped on them in the war.'

'Forty years ago.'

'Yes, but they still can't forget those wonderful dollars.'

We ate in silence for a while.

'Remember, too,' the indefatigable L'Evêque went on, 'the best French are not coming here now. Some are good, of course. Others are misfits, bombastic, here to feather their nests. The Tahitians notice these things.'

'Could they manage independence?'

'Oh, no. Tahiti runs on subventions from Paris. It exists on them. That's the power of the French here.'

After a while, I thanked him and said I would go and visit Gauguin's grave. I only had a day here.

'Gauguin's house – nothing remains of it now. They may be going to restore his *Maison de Jouir*, that's what I heard.' Gauguin's house had been a two-storey affair of wood and bamboo, with a large, six-windowed studio upstairs. Over the entrance he had put up a provocative sign, *Maison de Jouir* – House of Pleasure. That and his consumption of alcohol – two hundred and twenty-four bottles of wine, fifty-five litres of rum and thirty-two litres of absinthe in the single year before he died in Atuona, according to his liquor supplier's books – his habit of wearing a blue pareo, a green shirt and a green beret, and his deliberate cutting of officials and priests at every opportunity, had outraged the small, stuffy, white community of the day.

'The *Maison de Jouir* was more or less where the mayor's office is now,' L'Evêque had said. Yachties, male and female, were standing about there in scarlet baseball caps and tight shorts when I passed. No *curé* would be outraged by tight shorts today – not even in Atuona.

I puffed up the hill to the cemetery and was relieved to find it was empty. There was no church. Under frangipani trees anonymous, undecorated white crosses poked up indistinctly through long, unkempt grass. I had no need to search about for Gauguin's grave – round it, at least, the grass was cut, and the grave itself was not white like the others but composed of sombre, distinctive slabs of lava that made a coffin-shaped platform on the foot of which was carved in the lava – 'Paul Gauguin 1903'. Someone had draped a wreath of fresh flowers and garlands of seashells and coral over the tomb, and the overhanging trees had shed brown leaves and a few white, starlike blooms to brighten the sad lumps of lava. At the painter's head, like a fierce, ambivalent bodyguard, stood a copy of his ceramic statuette *Oviri*, the enigmatic Tahitian god-goddess.

Nothing could be more appropriate. Gauguin had found the burial place he wanted and deserved, eleven thousand miles from France. To his right is the tomb of the Belgian singer, Jacques Brel, who died here of cancer in 1978. Behind lie other memorials – one, ironically, is to a forgotten bishop – half lost in long grass and undergrowth. In front the cemetery slopes sharply down – simply by raising his head a fraction, Gauguin, like Stevenson on Mount Vaea, could look over his feet to the sea far below. Tilting his head farther back, he would see towering ridges; he is, you might say, perfectly suspended between mountain and sea.

The sun moved in and out of clouds, blurring or bringing into sharp focus the wooded crest of the mountain. Raw scars of rock began halfway down it, and then the tide of trees lapped up from the valley where Jésus L'Evêque lived. It was warm. I was alone at Gauguin's feet with a few whistling mynah birds. I was in no hurry; I wished I had a book and a picnic. I smelled the sun in the hot grass and began to think I was on a summer hillside in Provence. My eyes drooped. I slept.…

It was cooler when I woke, but the sun still warmed the lava boulders of the tomb. Oviri looked at me impassively. I got up and pushed into the long grass, wary for snakes, and squatted down, carefully avoiding some sharp, up-thrusting plants like green bayonets. A call of nature has to be dealt with even in a cemetery. I was busy dealing with it when I realized I was not alone. I heard the first step quite soon, but it was some time before the second followed it. Then, in quick succession, came a third and a fourth. Slowly and furtively, someone was approaching the spot where I crouched with such lack of dignity. The sexton? The *curé*? Would I be taken in charge? Would I return to the *Taporo* in company with a *gendarme*? – 'The charge, monsieur, is – *sacré nom d'un nom* – defecating on consecrated ground!' The steps continued to approach. An embarrassing exposure seemed imminent. I coughed – some small modest sign that I was there seemed appropriate. Meanwhile, I was not inactive. I wrestled extensively with my clothing and was still painfully wrestling (an aggressive sprig of cactus had entangled itself in my shirt-tail) when, with an exasperated snort, a head thrust out of the shrubbery. At my elbow, within touching distance. I froze. The head had a great, long, curving nose. Heavy-lidded eyes slowly blinked at me, then widened in astonishment; an upper lip as grey and thick as a slab of boiled beef curled back from monstrous discoloured teeth that pushed out towards me … I have the impression now that, for a hundredth of the second, I believed I was face to face with a hideous, outraged manifestation of Gauguin–Oviri. But, no. I put out a hand and patted the long, hairy, Bottom-like nose. I stroked the melancholy, drooping, hairy ears and I think I murmured, 'There, there,' in soothing tones. I have always loved horses. This one was small, old and lonely.

We took on board a jeep, twelve goats and a black and white pig. Leaving Hiva Oa our decks were cluttered with crates, sacks, bags, boxes and an outboard motor. The goats bleated and butted each other as if they were competing for the pig, which squealed continually. The upper part of the ship was festooned with banana plants and coconuts. We might have been part of one of Captain's Bligh's botanical expeditions. By the time we passed the mountainous outline of Ua Pou Island that claws the sky with the jagged fingers of a drowning witch – one of the least forgettable of all island outlines – the sweet *noa-noa* of Atuona had given way to more barnyard smells. But the image in my mind remained – still remains – of a foot-high statuette under a frangipani tree, dominant on a grassy hillside peopled by squabbling mynah birds, a lonely old horse and heaven knows how many Marquesan *tupapau* (the *aitus* of these islands). The spirit of Oviri, a frigate bird and several small terns travelled with us towards Nuku Hiva.

Twenty Seven

Tai-o-hae Bay.

'The *Snark* rested in a placid harbour that nestled in a vast amphitheatre, the towering walls of which seemed to rise direct from the water. Far up, to the east, we glimpsed the thin line of a trail, visible in one place, where it soured across the face of the wall. "The path by which Toby escaped from Typee!" we cried.'

Whether or not we (like Jack London) were looking at Toby Green's actual escape route, the word 'amphitheatre' was certainly the appropriate one to describe the main anchorage of Nuku Hiva. There was the glorious bay where in 1842 Melville had seen from the *Acushnet*'s deck the six-ship fleet of the French Admiral Du Petit Thouars in the process of sandbagging the Marquesas Islanders into the service of France. He made scornful remarks about the French warships calling there, 'floating batteries, which lay with their fatal tubes ostentatiously pointed at a handful of bamboo sheds, sheltered in a grove of coconuts!'

Herman Melville hardly had time to worry too much about the iniquities of French colonial conquest. The ship was soon entirely overrun by a laughing swarm of Marquesan girls – a 'dashing and irresistible party of boarders who succeeded in getting up the ship's side, where they clung dripping with the brine, their jet-black tresses streaming over their shoulders, and half enveloping their otherwise naked forms'. The debauch then – needless to say – began. 'But the feeblest barrier was interposed between the unholy passions of the crew and their unlimited gratification.... Alas for the poor savages...!'

No such welcome greeted the *Taporo*. I am sadly able to state that I walked down the jetty to which we tied up without so much as a handshake being offered to me by man, woman or beast.

Along the horseshoe of the bay a cluster of new buildings, some attempting an imitation of traditional Marquesan architecture – the *mairie*, *Travaux Publiques*, Banque de l'Indosuez. Yachts stood in the bay. There was nothing I wanted to see or do in this place with its wonderful scenery and its beautiful name like a sigh in a perfumed night – Tai-o-hae. It sounded like the name which Melville gave to the 'beauteous nymph Fayaway' with the 'strange blue eyes'. She was the only Typee who seemed truly to understand the distressful feelings of the two young American deserters when they found themselves the captives of a well-organized race of cannibal warriors.

Now it was the valley of the Typees I wished to visit. Not in the hope of finding my own Fayaway – I was well aware that the Typees were no more, victims of those all-too-familiar European invasions, alcohol and disease. Yet the valley Melville saw would be there; and even some vestiges of a civilization – for example, the immense stone platforms called *pae-paes* on which the Typees built houses and temples.

The French teacher on the *Taporo* had said I might go there on foot, on horseback or by jeep. I consulted Captain Alphonse, who in turn suggested a visit to Jim Hostetler's sister-in-law, a Marquesan who lived here. She was married to a prominent merchant, a Chinese Tahitian called Chin. 'Chin will know. Chin knows everything here,' Eric Maamaatua, the mate, confirmed and we went to Chin's for dinner together.

Chin and Michelle lived in a modern bungalow in a fine Marquesan garden. Michelle greeted us all with a kiss on the cheek and her husband was all smiles. It was impossible not to feel warmly towards such a friendly couple, who produced a meal of raw sailfish in a dark wine sauce, *langoustes* grilled on charcoal and French red wine.

'If Du Petit Thouars hadn't got here first,' I said after a while, 'we might be drinking warm English beer instead of wine.'

'Yes' Chin said. 'If he hadn't come, the Tahitians might all be speaking English.'

Michelle said, 'The Tahitians were doomed to be someone's plaything.'

'Capitaine Cook, *peut-être*,' Captain Alphonse suggested.

'Well,' said Michelle, 'he wasn't a religious man. There would have been more dancing hereabouts. Cook quite enjoyed all that.'

286

Chin said, 'Nowadays, young Tahitians don't dance spontaneously – okay, at weddings, on national days, yes. But normally they prefer video TV or cassette music. Or sleep.' As it happened, the Chin children were watching *Space Invaders* on the television set, transfixed. Later the news came on. There was nothing about the Falklands War, but a bomb had exploded in Paris, killing and wounding numerous passers-by. Shocked eye witnesses – a mechanic, a young butcher's assistant – gabbled to interviewers above the noise of ambulances and police sirens. 'I saw this car lifted bodily....' It seemed very good indeed to be in the Marquesas Islands. Give me a Typee warrior-cannibal any day, I thought, in preference to a twentieth-century idealist who believes that murder will bring the millennium.

Chin said, 'Go to the valley by jeep. The ship sails soon. It may rain and the track can get very bad. Be on the safe side. I know a good driver called Peine.'

And so next morning I set out with Peine to the valley of Typee. But I was not alone with him. 'Capitaine Cook', the chef of the *Taporo*, was with us, too – on business, he said. He was carrying a bunch of political tracts in a large manila envelope on behalf of the Parti Socialiste du Tahiti. There was an election coming on.

'I hope we won't all be arrested,' I said.

We wriggled up the side of that great amphitheatre in low gear. Terns and pure white birds which the driver said were parrots accompanied us until the dirt track climbed past a dense region of willows and reeds – the one, I supposed, that had given Melville and Toby such a devilish struggle as they pushed upwards out of sight of their ship. Wonderful vistas of cliff and sea met us at every turn. The air cooled and purified itself; far below, the *Taporo* and the yachts were toys to play with in the bath.

At the top of the ridge we dipped away down towards a valley which Melville wrote as Happar and which is now spelled Hapaa. The Happar people, he said, were good, while in the valley beyond them dwelt 'the dreaded Typees'. In Hapaa there was no sign of habitation now – there were no people, good or bad – and this may have accounted for Capitaine Cook's unusual excitement when we spotted human figures at the side of the track ahead. There were two of them – dark-skinned men who leaned on their pickaxes and watched our approach with expressions of wariness.

'Ah-ha! Hee!' cried Capitaine Cook triumphantly as we came up to them with undiminished speed, and he swiftly thrust a copy of the

287

manifesto at each in turn. 'Whee!' The driver seized a third copy and tossed it at random into the air. We bumped on, and looking back I saw the roadmen staring after us, awkwardly clutching their pamphlets. Only their two short-legged horses showed much interest; they gave up cropping the verge to snort suspiciously at the paper that fluttered on the ground.

We rose over another ridge and descended into a valley much greener than the first, with a bridge over a stream. Here we stopped. 'Taipivai,' announced Capitaine Cook, and got out of the jeep.

We had pulled up by a small bungalow on a track that crossed ours at right-angles and disappeared in one direction up the valley through thick avenues of trees. In the other direction it ran parallel to the stream towards the bay which, I knew from Melville's book and my map, was hidden behind the screen of vegetation. A fat, middle-aged man in shorts waddled out of the bungalow, recognized Peine and shook his hand. When Capitaine Cook eagerly gave him a pamphlet he folded it carefully and put it into his pocket. I was a writer, Capitaine Cook told him. The fat man seemed mildly interested to meet someone like me, a writer from outside. Speaking Marquesan, he gave me through Peine a few useful facts. There were now about one hundred and fifty inhabitants of Typee, he said. Half the coconuts here belonged to them, half to a company in Papeete. He was not quite sure what Typee (or Taipivai) meant, but he thought it meant 'where the river meets the sea'. He pointed out that his wooden bungalow stood on a platform of lava boulders like a chief's house in Samoa. There were several like it along the track.

Even in the shade of the breadfruit trees that screened the house the air was hot and oppressive. The midges were particularly militant. Melville had tried to protect himself from them by wrapping his body in a large roll of *tapa*. I could only curse and slap at them with one of Capitaine Cook's manifestos.

The valley was peaceful, though it could hardly help but seem melancholy. The magnificent, happy-go-lucky Typees whom Melville described in such glowing detail, and whom James Cook said were 'by far the most splendid islanders in the South Seas', had coughed and shivered their way to oblivion eight or nine decades ago. Melville saw the race of Typees during its finest hour. He had closely observed its chiefs, Marheyo, Mow-Mow, the war leader Mehevi; he had be-friended the hideous but devoted servant Kory-Kory, who wept in the waters of Typee Bay when he saw Melville escaping to freedom; and he had won the heart of the 'nymph' Fayaway. The valley was full now of birdsong and the sound of the stream rushing to the sea: and it was dead.

I asked Peine to drive us to the stream's mouth at Typee Bay. Here Melville had fled down a more primitive track, seizing his last chance of escape to the world of white men in an English whaling boat that had put by chance into the bay. We heard the same roar of surf and saw the same 'flash of billows through the trees' as he had done in a bay that was more like a deep cove with a beach of unexpected black sand – with only a boathook to fend off warriors armed with tomahawks, Melville would have had little time to notice the unusual colour of the sand, even though the 'beauteous sylph' Fayaway lay on it, sobbing to see him go. There, like a dog's head, was the stubby point of land at the bay's entrance from which Mow-Mow and his companions had dived in vain to intercept the whaling boat. Palm groves clustered on one side of the bay, and from a high ridge opposite a heavy, sweet smell floated down to us: the *noa-noa* of Typee.

'Hee! We go!' Capitaine Cook was impatient to distribute more pamphlets, so we drove back up the valley past a red-roofed church and a small store displaying shelves full of tinned pilchards, butter, jam and baby powder, where a sleepy boy sold us lemonade. The fat man was still outside his bungalow. Two hundred years ago, he said, this valley was full of temples and priests. I should see the *pae-paes*; some of the larger ones were burial grounds. All, I knew, were of extreme antiquity; the former inhabitants of the island had believed them to be the haunt of spirits.

I went on up the valley with Peine, leaving Capitaine Cook to distribute manifestos to other houses dotted about the valley. We had the only motor vehicle in Typee, and now and again we were obliged to edge past men leading small horses laden with bananas – the track was hardly wide enough to permit more than two such loads side by side. Beyond the houses we stopped at a tumbledown shed, and a woman sorting bananas outside it hailed Peine. When he had explained about my wish to see the *pae-paes*, she called to a girl who came yawning out of the shed and signalled to me in a bad-tempered way to follow her.

The girl was called Marie. She was the woman's daughter and she led me up a steep, slippery path through the palm trees at a rate that seemed deliberately designed to punish me for disturbing her. It was hard going. A faint breeze soon petered out, and low rain clouds pressing down on the treetops added humidity to the considerable heat.

Sweating and tormented by midges, I followed close behind Marie, trying to avoid humiliation by suppressing my increasing need to puff and wheeze like an old locomotive. As we climbed higher and higher up this infernal path, I had to fight off a desperate desire to stop and gasp for breath. We stumped on through the trees, my eyes hypnotized by Marie's muscular rump as it moved evenly and relentlessly under her pareo, evidently one the *curés* had missed. I tripped and fell over creepers, but she never looked back. I stumbled through piles of burnt human heads that were really coconuts rotted black by moisture. My towelling shirt clung to me as if I had taken a shower in it.

At last Marie stopped, and I saw with some satisfaction that even she was sweating. Sweating, but not smiling; scowling, in fact. She jerked a finger at a great jumble of high grass and creepers: 'Pae-pae,' she grumbled. Oblong shapes of stone as high as two-storey houses loomed half visible in the anarchy of grass and creepers. Here and there, black volcanic blocks thrust up menacingly like altars of Baal. Lurking dimly in the grass, three dark stone figures stood motionless, gazing back at us, like men surprised by enemies.

When I rejoined Marie's mother by the tumbledown shed, she told me there were eleven *pae-paes* up there – had I seen them all? She was quite angry with her lazy daughter for not having bothered to take me to them. So was I, having come all this way. But after all I had seen a *pae-pae* or two, and the three watching stone figures – and I felt I had sweated enough. Peine loaded a great branch of bananas into the pickup, Marie's mother kissed us both on the cheek and we drove down the valley. I tried to imagine what it had been like in the great days. The scenery Melville described was still there – the leafy canopies of enormous breadfruit trees and stately palms, for instance; and the romantic stream on whose banks he had watched chattering groups of naked beauties polishing coconut shells with small stones to make them into light, elegant drinking vessels like tortoiseshell goblets.

What then was missing? Life was missing. Gone were the taboo groves, once the scenes of the prolonged feasts and pagan rituals of these superstitious and cannibalistic Typees. You would need a flotilla of bulldozers, perhaps dynamite now, to uncover from the forest floor the man-made terraces, the amphitheatres, the idolatrous altars built of enormous blocks of black and polished stone, twelve or fifteen feet high, that once crouched, heavy with priestly mystique, in the cathedral-like gloom of the trees. Gone were those chattering beauties by the stream; gone every last descendant of gentle Kory-Kory and Fayaway; gone the chiefs and the warriors, their arts and their crafts. The magnificent Typees are gone – out of this valley, out of the world. For ever.

We collected Capitaine Cook and what was left of his socialist pamphlets from the fat man's bungalow, and Peine drove the pickup across the little bridge and up the Hapaa ridge once more. The low clouds threatened rain, but none fell. The road workers and their horses had disappeared. In the green wilderness of the Happaas we stopped and picked wild guavas, and then started down the winding path to Tai-o-hae and the horseshoe bay of Nuku Hiva. From the top of the amphitheatre of mountain and glen that had encircled Melville and Toby as they fled from the *Acushnet*, I could see the *Taporo* and bustling figures on her deck getting her ready to sail. But my mind loitered in the valley behind us where less than a hundred years ago the last of the Typees, miserable and disease-ridden, waited patiently for the end by their ancestral burial grounds. They had abandoned their *pae-paes*, believing them to have been made taboo by the spirits of their dying race, and already the great stone oblongs and altars had become, Stevenson thought, outposts of the kingdom of the grave.

Twenty-eight

The *Taporo* took me back to Papeete, its decks transformed as if for some Pacific Harvest Festival by stacked branches of bananas and the pungent presence of numerous goats and pigs. Captain Alphonse wore the baseball cap I had given him, and for some reason all the cockroaches had disappeared. Several young men had joined the ship as passengers at Atuona and one of them, named Hyacinthe, told me they were off to do their compulsory military service in the French navy. With any luck, he said, they would be sent to Toulon for training. They were handsome young men with pale toffee-coloured skins. I wondered how much pure Marquesan blood they had in them. How could a race so strongly muscled, so swift and graceful, have vanished in a mere flash of time? That it happened in a flash is beyond doubt. Melville's account of his adventures in *Typee* is a partly romanticized version of his actual experiences during a month-long captivity, but his depiction of Typee life was essentially accurate:

> There seemed to be no griefs, troubles, or vexations, in all Typee.... No foreclosures of mortgages, no protested notes, no bills payable, no debts of honour ... no duns, no assault and battery attorneys ... no destitute widows with their children starving on the cold charity of the world; no beggars; no debtors' prisons; no proud and hard-hearted nabobs; or to sum all up in one word — no money! All was mirth, fun, and high good humour. Perpetual hilarity reigned through the whole extent of the vale.

Yet only forty-six years later, Robert Louis Stevenson arrived in his yacht *Casco* to find the Typees and Hapaas — and all the other Marquesan islanders for that matter — on the point of extinction.

Stevenson witnessed the deaths of some of the last survivors, and he records that these doomed few were terribly aware of the horror that had befallen them. From Tai-o-hae he wrote: 'The Marquesan beholds with dismay the approaching extinction of his race. The thought of death sits down with him to meat, and rises with him from his bed; he lives and breathes under a shadow of mortality awful to support.'

Less than twenty years after Stevenson, Jack London sailed *his* yacht, the *Snark*, to Nuka Hiva – and found it virtually unpeopled. How was it that the Marquesans were decimated while the Samoans, say, survived the same afflictions – grog, blackbirders, firearms, smallpox, syphilis? Both Stevenson and Gauguin shared an answer to this question – as independent witnesses, neither man knowing the other.

'The Polynesian,' Stevenson wrote in *In the South Seas*, 'falls easily into despondency: the fear of novel visitations, the decay or proscription of ancient pleasures, easily incline him to be sad; and sadness detaches him from life.' This talk of 'the proscription of ancient pleasures' led him to the subject of missionaries. Stevenson was not congenitally opposed to all missionaries; he was, however, bitter against self-righteous persons who meddled with other people's lives for meddling's sake.

> We are here face to face with one of the difficulties of the missionary. In the Polynesian islands he easily obtains pre-eminent authority; he can proscribe, he can command; and the temptation is ever towards too much.... It is easy to blame the missionary. But it is his business to make changes. It is surely his business, for example, to prevent wars. On the other hand, it were, perhaps, easy for a missionary to proceed more gently, and to regard every change as an affair of weight. I take the average missionary; I am sure I do him no more than justice when I suppose that he would hesitate to bombard a village, even in order to convert an archipelago. Experience shows (at least in the Polynesian islands) that change of habit is bloodier than a bombardment.... Where there have been fewest changes, important or unimportant, salutary or hurtful, there the race survives.... There may seem, *a priori*, no comparison between the change from sour toddy (or kava) to bad gin, and that from the island kilt to a pair of European trousers. Yet I am far from persuaded that the one is any more hurtful than the other; and the unaccustomed race will sometimes die of pin-pricks.

How lucky Tolu's forebears had been. The missionaries, Catholic or Protestant, who converted them had not tampered much with *fa'a*

Samoa. There the pinpricks had not gone deep enough to be fatal. And so *fa'a Samoa* lives, while Typee is little more than the title of a book.

Again, it was the Marquesans' extreme misfortune to have been taken over that July of 1842 by Rear-Admiral Du Petit Thouars in the name of France. A valiant warrior doubtless, said Melville, 'but a prudent one, too, was this Rear-Admiral Du Petit Thouars ... 4 heavy, double-banked frigates and 3 corvettes to frighten a parcel of naked heathen into subjection! Sixty eight-pounders to demolish huts of coconut boughs, and the Congreve rockets to set on fire a few canoe sheds!' If one believes Stevenson and Melville and the evidence of the empty valley, French colonial officials, *gendarmes* and priests invaded these remote and innocent isles like so many grim nannies taking over a nursery full of cheerful children. 'Stop that!' they commanded the natives. 'Stop that or we shall give you a good hiding!' And in doing so they broke the natives' hearts.

Gauguin, glowering in his *Maison de Jouir* at Atuona, saw all this at close range. Between appalling rows with the local *gendarme* and the bishop, he made dismal jottings in his journal:

> Marquesan art has disappeared, thanks to the missionaries. The missionaries have considered that sculpture and decoration were fetishism and offensive to the God of the Christians.
>
> That is the whole story, and the unhappy people have yielded.
>
> From its very cradle, the new generation sings the canticles in incomprehensible French, recites the catechism, and after that.... Nothing ... as you can understand.
>
> If a young girl, having picked some flowers, artistically makes a pretty wreath and puts it on her head, his reverence flies into a rage! Soon the Marquesan will be incapable of climbing a coconut-tree, incapable of going up the mountain after the wild bananas that are so nourishing to him. The child who is kept at school, deprived of physical exercise, his body always clad (for the sake of decency), becomes delicate and incapable of enduring a night in the mountains. They are all beginning to wear shoes and their feet, which are tender now, cannot run over the rough paths and cross the torrents on stones. Thus we are witnessing the spectacle of the extinction of the race, a large part of which is tubercular, with barren loins and ovaries destroyed by mercury....

Gauguin, of course, could do more than write. The vanished people of the Marquesas Islands – indeed, all vanished Polynesians – have their most moving memorial in Paul Gauguin's paintings. In *Nevermore*, and

Where Do We come From? What Are We? Where Are We Going?, a bewildered awareness of impending extinction speaks to us in anguish from impassive Tahitian faces.

Yes: Tolu, Manino, Fili and Emma were lucky. Back in Papeete I lay on my hotel bed and in my mind's eye saw Fili and Amosa in the halo of sunlight at their hidden bathing place, the stream in the forest. Then I sadly copied out from Gauguin's *Oviri* an old Polynesian invocation he had loved:

> You, gentle breezes of the South and East, playing and caressing each other above my head – hurry! Run together to that other island: you will see there someone who has abandoned me seated in the shade of his favourite tree. Tell him that you have seen me in tears.

I would be leaving the Pacific in a few days, sadly and without quite believing it. In the *Tahitian Sun Press* ('Your weekly guide to sun and fun in Tahiti') I read:

> A crippled Australian anti-nuclear protest yacht is *en route* to Hawaii after a costly decision to try and visit the French nuclear bomb testing site in French Polynesia.
>
> That decision cost Bill Ethell, the skipper of the 54-foot *Pacific Peacemaker*, a broken mizzen mast, a 20,000 French Pacific franc court fine (about 180 US dollars) and a suspended three-month prison sentence....
>
> The decision also earned the *Pacific Peacemaker* a place in Tahiti's history as the first protest yacht in 10 years to have a confrontation with a French naval vessel off Mururoa, the Tuamotan atoll (about 500 miles from Papeete) where France conducts nuclear bomb tests – unofficially, 41 atmospheric tests between 1966 and 1974 and more than 50 underground tests since 1974.
>
> The confrontation, like the one in 1972 involving the Canadian protest yacht *Greenpeace II*, resulted in charges of a French Navy ship intentionally ramming a protest yacht, damaging the yacht....

Ratu Mara, the stately, Oxford-educated Prime Minister of Fiji, had wanted nuclear contamination of any kind expunged from the South Pacific. The New Zealand sailor's T-shirt, so surprising in the main street of Honiara, had said: '*Nuclear hem save killim iumi evriwan.*'

Was nuclear power to become the Pacific's final Fatal Impact? Perhaps it would fulfil the prophecy in the Tahitian saying:

The palm-tree shall grow,
The coral shall spread,
But man shall cease.

Twenty nine

The *African Star* had faded from my hopes. Her owners or agents in Sydney had cabled that they did not at all care for the idea of an unknown traveller hitching a lift on one of their ships to Valparaiso or anywhere else. I sat glumly in Raphael Tixier's office in Papeete with Jim Hostetler, wondering how to avoid taking a Lan Chile flight to Santiago.

'Jim, there wouldn't be anything like a cruise ship passing through here, would there?' It was a long shot; there aren't that many cruise ships in the world and I had turned my nose up at them in the past. But now anything was worth trying.

'No, nothing now. Not at this season – but wait, I'll look anyway.' He riffled through the shipping pages of *Dépêche de Tahiti*. After a minute he cried, 'Hey! There's the *Alexander Pushkin*. Arriving in two days. Going to Callao.'

'That'll do!' I may have yelled it – I was on my feet, I know that. 'Who's the agent?'

'C.G.M. Let's go.' We left the office and drove to the other side of town – crossing en route the Place Du Petit Thouars.

M. Hubert, the helpful French manager of the Compagnie Générale Maritime (I was getting a very favourable impression of most shipping agents on this second ship-hop) said, 'Yes, *Alexander Pushkin*, Soviet round-the-world cruise ship. A big one. Chartered out to a few hundred geriatric Germans. West Germans.'

'Never mind. West, east, north or south, I'll kiss them all if I'm allowed on board.'

'I'll certainly ask, at least. . . .'

Later that day came a message that the ship was full, but if I could see

297

the Russian purser when she arrived at Papeete he might arrange something. No passengers would be joining her after Papeete. Nobody could: the ship did not stop anywhere in the four thousand five hundred miles between here and Callao, the port of Lima in Peru.

Two days later I was fidgeting nervously about the wharf of Papeete under the black metal wall of the *Alexander Pushkin*'s side, waiting while Jim Hostetler went on board to find the purser. Three long rows of portholes stared down like unblinking, hostile eyes. Around me, well-dressed greying men and women with carefully permed hair doddered or pushed about, addressing each other in quavering or boisterous German. Jim returned eventually, saying, 'Come on and meet the purser. It's all right. They'll take you. The other passengers are going to be surprised to see you, but what do you care?' He seemed almost as pleased as I was that we'd succeeded. I owed a lot to Raphael Tixier and Jim Hostetler – they had arranged the voyage to the Marquesas and now this. I hoped I would meet them again in a place where I could repay them.

In a saloon the size of an average ballroom, a blond uniformed Russian with a baby face and glasses smiled and said, 'Your name is Gavin. I am the chief purser. My name is Alexander. Sacha.'

I said, 'Will you really take me to Callao?'

'Oh, yes. Of course, I shall need some money for your fare.'

Gladly I gave him eight hundred dollars out of my dwindling store of travellers' cheques for the eleven days' board and lodging. A lot of money, but four thousand five hundred miles is a long way and the air fare could hardly be much less. Jim went with us to inspect the cabin I was to be given. It was a good one on the promenade deck: large, clean, functional. The bed was narrow but, more important, there was a good reading light over it. The window was large and rectangular, more than a mere porthole. A sign by the telephone said I could call four stewardesses: Anna, Olga, Natasha and Tatanja. 'All at once?' Jim asked.

When we returned to the wharf, it was crowded. Not only the German passengers were milling about; half Papeete seemed to be there: men and women strolling in the sun with their children or their dogs, couples in cars, boys and girls on scooters. Above them all towered the *Alexander Pushkin*'s single great funnel, white with a wide red band carrying a yellow hammer and sickle.

'Well, I'll leave you,' said Jim. 'I hope you've had a good time. Gauguin is nothing but a syphilitic layabout to me. Who needs him?'

298

He laughed. 'Enjoy Cape Horn. If Mrs Thatcher lets you get there.'

He was gone and I was sad. But exultant, too. In my pocket I could feel my ticket to South America.

1705 hours. A last-minute swirl of Germans poured from a big smart tourist coach, cutting it fine. Men and women strung round with cameras and binoculars walked stiffly towards the gangway. One or two of the women had white Tahitian flowers in their hair, and some of the men wore flowery Hawaiian-style shirts. A well-preserved and affluent group had chartered this big ship.

A voice from somewhere near my elbow inquired, 'You haven't got a pencil, old boy, have you?' Was it a German being funny? I looked down in surprise. A small man smiled hopefully up at me. He had flat white hair brushed straight back and an open, humorous face; a monocle hung from a ribbon round his neck. He looked like a nice combination of Lord Carrington, the then British Foreign Secretary, and Mr Magoo, the animated cartoon character. The stature was Mr Magoo's; the voice was Lord Carrington's.

'Here you are,' I said, handing him the ballpoint in my outside pocket. He looked startled, then made a note on a list on a clipboard and handed it back.

'I say, old boy – you sound English.'

'I am. And I hope you're on this ship because I'm coming with you.'

'What?' He looked flabbergasted. 'Well, I *am* on the ship, old boy. But you mean to say they've let you board her here? That's *very* unusual, old boy. *Very* unusual. You actually have your ticket and a cabin, eh? I mean, I'm not doubting your word, but....'

I explained about my round-the-world adventure, about Jim Hostetler and C.G.M.'s M. Hubert, about my meeting with Sacha the purser.

Carrington-Magoo nodded his head, smiling. 'Oh, you've met Sacha. Ah, well – by jove, old boy, you're a lucky bugger, excuse the language. I've never heard of a stray passenger being taken on board a Russian chartered cruise ship before. I'm bloody delighted, old boy.'

He looked around at the Germans beginning to troop up the gangway, shepherded by smiling young Russian stewardesses, and lowered his voice. 'To tell the truth, I've done many cruises with the Russian ships – I organize the shore excursions – but this lot of passengers is a pretty ghastly bunch. A few nice Dutch and Austrians, though. And the Russians are no problem at all; a good lot, actually.'

People were converging on him with questions. 'To work. See you later. We must have a drink or two. Plenty of time for that in the next eleven days. I'm a brandy man m'self.' His stocky little figure and white head disappeared up the gangway. I followed him as the Russian deckhands prepared to pull it up.

I watched from the boat deck with a feeling of unreality as Papeete began to recede, slowly at first, then faster as the quiver of the deck increased. Evening sunlight gently washed the green mountainsides and the rose-coloured fingers of Moorea across the bay. Yachts darted about, and I wondered what had happened to the wretched fugitive Tony Carter had given a beer to – the blond skeleton with the wild hope of escaping from an island outpost of the French Foreign Legion without papers. Had some yachtsman found helping him a challenge worth taking?

Slowly my thoughts turned to quite another world. Even now half of my mind was wondering how tightly Mrs Thatcher's naval blockade was drawn round the area of Cape Horn. The last fragments of news I had heard were that a British destroyer had been sunk and an aircraft carrier seriously damaged. The Royal Navy seemed to have been a little careless.

Once the *Alexander Pushkin* was at sea I went to the purser's office to find out about the times of meals and to see where I should sit for them. A beautiful girl almost collided with me on the stairs. 'Hello,' she said. 'I'm Diana. From New York. I haven't seen *you* before. English?'

'Yes.'

'My husband's English,' she said. 'He's a magician. See you later.'

A blustering man with a near-Teutonic accent and a lapel badge saying 'Cruise Director' brayed, 'A *new* passenger. I haven't heard anything about a new passenger.' He stared at me without pleasure.

'Welcome,' said a young Russian woman in cool white uniform from the purser's desk. 'I'm glad you are joining us.'

At dinner I was a small sensation: the Flying Dutchman. Grey heads lifted from plates full of rollmops and potato salad; baleful eyes and a rustle of tongues followed me to the table the purser's assistant had indicated. Five Germans were seated there, irate. I didn't blame them; they had been sitting together since the ship had left Europe a couple of months before. They had a tightly knit, well-entrenched, Siegfried line look. I managed to get through my pea soup before the sniping began.

The first trigger was pulled by a thick-set man who had probably once been handsome, but by now his cheeks had fallen in, his chin had fallen down and his nose had ripened unhealthily under the influence of beer or Rhine wine like a plum in a heatwave. 'So. You are new here?' The accent was heavy. 'So surprising to see anozzer face at zis stage of our voyage. You don't speak German? A pity.'

I think his wife fired next. 'We are most surprised.' A pause. 'Welcome, of course.' Her smile was a very poor pretence. 'But I must tell you frankly that we are most – *bemused* – by you coming on board. You will go to Europe with us?'

'Only to Callao, the next stop,' I explained meekly. 'Peru.'

'And you have some permissions, of course?'

'It would be difficult, I imagine, to come aboard a Soviet round-the-world cruise ship without permission,' I said, keeping the annoyance out of my voice.

'But – excuse us, please, it is so interesting to us – the cruise director knows nothing about a new passenger. We have asked him. Of course.'

'Of course you have.'

'It is his duty to know.'

'Of course it is.' I ordered half a bottle of red wine from a passing Russian steward.

Another, thinner, man with fish-grey eyes leaned towards me. 'We haf nothing against you personally, please understand. But I zink ve all vould like to ask from vhere your permission to board vas coming.'

The wine arrived and I poured a glass with a steady hand.

'A matter of interest,' the woman said in a businesslike way. 'It concerns us all. For instance, you have paid to be here, or you are not paying? We all have paid. Round the world. Genoa to Hamburg.'

'Yes, don't worry,' I said. 'I have paid. From Tahiti to Peru. I have the receipt.' My hand moved towards my pocket.

'No, no,' Plum-nose said quickly. I suppose even he thought that to make me show my receipt would be forcing things too far. 'But, even so, who – forgive us, frankly we are very curious – has given you permission to come on board?'

'It is not the cruise director,' the businesslike woman informed the others again. 'We know that because Helmut asked him and he said not. He said not, quite firmly.'

'Who, pray, can it be, ve ask ourselves?' the thin man said to me. 'It is *such* a mystery,' he sighed. 'Frankly....'

To myself I said, enough of this. And out loud: 'Ladies and gentlemen, I see you are worried about this – mystery. I suggest you go after dinner to the captain's cabin, knock loudly on the door and tell him that you suspect he has an interloper on his ship. In cabin 208. You could ask him to do something about it. He might, for instance, turn the ship round and steam back to Tahiti to drop me off. Only a few hours out of his way. Or perhaps he could put me in the ship's prison. There's bound to be one.'

Astonished faces looked at me. Was I serious? I poured more wine and gulped it down.

'Of course,' I reassured them, 'I am only joking.'

'*Ach so*. Joking.'

'Actually, I have the personal permission of the captain of this vessel. That is good enough for me.' I looked round at them. 'I hope you can live with it, too. It's only as far as Callao.' I left them in the middle of their boiled veal, and a silence like a laser beam followed my back to the door.

'I hope the Germans weren't starting as they mean to continue,' said Carrington-Magoo over our first brandy. I felt I needed it. He looked very debonair with his eyeglass ribbon and a bow tie.

'Funny how they say, "Pray, would you this and that," like Winston

302

Churchill in a memorandum. Don't worry, for heaven's sake. We'll change your table. Just remember, you have the Russian captain on your side, old boy. After all, he didn't let you come aboard without giving it some thought.'

'No, I'm very surprised he did let me on. What's more, I'm very grateful to him.'

'Frankly I'm surprised, too. But he's a jolly good chap, is Vitaly Segal. A friend, really. I've known him since he was a junior officer.' He put out his hand. 'It's time I introduced myself, old boy. Should have done it before, but it's always a rush, sorting things out after sailing. The name's Eric Hart. Commander Hart when I'm in the Devonshire Club in London – I think that's fair, don't you, old boy? I *was* a commander RNR in the war.'

We sat at a small table in the smallest of the ship's bars. There were four or five, Hart said. He preferred this one – the Friendship Bar – because it was cosy and because he liked to watch the big, stately Russian barmaid.

'Nice looker, isn't she?' he said appreciatively, drawing my attention to her. 'She's called Ludmilla, old boy.' She looked as if she could bat out an aria from *Boris Godunov* between pouring one vodka and the next. She was splendid.

Little by little I learned about Eric Hart. I knew instinctively that he was totally reliable, and I knew after the German inquisition that I was going to be very glad he was on board.

He had been born in London – 'Quite a long time ago, old boy. Never mind how long exactly.' If you went by his thick white hair, his relatively unlined face, his brisk manner, you would have said he was anything between sixty-five and eighty. He had first been to sea in a tramp in 1928 and had then joined the old Orient Line as an assistant purser. Later, he went to the Blue Star Line and was promoted to purser of the *Almeda Star* on the South America route. When war came he volunteered for the navy, ending up in 1950 as paymaster lieutenant-commander RNR, with good experience of Iceland and the Russian convoys. He parted company with the sea for a stretch after that – 'Wanted to see something of the wife, old boy.' He tried tobacco farming in Rhodesia and then distributing liquor, but neither job suited him. He had appreciative friends, though, for a few years later he was managing a big hotel in Salisbury. Even so, he returned to England and to the sea. He joined a company that chartered out ships for cruises and became an excursion organizer. Some of the ships turned out to be

Russian, like the *Alexander Pushkin*, and I suppose because of his transparent honesty and no-nonsense amiability the Russians came to trust him.

'I've never been buggered about by the Russian captains and pursers,' he said. 'Never. They're very businesslike. They need to be. They earn a lot of hard currency with these cruises. And there's the prestige of having these big ships with the hammer and sickle on them going all round the world.'

He raised a smile and a beckoning finger for Ludmilla to bring us the same again. 'Don't get me wrong, old boy. I'm not a Commie. Far from it.'

'I didn't think you were, somehow.'

'Frankly, y'know, these Russians don't give a damn about anyone's politics on these ships – except their own, of course. No one talks politics. It'd be out of place, anyway. I get on very well with Russians on a business basis. We drink together. A man like Captain Vitaly Segal is simply a good sailor as far as I'm concerned.'

Ludmilla breezed up and laid two brandies down in front of us. 'Thank you very much, m'dear,' said Eric, smiling at her, and she gave us both a warm smile back.

Across the bar a tall man with strong straight-back hair the colour of gun metal, a white military moustache and a fierce red face was playing cards with a good-looking woman and a couple I hardly noticed. He looked like C. Aubrey Smith as Colonel Sapt in the film of *The Prisoner of Zenda*, about to see Rudolph crowned king of Strelsau if it was the last thing he did.

'Cheers, old boy,' Eric was saying, raising his glass. 'We might go up to the White Nights later. I think I ought to show you that.'

At the door of the White Nights nightclub, a fat old man with a paunch said pleasantly, 'Good evenink. Your first night on this ship, I belief. Most extraordinary. Pray may I ask you who gave you the go-ahead to come aboard?' He paused. 'You haf permission been granted, I suppose, *ja*?'

Would this never end?

'Mr Young is with me,' Eric said, pushing ahead.

Provoked, I smiled at the man. 'Actually, it's very simple . . . as long as you don't spread it around. The captain and I were at school together. That's why I call him Vitaly.'

'At school together. . . ?'

We left him with his mouth open.

The White Nights was better lit than the Pago Bar had been and far better aired. Soft taped music filled the plushy little room: a tiny bandstand at one end, a bar discreetly lit by pink neon at the other, a dance floor, tables and chairs, curtained windows in between. We had a drink or two. People came and went. A few danced. Eric indicated a female singer, accompanied by a pianist, who was singing 'Embraceable You'. 'Ricci from Lancashire,' he said.

Two hours later I was glad to get to bed. I seemed to have floated from one universe into quite another within a very few hours.

'Have you not heard the singer in the White Nights?' It was the pleasant-looking lady at my new table in the dining room. 'She is good. But she weeps a liddle.'

She was Austrian, she said, from Vienna. The girl with the sweet face and short gold-blonde hair was her daughter, Margit. They were nothing like the interrogators of the night before. Nor were the other two at the table, a young German couple called Pieter and Karol. I explained my sudden presence and added a bit of last night's dinner conversation.

'Pay no attention,' the mother from Vienna said.

And Pieter nodded. 'There are some pretty funny people aboard.'

Karol said quietly, 'This lady has had a very great misfortune.'

I looked at the Austrian. She was embarrassed and murmured, softly, 'No, no, no.'

'Ja. Her husband. . . .'

She finished the sentence herself. 'It is true. My husband died on this voyage. Some weeks ago. Just before Madang in Papua New Guinea. It was very sudden.'

Karol said, 'There was a . . . a burial at sea.'

'Yes, at sea. My daughter came out by plane immediately and met me at Madang. My husband used to sit where you are sitting.' She was quite composed. She just thought I might as well know.

The girl said, 'Mamma wanted to continue her voyage. It is better.'

'I am sure it is,' I said.

'Many people come on these trips to die,' Pieter said when mother and daughter had left us. Then he and Karol rose, too, smiling, 'Now we go for a tiring morning of Scrabble and such.'

Perhaps I would choose a cruise ship to die on, I thought. No fuss, no mess — a quiet splash in the ocean at three o'clock in the morning.

Thirty

I was drinking coffee next day with Eric Hart at his desk in the cruise director's office when the door opened and a large, sixty-ish man with flowing locks came in accompanied by a tall woman. They stood just inside the door.

'Good morning, excuse me and my wife, please. Oh, Eric, we thought maybe you are wanting some news from the Falkland Islands. I believe you have no radio.'

'Quite right, quite right, old boy,' Eric said. He dropped the monocle from his eye.

'Ah — then we can tell you. I am afraid — very bad news.' The man shook his head with a sort of *Schadenfreude*, like a sadistic doctor announcing a terminal disease. 'Several British warships sunken. One aircraft carrier gravely damaged. British forces trying to land on the islands also badly damaged.'

His wife turned her mouth down at the corners. 'We feel you should know, Eric.'

They disappeared, leaving Eric and me to stare at each other in dismay.

'I say, old boy,' after a moment. 'Seems pretty bad, eh? Bit of a British balls-up, that's what it sounds like.'

'It may not be accurate, Eric. We don't know where the news comes from. Let's just wait and see what comes next.'

'Right-o, old boy. We'll let each other know.'

On the sun deck elderly Germans of all shapes and sizes lay or sat on long chairs in the sun, gossiping, playing cards, reading or knitting. I took a chair and opened Darwin's *Voyage of the Beagle*.

'English?' A rumpled old German lying in a deckchair hailed me. 'I

306

like Englishmen. My sister married one. Lives now in Maidenhead. Tudor-style. Very nice.' He at least was not going to give me hell. He travelled a lot, he said, painting, showing his work here and there. Modest stuff. He would have a little show on board in a day or two.

He had had a rough war, he said later, but without the least rancour or self-pity. Just matter-of-fact.

'The Russian and Polish fronts. At Monte Cassino I was also. Then the Americans made me their prisoner in Holland.' He laughed. 'I was a tank driver. The American soldiers came up to me and said, "Hands up, you goddam fucking Nazi." So I put my hands up double quick, *ja*? The tank drivers wore uniform black like the SS. So I threw it away – *ach*!' He shook his head. Now he lived some of the time in the Richmond Hotel in Paris. He knew England and liked America. 'All that fighting for nothing.' I saw his exhibition in the saloon: pale watercolours of Penang, beaches in Sri Lanka, junks in Hong Kong, Indian fakirs – and a sketch of a fat German sunbathing entitled '*Deutscher* fakir'.

As the days went by the weather changed, becoming grey and perceptibly harsher. There was appreciably less sun, and the high winds at night had a cutting edge to them far sharper than the winds that rattled the bamboos at Tolu's house. The sea took on a bleak look and I felt the Pacific I knew was dying under the huge, thrusting keel of the *Alexander Pushkin*.

Days are long on a cruise ship – at least they are to me – in spite of all the arrangements to keep passengers amused. It was lucky I had brought my own few books; in the 'Kalinka' shop everything, reasonably enough, was in German. The only author I recognized was Ambrose Bierce but his solitary book was translated as *Die Spottdrossel* and I couldn't read it. Bookholders attached to the bulkheads near the stairs offered free copies of *Lenin on Cooperation*, and L.I. Brezhnev's *To Stop the Arms Race*; *To Prevent Nuclear War*; *To Start Disarmament*, but I couldn't get far with them. Dancing lessons were available, and Pieter and Karol were enthusiastic learners. I watched one of their energetic – almost erotic – tangos in the saloon; they waved to me when I applauded. There was wine tasting, too. People became muzzily chatty on Russian wines called Zinandali and Mukuzani, and I realized that many of the passengers were ordinary, amiable folk. Some foolhardy souls, of course, overdid the Ararat brandy or the deadly Peper or Ochotschnitschji vodka and spent the next few hours hanging over the ship's rail. Unfortunately these did not include our self-appointed war reporters.

Nearly every morning that smiling German couple put their heads round Eric's door. 'You have heard the news? Five more warships sunken. The *Canberra* badly hit. Thatcher is now having to send urgently heavy troop reinforcements.'

I felt puzzled and anxious, and even Eric's high spirits waned. In our gloom we sought the seclusion of the Friendship Bar and the attentions of the glorious Ludmilla. When she took her time off, the young barman, Dmitri, would play videotapes of *Tom and Jerry* cartoons, howling with laughter until Ludmilla came sailing back and turned them off with a grand, contemptuous gesture, like a duchess putting the cat out. Eric and I agreed that the war news must be Argentine propaganda from Buenos Aires Radio, but we couldn't be sure. And after a few days the Germans added a still more disconcerting clarification of their source — 'It is hunky-dory from the London Defence Ministry's mouth, you can be sure!'

'What on earth's happening?' Eric asked. 'Looks bloody bad, old boy.'

'Search me.'

Without any other source of news, what were we to think? Eric had no radio — 'Never had such a thing, old boy. To tell the truth, I was never much good with electrical gadgets.' The Russian officers, presumably, knew what was happening; the electronic equipment on a ship like this could pick up details of a tribal war on Mars. But understandably no one else was regaled with the news from Radio Moscow — this ship was rigidly non-political and Eric was adamant that it was more than his job was worth to question the captain about how Britain was doing in the Falklands War. I saw his point.

'More British troops killed. Troopships sunken. Many dead. A disaster. You have our wishes....' As the daily litany of catastrophe continued we realized that if there really had been a terrible débâcle in the South Atlantic there would soon be a violent crisis at home — if indeed there hadn't been one already. In imagination we saw Thatcher falling; Parliament in uproar; the country in economic ruin; riots. It would be a hundred times worse than the aftermath of the Suez fiasco. At this point thoughts of the final dissolution of Britain drove us back to Ludmilla.

'Thank God you're here, old boy.' Eric said over his brandy, fiddling nervously with his bow tie. 'I don't think I could have borne all this uncertainty alone, surrounded by bloody-minded Germans.' But he was the first to admit that almost any shipload of passengers – of any nationality – can be an appalling handful. 'The Brits can be bad, too,' he confessed. 'They can be disgusting, actually. On the *Baltica* the British passengers marched round the deck singing "There'll Always be an England". The Russians looked at them as if they couldn't express their contempt. And by the way, old boy, so did I.'

'I never knew West Germans felt such an affinity with the Argentines, Eric. Did you?'

'Well, I think they are Bavarians, old boy, some of them. Brought up around Hitler's place – Berchtesgaden, was it? They'd have been between twenty and thirty years old during the war. Perhaps one or two were Hitler Youths. They wouldn't care for the British anyway. Remember, we sank their Grand Fleet off the Falklands in 1915. Drowned their Admiral Graf von Spee – remember, old boy? The word "Falklands" might trigger some nasty ideas about us in German minds.' I had forgotten that story of a long time ago, a brave one for both sides. Perhaps the spirits of von Spee and his British adversary, Vice-Admiral Sturdee, were among us.

On the third night Eric and I went to the White Nights nightclub for a late nightcap and Ricci, the singer, came to our table when her act was over.

'You are a couple of darling Englishmen to turn up and clap. Keep the flag flying, eh?' Eric offered her a drink and when it came she said, 'Cheers! I must say cheers, mustn't I, love? For the old country's sake, darling.'

'Won't you sing some more?' Eric said.

'I'm only expected to sing twenty-five minutes and that's it. But to meet an Englishman, what a treat. You know what I really want to sing for you – "My Old Man Said Follow the Van". But we've got all these Germans, that's the trouble.' She waved at a large woman in a caftan at the bar, and called to a man at another table, 'Hello, Heinz. That last song was for you, love.'

After a while she said, 'I don't go much on some of these Germans – though Heinz over there is all right. Some are all hoity-toity; they think they can say anything they like to me. Ridiculous cheek. See that fat old girl in the caftan?' She jerked her head towards the bar. 'In good old showbiz language, she's a bike, darlings. If *ever* I saw one. And I did.'

'A what, m' dear?' Eric asked.

'A bike, love. You know – something that's always getting ridden. Get the joke? Sorry about that.'

Ricci was attractive, though no longer in her first youth. She had been through the mill, she said. 'The north-east of England, Birmingham – oh, I love Birmingham – and Manchester. And South Wales. I've had some good times in Swansea and Llantrisant. And Porthcawl, too.' Another drink came, and in a while she said, 'Oh, all right, darlings, I'll sing just one. You'll probably go to sleep.' But she sang Jerome Kern's 'My Bill' very well, accompanied by her French pianist.

'You darling Englishmen. And I've got the toothache as well.' After a lot more talk: 'You will come to see me, won't you, in Cardiff or anywhere? At the stage door.'

'We'll come and buy you lots of drinks,' I said.

'That'll be lovely. Well, people will know my name. You can ask. Including Lord Delfont. That's Bernie Delfont, you've heard of him, love. He knows me all right.'

'I'll give a good rap on your dressing room door,' Eric said gallantly, twirling his monocle.

She lowered her eyelashes and her voice. 'I'll bet you will, you old love.'

Ricci was a good person to meet in the White Nights at the end of a long day's war reporting from cold-eyed Germans. She, too, had had a 'Falklands incident'. 'Bloody cheek! Two Germans, man and woman, came up to me and said, "What is it about the English! Why do they always want to fight someone?"'

Eric spluttered, 'Damned sauce!'

Ricci laughed. 'I gave him sauce, *don't* you worry, my darling. I said, "Oh – so Adolf Hitler was a bleeding pacifist, was he?" They were *furious*. Said they'd boycott my next show. As if I cared.'

'She's got plenty of pluck, Ricci, hasn't she?' Eric said with warm approval as we went to our cabins. I had to agree she had.

I had forgotten about the magician whom Diana, the beautiful New Yorker, had said on my first evening on board was her husband. A few nights later, there was Mo performing in the ship's cabaret. He was good – or rather, they both were; they called their act the Molins, producing budgerigars and rabbits from unlikely places and making them disappear again in an impressively casual way.

Mo came from Reading, and his real name was Maurice Weller. He had once been a professional footballer, he told me, but was badly injured somehow and drifted into magic – that was the way he put it.

He and Diana had met while he was touring the Bahamas, entertaining passengers on a different cruise ship. 'She was a nurse,' he said, 'and I had quite a few problems with my health just then – sore throats, cut fingers, a nail in my foot. Diana was always getting my trousers down to give me injections. Well, after a while we bloomin' well *had* to get married.' He laughed.

The whole act was like a family affair. Showing me round their cages below decks, Mo spoke to the birds and animals as if they were his children.

'He's a funny chap, that white rabbit there. Fred. He's been a bit too nervous up to now. Oh no, I never give rabbits aspirins, though some people do, and I never clip the birds' wings neither.' Mo stroked a pair of budgies, one purple, one white. 'They were born in Hong Kong. And these two, look,' he added fondly, 'they were nothing more than eggs last time we came through the Panama Canal.' Apart from the budgerigars and the rabbits, there was a full dovecot. 'Java doves,' Mo said. 'Wonderful birds, quite hard to find. They've no nerves, y'see. You wave newspapers at 'em, clap your hands under their beaks, anything. It's like training police horses. I've had 'em eight years. I spray 'em with a little spray now and again. To kill the mites, y'know.'

We were getting near South America. The mornings were misty now. Booby birds began to appear round the ship; dozens of huge white creatures gliding sedately or folding their wings and diving into the water like collapsed umbrellas.

One morning soon after the German couple had announced 'Another fifteen thousand British troops landed,' Mo came into Eric's office. 'I say, Eric, what's all this about the Falklands – have we been defeated or something?'

'Wish we knew, old boy. Haven't you got a radio in your cabin? We really must get some BBC news.'

Mo did have a radio. He had bought it in Sydney or Hong Kong. It was big and covered with shining knobs. He wasn't sure how it worked.

'Never mind, old boy,' Eric said. 'Do us all a favour. You two go up top, onto the boat deck or somewhere high, tonight after your act, and fiddle with it. At midnight the airwaves should be calmer, better for reception. Just go up and have a good fiddle, old boy. It's very important for Britain, I'm sure you agree.'

That night Eric and I sat through the entire Fiesta cabaret, including a comedian whose jokes – '"What should I tip?" said the English aristo about to be guillotined' – received an ovation. The comic came back for a finale – '"My wife's an angel," said a man. "You're lucky," said his friend. "Mine's still alive"' – and in a moment I felt a tap on my elbow. 'Come on,' said Mo.

We lugged his heavy radio up companionways from deck to deck. On the boat deck we paused, but the roar of the funnel was too loud there, so we struggled up to the topmost deck where the wind seemed to be approaching gale force. 'We'll never hear a thing up here,' I yelled into Mo's ear.

'*What?*'

We heaved the set behind the shelter of a liferaft designed to keep sixty passengers afloat, and that gave some protection. Crouching there, Mo twiddled knobs and dials and the set began to whistle and squawk. After a minute or two the wind fell somewhat, but that made things worse – the whistles and squawks grew louder and louder; it sounded as if we were murdering an old woman and cutting her up. 'For God's sake, Mo!' There was not the slightest hint of a human voice reading news in any language. If my hair rose on the back of my head it had nothing to do with the wind. At any moment, I thought, the Russian duty officer on his rounds would hear the noise, summon his men and seize the two Englishmen, one a last-minute boarder from Papeete (said to be a writer), the other the ship's magician, whom he had surprised squatting over a massive radio receiver with a six-foot antenna. That might be good for several years' forced labour east of Omsk.

There was no point in shouting to make this point – I tugged Mo's coat and made vigorous gestures of instant departure. He nodded, evidently also longing to be gone. We stood up and tiptoed away – in the racket of that semi-hurricane – and not until we reached the warmth of the Friendship Bar did we breathe freely again. Eric sat there, tense, waiting.

'Well, old boy?'

'A drink, Eric, a drink,' Mo panted. 'No dice. That's all there is to say.'

'Oh, blimey. Lud-*milla!*'

Across the bar Colonel Sapt, at his cards, ran a long forefinger slowly and delicately along the curve of an eyebrow; then he reached for his glass of brandy and raised it, crooking a little finger like an old lady in a tea room. I suddenly saw that he was not C. Aubrey Smith after all; he probably ran the only unisex hair establishment in Strelsau.

Next day Eric looked conspiratorial. 'A word in your ear, Gavin old boy. The captain wants you and me to dine with him.'

'Eric, you don't think Mo and I were spotted last night?'

'Heavens, no, old boy, I don't think it's that.'

Captain Vitaly Segal was quiet-spoken, about forty, slim, black-haired and could have been Italian or Welsh as much as Russian. Eric and I, in our best clothes, were seated on either side of him; like all his officers, he wore a white uniform jacket without medals, dark trousers and black tie. He had a dove tattooed on one hand. Over the first three or four glasses of Peper vodka I broke the ice with a description of Tolu's tattoos. *Salade niçoise*, steak, fruit, came and went. Eric prattled on, completely at ease. The steward came round indefatigably. A sweet white wine followed the vodka and a hefty brandy chased the wine. Towards the end of the meal I was surprised to hear Eric venture a question I had thought was forbidden. 'I say, Captain,' he said in his most casual Carrington manner, 'any news at all of the Falklands?' It was a measure of his extreme concern, that question.

Captain Segal's voice was equally casual. 'No, Eric. No. We have heard nothing.' To me he said, 'There may be some changes in procedure at Peru because of the Falklands business. They must know who, what, enters their waters, and who is coming ashore.'

'I hope that won't be a problem for you. I am most grateful for your permission to come aboard.'

He smiled and tapped my wrist. 'There will be no problem. It is a pleasure to have you with us here. It will be all right.'

After more brandy, he said, 'I hear some German talk about the British. . . . Look, one German has said to me, "See how the British attack?" – as if the Russians will be pleased. You know what I replied? I shook my head, saying, "Why should we be pleased? If the Dutch and the Germans start fighting, is the Soviet Union pleased? Of course not."' I told him about Ricci's retort – 'Was Hitler a pacifist?' – and he laughed. The matter ended there.

Next morning Segal and Sacha the purser came to my cabin to say goodbye. I thanked the captain again and he asked for a souvenir. I gave him a book. In return he signed a large colour photograph of the *Alexander Pushkin*, and wrote: 'Dear Gavin! to good memory about your voyage on the *Alexander Pushkin*. Wish you good luck and many new interesting books! Captain Segal.' From the purser I got a set of Russian dolls, and from both a firm handshake. What I did not get was the reason why Captain Segal had agreed to come to my rescue in Papeete. No one, not even Eric Hart, had managed to explain that. I am inclined to believe there was one simple reason: Vitaly Segal has a kind heart.

When the *Alexander Pushkin* reached Callao, on a pink and misty morning, Eric and I had but a single thought – to get ashore, speed by taxi into the city of Lima some miles away, and find out once and for all if the British nation had suffered one of the greatest military and naval disasters in its history.

Our landfall was bleak. Captain Segal had allowed me onto the bridge for our approach into the wintry harbour where a hundred or so pelicans covered the water in an agitated blanket of white and grey. On the wharf a stall's sign said: 'Inca Cola', and two policemen stamped about in greatcoats. The formalities were quickly done; I had no problems. Eric had no excursions to organize here, and in no time at all we were leaping out of a taxi at the gate of the British Embassy, urgently explaining our visit to guards who had survived a bomb attack on the building a few days before: Peru, it seemed, had sided with Argentina. Thinking about it now, I suppose we burst into the Ambassador's office rather like a couple of terrorists. At the first sight of Eric's sleek white head, bow tie and eyeglass, he might even, for one astonished moment, have imagined that it was Lord Carrington himself who, wild and flushed, was demanding to know 'just what in the name of heaven is going on down in the Falkland Islands?' If so, His Excellency in Peru took it in an admirably calm and diplomatic way, grasping at once the nerve-racked state of ignorance we had endured for the last eleven days.

'Gentlemen, be seated,' he said soothingly. 'I am pleased to inform you that we have won in the Falklands perhaps the greatest victory since – ' Was it Trafalgar or Matapan? I have forgotten now, and when I asked Commander Hart RNR over a pink gin at the Devonshire Club in London several months later, he, too, was uncertain. In any case, the Ambassador's words were bracing. They sent us out into Lima like caged birds set free, only coming to rest at the Bolivar Hotel on the Plaza San Martin. There we sat in high-backed chairs in the panelled warmth of the English Bar and breathed deep breaths of patriotic relief

314

under a stuffed antelope's head. In the Plaza was a statue of General San Martin astride a horse; stall owners sold alpaca and llama skins, and small, highly coloured sketches of the snowy mountains of the Cordillera de Los Andes, condors and wild bulls. Mo and Diana passed by and we told them the news. More drinks came and then the lady from Vienna and her sweet daughter arrived. There was quite a party.

Next day, the *Alexander Pushkin* sailed on towards the Panama Canal. I took a lonely taxi down the long road to the airport.

In the British Embassy in Santiago I learned that Chile was not Peru. There had been no bombs in the capital – the Chileans were a hundred and one per cent pro-British in the Falklands affair. Since successive Argentine governments had claimed sovereignty over three Chilean islands and the Beagle Channel just north of Cape Horn, and had threatened to invade them despite a ruling from the Pope that the islands were Chilean, there had been no love for Argentina in Santiago. No ships were sailing south from Chilean ports into Argentine waters, or were likely to for some time. The British Embassy people told me that the Argentine forces on the Falklands, though hard-pressed, had not yet surrendered. British paratroopers, marines, guardsmen and Gurkhas were advancing over difficult, boggy ground, but they had not yet re-taken Port Stanley, the capital of the islands. Argentine news-papers on sale in the streets of Santiago boasted: 'Hundreds of Gurkha Mercenaries Dead Before Our Trenches'. These headlines were blat-antly deceptive. But even if the Argentines surrendered tomorrow, the state of hostility and the British naval blockade would continue one month, two, three ... who knew?

I had hoped to reach my last landfall in England at the end of the summer, because winter storms would close the little fishing harbour of Bude, and it was already June. I looked at the map. Chile lay as thin as a snake along the Pacific Ocean – a four-thousand-mile jumble of rock and water. It was the most extraordinary coastline in the world. South from the port of Valparaiso, islands, fjords, bays, inlets and straits were strewn like pieces of a dinosaur's shattered vertebrae, and at the very farthest tip of the dinosaur's coccyx lay the tiny Island of Cape Horn, the southernmost part of the earth. I had an ambition to be there.

Part Three

Uttermost Part of the Earth

In these still solitudes, Death instead of Life,
seemed the predominant spirit.

Charles Darwin: *Voyage of the Beagle*

thirty one

I had introductions from friends in London to two people in Santiago. Presenting letters of introduction to strangers embarrasses me so much that often I don't present them at all; but had I not met Tony Westcott I might have missed Alexander Selkirk's cave, and if I had veered away from Señor Don Hernan Cubillos I would not have slept on Cape Horn.

I went to Hernan Cubillos first. He had been Foreign Minister and resigned from the post, but I was not concerned with politics. He was also a businessman, but business does not interest me either. The important thing to me was that, apart from being an excellent host and a cultivated and amusing man, Hernan was an enthusiastic and expert sailor. He had served in the Chilean navy and now he owned a fine yacht, the *Caleuche*, famous in South American waters.

Nervously I rang him up and he invited me round to dinner in a house full of sailing mementoes, books, music and much more; Hernan's interests seem inexhaustible. We talked about the Falklands War, the blockade, and the Chileans' conviction that, if General Galtieri and his colleagues had succeeded in the Falklands, Argentine forces would have been let loose in a similar fashion on the islands of southern Chile.

'From what I hear, your way round to Argentina or Brazil will be blocked by the Royal Navy for some time,' Hernan said. 'I suppose you could fly to Rio de Janeiro and get a ship from there across to South or West Africa.'

He led me into his chart room and pulled out detailed maps of the Chilean coast, particularly of the far south. Below the Straits of Magellan, wider than I had thought but not as far south as I had imagined, below even the big island of Tierra del Fuego at the toecap of

319

the continent, Hernan's finger moved south. It reached the Beagle Channel and the three pinprick islands claimed by Argentina: Lennox, Picton and Nueva. 'You could go down there, perhaps,' he said. My finger moved lower still. To Navarino Island, to Cape Deceit, and at last reached the island to which Wilhelm Schouten of Hoorn in Holland had given a name: Isla de Cabo de Hornos – Cape Horn Island.

'That's where I want to be, Hernan.'

He laughed. 'Yes, well, I see what you mean, but it's not terribly easy. Particularly now. Still – give me a little time to arrange things. Go somewhere first. Any ideas?'

'Yes. Robinson Crusoe Island.'

'Good. A nice place. I've sailed there.' He shook my hand. 'But don't go away *too* long. Something may turn up.'

Tony Westcott turned out to be a bluff Chilean Englishman of an extreme good nature matching Hernan's. He kept a Plymouth-built ketch in a marina south of Valparaiso, Chile's main port, and from behind his desk in the Santiago printing business he owned with his brother he spent much time dreaming of the voyage he would one day make across the South Seas.

He was brisk. 'You have time to spare. Take a ship to the Juan Fernandez Islands. There are three of them, Robinson Crusoe, Alexander Selkirk and a tiny one called Santa Clara, but only Robinson Crusoe is populated. Barely. There's a ship of some sort. We'll have to find out about it.'

We drove together to Valparaiso, an old town that sprawled along the edge of a magnificent bay, its narrow streets creeping inland into encircling hills. The port's passenger wharfs were reached by way of a plaza dominated by heroic statues; and by probing behind a clutter of warehouses, diligently searching among a number of fishing trawlers, we found the diminutive vessel we sought. She crouched under the stone jetty as if exhausted – a tough but battered sea creature waiting to get its breath back after a long, hard struggle with the waves. She had a nice compact wheelhouse and a funnel like a retired boxer's nose. She was no beauty of the Seven Seas. But, as far as I was concerned, with her name she didn't have to be. *Carlos Darwin*, the painted letters said. She rode up and down in a fair swell, scraping her frayed hemp fenders against the jetty wall; huge gulls wheeled around her or fought screaming over refuse on the oily surface. Men with bored expressions

were arranging barrels, crates and tarpaulins on oily, unscrubbed decks.

'Now, let's find out when she sails to Juan Fernandez,' Tony said. 'You never can tell with the *Carlos Darwin*. The schedule is often, er, elastic.' He waved to a man with a beard who was watching us from the wheelhouse, and the man clambered down a ladder and swung across a rickety metal and wood gangway to where we stood. It was a long conversation, and transferred itself easily to a nearby bar, the walls of which were hung round with nets and fishermen's floats and lifebuoys from old ships of several nations.

The bearded man was called Pedro Espinoza Leon. The wavy hair that fell over his forehead and curved over his collar was a fine copper colour, and the bushy beard failed to disguise his relative youth. He was the captain of the *Carlos Darwin*. He had undertaken to carry a shipful of islanders back to their home four hundred miles away on Robinson Crusoe Island, he said, speaking fair English, but he would certainly find a bunk for me. 'A too small bunk, not too clean bunk, but a bunk,' he said, smiling. When would he sail? He shrugged – maybe in twelve hours, maybe later. It depended on the arrival of the cargo. In Valparaiso, you could never guarantee....

At the gangway, seeing Captain Pedro aboard, a crewman clutching a radio called '*Buenas tardes*. Hey, *gringo*! You comin' Juan Fernandez? Okay, see football – Mrs Thatcher play Galtieri. We see, okay?' he grinned, and we waved back.

Tony explained. 'The World Cup's on. Britain's playing Argentina or something. Look, when you get to Robinson Crusoe Island, stay with an old girlfriend of mine. Ask for Maria Eugenia at the Aldea Daniel Defoe. *Aldea* means *pension*. Stay there. You'll get on well.'

The *Carlos Darwin* sailed well after dark three days later, her decks cluttered with men, women, children and cargo. We sailed out into a Pacific that certainly was not the Pacific of Colson or Tolu or Gauguin. It rained and was cold. By the time the battered little bruiser of a vessel finally slogged off into the darkness I had shared a bottle of vodka with a blue-chinned man from Juan Fernandez, and was flat on my back in my clothes on a bunk in a fuggy little cabin without a porthole. I woke up five hours later to a strong smell of wet clothing, sweat and oil. Sea slapped the bulkhead near my ear like a fist; the metal sounded no thicker than a biscuit tin.

A lazy south-westerly swell accompanied us all the way to Robinson Crusoe Island, and the deck of the *Carlos Darwin* seemed hard put to it to stay above the level of the ocean. The little ship was full of men in boots and rough, high-necked sweaters that might have been knitted straight off the backs of living sheep. They wore knitted woollen caps, too, with pom-poms of wool on the crown, and anoraks of all shapes and colours. They were nothing at all like Polynesians. The five hundred inhabitants of Robinson Crusoe Island were Chileans of European origin, as racially mixed as you might expect in a country whose navy was founded by Lord Cochrane and whose two principal national heroes are called José San Martin and Bernardo O'Higgins.

Three times a day I squeezed into the vessel's cramped mess where two tattooed cooks ladled stew onto greasy plates. A television set high up in a corner poured out pictures of the World Cup without cease, and the hysterical one-note voice of a Spanish-speaking commentator sounded like a fire alarm that had gone off and got stuck. It was difficult for a mere *gringo* to know who was playing whom. Could England really be playing football against Argentina while there was a war in the Falklands? It seemed almost grotesquely improbable, but the crewman who had shouted 'Hey, *gringo*!' in Valparaiso harbour now shouted again: 'Hey, gringo! England *contra* Argentina. Mrs Thatcher against Galtieri – the score: Galtieri *zero*, Mrs Thatcher *uno*.' He held up the first finger and thumb of his left hand joined to make a zero, and the first finger of his right hand to signify the number one. Then he completed the dumb show by stabbing the single finger in and out of the zero, chanting as he did so, 'Mrs Thatcher *uno*, Galtieri *zero*. *Uno–zero. Uno–zero...*!' Later he pushed through the crowded mess and slapped my back. 'Armanduco,' he introduced himself.

Even on deck Chileans shook my hand and told me that Galtieri was bad, Mrs Thatcher was good. It would have warmed Eric Hart's soul. Armanduco's friendly shouts reached me at frequent intervals from the wheelhouse, from the galley door, from the fo'c'sle, anywhere, until in two days' time the spurs and headlands of the island of Mas a Tierra, more commonly known as Robinson Crusoe Island, hove into sight. Supreme among them was the flat top of El Yunque, the Anvil Mountain, on which Alexander Selkirk had sat year after year, staring out for a sail on an empty ocean, reluctant master of all he surveyed.

The *aldea* of Maria Eugenia, Tony's friend, was a group of simple log cabins on the edge of Cumberland Bay. Maria Eugenia herself was an attractive Chilean lady speaking perfect English, cheerful and energetic, who had a practical but easygoing way with guests. There was no formalilty at the *aldea* any more than there was in the whole bailiwick, except perhaps round the bungalow where the *alcalde*, the governor, had his office – it was not at all that sort of place.

The modest, wood-built settlement reminded me of a well-gardened and peaceful American frontier town in the 1890s, but the line of longboats drawn up along the beach on either side of the tiny wharf signalled otherwise. San Juan Bautista was inhabited mostly by fishermen, and wives and children of fishermen. Catching *langostas*, the giant crayfish, was the special industry here; there was no other that I could see. The day the *Carlos Darwin* pulled into Cumberland Bay most of the island's population crowded onto the wharf to lug away the cargo on their shoulders or in borrowed wheelbarrows. There was one jeep, I think; perhaps it was the only one on the island – it belonged to the *alcalde*.

Robinson Crusoe Island felt as remote as Nuku Hiva. The little town straggled in a thin semicircle along an unpaved track among pine trees and eucalyptus in such a tentative fashion that it seemed about to be nudged into the sea by the mountains that swept down on it from every side. Dominating everything, El Yunque spread its long, flat anvil's top under the clouds, and in the highlands at its feet were the goat-filled

323

caves once so familiar to Sailing Master Selkirk, late of Largo, in the county of Fife in Scotland.

It had been raining. I stamped and slipped down the track from the wharf to the *aldea*, saluted along the way by men with white faces and stubbled chins muffled by scarves or woolly caps. They could have been Swiss, German, Italian, Spanish or English – and they probably were a bit of a mixture of all these things – but they were not Polynesians. Certainly no one like Man Friday had ever lived on this island.

While his ship was at the wharf, Captain Pedro of the *Carlos Darwin* often came to Maria Eugenia's and seemed in no particular hurry to return to Valparaiso. He came for meals and long, cheerful drinking sessions with Maria Eugenia and myself, bringing Armanduco with him. We sat in the kitchen at a wooden table and drank the colourless Chilean brandy called *pisco* or the red wine called Concha y Toro that came in wicker-covered jars. Armanduco had taken a fancy to Maria Eugenia's cook, a plump young woman with a wall eye, and he was sometimes difficult to dislodge. Now and again, a group of boisterous young fishermen brought a guitar and sang songs they had written themselves about 'Juan Fernandez, island of fishermen, island of enchanted summits'. Into the night they roared, 'If only I could be buried on the Yunque, with my face towards the sea....' Then they coyly fingered the bottles, murmuring, '*Pisco – pocito, eh?*'

One of these singers, a pale youth, came to the *aldea* with a small animal half concealed in his jacket. A little wiggling, questing nose – almost a small trunk – poked out between the buttons and delicately tested the air. It was a coati, he said; there were quite a few of them on the island. Like his pet, he had melancholy eyes and a long nose that wriggled, so I called him Coati and he didn't seem to mind.

It was with Coati that I saw some relics of the *Dresden*. Of course, the ghosts of Admirals Sturdee and von Spee hung about Cumberland Bay, and no doubt that of Captain Luce, too, commander of the *Kent* and the *Glasgow*, who finally trapped the German cruiser.

The object of the Anglo–German naval contest in the South Atlantic in 1914 was control of the sea routes to and from the Pacific. It was sharp and very short – all over within the space of the thirty-eight days between the Battle of Coronel on 1 November and the Battle of the Falklands on 8 December. Off Coronel, on the south-western coast of Chile, the German East Asiatic Squadron, a powerful group of modern armoured cruisers commanded by Vice-Admiral Maximilian Graf von Spee, was attacked by a force of ageing warships under Rear-Admiral 'Kit' Cradock. Cradock was a dashing bachelor who had always wanted to die in the hunting field or in action, and he had his wish. He and his flagship, the *Good Hope*, went to the bottom after a futile engagement with von Spee's flagship the *Scharnhorst*, her sister ship the *Gneisenau*, and the light cruisers *Dresden*, *Nürnberg* and *Leipzig*.

Who was to blame for Cradock's ill-advised attack? Winston Churchill, then First Lord of the Admiralty, has been accused. But whoever it was, humiliation was soon followed by victory. Vice-Admiral Doveton Sturdee caught von Spee's ships off the Falkland Islands and sent nearly all of them to the bottom. Admiral von Spee himself perished when the *Scharnhorst* turned turtle and sank with her complement of 765 men. Only one light cruiser, the *Dresden*, escaped, and headed west to southern Chile. Trapped at last at anchor in Cumberland Bay, Captain Lüdecke of the *Dresden* had a cable in his pocket from the Kaiser telling him to let himself be interned by the Chilean Government. Captain Luce had received a different sort of cable from Winston Churchill: 'Object is destruction not internment.'

On 14 March 1915 the *Glasgow* opened fire, and within three minutes the *Dresden* had suffered enough damage for Lüdecke to hoist a white flag. Seeing this, Luce ordered 'Cease fire' and awaited the arrival of a boat from the *Dresden* flying a flag of truce brought to him by a lieutenant called Canaris – who lived to become an admiral and head of German Intelligence in the Second World War. It was a clever plan. While Canaris talked, Lüdecke scuttled the *Dresden*, not only opening her seacocks, condensers and torpedo tube doors but blowing up her magazine as well. As the *Dresden* sank for ever her ship's company cheered from the shore, and the British, moved by the sight, cheered too. Lüdecke and his men were interned by the neutral Chileans, but eight Germans had been killed.

With Coati I walked along the beach and tried, among driftwood, lumps of cork, plastic bottles and broken glass, to imagine the ear-splitting crack of the exploding magazine resounding round this little bay. The German colony in Valparaiso erected a monument after the war, and here it was, a small stone monolith with one of the *Dresden*'s lifebuoys and the ship's anchor. The inscription said:

In Treuer Pflicht-Erfüllung für das Deutsche
Vaterland Starben den Heldentod:
Ing. Asn. Lerche
Ob. Matr. Hunger
Heizer Reuter

S.M.S. Dresden 14 März 1915

Coati told me that on a clear, calm day it was possible to see the *Dresden* lying at the bottom of the bay. I peered down from the gunwale of his longboat but all I could see were the jellyfish called Portuguese men o' war, a large, hideously orange squid and the reflected sky. I made another attempt on the feast of San Pedro, the patron saint of all fishermen. Then a procession of *barcos-longos*, hung with gay bunting from masts to prows and sterns and carrying most of San Juan Bautista's women and children, made circles and figures of eight in the bay and rolled on down the coast, passing under cliffs where goats skipped blithely on rock faces that seemed to lack the minutest hoofhold. An exhilarating morning, but I got no glimpse of the *Dresden* that day either. Still, the story of the *Dresden* is by no means dead. The young fishermen of Cumberland Bay have commemorated it in a song which they sang to me, a lilting tune:

> The fourteenth of March, the naval battle began. The English opened fire with their heavy guns, and Juan Fernandez was witness to the heroic German cruiser and how the ship was sunk with her flag still flying. It is useless to forget that day, the fourteenth of March, when the naval battle started, the day Juan Fernandez saw the heroic German cruiser heel over with her flag flying....

But the islands were named after Robinson Crusoe and Alexander Selkirk, not after Luce and Lüdecke. *The Life and Strange Surprising*

Adventures of Robinson Crusoe of York, Mariner, a fiction from the mind of Daniel Defoe, was based on the almost equally surprising adventures of Alexander Selkirk of Largo in Fife, the tall and powerful sailing master, or first mate, of the 120-ton privateer *Cinque Ports* (Captain Stradling), who after a dispute with the master refused to sail on with him from Cumberland Bay in October 1704. With the *Cinque Ports* was a second privateer, the *St George*, commanded by the famous buccaneer, Captain William Dampier.

Luckily for Selkirk, when a Captain Woodes Rogers arrived off Juan Fernandez in 1709 the indefatigable Dampier was with him as pilot. Their two Bristol privateers, the *Duke* and the *Duchess*, had captured the Acapulco treasure ship carrying Mexican gold to the King of Spain and were about to take her to England, Woodes Rogers wrote, when their pinnace returned from the shore of Cumberland Bay 'with a Man cloth'd in Goat-Skins, who look'd wilder than the first Owners of them'. When Dampier assured Woodes that Selkirk had been on the *Cinque Ports* and the best man in her, 'I immediately agreed with him to be a Mate on board our Ship'.

Selkirk's subsequent appearance in London caused a stir. Woodes Rogers wrote his account of him. Sir Richard Steele, founder of the *Tatler* and co-founder of the *Spectator*, interviewed him. Daniel Defoe seized on the story, enlarged on it fore and aft, and by transferring it bodily to the Caribbean (the struggle between England, France and Spain for the West Indies was much in the public's mind just then), was able to give us Man Friday.

Hoping to see goats and caves and the umbrella-shaped plant that in some illustrations Crusoe is seen holding like a parasol, I set off on foot to walk the thirteen miles to the end of the island. Not alone. Three young islanders volunteered to come: Teddy, Miguel and Francisco. Miguel, small and sharp-nosed, brought a white mule named Mantequilla, or Butter, and Teddy, tall and gangling, an old, small dog called Cholo. In her sackcloth panniers Mantequilla carried a few metal dishes and spoons, knives and forks, bread and the ingredients of some sort of stew; also a kettle, a few blankets and useful odds and ends like matches and a bottle of *pisco*. We had, in fact, all that Selkirk took ashore from the *Cinque Ports* with the exception of a firelock, gunpowder, bullets, a hatchet, mathematical instruments and a Bible, none of which we seemed likely to need.

The track shot straight up through the scrub on the long, broken slopes behind the little town. In my heavy lace-up boots and thick sweater I soon began to pant as I had following Marie to see the *paepaes*, and even Mantequilla developed an increasingly melancholy expression. At the top of the steep escarpment called El Mirador de Selkirk, or Selkirk's Lookout, the three young islanders themselves were quite glad of the halt that I justified by pausing near a large rock to read the Spanish on a metal plaque embedded in it:

> On this spot, day after day, for more than four years, the Scottish sailor Alexander Selkirk searched the horizon expectantly, anxiously waiting for a rescue ship that would free him from isolation and permit him to return one day to his fellow human beings, perhaps even to the place of his birth.

A few steps further on the full length of the island was revealed, straggling away rather oddly. For the island was roughly the shape of a tadpole, the head of the tadpole ridged with mountain and at first shaggy with forest. Beyond the forest I could see a track winding like some yellow thread across hillsides and crevices as bare as the Sahara: the tail of the tadpole had withered. The green richness stopped as suddenly as if a terrible experiment in chemical warfare had completely defoliated half the island.

Teddy and Francisco hurried down the steep descent beyond the plaque; Miguel and I followed more sedately with Mantequilla: it was awkward going. The track was terribly uneven and we slid and stumbled along it over boulders and fallen trees, among monster ferns, cabbage trees and umbrella plants that looked like giant rhubarb. There were even clumps of palm trees in this strange forest.

'Hey! *Mula!*' Miguel shouted to encourage Mantequilla. '*Mula!* Oh!' He, like the others, wore nothing but ruined jeans, ragged shirt that hardly covered his bare chest, and battered shoes that in Europe would have been thrown away long before; yet it was far from warm. Teddy, the leader of the three, frequently left us to dash down the steep, rough hillside that dropped nearly sheer from the eroded ridge of the tadpole's back into the sea. This plunging hillside, I thought, was extremely dangerous; it was pitted and riven with hidden gullies, potholes and depressions, and covered with rocks and occasional bushes as well. But Teddy in his tattered shoes raced up and down, whooping and whistling encouragement to Cholo, whose tiny legs worked overtime as she dived in and out of the stone-filled ravines. Rabbits were the quarry. The hillsides were full of them; they sat in the weak sun like black and brown currants on a cake. An amazing number were black – descendants, I suppose, of all the sailors' pets that had ever escaped ashore. There had been no rabbits here in Selkirk's time; only cats, rats, and goats. Teddy, racing about so dangerously but with such ease, might have been Selkirk pursuing wild goats for food. Woodes Rogers had written:

> Agility in pursuing a Goat had once like to have cost him his Life; he pursu'd it with so much Eagerness that he catch'd hold of it on the brink of a Precipice, of which he was not aware the Bushes having hid it from him; so he fell with the Goat down the said Precipice a great height, and was so stunn'd and bruised with the Fall, that he narrowly escap'd with his Life, and when he came to his Senses, found the Goat dead under him.

'I am careful,' Teddy assured me when I remonstrated with him, and rushed off again as dangerously as before. 'We had a Bull-Dog,' Rogers went on, 'which we sent with several of our nimblest Runners ... but he distanc'd and tir'd both the Dog and the Men.' Teddy would have distanced and tired me in half a minute, so I watched him quite passively from the track with Miguel, Francisco and Mantequilla. He finally returned waving three rabbits over his head, saying that little short-legged Cholo, now dancing about his feet barking triumphantly, had caught them. It seemed something of a Selkirkian miracle.

'Bravo, Teddy,' I said.

'Bravo, Cholo,' he laughed, putting the rabbits in the pannier.

'Hey, *mula!*' Miguel cried to Mantequilla, and we went on.

It was cold and windy, and to keep warm we drank the *pisco* out of the bottle. After two or three hours we came to a cave the boys knew well that lay a little way off the track. There Teddy and Francisco laid a fire with wood they had collected on the way, heated the stew and made tea with water from a nearby stream. The cave was cosy. It was low and smelled of sheep; the ashes strewn among the blackened stones were relics of shepherds' fires. After the meal, we cloaked ourselves in blankets and I read bits of Woodes Rogers by torchlight. How had Selkirk passed the lonely weeks and months? He had sung psalms and prayed a good deal, and he had also invented odd pastimes. At first he was troubled a good deal by the wild cats and rats that had come ashore from ships and bred on the island. He told Sir Richard Steele he 'was extreamly pester'd with Rats, which gnaw'd his Cloaths and Feet when sleeping. To defend him against them, he fed and tamed numbers of young Kitlings, who lay about his Bed, and preserved him from the Enemy.' Odder still, he 'likewise tamed some Kids, and to divert himself would now and then sing and dance with them and his Cats'.

No one danced with Cholo or Mantequilla, but under Teddy's direction the three islanders sang island songs which the low roof amplified while the wind rose around us. Long after the songs were over I woke to hear snoring, and rain swishing about the mouth of the cave, and felt something – a small creature – moving about under my blanket. Remembering Selkirk's rats, I sat up quickly, took a look – and found the bright, apologetic eyes of Cholo looking back at me. The old bitch's fur was sodden with rain, so I rubbed her and covered her with my blanket. With the same blanket over my head and inhaling the rich smell of rain-sodden earth, sheep droppings and damp dog's fur, it was not difficult to feel a little like Alexander Selkirk. The trouble was that I was far too old to learn to catch goats as Cholo caught rabbits. Alone on this island I would have starved in no time. I heard Mantequilla stamping outside, and fell asleep.

Selkirk lived on turtles and the giant crayfish of the island as well as goat's meat, and he told of huge colonies of seals and sealions whose 'dreadful Howlings and Voices seemed too terrible to be made for human Ears — some bleating like lambs, some howling like dogs or wolves, others, making hideous noises of various sorts'.

Next day we saw a party of fur seals at the end of the island, a long way below us, slipping on and off some rocks in a diminutive bay and barking happily. But the immense colonies Selkirk knew have quite gone. And we had yet to see the famous wild goats.

We returned to San Juan Bautista along the same track in a gale and driving rain, soaked, frozen, yet somehow sweating at the same time. The scramble up the western slope of the Mirador de Selkirk was one of the most exhausting I have ever endured. I have known many steeper climbs, but the weight of the downpour battering my body turned my legs to rubber and seemed to fill my lungs with hot coals. There is no pride in such situations. I leaned abjectly against boulders and choked for breath, and the islanders kindly offered me Mantequilla's back. But the poor old *mula* had enough to carry up that agonizing mountainside without my hundred and ninety pounds. Slow step after slow step, we plodded upwards through the hubbub. It was like walking up a waterfall. 'Damn Alexander Selkirk,' I thought, feeling old and useless. The downhill slope to Cumberland Bay should have been easier going, but the steep rutted slopes of mud-covered rock had been made slippery by the rain, and while I sped on ahead, leaving the boys to help Mantequilla, my feet were continually sliding from under me and dumping me in mud and bushes. My final humiliation was a spectacular flying fall to splosh face-up into a deep mire of black mud. Scratched, sodden and bruised, I lay for a moment half stunned in a puddle, spreadeagled like a beetle. Rising, I staggered, cursing, through Maria Eugenia's front door. She stood there laughing. 'You look more like Man Friday than Robinson Crusoe,' she said.

'Very funny.' Wet and disgruntled, I watched steam rising from my clothes as if I might burst into flames, but then the boys arrived, bottles of *pisco* were opened, and when we had all dried out by the fire I felt a great feeling of satisfaction. I even apologized to Selkirk for cursing him. I was glad of that when, much later, I read Sir Richard Steele's thoughts on him, published in *The Englishman* in 1713:

> When I first saw him, I thought, if I had not been let into his Character and Story, I could have discerned that he had been much separated from Company, from his Aspect and Gesture; there was a strong but chearful

Seriousness in his Look, and a certain Disregard to the ordinary things about him, as if he had been sunk in Thought. When the Ship which brought him off the Island came in, he received them with the greatest Indifference, with relation to the Prospect of going off with them, but with great Satisfaction in an Opportunity to refresh and help them. *The Man frequently bewailed his Return to the World, which could not, he said, with all its Enjoyments, restore him to the Tranquility and his Solitude.*

The italics in the last sentence are mine.

One question still remained as I sat in the kitchen of the Aldea Daniel Defoe.

'Maria Eugenia, Teddy, Miguel, Francisco,' I addressed them all. 'Where *are* those wild goats? Crusoe made his hair suit from goatskins, stitching them together with a nail and worsted strands from his socks. But where are they?'

A chorus answered me. 'The wild goats stay high up near the Yunque, the Anvil Mountain.' They added wickedly, 'Would you like to go up there and see?'

'Of course,' I said, ostentatiously concentrating on squeezing lemon juice into a finger of *pisco*. 'But we'll leave that until I come back to Juan Fernandez.'

'Oh, not till *then*!' Teddy slapped me on the shoulder. I looked up, caught his teasing expression and we all laughed together.

Thirtytwo

'No sign of any ship running that British blockade,' Hernan Cubillos said over a drink when I was back in Santiago.

I had been away two weeks, returning again in the *Carlos Darwin*, this time with a dozen or two Juan Fernandez goats and sheep and four-foot *bacalao* fish hanging round the vessel like sides of beef in a butcher's shop. According to some mainland veterinary rule, all the animals were slaughtered on deck as we came within sight of Valparaiso, so that the decks were full of piteous bleating and ran with blood like the floor of a temple after a mass sacrifice. With the stink of slaughter and *bacalaos* heavy around us, and bodies and blood under our feet, we passengers spent our last hours aboard either leaning over the rail as far as we safely could to sniff fresh air, or below in the mess. I had an evening with Captain Pedro and his wife in their flat in Viña del Mar near Valparaiso, and several whiskies with Armanduco in a bar near the wharfside plaza while two *langostas* he was taking home scrabbled hopelessly on the sawdust-covered floor. Captain Pedro and Armanduco each gave me a ceramic vase decorated with flowers: the words *Al Escritor Gavin Young con Afecto Capitan Pedro* were inscribed on one, and *De la Isla Robinson Crusoe Amistosamente, Armanduco* on the other.

After that I took a bus to Santiago to think out my next move.

From the first, I had wanted to round the Horn; I had thought of doing it on a freighter – I couldn't see another way. But now that possibility had been ruled out by the British blockade and a more exciting idea struck me: to go down that two thousand miles of broken coastline and approach the Horn from its northern side. It was midwinter on the Horn, but that couldn't be helped. I would see it now or never.

'The blockade seems like staying for some time,' Hernan was saying. 'But I have done something for you. I've spoken to the head of the national shipping line. There's a Chilean cargo vessel sailing from Rio de Janeiro in a few days' time. To Cape Town. You could be on her, if you want to go in that direction.'

Yes, I said, I did want to get across the South Atlantic.

'But?'

'I've always wanted to see Cape Horn. . . .'

'And you're so near, is that it?' Hernan laughed. 'As a matter of fact, I rather thought you might choose to go south. It's precisely what I should do. You can't see Cape Horn every day of the week.'

The chart was on the table before us, with the toe of Tierra del Fuego jabbing out conspicuously into the Atlantic below the irregular sweep of the Straits of Magellan. But my eye drifted lower than that – to the Beagle Channel with the two tiny naval stations, Argentine Ushuaia on the northern shore, Puerto Williams to the south – and lower still, to Navarino Island, Ponsonby Sound, False Cape Horn, Cape Deceit, and at last to Cape Horn Island that hung like a drip at the extreme tip of a very battered nose.

'I told the shipping people that you might after all choose to stay on here a bit,' Hernan continued. 'The only thing is I must warn you that, with the Falklands business still unresolved, I can't guarantee you will get to the Horn. You see, the far south of Chile is in the hands of our navy. The officers at our naval station on the south side of the Channel at Puerto Williams may not have time for a strange British visitor. You understand?'

I understood perfectly. But to have arrived within striking distance of the Horn and to find the first major war there for nearly seventy years. . . .

'I'll consult,' Hernan said, 'and see what's to be done. But meanwhile, why not buy some really warm clothes?'

When he said that, I was certain I would be able to reach the south. But that did not mean I would see the Horn itself. That ambition seemed to rest in the uncertain hands of General Galtieri in Buenos Aires.

Within a week I was heading south. First, I took a train to Puerto Montt and made a detour from the direct route to the Straits of Magellan onto the large, bleak island of Chiloe. Darwin didn't think much of the place, failing in 1834 to buy either a pound of sugar or an ordinary knife there. He found some pure Indians hereabouts, but thought very little of the non-Indians: 'It was a pleasant thing to see the aborigines advanced to the same degree of civilization, however low that may be, which their white conquerors have attained.' I hurried past the houses on stilts that he had seen, and through the old cemeteries where the ancient tombs are as large and alarming as any in Père Lachaise in Paris.

Further down the coast, across valleys and over countless inlets and coves, near the island of San Pedro, I saw my first albatross. It was heavy with self-conscious arrogance, with its cold eye, its cruel beak and a head like the head of a wicked pope. At San Pedro, Darwin wrote:

> two of the [Beagle's] officers landed to take a round of angles with the theodolite. A fox (Canis fulvipes) of a kind said to be peculiar to the island, and very rare in it, and which is a new species, was sitting on the rocks. He was so intently absorbed in watching the work of the officers, that I was able by quietly walking up behind, to knock him on the head with my geological hammer. This fox, more curious or more scientific, but less wise, than the generality of his brethren, is now mounted in the museum of the Zoological Society.

A ferry carrying trucks took me to Punto Natales near the Straits of Magellan. The *Evangelistas* was a modern 'roll-on roll-off' vessel – the loaded lorries were driven directly on board up a wide ramp in the stern. I stayed on deck with my binoculars and a chart folded against the rail and watched the islands and sounds move past like the scattered pieces of an enormous jigsaw puzzle. The prospect was an unending one of stern headlands, bays, daunting hillsides and bleak inlets with sometimes, in the distance, a snow-covered volcano rising like a glorious pyramid above all the intervening ridges and chasms; a serene white sentinel in the sun. Austere but magnificent vistas were repeated with almost imperceptible variations. In days gone by, it must have been the easiest region in the world to get lost in. Fjord after silent fjord moved towards the *Evangelistas*' bows, echoed faintly the deep purr of her engines, and fell behind to merge silently once more into the tableau of a thousand other hillsides. Very rarely there was a huddle of houses by a wharf; little fishing villages which we passed by. Mile after mile, the only living things to keep us company were screaming gulls and a few ducks, the flapping 'steamer' ducks that skitter over the water's surface beating up spray like steam. If not truly beautiful, the desolation

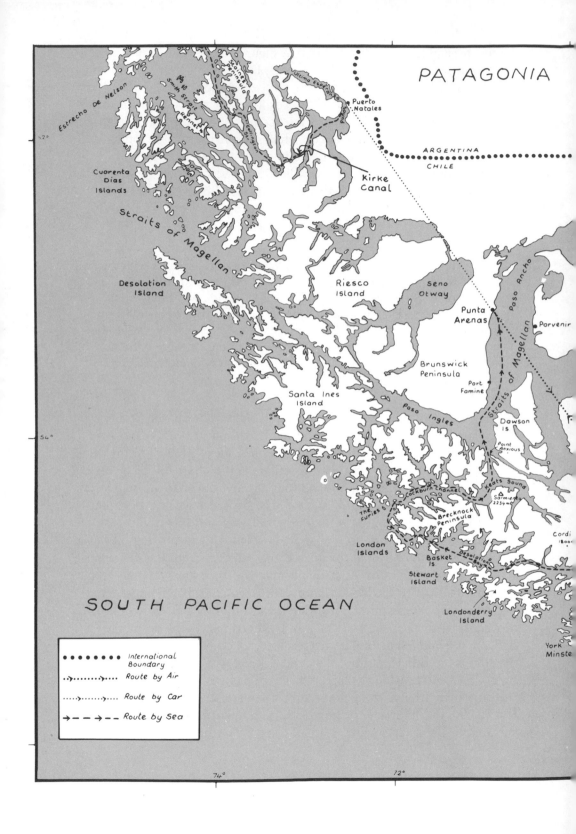

PATAGONIA

Estrecho De Nelson

Smith Strait

Rennell's

Peninsula

Ultima Esperanza Sound

Puerto Natales

ARGENTINA

CHILE

Kirke Canal

Cuorenta Dias Islands

Straits of Magellan

Riesco Island

Seno Otway

Punta Arenas

Porvenir

Paso Ancho

Desolation Island

Brunswick Peninsula

Port Famine

Santa Ines Island

Paso Ingles

Straits of Magellan

Dawson Is.

Point Anxious

Keats Sound

Sarmiento 2234 m.

Cockburn Channel

Brecknock Peninsula

The Furies

London Islands

Basket Is.

Stewart Island

Desolation Bay

Cordi 1800

Londonderry Island

York Minste

SOUTH   PACIFIC   OCEAN

56°

•••••• International Boundary

···>···>··· Route by Air

·····>·····>· Route by Car

→ – → – Route by Sea

74°

72°

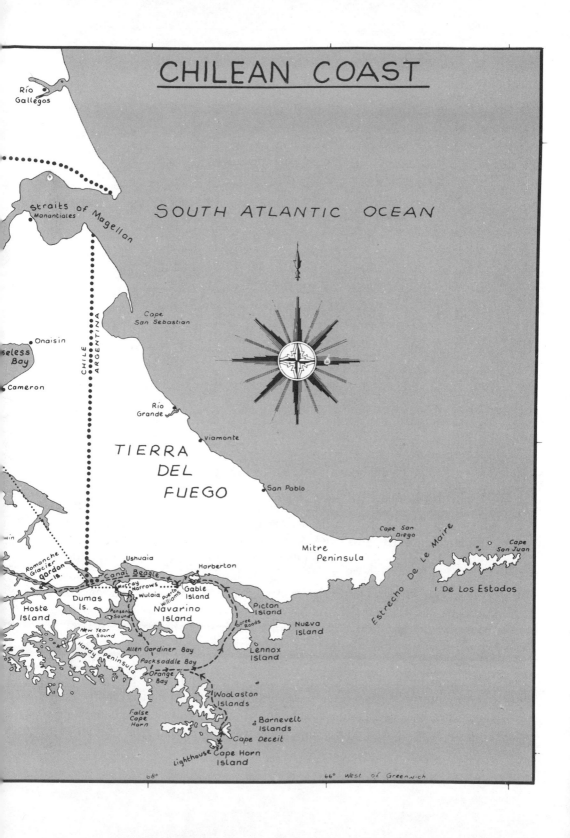

CHILEAN COAST

Río Gallegos

Straits of Magellan
Manantiales

SOUTH ATLANTIC OCEAN

Onaisin

seless Bay

Cameron

CHILE · ARGENTINA

Cape San Sebastian

Río Grande

Viamonte

TIERRA DEL FUEGO

San Pablo

Cape San Diego

Mitre Peninsula

Estrecho De Le Maire

Cape San Juan

I De Los Estados

win

Romonche Glacier
Gordon Is.

Ushuaia

Canal Beagle

Harberton

Hoste Island

Dumas Is.

Murray Narrows
Wulaia

Ponsonby Sound

puerto williams

Gable Island

Navarino Island

New Year Sound

Picton Island

Horne Roads

Nueva Island

Hardy Peninsula

Allen Gardiner Bay

Packsaddle Bay

Orange Bay

Lennox Island

Woolaston Islands

False Cape Horn

Barnevelt Islands

Cape Deceit

Lighthouse Cape Horn Island

68°

66° West of Greenwich

had a strange, monotonous allure. Inlets shaggy with evergreen beeches, wooded slopes piebald with snow rose on all sides: it was monotonous all right. Even the dangerous Bay of Peñas stayed flat as a millpond.

HMS *Beagle* had first crept this way in 1826 to chart the horrendous coast on behalf of the Admiralty in London. Captain Robert FitzRoy had spent four years here before tackling the far rougher regions round the Horn. While probing the western region around Desolation Bay, FitzRoy's men had lost a whaling boat to some mischievous Indians, and in retaliation FitzRoy had taken hostage four young Fuegians of the region whom eventually he took to England. One of the four, a boy called Boat Memory (after the incident of the lost whaling boat) died of smallpox in the naval hospital in Portsmouth, but the three others passed a cheerful year and a half in a clergyman's house in Walthamstow. This was the beginning of one of the world's strangest stories.

These were the three: York Minster, named after a prominent mountain west of Cape Horn, a 'thick powerful man' but morose; Jemmy Button (he had been 'purchased' for one pearl button), short, fat and vain, who in England became inordinately fond of gloves, mirrors and highly-polished shoes; and nine-year-old Fuegia Basket, named

338

after Basket Island near Desolation Bay where she was first taken on board the *Beagle*. By the time the unlikely trio had spent some while at school in London, they spoke a good deal of English, had acquired polished table manners and behaved with the utmost decorum when presented at Court to King William IV and Queen Adelaide. The King asked a good number of questions about their life at home, and gave little Fuegia a ring from his finger; Queen Adelaide gave her the lace cap from her own head. The true story of these three Indians reads like an exaggeration by Defoe: but it slowly came to life as I journeyed south to the Horn.

The Chilean charts generously retained the names FitzRoy had chosen. South of the Bay of Peñas, for example, I saw Adventure Bay, Benjamin Island, Wickham Sound, Patricio Lynch Island, MacPherson Island, Wellington Island, Evans Island and Kirke Channel, named after a lieutenant on the *Beagle* who would no doubt be glad to know that his strait will be forgotten by few who see it. It was as much as we could do to squeeze through the needle's-eye gap in its rock walls. Everyone on board came on deck to watch, and two crewmen stood by the two anchor winches in the bows, ready to let them go if the *Evangelistas* began to swing out of control. Beyond, a sound that seemed to stretch away for ever had been named Seno Ultima Esperanza or Last Hope Sound by Magellan, who, searching for a route through to the Pacific Ocean, had sailed exhausted and half frozen to the far end of it – and found it was a cul-de-sac.

At the little Patagonian town of Puerto Natales I disembarked. There was no waterway to the Straits of Magellan from here, so I hired a taxi and, pausing merely for a cup of tea for the driver and *pisco* for myself, bumped away south to Punta Arenas, the Chilean port halfway between the Atlantic and the Pacific.

I was getting on, I thought. Across the choppy Straits, several miles wide here, I could see the cone of Sarmiento Mountain behind Dawson Island, and range after range of snowy mountains running down to the Horn. Further to my right, the Straits spread lakelike to Point Famine and swept out of sight round the point of the Brunswick Peninsula. To my left the Straits curved up under the shore of southern Patagonia – Argentina now – and went on to meet the Atlantic at Dungeness Point beyond which, in the open sea, the patrolling warships of the Royal Navy had put a shield in front of the Falkland Islands.

I could see the northern shore of Tierra del Fuego, named the Land of Fire by the earliest European explorers whose first sight of it had been smoke from the countless fires of the Fuegian Indians. Fire had been the poor Fuegians' greatest comfort. They made their fires with tinder from birds' down or parts of a puffball common in these desolate regions, and set them going with the sparks from iron pyrites – firestones; they never wittingly permitted them to go out, caring for them almost as much as they cared for their babies. Required to travel, they carried their fires with them from shore to canoe and back again.

FitzRoy and Darwin found the Indians in the far south near Cape Deceit in a terrible state. They appeared in bark canoes out of curtains of heavy rain, stark naked, their skins filthy and greasy, their hair tangled. When bad weather prevented them from collecting the shellfish they lived on, they all but starved. When the *Beagle* entered Goree Roads to the east of Navarino Island, FitzRoy, who was anxious to find a way through from there to Ponsonby Sound to the west, sent off four boats through the channel he had earlier named after the *Beagle* and which Darwin compared to the valley of Loch Ness in Scotland. It was about a hundred and twenty miles long with an average breadth of about two miles, and crossed the south part of Tierra del Fuego in an east–west line. Nothing existed there except Indians, animals and birds.

FitzRoy's three Fuegian protégés were returned – at their own request – to the Land of Fire in 1832, laden down with clothing, books, tools, seeds and plates and accompanied by a missionary, Mr Richard Matthews. At first FitzRoy thought it advisable to land them exactly where they had first been found: in Jemmy's case, in Ponsonby Sound.

Here it was interesting – disturbing, too, no doubt – to watch the conduct of the resident 'savages' towards their 'civilized' relatives so recently at the Court of St James's. The Indians of Jemmy's family were not like the abject, naked wretches in the canoes nearer the Horn. The young men were powerfully built and often six feet tall. They wore cloaks of guanaco hides 'just thrown over their shoulders, leaving their persons as often exposed as covered', said Darwin. Not surprisingly, they looked distrustful, surprised and startled. An old man with a fillet of white feathers round his head, their chief spokesman, scarcely deserved, in Darwin's view, to be called articulate. The language was so odd that Captain Cook had compared it to a man clearing his throat. Poor, vain, overdressed Jemmy Button was acutely embarrassed.

> The Indians immediately perceived the difference between him and themselves and held much conversation one with another on the subject. The old man addressed a long harangue to Jemmy, which it seems was to invite him to stay with them. But Jemmy understood very little of their language, and was, moreover, ashamed of his countrymen. When York Minster afterwards came on shore, they noticed him in the same way, and told him he ought to shave; yet he had not twenty dwarf hairs on his face, whilst we all wore our untrimmed beards. They examined the colour of his skin, and compared it with ours. One of our arms being bare, they expressed the liveliest surprise and admiration of its whiteness. And their interest exceeded admiration: 'We thought that they mistook two or three of the officers, who were rather shorter and fairer, though adorned with large beards, for the ladies of our party.'

FitzRoy let himself be guided to a 'quiet, pretty little cove' called Wulaia and here Jemmy's mother and family soon appeared. But the family reunion lacked the warmth Darwin had expected of it; it was, he said, 'less interesting than that between a horse turned out into a field, when he joins an old companion'. Nevertheless, York Minster and Fuegia both decided to stay here instead of going to their homes further west.

The name Wulaia – or Woollya, as Darwin writes it – runs through the history of those desolate regions like an owl's cry of doom. Soon the whole party of Fuegians, and Mr Matthews too, were settled in the little cove there. Wigwams were erected, gardens dug, seeds sown. The *Beagle* sailed, but no sooner had she disappeared round a snowy headland than the local Indians ran amok, plundering all they could lay hands on. They terrorized Mr Matthews, showing him by signs that they wished to strip him naked and pluck all the hairs out of his face and body. When, luckily, FitzRoy returned unexpectedly, he found Jemmy wringing his hands, blaming his tribesmen and moaning, 'All bad men, no savvy nothing. Damned fools.' Matthews was taken off, quaking, and swiftly made his way to New Zealand.

A bad start, but a year later worse had befallen poor Jemmy. Returning yet again, FitzRoy and Darwin found the Wulaia settlement oddly quiet, but soon 'a canoe, with a little flag flying, was seen approaching, with one of the Indians in it washing the paint off his face. This man was poor Jemmy.' The once plump, mirror-loving dandy was by now only a 'thin haggard savage, with long disordered hair and naked, except for a bit of blanket round his waist. . . .' There had been fighting in the settlement, and York Minster and Fuegia, who had married each other, had deserted him, taking most of Jemmy's property with them to their home in the west. Nevertheless, Jemmy brought presents of spearheads and otter skins to the *Beagle* and ate dinner on board 'as tidily as formerly'. He, too, was married and, although FitzRoy offered to have him on board, he showed no sign of wanting to be taken away again. He returned ashore loaded with presents and 'every soul on board,' said Darwin, 'was heartily sorry to shake hands with him for the last time. . . .' As the *Beagle* stood out into the open sea a farewell curl of smoke rose from Jemmy's signal fire.

Punta Arenas is pleasant enough but I did not see much of it. I glimpsed a green city square, a modern hotel or two, a museum full of stuffed birds and wax models of Indians, and a small zoo containing live condors and guanacos, a species of llama with yellowy-red wool that used to be common on the Beagle Channel and Navarino Island.

To save time I flew to Navarino Island in a tiny twin-propellered plane carrying four Chilean naval petty officers. The Straits lay wide and placid in perfect weather. Beyond Useless Bay on the western shore of Tierra del Fuego Island, we came to the shimmering wasteland of the south.

Behind Sarmiento's seven-thousand-foot peak, walls of white spread south and east, entwined as waves are before breaking on a beach. Between them lakes or spreading tentacles of sea lay like blue mirrors in elaborate dead-white frames, and blue-green glaciers crept down to them under the wintry sun. A haze lay over the whole immense wilderness which stretched as far as I could see even at the plane's height, becoming bluer and bluer with distance until everything was swallowed up at last in the luminous, misty blue horizon.

It was breathtaking. And awesome too – for there was no human life in that whole region of earth and water, mountain and forest, snow and glacier. It was one of the angriest places on earth. The islands themselves had angry shapes; and their angry beaches were littered with the bones of ships and men.

The plane banked over the southern shore of Tierra del Fuego in clear, cold air and slid down the long, straight waterway called the Beagle Channel. Turning over the bare blob of Gable Island opposite the Argentine base at Ushuaia, the little machine landed smoothly on the airstrip of Chile's Puerto Williams. Small blue-grey torpedo boats lay alongside a jetty. Near them, a sailor in a sandbagged bunker gazed to the north shore through powerful binoculars mounted on a tripod at similarly coloured Argentine warships.

There was snow everywhere, and ice made walking dangerous. I followed the petty officers down a steep, narrow path from the airstrip to an area of jeeps, bungalows and a flagstaff flying the blue, white and red flag of Chile, where a board announced naval headquarters.

The Chilean naval officers seemed glad to see an outsider, particularly from Britain. The commanding officer, Captain Frederick Corthorn Besse, housed me in the navy's mess where I learned that the entire population of Puerto Williams, civilian and naval, had watched the progress of the Falklands War with intense concentration on their TV sets, as spectators stood on a hilltop overlooking Waterloo.

Here they had been living on the very edge of conflict. If war had come, the full force of Argentina would inevitably have fallen on Puerto Williams, and no one disputed, I found, that the Argentine armed forces were larger and stronger than Chile's. The Chilean south would have fallen, everybody admitted, but resistance would have been fierce. A scholarly-looking lieutenant said with conviction that the whole four thousand miles of Chile's frontier from Cape Horn to the border with Peru 'would have been set alight'. For the moment, no one knew what would happen next, since Galtieri was still in the presidential Casa Rosada in Buenos Aires and, as I could see, Argentine warships were just across the Channel in Ushuaia Bay.

Captain Besse was a friendly man. He understood what I wanted to see and would help me. There was only one thing, however: he could not put me onto the naval supply vessel going to the Horn without special permission from the admiral in Punta Arenas. I would have to apply for that permission in person; he wished, he said, that someone had told me that before I'd come south. Still, there was a small commercial vessel leaving at any minute for Punta Arenas; it would take me back there to see the admiral. He pointed out its course on his wall chart – it would take me through the most barren parts of the island wilderness, through the homelands of FitzRoy's Fuegians, even briefly out into the Pacific.

'See you in a few days,' he said, 'with the admiral's permission.'

The little cargo-passenger vessel back to Punta Arenas travelled west along the Beagle Channel, past the glum evergreen woods of Navarino Island, past the entrance to Jemmy Button's Ponsonby Sound. The land of York Minster and Fuegia Basket presented the most savage scenery. Through these snow-patched islands the little ship moved gamely on, battling the high winds and blizzards of midwinter, dwarfed to toy-size by the towering white peaks of the Cordillera Darwin lying under their permanent snow and often lost in heavy mist. The body heat of men in layers of wool and fur-lined anoraks made a good fug in the wheelhouse, and there was an electric heater, but on deck all the clothes I had bought in Santiago hardly kept out the cold: the thick woollen cap, the two sweaters, the three shirts, the long underwear, the heavy woollen socks, the lined leather boots and the woollen gloves.

We skirted the north of Gordon Island where the Beagle Channel divided into two, and slipped under O'Brien Island. Great lumps of ice floated alongside us there, and then, leaving Londonderry Island to port, we came into Whaleboat Sound where the saga of FitzRoy's Fuegian trio had begun. On the chart of these islands you see fierce, tortured shapes – snarling dogs' heads, dragons' claws, and the screaming mouths of drowning men. We entered Desolation Bay plunging and rolling, horribly exposed to the Pacific and the south-westerly wind, only regaining stability by ducking behind Basket Island, Fuegia's home. Island succeeded island, bay opened into bay and sound into sound. You could sing with relief that you were about to emerge from some claustrophobic, rockbound passage, only to discover that that passage led into another indistinguishable from it – and that one into yet another. No wonder the early navigators lost themselves here for months in this uncharted maze. No wonder crews went mad with fear. The landscape seems to stare at you with the fixed, thoughtful look of an idiot wondering whether to crush a beetle.

The passage behind Basket Island led into another open bay, in the mouth of which the seas pounded on the islet known, understandably, as the Furies. Near the Furies the *Beagle* had been all but overwhelmed by a huge wave, but I was, thank God, in a well-powered ship with radar and a master and crew who knew the region. While winds howled round us, we wallowed in a vicious maelstrom of waves and the wheelhouse jerked back and forth like a metronome gone berserk. A snowstorm struck as the vessel's nose swung northward into the Cockburn Channel up the side of Brecknock Island and the heavy white flakes piled up on the deck and glued themselves to the window of the wheelhouse, half blinding the helmsman; but by then we had the sea behind us.

Then it was plainer sailing. We skirted Bluff Cove, Point Anxious and Keats Sound quite comfortably, entering the Straits of Magellan near Dawson Island. Within a few hours we were tied up at Punta Arenas. A few hours more and the admiral had given me his permission to visit Cape Horn and I was sitting in the same twin-engined plane on the way back to Puerto Williams. There Captain Besse boomed 'Welcome back!' and, flourishing a cable from the admiral, told me to be ready to board a small naval craft loading supplies for Chilean posts round Cape Horn. 'Don't take too much baggage,' he said. I emptied my bag except for a camera, a spare pair of trousers, socks and a bottle of *pisco*, and that night I lay in bed sleepless. As Hernan Cubillos had said, 'You can't see Cape Horn every day of the week.' I had to read myself into oblivion with the story of the three Fuegians.

Darwin's tale was continued in a book as remarkable as his and called *Uttermost Part of the Earth*. Its author, Lucas Bridges, was born in 1847 at Ushuaia, then no more than a primitive mission station established by his father only five years earlier. Lucas knew all there was to know of the Fuegians. He was brought up with the Indian people, playing with them, hunting with them, speaking their language.

Sixteen years after Jemmy's farewell signal fire had sent up its hopeful plume of smoke just south of the Beagle Channel, a Royal Naval captain, Allen Gardiner, having recently found God, started the Patagonian Missionary Society and set sail for the Beagle Channel with six companions, one of whom, a Dr Richard Williams, gave his name much later to Puerto Williams. Gardiner tried to make contact with Jemmy Button and his tribe, but failed, and the expedition was a disaster. His party was pursued with homicidal intent wherever they went by the very Indians they had come all this way to convert, and finally died miserably, like rats, of starvation, exposure and scurvy in a freezing cave on the Beagle Channel. Gardiner died, according to Lucas Bridges, in a condition of ecstasy.

Three years after this tragedy another small mission ship, named in honour of Gardiner, reached Wulaia from the mission's headquarters on Keppel Island in the Falklands, and this time her captain easily found Jemmy Button, though the once dapper Indian was obliged to borrow a pair of trousers before being introduced to the captain's wife. Jemmy was next spotted in 1859, when the same mission ship arrived from the Falklands bringing three Indian families, a catechist called Garland Philips and an ambitious plan to set up a mission in Wulaia there and then. A hut was at once erected to serve as a church. Excited Indians swarmed round from far and wide and were incessantly importunate. The worst pest of all the Indians proved to be Jemmy Button, who never stopped begging and was thoroughly bad-tempered. 'Spoiled,' the captain thought, which proved to be something of an understatement.

Despite continuous harassment from the Indians, the first church service in Tierra del Fuego was arranged. In perfect weather, three hundred Indians packed the little church and the ship's company came too, leaving only one man on the *Allen Gardiner*, Alfred Cole, the cook. He was the sole non-Indian witness to survive the carnage that followed.

> He heard the first lines of the hymn, then, helpless and terrified, witnessed what followed.
>
> Some of the natives ran to the long-boat, carried off all the oars to a nearby wigwam and set the boat adrift. In the hut the hymn ceased abruptly, to be followed by a terrific hubbub. The natives had fallen on the party with clubs, stones and spears. But, wearing only loose cloaks, how had they concealed these things – so inappropriate in a Christian prayer meeting – when they came into the church?
>
> Garland Philips and a Swedish sailor named Agusto fought their way out of the hut and reached the sea under a hail of stones. Philips waded out to the drifting long-boat and waist-deep in water, was just scrambling into it when a stone flung by Tommy Button, Jimmy's [sic] brother, hit him on the temple. He fell back unconscious into the sea and was drowned. Agusto met with a similar fate, and ashore the rest of the little party were stoned, clubbed, or speared to death.

Cole escaped into the woods on the island opposite Wulaia, but capture was inevitable. 'The natives stripped him of all his clothes except his belt and a ring on his finger, and plucked out his beard, moustache and eyebrows.' (This, Bridges charitably remarks, was not necessarily prompted by cruelty, for, he says, it was in accordance with their own custom.) In fact, Cole's life was spared and he lived with the Indians for three months, mostly stark naked, until rescued – in a desperate physical state – by another mission ship that had been sent to search for the *Allen Gardiner*. Cole, naturally enough, was the principal witness at the subsequent inquiry, Jemmy Button being the only other. The inquiry found beyond all reasonable doubt that Jemmy had instigated the massacre with an eye to the loot on the *Allen Gardiner*.

Nothing much seems to have been done about Jemmy. The inquiry was only an inquiry after all, not a meting out of justice, and Jemmy was seen alive in Wulaia in 1863, four years after the massacre, by Lucas Bridges' father, Thomas, who was as determined as ever to set up a permanent mission in the region. By then Jemmy had three sons himself and one of them, known as Threeboy, was taken by the missionaries to the Falklands and later to London, as his father had been taken by Captain FitzRoy. Threeboy was not, however, received by Queen Victoria.

Thomas Bridges soon decided that Wulaia was not the ideal site for an agricultural mission intended to expand: the bay was too small and off the main canoe routes of the Beagle Channel. On the other hand Ushuaia, nearby on the northern shore of the Channel, offered a sheltered, accessible harbour, and so Ushuaia became the first and most famous Christian mission of Tierra del Fuego.

Yet even now the Button–Basket–York Minster saga was not played out. There was further news of Fuegia Basket in 1873, when she turned up at the Ushuaia mission. By then a hearty, if nearly toothless woman of over fifty, she was proud of her new husband, aged eighteen, who had come with her; York Minster, she said, had been killed in some tribal squabble. She remembered a little of London and of a Miss Jenkins who had looked after her in Walthamstow. She also remembered Captain FitzRoy. But when Thomas Bridges offered her a chair, she squatted beside it on the floor. And the missionary in him was sad to find she had lost her religion.

The last sight of Fuegia was recorded by Bridges ten years later on London Island, near the Furies. By then sixty-two, very weak and unhappy, she refused to respond to Thomas Bridges' attempts to cheer her up with 'the beautiful Biblical promises' and Lucas Bridges, in retrospect, thought she was lucky if she escaped *tabacana*, the Indians'

347

habit of hastening the end of aged relatives by strangling them. '*Tabacana*' – Bridges' wry comment – 'was kindly meant; it was carried out openly and with the approval of all except the victim, who was too inanimate to do anything about it.'

In *Uttermost Part of the Earth* Lucas Bridges, evidently an honest man who genuinely cared for the Indians, tells how white men in the early 1890s came to grab those parts of Tierra del Fuego that were excellent for sheep farming. Vast tracks of land were sold to companies and individuals on both sides of the Argentine–Chilean border. 'I need hardly state,' Bridges wrote, 'that the white invaders soon found it impossible to start farms they had planned in a country over-run by these wild, undisciplined nomads. A story – widely circulated and not yet forgotten – tells that certain of the newcomers paid a pound a head for every Indian killed.' The Indians were armed only with bows and arrows, while the white men were mounted and armed with repeating rifles. Some settlers paid five pounds for every Indian taken off their hands and transported to a mission. There were white men who looked upon all this as a meritorious act, clearing the country of predatory vermin and, at the same time, helping to reform the savages and make useful citizens of them. On the other hand, it could be regarded as condemning free natives – rightful owners of the land – to a kind of penal servitude.

Bridges follows his statement with an individual case in point – the case of Hektliohlh, 'one of the finest Indians I ever met'. Hektliohlh and a party of men, women and children were captured by the white men. They had been taken to the government settlement at Ushuaia from which after a while they were able to escape back to their lands. Four years later, Bridges happened to visit another Christian mission on Dawson Island where seven hundred Indians were confined, some making blankets under the supervision of nuns, others working in sawmills. The latter crowded round Bridges, who spoke their language, and to him they were pathetic in their secondhand, shop-soiled garments, generally several sizes too small. Looking at them, he 'could not help picturing them standing in their old haunts, proud and painted, dressed, as of yore, in head-dress, robe and mocassins'.

Among them was Hektliohlh, 'who stood out amongst them for his looks and bearing'. He had been recaptured by the settlers and handed over to the mission. He had no complaint about his treatment. But, gazing in the direction of his native mountains, he told Bridges: 'Longing is killing me.' Which was actually the case, Bridges admits, for he did not survive very long.

Nor did any of his race. At Puerto Williams I visited what the Chilean naval officers called 'the last of the Indians'. This lone survivor was a gnomelike woman, obviously of great age, who received me outside her hut behind the married quarters of the naval station. She spoke a few words in English, learned at a mission school years before, smiled, and let me look through the door at her table, her fire and her chair.

Bridges remained a committed missionary until his death. 'Allen Gardiner's plans,' he wrote in old age, 'were followed to a successful conclusion. Though I am well aware that, within less than a century, the Fuegians as a race have become almost extinct I deliberately used the word "successful"....' So modern Tierra del Fuego's history began with a massacre of the Christians by the Indians, and ended with the annihilation of the Indians by the Christians. No doubt a number of souls were saved in between.

Thirty three

Twilight was thickening when we left Puerto Williams, and a wind like a hungry rat scurried up and down the Beagle Channel, gnawing at my ears and cheeks.

'Murray Sound. Wulaia.' I could just hear the Chilean lieutenant shouting to me through the wheelhouse door at the gloom ahead. I edged along the deck and felt my way with gloved hands down a stubby iron ladder to the stern, somewhat protected. There was a passenger to be disembarked at Wulaia. She stood by me now, her two bags beside her, while the sailors prepared to lower the rubber dinghy

with the outboard motor that could run into rough or shallow bays. The supply vessel was a converted trawler; small enough – a barrel fitted with a powerful engine, radar and a wheelhouse, really – but some of the inlets here were smaller still, and the currents and shifts in the weather were dangeroug from here to Horn Island. She was painted dark blue and now that the sunlight had gone, her silhouette was black against the sky. There was a small island ahead of us, hardly more than a shadow, and a bay.

The dinghy splashed into the water. The ship's dog, a woolly animal with a high-curling tail and intelligent eyes, sprang about barking as though piratical boarders were imminent, appearing to be about to jump onto the gunwhale and down into the sea. I spoke to the woman in halting Spanish. She was bringing some shopping from Puerto Williams, she said, and had been lucky to find this lift home. Usually she couldn't count on the supply boat, because it sailed at infrequent and irregular intervals, and so she would take a motor boat, or anything going.

It was difficult to catch all she said, with the wind in my ears, the barking, the shouts of the crew, the crashing of the dinghy against the little ship's side and, of course, my appalling Spanish. I understood her to say she had a small farm, a husband, and some sheep at Wulaia, that her family came from Punta Arenas, that she would retire there shortly. She was lifed carefully over the side and lowered into the bouncing dinghy, and in a moment I heard the roar of the outboard motor. At the last second the dog did what I had feared. Over he went – up, and – down! I forced myself to look over the side, expecting to see him swimming for dear life, but instead he was seated calmly near the helmsman in what was evidently his accustomed place.

'Our dog, Tom, was born on ships,' a man said in good English at my shoulder. 'Engineer Menderez,' he added, introducing himself. 'Wherever men can go, Tom, too, can go.'

'A real seadog, then,' I said.

'*Claro.*'

The dinghy's white wake curved away noisily towards the shore. I

stared. Wulaia was just there, on the dark patch of land. Jemmy Button had groaned of his kith and kin 'Damned fools' to Captain FitzRoy and Charles Darwin, standing there in his polished shoes and trimmed hair, longing for a quick glance in a mirror. There York Minster had been ordered to pluck out the few miserable hairs from his chin. And there, in that place where the sounds of a half-finished hymn and the cries of the dying had risen to smite the terrified ears of Cole, the cook of the *Allen Gardiner*, a light – a torch, perhaps – was flickering as our lady passenger was helped ashore with her shopping bags of washing powder, toilet paper, beer and canned meat, and the only sound was the happy barking of Tom the dog.

A silence like that of outer space accompanied us south through the waters of Ponsonby Sound and into a bay where we could anchor and rest for the main part of the night. I did not sleep much. I hardly seemed to have squeezed into my tiny bunk before the engines were alive once more and it was time to struggle again into sweaters and boots, open the door and feel the blast of cold air like a slab of metal against the exposed bits of my face. No plumes of smoke rose from these shores. Any Indian here now would have to be a ghost. I stood on the deck outside my cabin, shivering with cold and excitement, and watched the oyster-gleam of dawn over the islands of the Horn.

After breakfast we began our Santa Claus-style round of duty calls. There were small Chilean garrisons on some of these islands, manning lookouts and tending radar installations. The Argentine navy regularly sent warships into these southern Chilean waters – just to provoke, to cock a snook, to say: 'See! You call these waters yours – and so does the world. But so what? Just try to keep us out!' Now and again small parties of Argentine seamen landed on Chilean islands, perhaps to spend a night there, perhaps to drink a cup of tea, perhaps just to have a good laugh, urinate, and go away at full speed ahead, curling a bow wave like an arrogant sneer. Contemptuous, buccaneering gestures like that would convey a serious message: Big Brother in Buenos Aires is watching you! The generals and admirals who ruled Argentina thought it was an amusing game; perhaps it made them feel like real warriors. So the Chilean garrisons kept watch and every two weeks or three, depending on the weather, the supply vessel went the rounds, dropping off food, spare parts, fuel, reading material and I don't know what else. We pottered about desolate bays and sounds and inlets, seeing a

Chilean flagpole here and there, the flag a minute splash of red and blue against the white and grey-green of the wilderness. At each outpost our crew lowered the rubber dinghy and loaded it with boxes and sacks. Each time Tom the dog barked with excitement, made his spectacular, perfectly timed flying leap seaward, and sat smiling in his place.

Muffled figures appeared on beaches hardly bigger than the supply ship itself. Through my binoculars I saw them waving as the dinghy dragged its white wake towards them across the freezing water and the growl of its outboard engine echoed back and forth between the rocky outcrops and the treeless headlands. We scouted Hardy Peninsula's south-eastern profile from Orange Bay almost as far as False Cape Horn, then turned across to the Wollastons. I shall never forget the scenes of those days – the islands at the end of the earth as silent as the moon, the whiplash of those hungry south-westerlies, green and snow-white patches in the pale blue bays – everything as cold and clear as a diamond. Most extraordinary of all was the stupendous backdrop of the Cordillera Darwin, the frozen chain of snow-covered peaks and ridges that lay across the north-western horizon, dominating everything else in sight like a frozen tidal wave over the icy turrets and battlements of the Snow Queen's Palace. In that breathtaking place, in that sublime and fearful silence, I doubt whether the Chileans, so accustomed to this routine 'run', felt as I did, like a miserable intruder.

We came down the sound between Herschel Island and Cape Deceit in the middle of the afternoon. The lieutenant tapped my arm and said, 'The wind is south-west. We can land the engineer, Menderez, from this side of Horn Island – the north-east side. But first, you want to see the Cape from the south side, don't you?' We passed the low island to starboard and felt at once the menacing heave of the open sea in Drake Sound. There it stood, Horn Island: low cliffs, a rocky bay, a mound of rock like a fist thrusting south. 'See the light?' the lieutenant said. It was not even a lighthouse – I had half expected a tall stone column with a glass crown flashing a thick beam, something like the Wolf on the Eddystone Lights. This little thing was a very modest affair, the southernmost light of the world.

We couldn't stay long off the point of Cape Horn; the sea was too high for the little souped-up ex-trawler. We rolled and plunged our way uncomfortably round the island and, arriving off its north-east corner again, lowered the dinghy once more. Men were waving from the shore.

'We'll drop Menderez here and come for him tomorrow or the next day. If the sea lets us.'

I decided at once what I must do.

'Lieutenant,' I said, 'I've come all this way. Drop me off here with Engineer Menderez. Will you?'

He looked doubtful. 'Well, if the weather is bad, maybe we come back in three days, or maybe three weeks.'

'Lieutenant, I have all the time in the world. You can leave me on Cape Horn for three weeks or three months.'

He laughed. 'Oh, no. Not so long.' He thought a moment, then took up the radio handset and spoke swiftly in Spanish.

A hoarse voice answered.

'All right,' the lieutenant said to me. 'Have you got a bag? Jump down into the boat with Tom. But don't take his place, or he can bite you.'

I think I embraced him, but I know that every member of the crew was laughing and making the thumbs-up sign as I slung my zip-bag over the side and followed it into the swaying dinghy. Tom didn't resent me at all. He licked my face.

All the same, when I put my foot on the shore of Cape Horn Island, my first experience was a dog bite in the calf. The aggressor was not Tom, I need hardly say; it was Tony, the fluffy mascot of the seven Chilean marines on the island, who probably thought I was an Argentine invader and decided on the spur of the moment to do his duty. It was a light snap rather than a serious bite, and did no damage – I was wearing far too many layers of clothing for that. In any case, Tony's attention was immediately diverted in umbrage to the interloper Tom, who was lifting his leg against a packing case.

The beach was stony and cramped and backed by a low escarpment with a crumbling track leading up to a hut. The tall marine in charge

354

shook my hand and ordered someone to take my bag. Then Engineer Menderez was helped ashore with his bag of tools, and for five minutes we scrambled, panting, up the slope to the unprotected crown of the island. There, as the wind pounded us like breakers against a shore, we turned and waved to the dark blue vessel, by now hardly bigger than a skiff bobbing across the water that separated us from Deceit Island. A moment later I was inside the hut with my hands outstretched to a stove in the centre of a small circle of goggling Chilean marines.

The tall man introduced himself. 'Sergeant-Major Nuñez.' He pushed a mug of tea at me, searching for a few words in English. 'We say ... *good morning.*' Everyone began to laugh, and at that early moment the ice was broken. Well, I thought, I've done it now: a few gales and I shall be here for weeks.

That evening and most of the next day, Engineer Menderez rallied a working party to the radio room attached to the little hut, where maintenance work was most needed. In the hut itself there was not much need for exploration. The first room faced south to the Antarctic and was furnished with a few tables and chairs. There was a radio set to listen to and the marines sat there reading sports magazines and comics, or playing patience, or chatting; they ate there, too. Further back there was a bathroom and toilets, and behind that a small dormitory with two-tiered metal bunks, and a smaller room with a similar bunk where the two sergeants slept, and two beds which now were allocated to Engineer Menderez and myself. There were doors to the bathroom — two showers and washbasins — and to the toilets, but no others, at least that I saw closed. Of course there was also a kitchen, from which two sweating marine cooks emerged to gawp at me and then smile and wave their ladles. Through the windows I could see the wave crests being thrashed into spray by the south-west wind, making the greybeards FitzRoy mentions, and from the flagpole the wind-torn Chilean flag flapped its ragged ends towards the north-east.

The marines were pleased to have a visitor, and I cursed once more my inability to speak even passable Spanish. Somehow we managed to communicate. Sergeant-Major Nuñez was concerned that I might not like their food, but during my time on the island there was little but bread and stews, which suited me perfectly. Nuñez introduced everyone by their first names: Sergeant Carlos, the second in seniority, Osorio, Patricio, Manuel, Miguel, Juan, Gonsalves. The two cooks were Cookie Uno and Cookie Dos, named in that Anglo–Spanish way that is Lord Cochrane's legacy. I might have called them Tweedledum and Tweedledee. Both were short, inclined to plumpness and particularly swarthy. Like all the others, apart from the two sergeants, they couldn't have been much more than twenty-three years old and had been posted to the island for the customary stint of duty which amounted to an extraordinarily long stretch. Was it three months? Something like that, I believe. Yet they did more than just survive; they were undoubtedly cheerful. No one has killed anyone else, Nuñez conveyed, laughing. It was a spartan life, of course, and I suppose it was sensible of the navy to ban alcohol on the island. Accordingly, I kept my *pisco* bottle out of sight.

The time passed oddly fast. The days are exceptionally short here in wintertime. To my mind, the Horn drew back the shutters to reveal its fullest drama just after sunset. Then the sea had turned its soft oyster-grey and soon, when the sun had quite disappeared, everything – sea, sky and this blunt stub of land – became obscure and drab and unconcerned with any human thing. The only presence then was the sighing, sobbing, nudging, teasing, bullying air. I asked permission from Nuñez to sit outside for a while on my own, not far from the door of the hut, just to admire the sudden black fall of cliffs to the ocean. I sat on a half-rotten bench and Tony came, too, and turned his nose to the wind. It made an odd noise, that wind. I felt the stress of it against me as its great gusts came and went, rose and fell. It was not the noise wind makes in sails, which is the reason for the old sailors' phrase 'blowing great guns'; nor had it anything to do with the eldritch howls and moans you can hear in mountains or round old houses (though they came later). Now, quite distinctly, as if they were just the other side of the clenched fist of rock behind the regular blink of the beacon, I heard the eager, deep, musical sound of baying hounds clamouring to be loosed.

I did not feel like sleep that first night on the Horn. Lying on the twanging springs of the military-issue bed, I slept very little, and when I did finally drop off almost at once a bleary grey dawn broke and the hut, well fugged up, was astir with yawning men fumbling their way out of the tracksuits and longjohns they had slept in into sweaters, khaki fatigues, ridge-soled boots and hooded anoraks to start on their duties outside.

I didn't regret the loss of sleep. On the contrary. That night and the next one I far preferred to stay awake as long as I could in order to savour the knowledge of where I was – to listen to the terrifying, unremitting wind that roamed round the island, rattling the flagstaff, roaring round our wooden walls like a monster in a story by Grimm, thrusting claws of steel between the floor and the rock beneath in an effort to wrench the hut loose, to hurl it and all of us into the ocean. That wind, and the thought of what it might do, was frightening and profoundly exhilarating at the same time. But most of all, huddled in my heavy underwear and two pairs of woollen socks, it was the sheer spiritual intoxication of being, of actually lying in a bed, on Cape Horn Island that kept me open-eyed and my nerves wide awake under those musty Chilean navy blankets.

Next morning Nuñez was busy but the other sergeant, Carlos, took me for one of the toughest walks of my life across the south-east prong of the island. Under a gloomy sky, butted and jostled by gusts of wind, we staggered along the cliffs towards a great knuckle of rock that punches out due south towards the South Pole. Cape Horn Island, I realized, lacks grandeur *per se*. It is perhaps the size of Hyde Park in London, a Hyde Park with no trees or bushes whatsoever. I had expected snow, but there was none. The wonderful sugary-white barrier of the Cordillera Darwin stood away to the north. Here, underfoot on the island, it was as snowless as a Scottish hillside in a mild winter. Clumps of what looked like heather were interspersed with tuffets of a livid, unhealthy-looking green.

The island is not quite flat. It undulates; here and there it pushes up hillocks. It looked as though it would be easy to walk from one end of the island to the other, but I very soon realized it was the opposite of easy. Heather doesn't mean a firm Scottish hillside. The ground was horribly boggy. Each clump of heather or livid green was surrounded by a solid-seeming mass into which, at every step, my booted foot sank at least as far as the calf. Following Sergeant Carlos's practised progress with difficulty, I squelched my way across Cape Horn Island, trying at times to leap from patch to patch, my lungs feeling more and more like antique bellows that had been left for far too long in somebody's attic. Oddly enough, the green tuffets which looked so treacherous were in fact the solidest; the trouble was there were so few of them. These marines must be in very good condition, I thought. Three months of pulling my legs out of the bogs of Cape Horn and I would be, too. For now, Carlos treated me with solicitude. So did Tony, who, having given me what I suppose was the statutory defensive nip when I landed, was treating me now as a long-awaited friend of whom he expected much. He was smaller than sturdy Tom and much fluffier; but he had the same curling, feathery tail. He, of course, negotiated the quagmire without

357

difficulty, rushing back and forth on rocks or tufts, looking round at my floundering figure from time to time like an anxious boxing trainer who wonders whether his boy is going to make it. I understood his doubts and summoned up enough breath for an occasional whistle downwind for his benefit.

We walked to a hilltop and stared at the sea. There had been seals on the rocks in the bay under the beacon, Carlos said, but they had moved on for the winter. There was no sign of life there now. Soon, other marines came out of the hut and began doing physical jerks. Osorio, the marine who had carried my bag up from the beach, came over, smiling 'Hello' at me, and began chasing Tony round and round. I watched them for a while, then looked across the sea. We were standing on a point, I saw; the whole of the island itself lay at the point of an arrowhead of islands. Facing south, Cape Deceit was a little behind us to our left, Hermit Island and False Cape Horn rather further behind to our right. Just there Darwin had seen six naked Fuegians in a canoe, surviving on putrid whale blubber. They slept on the wet ground, he said, coiled up like animals. Straight ahead – the Antarctic. I expected to see ships passing on the horizon of Drake Sound, but Carlos said he had spotted very few, not more than a dozen in a week. Not simply as a result of the blockade, he thought. They preferred the easier passage over two hundred miles north through the Straits of Magellan.

Osorio and Tony showed me the island's church. It was no bigger, I imagined, and probably much smaller, than the first little church at Wulaia the day of the *Allen Gardiner* massacre. It was simply a wooden hut made by the marines; outside it they had planted a wooden cross that swayed now, silhouetted against a sky the colour of dirty snow. The flagpole trembled beside it, its ragged flag writhing in the wind.

There is not much to do on Cape Horn Island except walk, run where you can, look at the scenery – and think just how extraordinary it is that you are where you are. Like Osorio, I played with Tony to keep warm, chasing him round the church and the flagpole while the marines peered out from their living hut and laughed. When I went inside I found those not on duty poring over the comics we had brought them from the supply ship the day before. One man was doing a crossword; one was darning a pair of discoloured woollen socks; two or three were interested in my binoculars, the *South American Handbook* and a few photographs I had with me of Samoa. A picture of Emma sitting on the beach while Fili and Amosa bathed in the lagoon brought whistles and laughter. Calloused fingers reached out to touch her. There could hardly have been a greater contrast between the picture and present reality – this austere hut of pale-skinned men wearing military fatigues in a drab, cold wilderness, and the reds and yellows of Emma's lava-lava, the glow of sun on skin, the hibiscus in her hair, against the warm blue of the lagoon.

'That's Emma,' I told them.

'Oh? Emma! Emma!' they echoed appreciatively. In a cloud of steam Cookie Uno and Cookie Dos left their kitchen and gazed at Emma as if she were a mermaid who might swim ashore at any moment. It was as much as I could do to keep their greasy fingerprints from blotting her out.

They were a cheerful lot, these marines, despite the long stint they had to endure on the island. Such isolation cannot have been easy for such young men. But I soon had the impression that Nuñez was an excellent commander, managing to combine authority – his deep, grating voice helped as well as his height – with a warm paternalism. I suppose he had been specially selected for the patience and self-sufficiency necessary in such a solitary post. He had humour, too, of a soldierly kind.

Towards noon, in a more serious vein, he said, 'English kill Argentina ship *Belgrano*. Good. *Pero*, why no kill more Argentina ships?' He added something to Engineer Menderez.

'You know what he want to say?' Menderez translated. 'He want to say this: Chilean navy has a saint, its name Santa Carmen. From now the Chilean navy has two saints. The second saint is Santa Margarita.'

'Santa Margarita?'

'Yes! Santa Margarita Thatcher.'

'Hey – Santa Margarita!' Osorio patted my shoulder. *'Buen!'*

'Santa Margarita!' cried Gonsalves and the other marines standing round.

'Please tell her what we say,' Engineer Menderez continued. 'Sergeant Nuñez says will you see her in London?'

'It's possible,' I said evasively, not wanting to spoil their pleasure.

'We called her General Galtieri's widow,' Menderez smiled. It took me a moment to work that out.

The radio from the supply ship announced that she would be back next morning, so my stay was not going to be a long one. I was sorry. I walked about the southern tip of the island as much as possible, trying to take in whatever I could of this place where I would probably never set foot again. When night fell and the lights in the hut had been lowered, Osorio mounted guard on the front door, Tony was put outside in a guard hut of his own, and the marines shed their heavy clothes, pulled on their tracksuits and climbed into their squeaking bunks.

Carlos was busy with the radio that night. In our room, Nuñez made sure that Menderez and myself were ready to sleep and then turned out the light. I drew the blankets up to my chin and closed my eyes. I felt like sleep. The wind scrabbling at my face and grabbing at my clothes all day had been tiring. One was forever having to push forward or resist being pushed forward or sideways. It was as wild as ever now. It howled and tore at the windowframes and rattled the doors. Sometimes, in a lull, it seemed to lean on the little hut like an animal of unimaginable size getting its breath back. Once again I felt it infiltrating beneath the hut – by far the most alarming thing it did. Unpleasant thoughts were unexpectedly interrupted. A great snore rose from the bed next to me. It filled the room with a shuddering crescendo. I had never heard a snore like it. It drowned out the noise of the wind. It had a deep, rather mellifluous liquid tone to it. And it was repeated. Engineer Menderez was a champion snorer and was showing his paces. It was impossible to sleep now; the snores went on and on. How Nuñez breathed on peacefully I couldn't understand – was he deaf? Yet he was the man in charge, who must do something. Wasn't snoring a disciplinary matter? The engineer, I thought, might easily resent any action that I, a foreign guest, might take. I tapped the iron of the engineer's bed with my pencil. I might have tapped it with a feather for all the effect that had. I rapped with my knuckles. Yet another snore rattled the windows, and still Nuñez was silent. I drew back the bedclothes and slid my legs floorwards.

Nuñez sat up and flipped on the light. '*Que!*'

I put my finger to my lips and uttered a demonstration snore, pointing. As if in answer another Menderez snore reverberated through the comparative silence of the room. Nuñez began to laugh. The laugh started quite quietly, but grew into a colossal roar – he was a big man, after all. As he roared, sitting up in bed with his head far back and letting it rip, the engineer's shattering snores continued, if anything louder than before.

The extraordinary racket from our room had already roused the marines lying in the bunks beyond the open door, and laughter shook the hut inside as the wind shook it from without. Several marines began grunting in exaggerated imitation of Menderez's snores, and soon the bunkhouse sounded as if the Big Bad Wolf had penetrated a pigsty.

'Never mind,' I whispered and signed to the still convulsed Nuñez. 'I'll take a chair in the mess.'

He was out of his bunk in a flash, dragging blankets and a pillow from my bed, through the marines' sleeping quarters and into the front room where Osorio, on guard, was sitting wide-eyed in a comfortable chair and full Cape Horn marching order, listening to the din. Tony was awake, too, and barking to be let in.

'Ha! Osorio!' Nuñez yelled. He grabbed a rigid, upright chair and gestured to the bewildered marine to transfer himself to it immediately. Then, still laughing, as if explaining to me something of extreme importance, 'Osorio is *pajero. Comprende?*'

I didn't understand at all. *Pajero* – what on earth could that mean? Nuñez had been overheard by the marines next door. '*Pajero!*' they shouted. 'Osorio, *pajero, si.*' As for Osorio, he blushed, spread his hands and shrugged. I looked, I suppose, as baffled as I felt.

In time silence, except for the wind, fell once more on Cape Horn. Everyone slept. Even I slept, in Osorio's comfortable chair.

Engineer Menderez apologized in the morning – to my extreme embarrassment – for his snoring. I assured him it was of no importance whatsoever. But what, in heaven's name, was *pajero*?

'*Pa...*' the poor engineer stared at me as if I had turned into Margaret Thatcher before his eyes. '*Pájero?*' he stammered, and in an urgent whisper he told me.

It was my turn to apologize. How could I have guessed it was Spanish for *fu-fu*?

I could see the supply vessel coming from a long way off: a speck no bigger than a waterboatman on a good-sized pond. I was sorry to see it, and I really believe the marines were sorry, too. The happy uproar of the night before had made us all friends, and with nothing much except routine duties and comic magazines to keep them occupied, a diversion such as my arrival must have been better than no diversion at all.

I began to say my goodbyes in the hut while some of the crates and boxes were being carried down the ragged escarpment track to the beach. I suppose the goodbyes were surprisingly unmilitary. I was hugged by Cookies Uno and Dos, one of whom spilled hot cigarette ash into the hood of my anorak so that I bore away a tiny burn mark as a souvenir. Other bear hugs followed from Osorio, Gonsalves and some of the others. The surprise came from Nuñez and Carlos. With great ceremony, grinning shyly amid cries of '*Silencio*', they handed me a strange, multicoloured bundle.

Engineer Menderez at my elbow nudged me and said, 'Look after it after we go.' But I couldn't wait to do that, and anyway I thought I knew what this present was because I'd noticed something missing from the paucity of the scene outside the hut. It was the best present anyone ever contrived. They had given me the Chilean flag from the mast by the church. True, it had been partly shredded by the wind, but not only did that not matter, it actually added something, because just by looking at it I could always recall the wind of Cape Horn. And it was not just the flag. The marines had signed their names on it – every one of them. When had they done it? It had been a great labour: it is not easy to write anything legibly on a torn flag. But these men had not only painstakingly written their names; one or two of them had drawn on it the elaborate crest of the Chilean navy as well, and a sketch of the island with its name, 'Isla Cabo de Hornos'; and they had marked its longitude, latitude and the date of my visit. They had given it thought. And affection. There was even a special signature: 'Tony the Dog'.

I stood there in the hut staring at the blue, red and white cloth in my hands, stunned by this unexpected and priceless souvenir. I couldn't speak to thank them; I could barely move. But there were shouts now beyond the door. Two marines panted in: the supply boat was entering the bay. I looked at Nuñez. He took my arm and we went outside together, skirting the boggy ground and a wired-off patch where I suspect there were mines, and stamped and slid carefully down the narrow crumbling track. Osorio took my bag and my other elbow.

The rubber dinghy soon grounded on the shore. It was time to leave. I shook hands slowly with each one in turn, thanking them carefully in Spanish. At the last minute Nuñez made a playful grab at my head as if to snatch off the sheep's wool cap I had bought in Puerto Montt; and instinctively I ducked back to frustrate him. It is an action I have deeply regretted ever since. I should have let him have it – I realize now he was not playing, he was serious. He wanted the hat for a souvenir and I should have let him have it. I should have pressed it on him. So as I write this I can see that torn flag above my head as a triumph and a reproach. There are the names – Nuñez, Carlos, Osorio, Gonsalves and the rest, not forgetting Tony the Dog. I have had it framed and I hope it will hang on my wall for ever.

Five minutes later, the supply boat's engines surged and we began to move across the water towards Deceit Island on our way back to Picton Island and Puerto Williams. 'Well,' the lieutenant said, smiling, 'was it worth it?'

I nodded. I couldn't trust myself to do more than that. The frozen air stung my cheeks and brought water to my eyes as I stared back at the island and that little band of men waving.

Part Four

Rolling Home From Rio

At my age and with my disposition, one gets to care
less for everything except downright good feeling.

Herman Melville, aged fifty-eight, in a letter

Mrs Thatcher did not slacken the grip her blockade had imposed on shipping in the Falklands area. From Chile, there was only one way to escape from the Pacific into the Atlantic – making a detour north through the Panama Canal – and from way down on the Horn I did not feel like doing that. Every shipping agent and ship owner in Chile assured me I might easily end up being stranded for an indefinite time on the wrong side of South America. Because of the only recently ended Falklands War, they said, shaking their heads, these were difficult times.

I had spent several days in Santiago after returning from Cape Horn, and after numerous cables and telephone calls I had managed at last to arrange the next part of my voyage. The *Piranha*, a cargo ship with a Liberian flag, would be sailing soon from Rio for Cape Town, stopping at two other Brazilian ports before making the twelve-day leap across the South Atlantic to South Africa. The company had agreed to take me and so had the master. So, after giving my thanks to Hernan Cubillos for his invaluable help, I was soon looking down on the snows of the Andes from a Lan Chile jet on its way to Rio. Before leaving Santiago I had also learned of a British ship, the *Centaur*, carrying passengers from Cape Town to Avonmouth in England, which appeared to have just the right departure date to take me to her first stop, St Helena, far out in the middle of the South Atlantic.

'Does the master allow alcohol on board?' I asked the *Piranha*'s agent in Rio.

'I believe so. Why?'

'You said the captain was a Dutchman and lives in South Africa. I wondered if he was a member of the Dutch Reformed Church or some puritanical sect.'

The agent laughed. 'There's nothing reformed about Captain Cornelius Brand, as far as I know. Oh, goodness no. Zulu crew, by the way.'

In a few days I was climbing up yet another steep companionway between cream-painted metal bulkheads towards yet another captain's cabin. Or rather, it seemed like any other until I heard the master's voice. The first words I heard from Captain Brand, still invisible behind the half drawn curtain of his doorway, were spoken in a rumbling, heavily accented growl: 'And I do not care a damn what oders do on dere ships. On my ship I do what I want to do.'

I followed the agent in. 'Captain, this is the passenger,' he said, and Captain Brand called to a man going out of the cabin: 'Steward, two more for lunch. Put some water in de soup, *ja*?' Then he turned to me.

His hand was a bonecrusher; his handshake of welcome amounted almost to physical assault. He was tall, about fifty, lean and powerful, with brown hair slicked back close to his head. He had a face to remember. Overhung by a heavy brow, pale blue eyes seemed to crouch like small, wary animals. A large fleshy nose, curved as a scimitar, projected like a prominent part of Mount Rushmore from rough, red, weathered skin – not the face of an abstainer. His mouth was large, too, and through a ragged, tobacco-coloured moustache and 'torpedo' beard I could see the ugly gap where a number of front teeth should have been. His smile, however benign, was made ferocious by those missing teeth.

I watched him as he poured whisky and told the agent, 'After dis trip, I will take a holiday. I've had it op to here.' The flat of his hand came level with the bearded mouth. 'Op to here. Or joost over here.'

'Will you go somewhere nice?' the agent asked.

'Nowhere. Joost go home to my wife and do noding. Well, I'll do someding, but I'll not tell you what!' He laughed and gave me a wicked wink. My first impression was of an old-style, rough-and-tumble, coarse-humoured, weather-beaten captain sipping whisky at ease in the cabin of a familiar command on a coast he knew well.

There was, however, an unusual aspect to the *Piranha*'s chain of command – unusual to me, at least. The chief officer, Ken Wishart, was roughly the same age as Captain Brand, with white hair and a quiet English manner – and he was an experienced master in his own right; normally he would wear four gold rings on his shoulder but now, because of his temporary position, he wore only three: the company, like many others, it seemed, had more senior deck officers than it had ships. The chief engineer and his number two were South Africans, the deck officers were South Africans of English origin, and the young engineers and cadets were a mixture of English and South African whites and coloureds; a real Anglo–South African stew. I wondered why. Later, in Cape Town, a shipping man explained: 'South Africa is not a sea-going country. South Africans are not sea-goers. It's not like Britain. People in Britain hanker for the sea. Seafaring there has great prestige. Here, no. South Africans think you must be a failure if you get a job at sea.'

After five minutes with Ken I knew we were going to get on. Over our first quiet drink together before sailing he said, 'One problem here. I should warn you. There's a lot of anti-British sentiment around on this ship. Don't be surprised when it hits you.'

He had just told me that the white South African officers were all of English origin. Surely – 'That's the trouble,' he said. 'English South Africans are a mixed-up bunch. They don't know rightly who the hell they are, English or South Africans. They get mocked by the Afrikaaners, of course. So they take it out on the Poms.' He handed me a glass. 'I'd just warn you, I thought.'

I half forgot his warning in the bustle and excitement of sailing and a turn of events that presaged dissension – or much worse – on the coming voyage. I had settled into the pilot's cabin – a small two-bunk room behind the wheelhouse – and met my cabin steward, a shy Zulu called Reginald. Then I went down to watch our departure from near the top of the gangway. A large, fat, white man stood there holding out a hand. 'Roy Taylor,' he said. 'Chief engineer.'

He was wearing a light khaki shirt several sizes too small and open much of the way down the front, hanging outside his belt; thick arms like overcooked hams stuck out of the short sleeves. He wore sandals, and above them long shorts that stopped just above fat, white knees gave him the look of a boy scout who has long since bulged out of his uniform. When he narrowed his eyes to scrutinize me through thick glasses he reminded me of Billy Bunter sizing up a new boy at Greyfriars School, and not much liking what he saw.

'Very civilized hour for sailing,' he said in a noticeably South African accent. At bows and stern, a few young white officers were watching Zulu seamen preparing to cast off.

But the hour for sailing was delayed. Soon Captain Brand was down on the deck, muttering to me: 'De Black Gang is aboard.'

The Black Gang?

'De customs officers,' he explained. 'First time on dis ship.'

And there they were, uniformed Brazilians, swarming over the foredeck, into the accommodation, here, there and everywhere.

'Are they looking in the funnel?' Billy Bunter grumbled.

But the officials had not come aboard in vain. Soon, there was a sudden angry jabber of voices and a swirl of men round the fo'c'sle; people were pointing and stooping and heaving. The captain was there and so was the huge-bellied chief engineer, waving his leg-of-mutton arms. Great strips of what looked like hides were being carried back towards me by a couple of young officers.

'Fokken, stinkin'....' I heard the captain's furious voice like ocean thunder across the forehatch. Something bad was up. There had been a theft of cargo.

After a time the customs men left the *Piranha*, smiling, unconcerned, appearing to wash their hands of anything they had found that was out of the ordinary. In a moment Captain Brand, who had come to the head of the gangway to see them off his ship, turned his hard, red face to me and said: 'De crew have stolen de hides, de cargo from Montevideo. It's expensive leather for makin' jackets, dat sort of thing.' He shook his heavy head. 'Stevedores' thievin' is bad, but when your own fokken crew start stealin' it's very fokken bad.' He turned grimly towards the door to the accommodation. 'Now I must give de crew a liddle talkin'-to.'

We sailed in that atmosphere of crime and betrayal. Ken told me later that the Brazilian customs check of the ship had been sheer chance, and the fo'c'sle was most unlikely to be searched in the normal way. The captain and the chief engineer were certain some of the crew were responsible, but no crewman would admit having anything to do with it. The Zulu bosun, looking agitated, was at a loss – or said he was. And there was no proof. So now the entire Zulu crew, guilty or not guilty, had undergone 'a liddle talkin'-to' and faced the prospect of dismissal in Cape Town. All of a sudden the atmosphere had become the worst possible in which to set off up the coast of Brazil and then start a twelve-day run across the South Atlantic.

The chief engineer's role during the hubbub on the foredeck had surprised me. A chief engineer, after all, is responsible for the engine room staff and the efficient working of the ship's engines; he is not required to oversee the situation on deck or the behaviour of a deck crew. That is the business of the chief officer – in this case Ken. But Ken, though he must have been aware of this trespass, didn't seem to worry about it; so why, I thought, should I?

At meals I sat at a table with the captain at the head, Ken on his right side and Roy on his left. I was next to Roy and opposite Pete, a quiet, coloured second engineer. It was immediately obvious what a dominant character Roy set out to be. Between mouthfuls of food and with a cruel and monotonous persistence, he continually goaded Ken with a range of supercilious attacks on anything from his seamanship to the British royal family. It was Billy Bunterish Pom-baiting stuff and delivered sufficiently loudly to carry to the only other table in the officers' mess, where seven junior officers and four cadets – a mixture of South Africans and Englishmen – sat nudging one another. I was surprised that such an evidently strong-minded captain as Brand would tolerate quite so easily two senior officers making mutually humiliating spectacles of themselves; yet his only reaction was an occasional amused wink at me. I thought it extremely lucky that Ken, so obviously a phlegmatic, good-natured man, refused to be provoked into anything more than an occasional gently flippant response to some gross disparagement of his professionalism, or an impatient wave of the hand if the royal family became the target. There was a self-pleasuring venom about the chief engineer's scorn that seemed to be as uncontrollable as scalding water spouting from a geyser.

After a meal made embarrassing by such exchanges Ken said to me, 'Roy's just a pussy cat underneath.' Perhaps he was. All ships have their neuroses, I suppose, but this one had a few extra. I asked Ken about the captain's missing teeth; the gap was so obvious and so ugly it was a wonder he didn't have new ones fitted. Oh, Cornie's teeth, he smiled – the chief engineer had knocked them out, in the days when he used to drink. Roy had been a terrible drinker, he said. But he and Cornie were thick as thieves – still were – and one night, when they were drinking hard together on board, Roy had said something that enraged Cornie. 'Say that again!' Cornie had said – and Roy had said it again.

'Oh, dear,' Ken laughed. 'Roy's first punch dislodged the teeth – teeth were all over the floor – but Cornie got his hands round Roy's throat in no time and was all set to kill him – or so it seemed. Of course, they were separated.' I tried to imagine these two men fighting like Godzilla and King Kong. Roy had given up drinking for good after that, and the two remained inseparable. As before, Cornie seemed to rely on Roy for all manner of things.

The *Piranha* progressed smoothly up the coast and into the mouth of
the bay of Porto Albino. She was a neat, brightly painted ship.
Somebody or other might be stealing the cargo, and the chief officer and
the chief engineer might behave like a bad vaudeville act, but the ship
herself seemed beyond reproach. This, of course, said a good deal for
Captain Brand.

'Cornie' was a hospitable man under the ferocious beard and
watchful eyes. At his invitation I began to take a whisky or two with
him in his cabin at noon, and then he relaxed enough to tell me
something of his earlier days. His father, a printer, had not thought
much of a sailor's life, and young Cornelius had to run off to sea as a
deckhand at the age of seventeen. He had come, as he said, 'op through
de ranks', determined to be an officer as soon as he saw the officers
wearing a fine style in shirts. 'I said if dey have dat, why not I?' He was
a hard worker and soon improved the quality of his shirts. His first
command had been a ship plying between the Baltic and Bermuda,
twenty years ago now, in the days when he had been happy to live in
Holland. Unfortunately, his successful professional life was not
equalled on shore.

'She went and took op wid de Jehovah, y'see,' he said of his first wife.

'The Jehovah?'

'Dis religious business. I couldn't stand dat. Politics and religion –
two things I cannot stand. And it was Jehovah, Jehovah all day in de
house, and she tryin' to get me involved, y'see – *pouf*! So I don't go
back dere. I stay in South Africa. Now I have anoder wife down dere.'
He gave me a wolfish grin. 'Here, take a look.' The photograph showed
a handsome blonde woman.

The *Piranha* slid into the little port of Porto Albino and tied up at a
wharf a very short walk from the bars of the red-light district. Except for
Ken – 'I've seen it all and I never leave the ship unless my wife's here,' he
smiled – most of the officers went ashore the first night. They favoured a
barnlike disco full of dark-skinned 'girls' in spangled dresses and lipstick
as red as a London bus. Metal tables and chairs scraped on a cement
floor; smoke and cheap scent was the standard atmospheric mix. Urine
had overflowed in the toilet and stood two pungent inches deep.

Pete, the coloured second engineer, I now discovered, had a hanker-
ing to travel by land. Nepal attracted him. He would even have been

prepared to leave the sea and get a shore job in order to travel there. He was tall, and rather grey-skinned, a prematurely balding man of about thirty with a pleasant face. He had a serious side, I think – I had glimpsed Conrad's *Life and Letters* on his cabin table – but he was pathetically influenced by the young white South African officers and frequently joined them in their shrill schoolboy talk of 'pomping' and 'sluts' (South African English for screwing and girls) which, repeated *ad nauseam*, drove out all other conversation.

'I'd like to travel and take photographs,' he said. 'Do you think one could become a travelling photojournalist and make a living?'

'Why not? People do, you know. I'll find out from my photographer friends, if you like, and drop you a line. Or get someone else to.'

'That would be –'

But it was no good. A young English South African who had been listening decided we were being too serious. He sidled up now with a fatuous laugh. 'Hey, Pete, do they pomp in Nepal, do you think?'

'I guess so,' Pete said, turning and smiling.

'Big, rough, pomping girls, eh?'

'Ya-hoo!' Pete cried and they went off together, sniggering.

Drink after drink went down the hatch and things became a trifle wild. The South African who had interrupted Pete's vision of a walk in Nepal was revealing his bare torso on the dance floor, and someone else was flashing a buttock: an impromptu male strip seemed imminent. Girls and transvestites fought over drinks, screaming and tugging at each other's wigs, and eventually through the haze and commotion I saw Captain Brand and Roy leave the bar for another.

I, too, had had enough. Next door I found my cabin steward at a table with a friend from the *Piranha*'s crew. 'Join us,' he called, and I was glad to. Reginald introduced his friend. 'This is Henry. He works in the engine room.'

Henry was thick-set and had intelligent eyes. We talked easily of this and that. Beer came, and still more, and soon Henry said, 'I like Brazil. Black and white are about the same here.' He looked fussed. 'Maybe you don't know what I'm on about. Do y'know, in South Africa, you'd have to get a special permit to visit Reg in his township outside Durban? Or me. And here we can drink together.'

After a while, he added, 'The crew is very unhappy.'

'Unhappy?'

Unhappy, he said, about bullying from their officers. The accusations of thieving against the deck crew. There was going to be trouble for the crew when the ship got to Cape Town, he went on. Police trouble.

'Be reasonable, Henry. Surely the captain has to do something about theft,' I said. 'How could he just let it go?'

'I have written to my lawyer,' Henry said, without seeming to hear me. 'It's not the captain. The captain's fierce to look at, a lion, but he's really as weak as a lamb.' He knocked on the table with his knuckles. 'It's the chief engineer!' he cried with passion. 'He thinks he's the king of this ship.'

'Come on now, Henry. Let's just –'

He cut me short. 'We know him, man. I tell you he thinks he's a king.'

I put Henry's sense of grievance down to drink – wild talk after a skinful – and went ashore alone next morning for a stroll about the town. There was not much to see. I looked for an outdoor cafe in which to sit and read in the sun, but couldn't find one. I hoped we wouldn't stay here long. I wanted to get on.

I enjoyed talking to sensible Ken, sitting in his cabin surrounded by a jungle of ferns, deer-horn cactus and assorted creepers. I half expected a glimpse of exotic birds. He told me he had a flat in Durban, but had kept his British passport – not that he didn't feel safe in South Africa: 'I don't think the place will blow up in my lifetime,' he said. 'The racial thing is very well sewn up, you know. Of course, I worry about the children sometimes, or the grandchildren.'

Ken admired Captain Brand and regarded him as a good honest seaman. I should bear in mind, he said, that Cornie had not been overjoyed when the company asked him to take a passenger up the Brazilian coast. Across to Cape Town he didn't mind taking me, but he had become used to having his current Brazilian girlfriend aboard with him on the coastal run – after years in these ports he had made a number of 'sweeties'. With me on board he decided he had better leave the current sweetie ashore.

Hearing this, I was even more grateful for the invitations to drink in the captain's cabin. There I could sometimes spot what a lonely man he was. He was only happy at sea, he said. 'Only a ship is important to me. I don't trust de friends, y'see. I don't trust anyone out of de sight. No one. If you cannot see dem how do you know what dey're op to?' Tortured by such self-doubt, I thought, no wonder he clings to Roy so much.

Towards sunset the ship's bar was crowded; the captain and Ken were in their cabins, but others were having their first drink of the evening. The looming figure of Roy dominated one end of the room.

'Let's go off to a good, quiet bar in the town,' he said to everyone in general. 'To sit outside. It's hot.'

'It's odd, Roy,' I said. 'I couldn't find anywhere like that in town. There's nowhere to sit outside.' Then, looking up, I saw the chief engineer staring at me with what melodramatic novelists would call sheer naked hate.

'What the fuck do you know about it?' he bellowed.

The unexpectedness of it and the loathing in his voice were staggering. Total silence fell in the bar except for a giggle from one of the South Africans. Astonishment gave way almost at once with me to intense anger. I had to make an enormous effort to control my expression and to sound flippant and unconcerned, but I managed to say quite mildly, 'Take it easy, Roy. You're not talking to the chief officer now.'

'I don't give a fuck who I'm talking to,' he roared, the hate still there, glaring out at me through the Billy Bunter spectacles. Then he left the bar. A long, embarrassed silence lasted while, at a deliberately slow pace, I finished my drink.

Then Lionel, the coloured chief steward, shook his head. 'What's the matter with the chief tonight, I wonder?' There was no answer, and I didn't need one. Ken had given me a warning to expect anti-British feeling – and I hadn't taken it seriously. I would do so from now on.

Later, when the bar was nearly empty, a British engineer, nicknamed the Pope because of a bald patch like a skullcap surrounded by white hair, sat down by me and said quietly, 'I sympathize. But a word in your ear. It's no good, y'know, talking to the Old Man about that outburst of the chief's. Like banging your head on a brick wall.'

'But it's not important, Popie. I wouldn't want to trouble the Old Man anyway.'

'You see, he's completely under the chief's thumb.'

'Someone has told me that already,' I said. Then, as he got me a drink, I suddenly began to wonder how I was going to stand another fourteen days on this ship.

'The company wouldn't approve of that behaviour,' Pope said when he came back. 'You can be quite sure of that.'

Next day, halfway to Bragança, the third officer asked me to report to the captain in his cabin. I found Ken sitting with Cornie. Both men looked grave.

'I want to say somedin',' the captain said. 'Please do not from now on have anydin' to do wid de crew. You see, it is very serious when de crew begins to steal de cargo. It's a fokken, stinkin' business. I told dem dey should own op or dey'll be discharged in Durban. Dey answered, "We are innocent." Well, dis is stinkin' lies, y'see.'

Roy came in. I had hardly spoken to him since the incident in the bar.

'Did you tell Gavin about my motorbike?' he asked. And to me: 'The crew threw it into the ocean in the night.'

'Overboard?' I was flabbergasted. It was an astounding thing to happen at sea. Now I understood Cornie's grave expression. The motorbike had been lashed to a handrail on deck. Roy had put the most junior engine room cadet in charge of maintaining it and cleaning it daily. 'Do you know who did it?'

'Well, of course no one will talk.'

'Dere's no proof again, y'see,' the captain said.

Someone's trying to tell somebody something, I thought. I remembered immediately my short talk with Henry, the angry Zulu, in the dockside bar. Perhaps my imagination, overheated by the incidents of the theft and the chief officer's fury, ran away with me, because it suddenly came into my head that the crew might start throwing all of us overboard one after the other, like a maritime adaptation of the Agatha Christie thriller *And Then There Were None*. True, eleven crewmen were up against sixteen officers and cadets, but the crew would have the advantage of surprise. Perhaps in 1985 such thoughts seem melodramatic to landsmen, but the dockside bars of the world abound with stories of recent acts of piracy, violence and mutiny on the high seas.

Brand said: 'Now, look. All doors must be kept locked day and night. Drawers, too. Cupboards. Everydin'. Nodin' is safe.'

I had a vision of Zulus trying vainly to break open my metal case and throwing it over the side in disgust. 'You've got no guns aboard, I suppose,' I said.

'*Dey* may have guns,' the captain answered grimly. 'Dey could have bought dem in Brazil.' This old seaman, I noticed, didn't find my talk of guns at all unreal.

'Haven't you any at all?' It would be nice to be able to defend the bridge and the radio room.

'Ha! And if I have where do I keep dem? On de bridge? And say to de mutineers when dey come, "Joost a moment please while I run op and get de guns"? Wherever dey are you would never get dem in time. Even in de cabin. Dat's why I say simply, to all our chaps – keep away from de crew.'

'At least the engine room crew are okay,' Roy assured me.

I thought of Henry again. Did Roy really think the engine room staff were on his side? Well, it wasn't my business. I was only a passenger.

None of the crew went ashore at Bragança. The bosun had been threatened and no one owned up to dumping the bike over the side so their shore leave was stopped. What were the Zulus plotting next? I was glad they weren't a Chinese crew. If they had been, I had a feeling the chief engineer might have been stabbed in the belly with a screwdriver – and maybe myself as well.

'Perhaps things have been handled in a rather high-handed way,' Ken commented. 'If things go from bad to worse and there's a strike in the engine room, we can handle that with the officers and cadets. That's no problem. Actually, even if the whole of the crew refuse to work, we could sail the ship with no difficulty.'

'Surely Pete should be on good terms with the engine room Zulus? He's a coloured.'

'That shows how little you know about South Africa, Gavin. The blacks dislike the coloureds almost to the point that they hate the whites.'

The stop in Bragança was intended to be short – just time enough to take on a cargo of timber. The officers, with mutiny in the air, vanished ashore to forget their problems at an establishment offering a bar, a disco and bedrooms that accommodated anyone until morning. Giving it the once-over with the Pope, I tramped over a yard of flattened mud to an open-air bar where the stench of urine hit my nostrils as inevitably as lavender in a Victorian lady's chemise. Here the captain found his sweetie waiting for him – thank God, because that cheered him up when a good cheering-up was what he most needed. He sat in the bar with his arm round her and her black shock of hair on his shoulder, his smiling, bearded lips happily exhibiting his great want of teeth.

The odd goings-on aboard the *Piranha* made everyone behave in an exaggerated way. The young men, seeing their captain's attention single-mindedly focused on his sweetie, gave way to inanity to a degree which Captains Carter or Gomersall, or even Steve Komorowski or young Graham Harris might have thought excessive. They threw away their money with the witless zest of men ridding themselves of useless currency, their shouts of 'pomp' and 'shit' filling the unsanitized air. A

Brazilian doxy nicknamed 'La Specialista' (she specialized in short times but many of them) suddenly achieved superstar status. I wouldn't be surprised if the bedroom block broke all occupancy records with the arrival of the *Piranha*. Feydeau-esque sounds of doors opening and closing might have been mistaken for the first fusillades in an armed uprising by the Zulu crew. I found myself lending money to the young officers and cadets, who were desperate to do anything rather than return to the ship before dawn.

The radio officer spent less than the others but suffered more, seemingly as dedicated to provoking drunken Brazilian seamen to beat him to a pulp as missionaries are to making converts. He began to look like a walking traffic accident, reappearing on board in the early morning with blood oozing from the corners of his swollen lips, fearful cuts round both his eyes, and his glasses reduced to splinters and tangled wire. The electrician, an Afrikaaner, was found at first light actually lying senseless in the harbour. Popie told me about it in tones of wonder. 'We came to get the launch back to the ship at seven o'clock. To our horror, there he was floating in the water. Like dead. Toes up – head back – eyes closed. Stiff.' Was he dead? He could have been. Popie shook his bald head. 'He began to sink as we watched 'im and I saw his eyes open and staring at us, I tell you, three feet under the water. Gave us all the creeps. It took us twenty bloody minutes to pull him to land.'

The chief steward had watched the radio officer fumbling his way back on board to lock himself away in his cabin. With his dignified yet gentle, watchful way, he reminded me of P.G. Wodehouse's Jeeves. He told me later, 'The radio officer only just made it back at dawn again today.'

'Speechless, I suppose?' I said.

'Well, I hear he insulted the captain.'

'Luckily the captain is a big enough man to weather that.'

Lionel nodded. 'Oh, yes. But it must be a very serious, very personal problem, the radio officer's. I told the captain that. Mind you – he's excellent at his job; he never takes a drop at sea.'

'Poor chap, Lionel.'

'Exactly, Gavin.'

We prepared to sail from Bragança and I breathed a sigh of relief. We took the pilot on board and moved astern into the wide bay. We went astern across the innocent face of that empty bay and within five minutes the *Piranha* lay motionless, her rudder jammed and her propeller shattered, incapable of going anywhere else at all.

Thirtyfive

There is something in the sound of the sailors' word 'stranding', meaning a ship touching the ground, that implies a rather slow, drawn-out process. But there was nothing slow about the stranding of the *Piranha*. Inside two minutes she was as dead as a withered arm. I was in the wheelhouse and it was as if a sea monster had punched her stern with a huge, scaly fist before taking her whole afterpart between finger and thumb and giving it a vicious tweak. The *Piranha* stopped – bang! – and began to roar and tremble and buck like a pony with a botfly under its tail. And then all at once she died.

Feeling the tremendous vibrations that shook the bridge and the sudden upward thrust of the stern tilting to port, I instinctively grasped at a nearby ledge. I have sailed in a good many ships but I remain an ignorant landlubber. What had happened? Had we hit the tug astern of us? Perhaps one should simply put it down to a not very friendly Act of God.

If so, it left Captain Cornie, Ken, Roy, the Brazilian pilot and myself gazing forward into space with a surmise that seemed wilder, if anything, than that of stout Cortez first sighting the Pacific.

I think it was Ken who first murmured, 'We've hit something.'

Cornie said in a quiet voice, 'Half ahead, pilot?' and the pilot replied, 'Yeah, half ahead.'

But half ahead or full ahead, I think everyone on the bridge grasped that the *Piranha* was not going very far that day.

Of course, there were theories. Roy said, 'We hit something that stopped the engine dead. Something like a pillar of rock.' And Pete, from the engine room's control panel, said on the intercom, 'Something big, I reckon. A six-thousand-horsepower engine knocked dead.' We didn't know what the hell was happening. The Pope, standing in the stern, had seen 'a lot of mud flying around in the water'. Eventually the ship's log simply said: '09.47: Ship took bottom.'

Hours – days – of controlled confusion followed.

'It is necessary for a tug and a diver,' Captain Brand said in a voice that might have been filtered through all the silt at the bottom of the bay. 'We have no steerin' and no engine. A tug will pull us to deep water and dere we anchor.'

And indeed, eventually a tug came out to us from somewhere near the wharf we had left with such relief a little earlier. Lines went back and forth and were secured. The *Piranha*'s lifeless hulk was lugged a little further down the middle of the bay, and lay there as inert as the victim of a sudden stroke.

The diver, arriving after a few more hours, confirmed what by then the ship's officers had already guessed – that the *Piranha*'s propeller blades were hopelessly bent. We also learned that her rudder was jammed at an unworkable twenty-degree angle to her hull. 'It takes a long time to repair a rudder. This one will have to be cut with an oxyacetylene torch,' Ken said. 'We shall have to replace the propeller, too. That means dry dock. Rio de Janeiro. And a long tow to get from here to there.'

I looked round the bay, its surrounding smudge of hills, the white dots of fishermen's huts along the shore. The low, unappealing port we had so recently been about to leave for ever seemed now to be watching us with a complacent contempt.

A continuous coming and going by launch to and from the shore began.

'You'll go with me to de port office?' Cornie said anxiously to Roy.

'Don't worry, I'll go with you, man,' Roy rumbled reassuringly. They went off, followed by Ken and one of the cadets. The Brazilian port officer was a careful man who wanted full accounts of what had happened from everyone on the bridge except myself. Furthermore he arranged to question each officer and cadet separately, rather like a police inspector to whom everyone, including the vicar, is suspect. This infuriated Captain Cornie who, I think, regarded his attitude as unnecessarily hostile. None of the *Piranha*'s officers blamed him, but after giving his own evidence he returned to the ship in a towering rage, muttering, 'Fokken, stinkin' business. . . .' Lunch that day was the first of a series of dire mealtimes at which his heavy silence and furious frown cowed us all.

That first day's interviews, even I realized, were to be the beginning of a long process of inquiry that might last months, even years. There would be convocations of surveyors and marine insurance assessors, damage would be inspected, numerous reports scrutinized by expensive lawyers, testimonies studied for telltale inaccuracies, and finally blame would be allotted, punishments doled out and the huge costs paid. It would affect Brazilian pilots, port officials, cartographers – anyone who might in some way be held responsible for the cost of divers, repairs, towage, heaven knows what. That day as we lay there cursing our fate, the messages began to pass between Bragança, Rio, South Africa, and for all I know may be passing to this day. There were more and bigger tugs to be ordered in preparation for the long, tricky, deep-sea tow down the coast to Rio.

A young English-speaking Brazilian called Osvaldo came on board to relay orders and observations in two languages between the *Piranha*'s officers and the Brazilian tugmasters. To be handy to the bridge, he took my cabin and I moved down two decks to another one. I don't think anyone aboard had experienced a long tow before. No one could predict what the weather would be like between Bragança and Rio – no one could even predict when the tow would actually begin. The still waters of the bay seemed to be listening to the echo of our feet in the hollow silences of a motionless mechanical box that had suddenly lost the reason for its existence, like a clock with a broken spring. In a sudden doldrum period of enforced and unexpected inactivity, which contrasted disturbingly with the normal bustle of a working ship at sea, the young officers played darts in the bar and mealtimes came and went in gloom. People mooched listlessly about the deck. The Zulus had gone to ground, invisible below decks. There was ample time to wonder how, in a surveyed and charted harbour, a Brazilian pilot – a local man, I suppose – could permit a ship to run herself astern onto a large rock pinnacle, or even to go anywhere near such a dangerous object. Finding no answer, I slunk away to my cabin and dug about in my metal suitcase for a suitable book – a volume of short stories by Saki. I needed something to make me laugh and I would need it even more quite soon. Act of God (Part Two) was only a few hours' sleep away.

The moment I opened my eyes I knew that something very odd had happened. It was like half waking from a nightmare. It seemed I was in the wrong bunk in the wrong cabin and someone with a tuba was blasting away on the same note over and over again very close to my ear. I lay hazily collecting my wits, fighting an almost irresistible gravitational force that seemed bent on toppling me out of the bunk onto my head. I twisted about to find a more stable position but it was no good: I kept rolling back with only the raised wooden edge of the bunk to keep me from pitching out. What on earth had happened?

I sat up and blinked. The room was grey with the dawn light but it was clearly my own cabin. My eyes focused on a pale gleam, reflected through the porthole from the water outside, that flickered on the cabin wall in little moving ripples of gold. The sight of that really woke me up. I knew from other dawns that the ripples should have been waving to me from the ceiling, not from that bulkhead. A second later I noticed that my suitcase, a half empty bottle of gin and most of the books I kept on a shelf by my bunk were now gathered in the corner of the cabin farthest from me, like a huddle of frightened refugees. *Barp! Barp!* – that was no tuba. It was the ship's hooter roaring away – one, two, three, four, how many times? The *Piranha* was bellowing for help.

With a rapidly heightened pulse I rolled myself out of my bunk, slid down the sloping deck of the cabin and looked out of the porthole. The muddy water of the bay was an abnormally short distance from my nose and beckoning me to dive in. I knew now what was happening. The ship was going over. She gave another tiny lurch to port as I stood there.

To be trapped in a sinking ship has always been one of my nightmares, and if I have ever dressed more quickly than I did then I can't remember the occasion. Trousers, sweater, shoes – to hell with socks – were on me in a flash. I struggled up the slope to the door, yanked it open inwards, grabbed the lintel with both hands, heaved my body into the opening and stuck my head out into the alleyway. To the right, the corridor was tilted like a camera shot from an avant-garde film of the thirties, and it was empty. To the left, there was the same tilt but a good deal more to see. A group of Zulus was clustered round a large door leading onto the deck, looking out, wide-eyed with alarm. They were not there to admire the view. They wore bright orange lifejackets on top of their overalls and each one clutched a small suitcase. Their intention was obvious. The crew of the *Piranha* was prepared to abandon ship.

For a moment I had the idea of dashing back to my cabin to rescue my metal case, notes and camera, but then I thought I felt the deck give yet another little jerk, and the sight of experienced Zulu seamen about to take urgent leave of the vessel decided me that the bridge, being high, was the best place to make for. I began to move in the direction, heaving myself up the stairway by the rail. Only one deck up I was delayed by another startling sight: Lionel, the chief steward, and Barry, the youngest and quietest South African cadet, were poised in a doorway on the starboard side. Like the Zulus, they had their lifejackets with them.

'Hey, man.' Barry greeted me with a nervous smile. 'No lifejacket? Have you heard? Daisy's been told to unlock all the emergency doors. Ah don' like it.' Daisy was one of the cadets.

'Well, well,' I said. I had no idea what emergency doors Barry was talking about, but I didn't like it either.

We leaned against the tilt, looking like three Towers of Pisa. Overhead, the ship's hooter continued to roar.

'Strange goings-on, Lionel,' I said, still panting from my climb.

'You could say that again, Gavin.' He was calm but his eyes were worried. 'It's a puzzle to know what it all means.'

'That it is.' I was glad to see he was as nervous as me. 'I think I shall go aloft and try to find out what the matter is.' It may seem odd that being with Lionel somehow made me talk like a character from *Uncle Fred in the Springtime*, but my notes tell me that this was so. 'Excuse me,' I added. Finding my way to the next stairway, I continued to the bridge.

There Captain Brand was standing with the pilot, Ken and Roy. 'What is she now?' he demanded. He let his hand drop from an overhead valve and the hooter's mournful blasts died into a reverberating silence. 'Where's dat fokken tug?'

'Nine degrees,' said Roy calmly.

Ken added, 'And five metres of water on either side.'

'Den we must be stuck on somedin' in de middle.'

'That's what it looks like,' Ken agreed, adding in low tones, 'Morning, Gavin.'

'Sittin' on de bottom on de port side, are we?' Captain Cornie said to the pilot, in a tight voice.

'Yes, captain. And you know, of course, this is not your original position. The ship has moved.'

'No, no.'

'You can see by those buoys and beacons.'

'*Ja?*' The captain's face was as expressionless as the bulkhead behind him.

We had certainly moved. And that meant we had dragged our anchor. Here was another mystery. How had that happened without anyone noticing? At that time no explanation was forthcoming, but from scraps of conversation in the day or two that followed I pieced together an impression of events that began with a sudden forty-mile-an-hour gale charging up the bay before dawn and heaving the sleeping *Piranha*, anchor and all, onto a bank. Then the tide began to ebb. Heavy rain and the dim light of dawn obsured the all-important landmarks from the presumably unsleeping eyes of the officer of the watch. The slow dragging of an anchor and a stealthy shift in a ship's position can go unnoticed in the distracting commotion of a sudden blast of wind and rain; or so I have been told. Even dragging an anchor might not have mattered if the tide had not turned at that moment, leaving us high and dry like a toy duck in a plugless bathtub.

'It is low water, captain,' the pilot said. 'Better wait for the tide.' The captain's reply was a wordless, guttural groan like a wounded lion in the night.

The officers paced up and down the tilted deck. In an atmosphere so tense with professional drama I tried to make myself invisible. We waited – how long? Time meant nothing – but at last, like a corpse reviving, the *Piranha* seemed to blink her eyes and breathe. A slight tremble ran through the stricken ship as though she had sighed, and soon there came another, stronger, shudder. In a moment I felt a gentle bumping under my feet and the deck began to heave, rising and falling almost imperceptibly, the slowly rising water restoring, almost tenderly, a buoyancy to her hull, though it still touched the bank beneath as if with soft, rhythmic kisses. After a while the bumping became heavier as the space widened between the ship and the bank – a worrying sensation; but then the tide took up her stern and she rode free. She was upright again, and alive. There was no cause to cheer because we were still immobile, but at least the Zulus could begin unpacking. As for me, I went below, rescued my belongings from the corner of the cabin, and put on my socks.

Within hours the middle-aged Brazilian diver was back, flopping into the water from his launch and vanishing with a flick of his flippers under the muddy surface. Two or three of the *Piranha*'s young officers watched him, whistling and hooting when he reappeared and making obscene gestures like urchins at a funfair, and they were watched in turn by some of the Zulu crewmen, who leaned over a rail looking down with blank expressions which, it seemed to me, could only mask contempt. The diver's verdict was that the ship had sustained more serious damage. He had found a long, deep depression in her plates well below the waterline.

'I've never heard of such a big dent,' Ken said later. 'It sounded as big as my living room. If the plates weren't extra thick we'd still be sitting on the bottom.'

Captain Brand's heavy expression became heavier and darker. 'I may be in South Africa before you, Gavin,' he said glumly, like a defeated general predicting his own recall and court martial. In *The Mirror of the Sea*, Conrad had asked:

> Does a passenger ever feel the life of a ship in which he is being carried like a sort of honoured bale of highly sensitive cargo? For a man who has never been a passenger it is impossible to say. But I know that there is no harder trial for a seaman than to feel a dead ship under his feet.... The grip of the land upon the keel of your ship, even if nothing worse comes of it than the wear and tear of tackle and the loss of time, remains in a seaman's memory an indelibly fixed taste of disaster.... To be 'run ashore' has the littleness, poignancy, and bitterness of human error.... A man may be the better for it but he will not be the same.

I have never been anything else on a ship but a passenger, and I could have answered Conrad: yes, it is as possible for a passenger to feel life in a ship, as it is for someone on an elephant's back to feel the life of the elephant; you don't have to be a mahout for that. Something mournful in the way a captain says 'Finished with engines' has always reminded me of a doctor at a deathbed reaching out to close the eyes of a corpse. So, passenger though I was on the *Piranha*, I could suffer for Captain Cornelius Brand.

That stranding changed things inside as much as outside the *Piranha*. First, there was the captain's brooding; that threw a terrible pall over us all. In contrast, however, Roy, the ship's baleful Billy Bunter, became genial and talkative; I supposed that his public outburst against me had satisfied his irresistible urge for Pom-baiting: he had made his one-upman's point and now seemed disposed to behave in a normal, friendly way. For this I felt relief. As for Ken, he took our catastrophes with his usual calm, but I could see that both he and Roy were worried about the effect of the double disaster on Cornie's nerves.

'I hope the Old Man won't crack up,' Ken said, puffing tobacco in his plant-filled cabin. 'There are only two men on this ship who really know what a captain feels like in this situation: me and himself. A ship's a master's baby, y'know.'

I did know. Still, I didn't expect Cornie – a hard man, after all – to go berserk, although I could see his temper might give us all a very rough ride. Lionel and Popie began to go about looking decidedly thoughtful, and the Zulu crew, who had faded silently below decks after the first stranding, mostly remained there. It was the junior officers who were most vociferously affected by our sudden immobility and isolation from the shore. Shrill bursts of hysterical shouting rang about the ship. One young officer, a South African of English origin, took to hooting and barking like a dog – 'Arf! Arf! Arf!' – up and down the companion-ways. Even before the accident he had affected a mad, whinnying laugh to amuse his mates, and now they began to imitate him. Non-stop obscenities filled the officers' bar much of the day and most of the night, and there was no one to control them. Lionel now wore a constant frown, wondering aloud where it would all end. One could only hope it would end quite soon.

But it did not end quite soon. We waited for tugs – and waited again. How long would they take to get to us? Nobody knew. Days went by. An order came from the captain to ration fresh water: its use was now banned except between the hours of 0600 and 0830, between 1200 and 1300, and between 1700 and 2030. No one was to wash or flush a toilet except between these precise times. That was only the start. By the next day, Captain Cornie had had time to worry a little more about the situation.

Popie came on deck with a long face. 'More rationing,' he announced. 'Can you believe it? Water for only one hour in the early morning, half an hour at midday and one hour from five-thirty in the afternoon. The Old Man's becoming very strange, if you ask me.'

First the water, then the grog. At lunch that day Captain Brand drained his wineglass and looked round the table at us. 'Dat's dat,' he said flatly. 'No more whisky now. And no more wine. Until we are at sea.' We nodded and smiled nervously. 'If we ever are,' he added in a haggard voice.

That afternoon Lionel shook his head as we sat alone over a cup of tea. 'Something strange is going on,' he sighed. 'I worry what will happen next. In twenty-five years at sea I've not known anything like this.'

'The tugs will be here soon,' I said soothingly, and added: 'Anyway, the kipper fillets were good at breakfast.'

'Good of you to say so. But you wait, the next thing they'll start complaining about is the catering.'

'The food is absolutely fine.'

'That's what happens when things go wrong. The food gets blamed. You'll see.'

'We're expecting a tug today, Lionel.'

But later that day Popie and Lionel approached me like mutes at a funeral, and Popie burst out: 'Shall we tell 'im, Lionel? Eh? Shall we?'

'Oh, go on, for God's sake,' I said, laughing. Popie laughed, too. 'The tug won't be here for two days more. That's what.'

So for two more long, dragging days we stared at the same bay, at the same shore, at the same wharf. People looked for ways to beat the boredom. Roy, a mountain of geniality, asked me for a book and I lent him Conrad's *The End of the Tether*, not simply because the title seemed appropriate but because I thought he might appreciate the seamanship in it. He took it and thanked me, and for once we had a conversation uninterrupted by obscenities. He talked interestingly of South Africa. I had wondered what, in the maze of racial complexities, his relations might be with Pete, who shared his table at mealtimes and drank with him in the ship's bar every normal evening at sea. What happened once they were ashore in Cape Town or Durban. Could they go to a pub together? To a theatre?

'Go to a bar with Pete – to all intents and purposes, no,' he said. 'Nor to the theatre. Maybe to some cinemas, but not to all. We'd have no trouble drinking together in a big international-class hotel, of course. They have no rules on colour.'

'What about in your house?'

'The government rule is that he could come to my house but couldn't stay the night there. But' – he put his elbows on his desk and stared unblinkingly through his gold rims like a police inspector confronting a suspected terrorist – 'I'd like to see the man who'd throw anyone out of *my* house. Pete's the finest shipmate you could wish for. Of course, it annoys me. I don't believe in one man one vote, and I think we need a dictatorship. But it annoys me about the coloureds, like Pete. The situation makes me feel fucked up in my mind.'

At last there was a tug. It dodged under our bows and linked up with our anchor chain and pulled us to the mouth of the bay. A blessing – even a limited move like that was a blessing.

387

'Tomorrow eight o'clock we go to Rio,' Captain Cornie said. 'We'll all be very happy.'

'Above all you, I hope.'

He gave me a wolfish grin. '*Ja*, dat's so, dat's so.'

But there was no happiness for anyone next day. Someone sent a message that the tug had broken down somewhere, and it never came. The silence at lunch was terrible. Cornie's eyes developed a pink, watery look. While the meal lasted we kept our heads down like soldiers in a trench while the 'fokkens' and 'stinkin's' exploded round us. Next morning another tug came and pulled us about aimlessly for a while before the tugmaster informed Cornie he didn't feel he could manage to tow us to Rio, and called it a day.

As meal followed silent meal, I read and re-read the manufacturer's stamp on the knives and forks – 'Status Stainless Steel' – and the small print on the labels of sauce bottles; 'Mrs H. S. Ball's Chutney' began to mesmerize me. It wasn't much by way of distraction, but it was something. Dinner was the worst torture. It was eaten at five o'clock in the afternoon now, by the captain's edict, and the nights seemed endless. The bar had become intolerable, filled with a confused racket of shouts from junior officers and cassettes of hard rock. Otherwise the ship's social life ground to a dismal halt. Ken retired into the quiet of his cabin. Jock, the radio officer, was, I presume, fiddling with his dials behind the locked door of the radio room. The Pope and Lionel watched Brazilian television with the sound off, which didn't appeal to me.

'The crew,' Lionel said, sorting some linen in a cupboard near my cabin door, 'they are *very* unhappy, Gavin.'

I hadn't seen a Zulu for days. 'What are they doing – playing darts? Watching Brazilian TV?' If I hadn't been forbidden to speak to them I would have gone down and asked them myself.

'They play cards a lot.'

'I haven't seen you near the bar lately.'

He shook his head. 'I can't stand the noise, the obscenities. These youngsters don't get enough sex in South Africa. That's the trouble.'

'No girls in South Africa, Lionel?'

'Well, the girls there are choosy. And they wouldn't choose this lot, I can tell you. In Brazilian bars, as you've seen, they only have to pay a girl to get it. And so when they can't get ashore, like now, like teenage boys they go all stupid. Trouble is the Old Man doesn't seem to mind the din.'

'The Old Man has other things on his mind.'

'That is indeed the case,' Lionel said sadly.

By now I had to think seriously of dates. It wouldn't be long before the *Centaur* sailed from Cape Town to St Helena, and if things had gone right with the *Piranha* we should have been in Cape Town already. I mentioned this to Captain Brand, who said, 'Leave de ship here if you like, Gavin. Joost take de agent's launch ashore.'

'I'd like to see the end of this,' I said. 'Can I give it another two or three days?' I reckoned I could afford that amount of time.

'As long as you like. Why not see if dis next fokken tow is workin' out?' So I waited for the next tow.

Next day, another tug maundered out to us. Once more the anchor chain was attached to the tug's stern. Now, I thought, the tug will go ahead of us, stretch the line tight and draw us cautiously to Rio. Like towing a bus with no brakes: tricky but possible, when you are a tugmaster and know how. But none of this happened. The tug shot off to port at right-angles, pottered daintily about there for a time, then, appearing to become bored, danced off back to base in time for breakfast.

'I dink I am goin' to have a heart attack,' Cornie groaned, raising his red, bearded face to the indifferent heavens.

'Tugmaster was scared,' Roy snorted with uncontrolled contempt.

'*Ja*, fokken, stinkin' scared.'

That day's lunch was indescribable.

At last, one day at dawn – I was learning that one day is much like another in purgatory – two tugs appeared. There was mist, rain and a noticeable swell. Once more the *Piranha*'s officers stumbled expectantly into the wheelhouse. Once more young Osvaldo, the interpreter, gripped the loudhailer. Once more our anchor chain was hauled up; once more it was laid over the stern of a tug and attached to its massive, swivelling towing hook. While the second tug looked on, the *Piranha* slowly moved ahead. Rising and falling with the swell, feeling once more the open sea under her bows, she silently approached the ocean. I saw an attentive phalanx of seagulls standing shoulder to shoulder on an exposed mudbank, like sailors lining the side of a warship leaving port; their sea-grey eyes watched us sceptically.

Captain Cornelius stared hopefully at the tug, a smile lurking. 'Away to sea,' he said, rolling up the sleeves of his old grey sweater. 'Away back to the fokken sea.'

'Just think — a few days in Rio,' Roy said. 'Hot baths.'

But the seagulls were right. I heard Cornie say very suddenly and very harshly — 'Keep de anchor outside the hawse-pipe, ready to let go again!'

I hadn't expected quite so exact a replay. The tug's captain was waggling his hands in some mad semaphore; the little snub-nosed tug scuttled across our bows to port and soon fetched up at the customary right-angles to our hull, where it sat bobbing and nodding like a complacent duck but incapable of pulling us in any direction we wanted to go.

Soon worse followed. The tug let the towline go slack, but for a moment the swell drew her away from us again and the line came out of the sea in a flash, rigid, white with spray, sizzling as if it were a steaming hot iron bar dipped in cold water. Drawing taut, it snapped, and almost faster than the eye could follow it sprang back wickedly like a striking black mamba. It lashed itself against the sternbar of the tug, wrenching one heavy metal leg of it out of the tug's deck and leaving a gaping hole in its plates. The sound was that of a blacksmith's hammer striking a cracked bell; the effect, disastrous. It was the knell of my voyage on the *Piranha*.

'Bedder get your bags packed, Gavin.' Cornie's despairing croak was barely audible above the roar of static from the handset that connected him to Ken and the anchor party in the bow. 'Dat's de end of de tow.' His mouth was twisting about in the ragged beard, but when at last he said into his handset, 'Drop de hook,' he sounded sad and tired rather than angry; he didn't even say 'fokken'.

It would probably have been a mistake to express the sympathy I felt, so I didn't try, and when he came over to me near the chart table I was surprised to see he was smiling.

'Gavin, you'd bedder leave us. You'll be late at Cape Town.' He made a sweeping gesture. 'I am commandin' a dead ship.' His big paw pressed down on a chart, on the finely drawn swirls and meticulous depth marks depicting the details of that infernal bay. 'I am commandin' a dead ship.'

He had been commanding a dead ship for three weeks.

The agent's launch would be coming out to us in an hour or so. I went below and threw my things into my bags, tilted the last finger of gin — one I had hoarded for so long — into a tooth mug and knocked it back.

Reginald, my gentle cabin steward, came in to lend a hand, and when everything was ready I gave him some money.

'Tell Henry I wish him luck,' I said, 'and good luck to you, Reginald. I hope you get to Rio by Christmas.' We laughed. 'Try not to spend all your money there.'

'No, no,' he said seriously. 'I am saving to buy some shoes.'

Lionel was next. 'Goodbye,' I said. 'If there's anything I can do. . . .'

'If you would call my wife, she'd like to know I am all right. She'll have read something about this in the papers back home.'

On the stairs I ran into Henry in grey overalls, going below, I suppose, after the towline fiasco. I hadn't set eyes on him since he'd complained in the dockside bar that the chief officer was behaving like the king of the ship. The chief's motorbike had gone over the side a night or two later.

'Goodbye, Henry.' I smiled. 'You're crew. I'm not meant to talk to you, but goodbye.'

'You off?' He held out a hand and I took it. 'You know – my lawyer? Yeah, well, I did write to him.' He gave me a short, friendly nod. 'We'll see what happens. 'Bye.'

When I wished Ken a happy tow, he said, 'Oh, we'll get one in the end. It's been a bad experience for all of us. Especially for Cornie, of course.' He sat in his easy chair, surrounded by his jungle. 'First-rate is Cornie. A bloody fine seaman.'

I forget what I said to Captain Brand – 'Goodbye and thank you' – something simple like that. I couldn't attempt to convey my appreciation of that rough, simple good-natured seaman who, just as I came aboard, suffered some of the worst strokes of misfortune – stranding and a disaffected crew – known to a ship's master.

Dressed as usual in khaki shorts, Roy looked at me through his Billy Bunter glasses and smiled. A pussy cat? Ken was probably right. At the same time, Roy, like many another ship's officer, might – as Henry alleged – have found a dreamed-of kingdom in the confined, autocratic world of ships; and, aware as he was that the most expert engineer can never become a master, might have discovered how at sea, as much as on land, the power of a grand vizier can be almost as great as that of the caliph himself. We shook hands. 'No hard feelings,' we said to each other, and these were all the goodbyes I had time for. The launch was waiting. Daisy gave me a hand over the side, and in a moment we were heading up the too-familiar bay towards a place I had had no desire to set foot in ever again. I took out my diary and flipped its pages. The

Piranha had put in here for a short weekend at most. We had stayed for four weeks and a few days more – some of the longest days I have ever known.

For the next two days I battled my way through the sluggish immigration system of Bragança and sank thankfully at last into a seat on a plane back to Rio. I fell asleep at once and dreamed I was at sea again on the *Piranha*. She was helpless in a terrible storm. Zulu deckhands were struggling to throw over the side a gigantic container of contraband potatoes before the weight of it took the ship down. I wanted to help them, but I was slammed against a bulkhead by two or three hysterical young officers screaming 'Sluts! Sluts!' and when I appealed to Captain Brand and Roy they only frowned and turned their backs. Just then the ship's bows dived for ever into a wave and I was in the sea. In a moment the captain's dripping, bearded face surfaced beside me, spluttering, 'Fokken, stinkin' business,' then disappeared below the water again, leaving me fighting to put on a lifejacket that kept turning into a metal suitcase....

I jerked awake, sweating, and ordered a double brandy to take the taste of nightmare out of my mouth. With the brandy inside me and the feel of the plane dipping down to Rio, my heart rose at once like the lark and gloried in the high places.

After a day of relaxation in Rio I made the change I really needed – a change of continent – and flew to Cape Town, where I had heard from the agents that the *Centaur* was waiting to leave on schedule. Her first stop was still St Helena, and I had time enough to catch her.

As for the *Piranha*, she reached Rio at last and sat in dry dock while they worked on her bent rudder and replaced her buckled propeller blades and hammered out her plates or maybe replaced them. The Zulus had taken matters into their own hands long before that, and had gone on strike soon after I left the ship in that God-forsaken bay. Rightly or wrongly, they believed that some of their officers were bullies. They knew the accusations of stealing the leather lacked proof, and I suppose they regarded the cancellation of overtime and the stopping of shore leave as high-handed treatment. Were they right? Or had they brought it all on themselves? There would be at least two opinions about that. At any rate they had been put ashore in Brazil and flown home, and thereafter the *Piranha* had been worked first by the officers and later by a skeleton crew flown in from South Africa.

Perhaps Henry's lawyer wasn't needed after all. It seemed to me unlikely that the company would drag an entire Zulu crew into the dock. But I don't know. Nor do I yet know — lawyers will keep such legal pots a-boiling for years if they can — who was to blame for knocking the tail out of the poor *Piranha* on a pinnacle of Brazilian rock.

Thirty Six

I was glad that my departure from Cape Town was as unlike my attempted departure from Bragança as anything could be.

A pink roll of cloud covered the flat top of Table Mountain that beautiful evening, a fringe of it spilling over one edge like candyfloss. The RMS *Centaur* was carrying a hundred and eighty passengers as well as cargo, partly destined for her first stop, St Helena, and her wide decks had a fairground atmosphere. We moved serenely towards the mouth of the harbour and took to the open sea without hitting a thing. Loudspeakers were relaying a brass band's rendering of 'A Life on the Ocean Wave'. Soon a demure English voice announced that dinner would be served at eight o'clock, and that this was Dusty Miller, your head waiter.

Presently, across a white linen cloth, I found myself facing the captain, George Coupar, a greying veteran of south-east Asian shipping, unbearded and benign, flanked by a pair of English businessmen and their wives. The larger of the two men, with a suntan that had turned him almost dangerously maroon, soon started on the Second World War, a novel topic after Brazilian tugmasters, water rationing and stolen cargo.

'. . . and they issued us with pith helmets. Pith helmets! So of course we knew at once —'

'— you were off to Iceland.' His neighbour, less sunburnt, managed a ventilation company in Sussex: a nice man who played the clarinet quite well in his cups.

'No. Actually it was double bluff,' the maroon man said. 'We really went to India.' He forked up egg mayonnaise as if eggs were going out of season. 'I'll never forget standing there on parade in Poona and

394

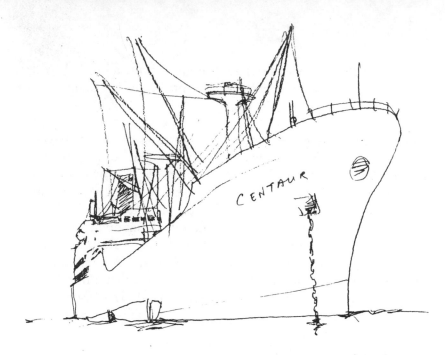

seeing officers on horses. Officers on *horses*. Clip-clop, clip-clop. Riding down the ranks. In 1942, Hitler's war. More like 1870. Made you think.'

'The King's Royal African Rifles, m'self, old boy. West Africa –'

'East, surely?'

'Come again?'

'King's Royal African Rifles. *East* Africa.'

'That's right. Kenya. Abyssinia way. Place called Hargeisa. Know it? Gave me a whole bunch of Italian prisoners to look after. Imagine. No Italian to my name –'

'Shipped in tiny ships to Basra –' Maroon Face said.

'Where did you go from – Poona?' Captain Coupar put in, addressing him.

'– and sure enough the Eyeties, one morning, when I woke up, had disappeared. Gone. Every one.'

Two stories now; you took your choice.

'– and up to Baghdad. Stinking hole.'

'– I'm for the high jump now, I thought. So I found the local British district officer feller. Intelligent man. Knew the area –'

'– didn't know Baghdad existed outside the fairy stories –'

'– "Sure to come back when they're hungry," he said. And he was right. Knew his onions. Soon came back in dribs and drabs. The Eyeties like a square meal, y'know.'

'Don't we all?' my neighbour said, pouring wine all round. A quiet man with a serious yet whimsical expression, he gave me a quick wink.

In the upper bar there were unexplained pictures of governors-general of Australia round the walls; it was a cosy little place of dark wood and crimson plush and bits of brass. Elderly passengers sat over brandy, dressed for an evening out. It seemed an age since I had worn a suit and tie on a ship – at Captain Segal's table on the *Alexander Pushkin*.

The barman was short and round, and two things about him puzzled me. He was dark without looking Indian, Latin, African or Oriental; and on his lapel a name tag proclaimed 'Brian Bar'. An unusual name.

'I'm a Saint,' he said, smiling. 'Not, I mean, that I'm saintly, of course.' He laughed. 'But from St Helena Island. That's what people from there are called.' He spoke with a soft, attractive burr like that of Devonshire or Dorset.

'And Brian Bar is your name?'

He laughed again. 'Well, Brian is my name, sir. Bar is my place of work.' He tapped the hard wooden counter between us.

'Nice piece of wood you've got here.'

'It *is* good. I am a cabinetmaker by trade, sir. Like all Saints I like to travel.'

'Will you ever go back to St Helena now you've seen the world?'

'Oh, yes. Very few of us leave the island for good.'

'It must be a good place to visit, then.'

'Captain Coupar and the Ship's Company welcome aboard R M S *Centaur* all those passengers who joined in Cape Town,' said the daily information leaflet pushed under my cabin door. It went on to announce: '*Rig of the Day*. The Captain and Officers will wear white uniforms during the day and Red Sea rig in the evening.' Red Sea rig meant black trousers, black cummerbund, black tie and white shirts with long sleeves. I tried vainly to imagine Roy of the *Piranha* in Red Sea rig. The leaflet advertised the usual soothing shipboard things. Boat drill and the captain's cocktail party; dancing in the Lido Lounge; whist in the library: deck quoits, Scrabble, chess and draughts tournaments organized by Jeannie, the assistant purser. Mike, the organist, would entertain in the Lido Lounge from 7 p.m. to 8 p.m. By the second day, passengers needed to be advised that the navigation bridge and the crew quarters were restricted to crew only. They were also reminded that it would be useless to try to post an airmail letter from St Helena: the island had no airport.

In the Lido Lounge a young man sat at my table, ordered a drink and handed me a card. Was he selling something? The card read:

Congratulations!!
You Have Just Been Killed by 44 Para Pathfinder Company.
Thank You!
(Families Catered For)

It had an ace of spades on its back.

'I'm Jacques,' he said with a broad, guileless grin, and held out his hand. 'I'll explain.' He was a mercenary, Belgian, but living in Paris. He was a killer, he said. He had been with South African irregular forces against the African guerrillas of SWAPO, the South West African People's Organization fighting for the independence of Namibia.

'I've killed a Soviet colonel and a Soviet woman there,' he said. 'Cubans, too.' The Soviet colonel and the woman had been caught in crossfire inside Angola. His card was similar to others left on the bodies of dead African guerrillas.

'You taking some leave?' I asked.

No, he was packing it in for good, he said. He hadn't been getting on with the South Africans. No foreign mercenaries did. The South Africans didn't make very good irregular soldiers and the mercenaries brought a lot of expertise with them and that made the South Africans jealous.

'I don't know about the South African high command,' Jacques said, 'but junior officers are very inflexible. Not like the Rhodesians, who are really terrific bush fighters. South Africans haven't much idea.' He held up both hands, palms flat, fingers together, and placed them either side of his head. 'Blinkered. Narrow view. So a lot of us leave.' He laughed. 'It's their loss.'

Jacques' Para Pathfinder Company had patrolled the bush, hiding all day, moving at night, using black trackers. 'Wonderful chaps. They'd say, "Oh, thirty men passed this way, going north-west, a bit less than an hour ago," and we'd follow and find them.'

What a world! We sat in the lounge, he drinking tomato juice and I a Bloody Mary, among middle-aged couples on holiday, on our way to a peaceful island far from everything, with that loathsome card lying on the table between us.

'Take a look,' he was saying casually, drawing out of his hip pocket photographs of captured machine guns, anti-aircraft guns, mortars, multiple grenade launchers, even tanks. 'The SWAPO people can't use those useless tanks,' Jacques said. There was a picture of a black corpse and another of mercenaries smiling at the camera in front of high clumps of what looked like elephant grass.

'See – all NCOs and all foreigners. From left: Rhodesian, Rhodesian, Rhodesian, New Zealand, British, Irish, Rhodesian, Belgian (ha, that's me), Irish, Australian, Australian, American, Costa Rican (yes!), Rhodesian (he's dead). . . .' Perhaps he'd publish his experiences, he said, in France or Belgium.

As the *Centaur* moved up north-west of Namibia, where the killing was still going on without him, I saw him again a couple of times during the voyage. Once we waved to each other across the Scrabble boards, and later he cheerfully raised his glass across the Lido Lounge during a dance party, while his other hand comforted a sad-looking woman with wilting shoulders.

At dinner one night an eccentric-looking woman, expensively dressed, teetered past our table, winking outrageously at Captain Coupar. 'Yoo-hoo, big boy,' she carolled, stopping the conversation. 'Haven't I seen you before? On the *Orontes*, wasn't it, darling? Or was it on the *What's-it*? You've aged, darling.' She leaned forward. 'I'm cabin 205; you've got the master key, haven't you, sweet?'

The captain took it easily and went on talking to the wife from Sussex. 'Er . . . so the pirates just throw a rope with a hook on it up the side of the ship and shin up. Off Singapore there are more pirates than you'd read about in the papers there. Container ships have very few crew. So the pirates climb aboard, go into the engine room – often without seeing a soul – and take the brass fittings and instruments.'

'Oh dear,' the woman said.

After a while I heard the serious man with the whimsical expression saying something interesting. 'A useful experience, running a ferry service in East Nigeria, shifting a million passengers a year.'

'Did you do that?' I asked him.

'Oh yes.'

'Sounds real Sanders of the River stuff.'

He laughed. 'It was. The Nigerian commodore was a great seaman in or out of the navy. A great character, too. He had three wives and girlfriends he rotated round his mansion and two farms. He said to me once, "Look, if we sail on the ferry to Fernando Po one day, we could sell the passengers there and return empty without anybody noticing."'

'Have you been on the *Centaur* before?'

'No. But I own her.'

It sounded a good conversational line.

'Actually, I've chartered her to see if she's what we want on the Avonmouth–St Helena–Cape Town route. My name's Bell. Andrew Bell.'

Andrew Bell was the sort of friendly ship-owner you would like to meet on a ship, but ship-owners usually prefer to travel by jumbo jet. At meals between Cape Town and Jamestown, the port of St Helena, I learned a bit about him.

'Much of my education,' he said, 'came from watching shipping in and out of Sydney harbour. I was with the Blue Funnel line. I had the ambition of working in shipping ashore, but I couldn't see how to get a good shore job at the age of twenty-one with a second officer's ticket, so I joined the Australian Navy and wangled a commission.'

You could almost warm your hands at the fire of Andrew Bell's confidence. I didn't think it would have needed much 'wangling' for him to get a commission in any navy. After that he'd been a management trainee with Elder Dempster; two years in Liverpool, two years in West Africa, where he'd met the Nigerian commodore with the rotating girlfriends. By 1973 he had decided to take a plunge.

'I put every penny I'd saved into a 500-ton coaster. Things went well, so I bought a 1000-tonner.' About this time he'd read a report on the need to do something about a sea supply route from Britain to the colony of St Helena, after the withdrawal of the Union Castle mail ships. The British Commonwealth Office asked him if he was interested in it.

'They said they liked the look of my shipping company even though it was pretty obscure. So we raised some money and bought a ship in Canada and put her on the St Helena run. The Royal Mail Ship *St Helena*.' Bell smiled. 'Named by Princess Margaret and all. She's making the round trip from Avonmouth to St Helena. Later she may go on down to South Africa. Or we'll use her in tandem with the *Centaur*. I'm here to look things over and come to some conclusion.'

The mad woman went by again, yoo-hooing at the captain.

'When the Falklands War began, the Royal Navy called the *St Helena* up,' Andrew Bell was saying, imperturbably. '"Taken up" was the nice official expression – like being raised up to the Pearly Gates by St Peter. She was fitted with a helicopter pad, Oerlikon guns – they weren't used in anger, by the way – and the Royal Naval ratings were integrated with our Saints and our British officers.'

'She deserves a medal,' I said.

Bell laughed. 'She got a plaque instead.' Probably *he* deserves a medal, I thought. For enterprise. At any rate, that was how I came to meet the founder and owner of the Curnow Shipping Company Ltd, based at the seaside town of Helston in Cornwall. I soon dubbed it 'the greatest little shipping company in the West'.

I had written to the British Governor of St Helena some time before, and his reply had reached me in Chile:

> You will, of course, be very welcome here: *bona fide* travellers always are in remote small communities. They are like the lemon slice in the g-and-t, a touch of 'zest'....

It was an encouraging letter.

> Inevitably Bonaparte's short stay here drew attention to the island. But much happened here before he came and more – though not enough – since. He is not a local folk hero and he is irrelevant to modern St Helena. I suspect local people resent being known for having had per force to accommodate a dangerous and ruthless 'war criminal' who was never recognised in his lifetime by a British Government for anything more than that. Longwood House is maintained by a dedicated and scholarly Conservateur des Bâtiments Français as a shrine.

The letter was signed 'John Massingham'.

'He's a very active and popular Governor,' Andrew Bell told me. 'Ex-BBC, I think.'

If Andrew Bell liked him he couldn't be bad, I thought. I saw the point about modern St Helena, but I certainly had every intention of visiting Longwood House. The Napoleonic period of European history had fascinated me from my schooldays. General Bertrand, Emmanuel Las Cases, the mystery-shrouded figure of Mme de Montholon – they were all there, flitting about under the no doubt hawkish eye of that 'dedicated and scholarly' French curator.

My first sight of St Helena must have been much the same one that met the eyes of the island's discoverer, the Portuguese navigator Joan da Nova Castella – the man who, arriving on the name day of Constantine the Great's mother in 1502, named it after her. The island sat in the middle of the South Atlantic – twelve hundred miles from South West Africa and eighteen hundred miles east of South America – as composed as a rock in a fishpond.

A voice was singing:

Where be that blackbird to?
I know where 'e be.
'E be up that worzel tree
And I be after 'e.

Now 'e sees I
And I sees 'e.
Bugger'd if I don't get 'im
With a girt big stick –

I recognized a ragged Cornish song and it might have been a Cornish voice – or perhaps a Saint's. At any rate, the song was cut off by the roar of the *Centaur*'s horn announcing our arrival to the people of St Helena. It was a great day for them. A ship only called there once every eight or nine weeks.

Thirty Seven

'I think that's Frieda, sir,' the boy said. 'Or it's Martha.' He stooped and peered. 'No, it's Frieda.' John Massingham stood with me in the paddock that lies the other side of the gravelled driveway outside the porticoed front door of Plantation House, the Governor of St Helena's handsome residence. He regarded the tortoise at his feet speculatively. It lay there like a large boulder.

'I think you ought to know who it is by now, Faron,' Massingham said with a smile. He was a bustling man with glasses and a tendency to portliness in a Pickwickian way. With an utter lack of pomposity he had made me feel at home at once. 'And where on earth is Jonathan? I think Mr Young should see Jonathan, don't you?' He turned to me. 'Jonathan is the oldest tortoise here. He's been here almost for ever. They're all Seychelles tortoises, I believe.'

'Napoleon knew him, then?'

'No, I don't think he's been here quite *that* long.'

The boy said, 'Jonathan is in the pampas grass, sir. It's a bit cold and damp at the moment. I daresay he'll come out later.' In his Saint's accent I recognized once again the good, warm burr of the south-west of England.

'Oh, good. . . . Jonathan has been here a hundred years, though, I should think,' Massingham went on. 'We don't know how old he is exactly. We had an expert in reptiles out and he said you can't date them. You know, you can't measure age by the rings on their backs or anything like that.'

'I've searched for Emma, sir. She's in some undergrowth on the other side of the lawn.'

Taking what seemed an infinity of time, Frieda – if it wasn't Martha

402

– poked her leathery head out of her shell and cautiously looked around.

'Do they bite?' I asked Faron.

'No. They don't bite. They just seem to dig themselves into holes a lot of the time.'

'So they can dig?'

'No, sir. They don't make holes. Frieda's just found that hole ready there.' Frieda looked nervous and snatched her head in sharply. John Massingham made a tut-tut noise.

'Old Jonathan leaves his head sticking out all the time,' the boy said.

'Ah – he's old and wise, so he's not afraid.'

'He's old and wise. Yes, sir, he is.'

Stepping ashore in the tiny port of Jamestown was not just a step back into the architectural past, it was like stepping into Toy Town. Everything seemed to be at peace and in miniature, a relief after the racket of Rio de Janeiro. There was a small and simple stone jetty to disembark at. In the main street here you could have shot a film about Napoleon's exile or the life of Nelson or the Duke of Wellington without doing much more than remove a telephone line or two.

With Andrew Bell I had passed through a rampart, over a moat, and under a royal coat of arms and a St George's cross into a little square, with a spired church on the right and a low, whitewashed seventeenth-century castle on the left. Here we had met Governor John Massingham in his high-ceilinged office, approached through a white arch guarded by brass cannons and then by a wide, old-fashioned staircase.

Under the royal portraits John Massingham said, 'It costs the British Government, oh, about four million pounds a year in subsidies to keep the island going. The RMS *St Helena* takes some of that, doesn't it?' This to Andrew, who nodded. He went on: 'We need things here very badly. A new power station, for instance – the system is overloaded now; there's no reservoir. A reorganized fishing industry. A secondary school. Things like that. Two million pounds would cover it.'

We walked out of his office in the toy fort. People said 'Mornin'' as we strolled slowly up the main street, running through a narrow valley with steep sides. Few of its two-storey buildings looked as if they had been built much later than the early 1800s, and when I asked I found that this was indeed more or less the case. The Dickens film set police

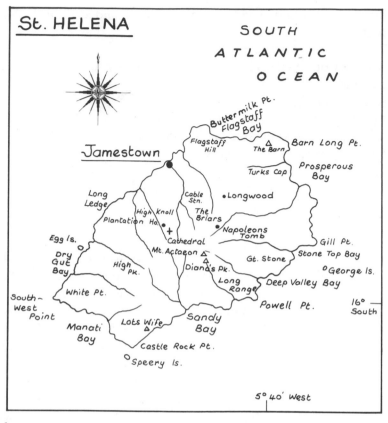

St. HELENA

SOUTH ATLANTIC OCEAN

Jamestown

Buttermilk Pt.
Flagstaff Bay
Flagstaff Hill
The Barn
Barn Long Pt.
Turks Cap
Prosperous Bay
Cable Stn.
•Longwood
Long Ledge
High Knoll
Plantation Ho.
The Briars
•Napoleons Tomb
Egg Is.
Cathedral
Gill Pt.
Dry Gut Bay
Mt. Actaeon
Gt. Stone
Stone Top Bay
High Pk.
Diana's Pk.
George Is.
Long Range
Deep Valley Bay
White Pt.
South-West Point
Powell Pt.
16° South
Manati Bay
Lots Wife
Sandy Bay
Castle Rock Pt.
Speery Is.

5° 40' West

headquarters, for example, had been built in 1817; the unforbidding prison, an attractive (empty) building of thick stone walls with a pleasant first-floor balcony, in 1827; the Cattle Market in 1865; the offices of Solomons & Co., with arched windows, were housed in what had been known in 1843 as Mr Corker's House.

'We're not simply living on Napoleon,' Massingham said. 'I do all I can. I've dropped the "His Excellency" from my title. I give old islanders lifts. Try to be human. Unstuffy. I'm devoted to the people here, but the Government at home –' He stopped, frowning, in mid-stride. 'You've no idea. Look.' He faced Andrew Bell and myself so that we made a little human island in the road. 'That reservoir we need so much. The Royal Engineers have taken seven months – *seven months*! – to submit a report on it. It's intolerable. No civilian contractor would stand for that. I write to the British Government saying, "For God's sake, let's get a civilian set-up." If we were Afghan refugees or from Zimbabwe or somewhere.... But St Helena has no political clout in

Britain. I shout and scream on the islanders' behalf – I may be sent to Outer Mongolia next!' He laughed.

'Yes, I'm devoted to the people here. Trouble is, the Saints have been used to very pompous governors who made themselves practically unapproachable – wearing dinner jackets at dinner, all that sort of thing. Plantation House is a fine place, but it isolates me. Sir Hudson Lowe lived in it, of course, Napoleon's Governor. By the way, I should go and see our archives if I were you. The Napoleonic ones, I mean. I wrote in my letter that there was more to St Helena than Bonaparte, but of course you're interested – anyone is – and there's the museum and so on at Longwood House.'

The Duke of Wellington had stayed on St Helena, too, at Mrs Ethel Yon's Cafe, in Wellington House, and I would not have been astonished to see on its ageless steps a Roman-nosed figure waving a cocked hat. Wellington had come here as Arthur Wellesley, on his way home from India in the late 1700s.

Brian Bar had given me a pamphlet advertising Mrs Yon's accommodation – he may have been some relative; many people on the island seem to be related.

'Not being a licensed premises,' Mrs Yon soberly announced, 'adds greatly to the quiet and homely atmosphere that prevails.' She provided a twenty-four-hour electricity service of 230 volts and a 'good variety of Mineral Waters (Tonic, Soda, Ginger Ale, Bitter Lemon, etc.) are manufactured on the premises'. The heavy drinking was done, I soon discovered, at the Consulate Hotel ('Patrick G. Joshua, Licensed to sell by retail wine, spirits and beer') which had a beautiful yellow stone façade and blue wrought-iron railings on its front steps, and graceful iron pillars supporting its balcony. Up Napoleon Street lay such venerable establishments as Darling's, Truebody's, Miss Short's School and two pubs – the Crown and Anchor, and the Victoria.

The island's archives were in the fort overlooking the rampart to the Atlantic. 'Ask for Mr Maggott,' John Massingham had said.

'I'm Maggott.' A friendly middle-aged Saint led me into a room under the battlements like an ancient wine cellar, but with racks of heavily bound tomes in place of bottles. 'Cecil Maggott, archivist.' He pointed to a spotty young man. 'And this is my assistant, Hansel Williams. He's the fast bowler of the Sandy Beach team, is Hansel. Yes. Now, what would you like to see?'

'Anything here from Napoleon's time, Mr Maggott, please.'
'Hear that, Hansel? Napoleon.'
'Who?'
'Napoleon Bonaparte, Hansel. Now then.'
There was a long table and soon a good number of books were on it, smelling dusty and old.

'See this, perhaps,' recommended Hansel Williams. He opened St James's Church Burials Registry and I read in old writing:

May 9th,
Napoleon Buonaparte, late Emperor of France, he died on the 5th Instant at the old House at Longwood, and was interred on Mr Richard Torbett's Estate.

The Emperor's name lay between 'Edmond Hawes, Inhabitant' and 'Maria Mills, wife of the late Major Mills, St Helena Artillery'.

John Massingham had mentioned Sir Hudson Lowe, the Governor appointed from his command in Marseilles to St Helena, with a heavily augmented garrison, specifically to keep an eye on the great exile, who, after all, had already escaped from Elba to perpetrate his own second downfall at Waterloo. Lowe was a man whom Napoleon and his entourage swiftly came to hate. Under the eyes of Sandy Bay's fast bowler, I read the careful instructions to Lowe, signed in London by Lord Bathurst of the War Department in July 1815, concerning the treatment of the prisoner who is referred to merely as 'the General':

He's to be allowed his plate, furniture, books and wine, but his money, diamonds, and negotiable bills are to be given up, and it is to be explained to the General that it is not the intention of the British Government to confiscate his property, but to prevent their being converted by him into an instrument of escape.

'The General's' escape was an English obsession. 'The General must always be attended by an officer,' London's orders stressed. 'The General must be given to understand that in the event of his attempting to escape, he will be afterwards subject to close custody.' Any letters, written or received, were to be censored. Ships of every description were to be prevented from touching at the island with the exception of those belonging to HM Service, or to the East India Company.

Hansel Williams brought me tome after tome. Angry old letters came to life again and began to fly back and forth under my nose as though

Napoleon was still at Longwood. General Count de Montholon, of Napoleon's suite, wrote thus to Lowe:

> This rock ... two thousand leagues from Europe, situated in the tropics five hundred leagues from any continent at all, and subject to a consuming heat; covered with clouds and fogs for three quarters of the year; it is at once the driest of countries and the most humid. This climate is most inimical to the health of the Emperor.... It is hate that has determined the choice of this place, just as it has determined the instructions given to the commanding officer here ... to call the Emperor Napoleon 'general', wishing to oblige us to recognise that he never reigned in France.

De Montholon's letter then took wing.

> Are your ministers unaware that the spectacle of a great man trapped by adversity is the most sublime of spectacles? Are they unaware that Napoleon on St Helena, among persecutions of all kinds which he opposes with nothing but serenity, is greater, more holy, more venerable than when he was on the premier throne in the world from which he was the arbiter of kings.

To this the British Admiral Sir George Cockburn, who had transported Napoleon to St Helena on his flagship *Northumberland*, gave a reply that must have flown in through the front door at Longwood like a cannonball:

> Sir, You oblige me officially to explain to you that I have no cognisance of an Emperor being actually upon this island, or of any person possessing such Dignity, having come hither with me in the *Northumberland*....

Napoleon had approached St Helena standing, as even I had done, on the bridge of a ship and staring at its cliffs rising from a blue sea. To me it was a charming prospect, and I daresay Admiral Cockburn had been mildly irritated by Napoleon's quite different view of things. As he peered at Jamestown through the little spyglass with which he had surveyed so many battlefields, including Waterloo, he grumbled, 'I would have done better to stay in Egypt; I would be today emperor of the whole Orient.'

'Napoleon didn't like your island, Hansel,' I said.

'Oh, did he not? Well, it is smaller than France, of course.'

'That's true.' A pause. 'But still, look at this –' Hansel had dropped another heavy volume in front of me. 'He wasn't all that uncomfortable. See this letter to the Governor of the island, Sir Hudson Lowe.'

Hansel traced the writing with his calloused fast bowler's forefinger and read in his Devonshire burr: '"It is also desired that you should take steps for the providing and shipping of wines, groceries, and other articles necessary for supply of Buonaparte's table – Particularly French wines [he turned a page] of which there is reason to believe that consumption will be unusually great."' Hansel broke off here. 'I wonder how much they ...' but the answer appeared there before he completed the question: '"Wines, clarets, graves, champagnes and madeira ... £2445. 10s. 0d. per annum."' And soon, searching around with Hansel's help, I found that that considerable sum formed part of a total annual expenditure on the Emperor of £19,152. 2s. 7d., which sum included food, carpenters, masons, mules, transport, horses, etc. The only things not mentioned were books and Napoleon's newspaper bill. But in a little while we discovered something about that, too. One of General Bertrand's letters complained that the exile had been unable to obtain a subscription to the *Morning Post* or the *Morning Chronicle* of London, or to any French newspapers. All Napoleon got from time to time was an old copy or two of *The Times*. Furthermore, Bertrand went on, several books sent by their authors had not been delivered, simply because they were inscribed either to 'Napoleon the Great', or to 'The Emperor Napoleon'. Since when had it been forbidden for prisoners of war to be subscribers to newspapers or to receive books?

Lowe contented himself with two sharp comments. First, he said that not merely odd *copies* of *The Times* but whole series of that newspaper had been sent to Longwood, and if any copies were missing probably members of Napoleon's entourage had pinched them. Secondly, Lowe said, if you asked *him*, the title of 'Napoleon the Great' had had its *coup de grâce* at Waterloo.

I had enjoyed the historical cut and thrust of the archives department. I warmly thanked Cecil Maggott and gladly accepted his offer to arrange for me to rent the only car available and tour the island with Hansel as guide. The car belonged to Mr Yeo – a good West Country name. Meanwhile I reported to John Massingham on the archives. We stood at a tall window in Plantation House, surveying a view once very familiar to Sir Hudson Lowe. A brown lump in the grass opposite like a small outcrop on the move might have been Frieda or even old Jonathan.

'Frankly, the way I look at it,' he said, 'Bonaparte was a war criminal. He introduced a new form of warfare to Europe – total war. His picture was on the wall here. It seemed to have no place among the British royal family so I took it down. I've been attacked by the Napoleon lobby for doing so, of course.'

'I really must go and see Longwood, anyway.'

'Of course you must. And you must meet Gilbert Martineau, who's in charge there; honorary consul and curator. Longwood's a bit of France, you know. We gave it to them in 1858. I have to admit he's very hospitable.' He pondered for a moment. 'Martineau. . . . Frankly, we don't really speak much. I forget the reason. Oh, yes, I know why. The trouble between him and me started when I put a lot of chidren's swings – playground swings – on the green at Longwood. He regards the whole place as a French shrine and protested really quite vigorously. He said, "The French would never stick such things just outside a war cemetery."'

He considered the matter again. 'Yes, Martineau. He really is a most extraordinary chap. I mean, when his old mother died quite recently, he had her shipped back to France in a barrel of brandy.'

'A barrel of –'

'Oh, yes. Good brandy, too. He actually had a lot of good brandy poured into a barrel with her in it. Of course they'd eviscerated her beforehand, I dare say. But still. . . .'

In Mr Yeo's little car I drove to the hamlet of Longwood through green lanes and hedges of spiky flax. It was very seldom that I met another car, but when I did and we squeezed past each other, or when I came upon a man driving donkeys laden with grapes, the Saints always waved or called a greeting. I had a beer in the little pub on the green and then went round it to the huddle of trees on the far side. Gilbert Martineau was waiting at the gate to the garden of Longwood House with an abstracted air.

'What can I do for you?' he asked me in breezy tones. I had expected a portly, moustachioed mixture of Hercule Poirot and the French actor Jean Gabin – that was what to me the word *conservateur* seemed to imply. Not at all. What I saw was an elegant, good-looking man, tall, slim and well-dressed in a pale blue seersucker suit and a dark blue knitted tie (he had bought it at Harrods, he told me later): a dandy, in fact.

'You invited me to lunch,' I said. 'I'm writing –'

He interrupted. 'I'm writing, too. Oh, yes, indeed. In fact I've written fifteen books and three more are in progress. I'm working on Byron and preparing something else on Berlioz.' He waved an elegantly deprecating hand. 'And Tchaikovsky as well. Apart from that I have written plays and film scripts. And I've just won a prize. So?'

I was glad that he had to stop to draw breath. 'So. You invited me to lunch. And to see Napoleon, I hope.'

'Of course, of course. Come in.' He led the way through a well-tended garden into a wing of an attractive single-storey house painted a pleasing, delicate shade of pink. This was Longwood – or rather the part of it Martineau lived in. It was beautifully furnished with things he had brought from France, as elegant as he was. On occasional tables stood framed portraits of de Gaulle, Churchill and Serge Lifar, the ballet dancer.

'Do sit down,' Martineau said. 'By the way, if you think my English is very good, it's because I was with the Royal Navy in the war.'

A servant appeared carrying a bottle and two glasses on a tray.

'It is *very* good.'

'Thank you. Champagne?' He popped a cork, pouring into a fine glass. '*Salut!*'

I liked Martineau. He was not only a good host, as John Massingham had acknowledged, but also an intelligent and indefatigable talker – a facet of his nature no doubt aggrandized by isolation. Not that he regretted Longwood's isolation. He said he adored Longwood and hoped to stay for ever – with periodic visits to France, of course. Actually, he had his eye on a flat in Monaco.

He showed me his books. Many of them were about Napoleon and the imperial family or about his entourage on St Helena. He talked affectionately of them rather as though he knew them all personally. He had written a bestseller about Madame Mère, Napoleon's formidable and long-suffering mother. 'I call her the Corsican Niobe,' he said. 'Am I lonely, you will ask? Let me only quote Napoleon. He said of St Helena, "Here, one must socialize with a budgerigar if that's all the company one has." I have people out to stay. I have books. The ship brings pilgrims to the shrine.'

'What Napoleon said about the budgerigar was not very complimentary to the people exiled here with him – Montholon and the rest.'

Martineau laughed. 'No, not very. People say Napoleon had an affair with Mme de Montholon. But no.' He seemed to be bringing me up to date on the subject of present gossip about people still living, whom we both knew well. 'Life here was all too cluttered. Too crowded for that sort of thing. An affair? No, not that. People say so, but I doubt it.'

Martineau's exile was self-imposed and a good deal more comfortable than Napoleon's. His cook was every bit as good as Napoleon's Cipriani, and his equivalent of Napoleon's Mameluk servant Ali was an old Saint called George Benjamin who, after lunch, showed me round while Martineau wrote a letter or two for me to post in Europe.

Longwood House was a pleasant building, surrounded by trim lawns and carefully sculptured hedges. Some of the paths had been sunk into the turf to enable Napoleon to stroll about below the level of prying eyes. By a door in a second wing we entered the part of the house kept as a museum, and more or less as Napoleon knew it.

We came first into the billiard room, which had also served as antechamber for those who had applied for audiences with the Emperor. 'See that billiard table, sir,' said old Mr Benjamin. 'Made by Thurston & Co. No slate. All wood.' I crossed the teak floor and looked at the pictures on the walls. There was a print of Napoleon saying farewell to his troops at Fontainebleau, portraits of him by David, Gérard and Delaroche. There was a white marble bust; the room was full of busts.

'Cold, isn't it?' Mr Benjamin said. I looked at a print by Steuben of the Emperor and his baby son, the King of Rome.

'I've got swollen legs,' Mr Benjamin remarked.

'I'm in no hurry,' I said. 'Please take your time.'

The salon where Napoleon received his guests was next to the billiard room. Here the Grand Marshal, Bertrand, had announced visitors as if they were all still in the Tuileries, and Napoleon was waiting at the mantelpiece, leaning against it standing up, as he had taken to doing since brusque Admiral Cockburn had one day ignored all the flummery and simply barged in muttering 'Mornin'' and grabbed a chair without so much as a by-your-leave.

Though there must have been quite a few, the only direct exchange I found between the long-suffering Lowe and his tyrannical prisoner was quoted in one of Martineau's pamphlets:

> *Napoleon*: 'You are our greatest scourge of all the miseries on this infernal rock.'
> *Lowe*: 'Sir, you do not know me.'
> *Napoleon*: 'Where should I have got to know you? I did not see you on any battlefield.'

Even after what had gone before, that seemed to me a bit of a low blow.

I, too, leaned on the mantelpiece, with old Benjamin beside me blowing dust off the back of an elegant dark wood chair with gold-leaf mouldings. The great battle pictures were here, or prints of them. David's *Bonaparte, Commander in Chief of the Army in Italy*, and Delaroche's *Bonaparte Crossing the Alps*. Looking at them, I could understand the anguish of the man confined to this upholstered prison. It was easy to let the mind wander in this room; one could almost imagine the hum of the golden imperial bees; see the valets, Marchand and Ali, in their gold- and silver-embroidered uniforms moving discreetly round the dying man. Examining the pictures, my imagination swept me far from this cold house in the South Atlantic — to the swirl of the massed cuirassiers at Friedland, the irresistible charge across the bridge at Arcole, the earth-shaking thunder of the horses, the sun flashing on helmets and swords, the frozen exhaustion of the Grande Armée's arrival on the banks of the Beresina at the end of the Russian disaster. And at Waterloo, at the end of everything, the hoarse cries of '*Vive l'Empéreur!*' as the grenadiers of the Old Guard in their long white gaiters followed frantic, red-headed Ney, his bullet-torn coat and broken sword, up the slope in the last, hopeless throw.

'I have to wear a couple of sweaters all the time,' Mr Benjamin was saying. 'I've had a heart attack.'

We moved from room to room — eleven of them, none of them large and all with low ceilings. Some rooms retained the original wallpaper, or perhaps it was a reproduction: a plain cream with blue stars in one room; in the dining room, a rich red with golden laurel leaves. In a cramped room I came across the camp bed Napoleon had used at

Austerlitz, tested it and found it hard. In size it was like a child's cot, unsprung, with a mattress that might have been stuffed with straw. It had been very damp in Napoleon's time, but it was an attractive house and I would have been pleased to live in it given adequate heating. With Longwood to myself I would never, as Napoleon had done, have cast covetous eyes at Plantation House; but then I have never been Emperor of France.

I bent over the Emperor's death mask, noticing that it seemed unnaturally small, diminished perhaps by the process of moulding. The closed eyes were deeply sunk into their sockets, the cheekbones harshly prominent, the nose under its fine long sweep of hairless brow as thin and sharp as a quill. '... at the head of the army' – those were his last words, and then he had lain on view in this room in the uniform of the Guard and the cloak he had worn at Marengo.

I had expected to find Gilbert Martineau as rabidly pro-Napoleonic as John Massingham was clearly anti, but he didn't seem to be much of a chauvinist. When I mentioned the story promulgated by some Napoleon worshippers, that the British – Sir Hudson Lowe again – had had Napoleon poisoned with arsenic, Martineau laughed the idea away without hesitation.

'Ha! That was a story thought up by a weightlifter in Canada in cahoots with a dentist in Sweden. Well, that's what I say. The obstacles to a methodical investigation of the Emperor's medical dossier are innumerable. The doctors at his deathbed were notably mediocre. The journals of Bertrand and of the valet Marchand – well, neither was a doctor. You see, the autopsy showed a perforation in Napoleon's stomach wall. When they opened up the stomach, Mme de Montholon found she could put her little finger into the hole. Symptoms were – exhaustion, loss of appetite, fever, vomiting of blood. The experts hesitated between a peptic ulcer and cancer.'

Martineau certainly knew the details. 'As for the arsenic, that came from the arsenic powder they used then to preserve people's locks of hair. That's all. Napoleon had an internal haemorrhage. His heart rate was below fifty all his life. Very unusual. He had always vomited when he flew into his furious rages and he ate all his meals in seven minutes. He'd have the whole meal set out, and he'd pick a bit of ice cream here, a bit of mutton there. Actually eating very little and drinking not much at all. He was a very sober man; like a camel.'

So all those wines I had read about in the castle archives had been swilled down by the Bertrands, the de Montholons and the rest. They had to relieve the boredom somehow, so who could blame them?

A sharp wind whisked through the hibiscus bushes beyond the window. 'Cold,' said Martineau. 'But it's not always like this. Sometimes the Emperor used to sit out of doors, reading Racine – *Andromache* was a favourite – to his entourage. He read badly and Mme de Montholon would fall asleep.' I had the feeling that a short, stout figure with a sharp nose and wearing a cut-away coat might stalk in at any moment and order us to stop gossiping.

'Napoleon was only fifty-two years old, you know.' When I commented that the camp bed seemed hardly big enough for a boy scout, he said, 'Well, Napoleon was about five foot six or seven.'

Martineau even had a compassionate word for John Massingham's remote predecessor, Sir Hudson Lowe. 'You know what happened to Lowe?' he asked me. 'Well, after St Helena he was offered the Governorship of Ceylon, but by the time he got there someone else had the job. He died in poverty in Chelsea. Without a *sou*. And that was his reward for doing what he was told to do.'

Before I left Longwood, Martineau talked of his new book – '*Byron: Pilgrim of Eternity*,' he said. 'Good title?' He had a ouija board at Longwood and sometimes Byron spoke to him.

'Byron talks to you? What on earth does he say?'

'Oh, terrible things. Things like, "You are a very clever bastard. Why do you take the piss out of me?" That sort of thing.' Martineau's English *was* very good.

'Byron says that to you?'

'Oh, yes. And worse. What a fellow! What a diabolical fellow! Do you know what he said once? He said, "Shakespeare's *Midsummer Night's Dream* is a real fuck-up." What a devil! But what a fabulous letter writer.'

He walked with me to the garden gate and looked calmly across the village green without noticeable scorn for its children's swings.

'Young people like the idea of Napoleon,' he said. 'I think it's because he pushed things to extremes. You can't do more, can you? Goodbye.'

Martineau was doing a good job of looking after the pink house and the trim garden, that was certain. In a lonely place I was glad he had Byron for company.

Back in Jamestown I had time to say goodbye to Andrew Bell before he sailed off to England on the *Centaur*. Before leaving, he showed me a picture of his ship, the RMS *St Helena*, the only means of transport to and from their homeland that the islanders possessed. 'Any time you want to come back here, I'll arrange a cabin.' I saw a neat little vessel, much smaller than the *Centaur*, a pleasing size, with a pale green hull and a white superstructure.

'You can find me at the office in Helston. Curnow Shipping.'

'I'll be there as soon as I can,' I said. 'Hold that cabin.' Then I set off with Hansel Williams and his friend Stedson Stroud to tour the little island. St Helena is perfectly preserved, like a piece of old English countryside of the seventeenth century, long before the intrusion of pylons, airports, motorways or factory chimneys. It was as green and lush as the Vale of Evesham in summertime. Houses like dwellings in Jane Austen novels and tiny Georgian farmhouses sprang into view from behind folds in the hills and in terraced valleys full of spreading trees. Napoleon had chosen one such fold to be buried in; tucked away in a deep dell, it was quite hard to find. We walked down a short, wide path springy with grass to his original tomb – a slab of concrete enclosed by railings and clumps of amarylis and hibiscus and tall dark cypresses that stood to attention like grenadiers. Mynah birds chatted round a spring nearby and bees hummed round the stiff bayonetlike leaves of flax. Of course, the Emperor himself lay in Les Invalides in Paris. His body had been exhumed in 1840, nineteen years after his death, so the grave here was empty.

I had brought a map of St Helena with me and spread it out on the car. It was crowded with marvellous Stevensonian names: Egg Island, Dry Gut Bay, Half Tree Hollow, Lemon Valley, Buttermilk Point, Prosperous Bay and, of course, Sandy Bay, of which Hansel was the champion fast bowler. As we drove on through it, I saw that the island was not all green and English. At its centre there were knobs of rock high enough to be veiled in cloud. In Sandy Bay, passing the cottage where Hansel Williams' family lived, a man waved from the roadside. 'That's Peter Mercury,' Hansel said, waving back.

'Nice name.'

Stedson Stroud had spent two years in England as a domestic servant; a footman at first, then butler to the Duke of Bradford.

'But I wanted to travel,' he said. 'So from the Duke I went to a château in France belonging to racehorse owners who spent six months in France and six months in Palm Beach.'

'You certainly did travel, then.'

'I did indeed. Africa, Europe, the Middle East. Now I want to stay in St Helena. Most Saints want to come back. Just to fish and do some gardening. We've a special magic here. Saints *are* special. If ever I was at a party in England I would know another Saint at once by his warmth, humour, friendliness.'

'I've noticed that myself,' I said.

'We like the English, you know. Most houses have portraits of the Queen and the royal family on the wall. It's a very genuine liking, you see.'

A small stone chapel stood on a hillside, apparently quite unattached to any village. There were only one or two villages on the island. We could see the sea and a farmhouse out of which Fielding's Squire Weston might have appeared.

Two oddly shaped basalt columns dominated Sandy Bay, one named Lot, the other Lot's Wife.

'Don't you miss the bright lights here?'

Hansel shook his head. 'I don't go to movies or dances much.'

I repeated the remarks I had overheard in the Consulate Hotel in Jamestown of two passengers from the *Centaur*, an American and an Englishman, discussing the island.

'If only they'd do something here,' one had said. 'Build an airport. Build a marina. A decent hotel. Bring tourists in.'

'Quite. A Holiday Inn or something. Bring St Helena to the twentieth century.'

Hansel said, 'I don't rightly think people can ever leave anything alone.'

'There's not much we need,' Stedson added. 'Nobody starves on this island. Saints go off to work on Ascension Island, on Mr Bell's ship or in Europe, and send money back. We don't need no airport or things like that.'

416

Had I discovered at last a place where everyone was content? Had there been no Fatal Impact here? An infinitesimal one, perhaps. I had had boiled eggs, bread, butter, cake and tea provided by the Consulate Hotel for the three of us. When it came to eating the eggs, Hansel took one bite, made a hideous face, and cried, 'What egg is this, then?'

'A hen's egg, of course,' I said. 'What do you think it is? An ostrich egg?'

'This ain't no hen's egg. Maybe it's a wirebird's egg,' he answered with a laugh.

'A wirebird?'

'A bird only found here. It's got big wiry feet and long legs.'

Stedson Stroud laughed, too. 'He means it's an imported egg. South African, probably. We hate imported eggs. They're not the same at all. Our hens wander about freely all over the place eating this and that, and so their eggs are real. These imported eggs – well, we can't hardly eat 'em.'

'So even the hens are happier here than anywhere else,' I said. 'That's why Saint eggs are better.'

'Hey, yes. Saint eggs are best.'

Not only to detect an imported egg but to find it uneatable.... That shows how far our civilized taste has degenerated. I took the imported horrors and hurled them far away over a hedge.

I had to find a ship for the next stage homeward, and I was in luck. Solomons & Co., the island's shipping agents, let me know through John Massingham that a small Dutch cargo ship would be calling in a day or two, bound for Portugal via Ascension Island and Senegal. In response to a radioed request, the captain had agreed to take me.

'How would that do?' John Massingham asked.

It would do perfectly. From Portugal there should be little difficulty in finding something to take me to England.

'*Pep Sirius*,' John Massingham said, 'is the ship's name. Rather an odd one. It sounds to me like some sort of toothpaste.'

Thirty Eight

'It's called the Nursery, because that's where all the dead children are,' had said the pleasant wife of the Cable and Wireless Company manager. Ascension Island, seven hundred miles to the north, was not in the least like St Helena. It is in fact little more than a big clinker seven miles wide. But a lot of people have died there.

'Then I'll go and look for them,' I told her.

The cemetery lay under a red, cone-shaped hill, and the wind lifted the dust off it in trailing clouds. The children were by the sea. I stood ankle deep in thick red powder and tiny crunching clinkers and read the stones.

One said: 'Two-year-old Kate accidentally drowned in the Turtle Pond July 1855.'

On a marble likeness of an open Domesday book was carved: 'Baby Boy Obey, aged 5 hours. Remembered by his parents. Jesus said Suffer little children to come unto me.' Remembered then by his parents, but who remembers now?

Someone had used part of a rusted cot to make a cross. I read:

> To
> Jacqueline Rose.
>
> Jacquie's gone to live up yonder
> How we miss her smiling face
> Though we very sadly miss her
> None will ever take her place.

Further along the coast, in a place well named Comfortless Cove, I came across other old graves, many of them those of yellow fever victims. The winds of centuries had whipped the soft volcanic rocks into fantastic and frightening shapes round a kind of natural amphitheatre – I seemed to be encircled by leering gargoyles, the ravening heads of monstrous vultures, the snarling fangs of werewolves. In the centre of this terrible place stood a six-foot obelisk, a memorial to 'Charles Baldwin Dyke Acland – 10 May 1837. Lieut RN. A beloved son. HMS *Scout.*' Out at sea, two ships lay unloading cargo into barges. Here among the lonely graves and weird rocks, in a wind that wailed like an abandoned baby, I felt a shiver of fear, and scrunched my way back to the track from Georgetown, Ascension's village-port.

It was a relief to see living, smiling human beings again, but I hadn't quite finished with the dead past yet. The central building, a low, white church, looked interesting and in it I found yet more naval memorials. One in particular was instructive. It was dedicated to the memory of twenty-two officers and men of Acland's HMS *Scout*, and to 'John Giles, James Bray, John Brison, boys of the 1st Class and John Reed boy of the 2nd Class. Also a landsman, a caulker and a college man.' All died between 1836 and 1839, though some were actually buried in Sierra Leone. Nineteenth-century West Africa – the White Man's Grave.

I had felt a little ashamed of my *frisson* of fear at Comfortless Cove, but later I discovered a book about Ascension which quoted an article in a Scottish magazine called the *Bulletin*, written in 1936:

This much is certain, men and women, walking alone on the island amidst the volcanic clinkers, are liable to take sudden panic, running this

way or that, or collapsing to the ground and remaining motionless with terror. Some have been known to disappear. This is why the British community arrange some social function or sporting event for every day of the week to keep them from brooding about the mysterious atmosphere.

The Cable and Wireless people on the island laugh at this, but Alan Nicholson, a communications expert, rattled off a list of recent ghostly apparitions he had heard of from apparently level-headed people – a woman in white, an invisible man who clambered into bed with almost anyone who slept in a particular house, an evil-faced marine in a nineteenth-century red uniform coat, and more. I didn't feel quite so ashamed after that.

The *Pep Sirius* would only be a day or two in Ascension – the chief engineer had broken his leg falling on deck and the island's doctor was making sure it was well plastered. The island was an air base, an essential refuelling stop conveniently situated between Britain and the Falkland Islands. All visitors to the Falklands had perforce to fly via Ascension; Thatcher herself had done so. But fortunately for me, since I find air bases as boring as factories, most of that technical activity was tucked away on another side of the island.

It is an odd and unappealing place. Unlike Robinson Crusoe and St Helena, it has a dead feeling. The boobies, wideawake terns, noddies, canaries and waxbills are its only natural inhabitants, somehow surviving the roar of military aircraft over their nesting grounds. But there are no indigenous humans, just British and American servicemen and communications experts, a few Saints to serve them, and a large number of graves and ghosts. I took away a souvenir lump of shiny black obsidian that I found in a shallow valley in a volcanic waste where several wild donkeys snuffled among the clinkers looking for God knows what.

I was delighted to come once more upon the tracks of that 'eminent and excellent buccaneer' Captain William Dampier, whom I had last seen, so to speak, on Juan Fernandez in company with Captain Woodes Rogers in 1709, rescuing Alexander Selkirk. Returning from the Far East, Dampier's ship *Roebuck* had been wrecked on Ascension Island in 1701. He and his men scrambled ashore with sufficient stores but no drinking water, a serious predicament on what was little more than a burnt-out volcano. Needless to say, the dauntless Dampier discovered a tree with an anchor carved on it and a date, 1642, near which a tiny spring gave forth a drip of water but enough to wash down the land crabs, boobies and goats that were their basic diet. I trudged up to the

spring, known to this day as Dampier's Drip, and paid my respects to the old seadog once again.

The *Pep Sirius* was a four-year-old vessel of 1500 tons with a crew of four Spaniards, all short, stocky and cheerful, and six officers of whom five were Danes and one, the chief officer, was Greek. I had taken to them at once. They were all, except two, heavily bearded. The captain, Kurt Sorensen, was hardly older than the other Danes, who looked to me barely thirty, though all that golden hair may have been misleading. Marcos, the Greek chief officer, was built like a tub; his beard was bushy and the colour of salt and pepper, with salt predominating. The chief engineer, Jan, had been advised by the doctor on Ascension Island to fly home with his broken leg in plaster, but he had refused to leave his wife, Elsa, the ship's cook. Jan spent most of the voyage with his leg up in his cabin, but joined us in the saloon for meals. His second engineer, Tom Rasmussen, a prototypically blond Scandinavian giant, managed the engine and we had no breakdowns.

We crossed from the South Atlantic into the North Atlantic, heading for a river in Senegal. Christmas at sea and then New Year were celebrated by the Danes with the heady desperation of men who

suspected that all alcohol was to be banned in Scandinavia on
2 January. Dolphins leapt joyously out of six-foot waves while inside
the *Pep Sirius*'s neat, freshly painted hull the saloon joyously reverberated with 'Kender i den om Rudolf', otherwise known as 'Rudolph the
Red-nosed Reindeer', 'Jingle Bells' and a happy jazzy Danish number
called 'From the Top of the Christmas Tree'. Elsa covered the portholes
with artificial snow and stars. Coloured streamers and paper bells criss-
crossed the ceilings. The drinks locker was thrown open; toasts were
drunk and drunk again. I made a note of the total Christmas Day
consumption of alcohol by six officers and one passenger – not
forgetting that Marcos was a teetotaller. Two bottles of akvavit, two
bottles of Scotch whisky and two cases of Carlsberg lager was the final
tally for the day. The sickly taste of the akvavit, a rich, raw aniseed,
clung tenaciously to the back of my throat for days.

Luckily Marcos was quite prepared to spend most of his time on the
bridge while the others made merry below. Sometimes he sang, at other
times he drank tea and talked and I joined him to listen. He was an
indefatigable artist, too. The margins of the ship's charts were covered with
sketches whose subject was always the same – parrots. The first one I saw, a
parrot man in a straw hat, was drawn over part of the Spanish Sahara.

'Who's that, Marcos? A tourist?'

'Oh, I don't know,' he said, shrugging. 'It could be. Look at these.'

From a drawer he dragged out other charts. One was of the Red Sea
coast and there, around Medina, were the domes and cupolas of
mosques that his pencil had made to burgeon among the arid contour
lines – and big-beaked Arab parrots in headcloths were walking about,
leading camels. Above Mount Sinai, a bearded parrot monk – not
unlike Marcos himself – stuck a head wearing a stovepipe hat out of a
monastery door. I still have a sheet or two of Marcos's doodlings –
Hebrew parrots with little skullcaps, Chinese parrots wearing mollusc
hats, Indian parrots with turbans, long-nosed parrots, bespectacled
parrots, even a Red Indian parrot with long hair tied with a fillet and
two feathers (parrot feathers, I suppose) sticking up at the back.

Marcos was married to a Danish woman, which is why he worked
on the *Pep Sirius* for a Danish company. He liked Denmark, but he
thought all Danes were far too gloomy. 'Everyone is deep down a
Hamlet. That's why they drink so.' Not that he was against drink, but
he thought Scandinavians made pigs of themselves in liquor, unable to
stop drinking once they had started. When, as I soon did, I came to
appreciate Marcos's humanity and humour, I also discovered a down-

to-earth commonsense. The Spanish crewmen were a good lot, he said.

'But why do you think we have a Spanish crew?' he asked me.

'Cheap labour?' I said, thinking of the Filipinos.

'No, no, no. I tell you. In Denmark shipping companies all employ foreign crewmen, eh? *But*' – he wagged a stubby finger at me – 'there are hundreds, maybe thousands of Danish seamen unemployed in Denmark. Why is this? Simple, my friend. Because the Danish seamen are a lot of useless, lazy, drunken bastards, always stealing, sleeping, fighting.' He shook his great bearded head. 'Ay-ay-ay, Gavin! You know that a Danish crew threw a captain and his chief officer into the sea – yes! In full uniform – from a Danish ferry? Ha, captain and chief officer – over the side. Po-po-po! With Danish seamen it's that kind of thing all the time.'

'What happened to the crew?'

'Oh, I don't know. Probably nothing. Probably they sent them to some pretty girl psychiatrist and she asked them very kindly about their background. All that bloody nonsense.'

He drew a quick irritated sketch of a parrot in a bowler hat and smoking a pipe, partly obscuring Seville.

'In Denmark people won't go ten miles to work. The unemployment wage is about eighty per cent of the working wage, maybe more. So many say, "Why work for twenty per cent? Not worth it." So unemployment figures are not real. You know I come from Greece. It's different from northern Europe. Poor. In the West we don't know what life is like in the rest of the world.' He sniffed sadly, adding a briefcase to the bowler-hatted parrot.

'I am sure we don't,' I said. 'I don't think we care. Asians would trek ten thousand miles on their knees to find work; or swim in water full of sharks. Risk their lives for work.'

'In Denmark,' Marcos said, 'nobody would go *by car* ten miles. But Greeks work. So do Spanish. This Spanish crew on *Pep Sirius* is not paid less than Danish crewmen. They are not cheap labour. But see how they are good and quiet and how they work.'

He looked quite put out but soon he was singing again and we made more tea. While we drank it I heard a voice a long way off saying, 'Ah Po cannot get sick. Not allowed' – the voice of Wei Kuen telling me how Ah Po and Ching Man would have to send their new baby to Shanghai because both their salaries were needed to pay the rent of a room hardly bigger than my outstretched arms.

*   *   *

In a day or two a coastline appeared, and then the mouth of a river bordered by low banks and mangrove swamps. We would load a cargo for Lisbon at the little port here. Bjarne, the second officer, and Tom Rasmussen leaned over the rail, watching canoes full of waving black figures converging on us.

'Take care,' Bjarne said. 'We'll soon be surrounded by businessmen in canoes. *Ja*, I think so.'

'Businessmen?'

'*Ja*. Selling masks and heads and such.'

The little port was a dusty market town with storks rattling their bills in skeletal trees, and grave, dignified men in long, delicately coloured robes, and handsome women with intricately braided hair. They were not wholly negroid; their jet-black skins were moulded over fine Arab bones and many of the men wore neat, closely trimmed jawline beards – they looked to me like so many Laurence Oliviers playing Othello. We loaded some sort of local seed, I think, while Bjarne was careful to keep all our doors shut against mosquitoes and businessmen. Elsa cooked sauerkraut and put out tuna fish and soused mackerel and cold pork to go with the whisky and Carlsberg.

'She is a spotless cook,' Kurt the captain said. 'And you notice how we are not being wicked, notice?'

'Wicked?'

'We are not talking so dirty. Danish seamen respect women so.' He said this with a big wink. Later he told me, 'You can have big trouble with women on board. Big trouble, and maybe have to send one or more people home from the ship.'

Jan, despite the plastered leg, kept a watch on Elsa, supposing one was needed. For the rest of us there were video films often starring the officers' favourite, Clint Eastwood, and sometimes Dudley Moore. Of course, there was booze. More drinking was done on the *Pep Sirius* than on any other ship I had been on, no question of that. I heard the thump of a large Danish body falling inert in an alleyway late at night after a film and a few bottles, even long after the official New Year celebrations were over. Most mornings two or more of us – I have to include myself in this – silently compared bloodshot eyes, secretly yearned for the first lager of the day. I even heard, very occasionally, the unmistakable sounds of a late-night punch-up: guttural cries and the thud of fists on bearded chins, barely muffled by metal bulkheads. In the morning Marcos simply smiled over his tea and murmured, 'I thought I heard some loud noises on the bridge. Danish games, wasn't it?' No hard feelings resulted from any of this.

After Senegal, our clocks went back an hour. Europe was upon us again. Approaching Portugal, a slow, heavy swell got up and a cold wind; we pulled on sweaters and windcheaters. Marcos became philosophical and drew a parrot with a halo. 'At sea,' he said, seeing me shivering with the sudden cold, 'you can't always have fine weather. Life is the same.'

Seagulls gathered over our bows.

Bjarne came onto the bridge. 'Why these gulls don't go somewhere warm?' he said. 'If they go south slowly, in three days they'll be in Dakar.'

Marcos made a small adjustment in our course, ignoring this talk of gulls. 'The West. Civilization. Where is the love? Ecclesiastes says if you have no love you are like a drum.'

Bjarne said, interested, 'You are a godly man, Marcos? Marcos is a priest,' he explained to me with a wink, 'that's why the beard.'

'I believe in the small voice inside us,' Marcos said unruffled. 'We can't kill that even if we try. This continuous critic inside us.'

The Algarve was in sight to starboard. Kurt came up shortly to say he had new instructions from the company. We would avoid Lisbon and go up to the port of Leixoes instead. After that even the company did not know where the *Pip Sirius* would go; it would depend on the cargo she picked up.

'She might go to Watchet in Somerset,' he said. 'We do that sometimes. A good little port. All little ports are good in England. Your unions have killed all the big ones. London, Southampton, Birkenhead, Liverpool – all dead. In Birkenhead, you could say to a stevedore foreman you prefer this container stowed here, not there, and he says, "That's my business. If you insist, I'm off." And the next thing, the whole port's out. Crazy.'

I made plans to leave the ship at Leixoes. There were forecasts of bad storms in the Channel and the Bay of Biscay and my hope of reaching Bude had gone. In this winter weather it would be absurd to attempt it even if I could find a yachtsman rash enough to try for the tiny channel that sneaked past the breakwater up to the lock gates. I would have to take what I could from Portugal for my last leg. Anything would do – I was keen to reach home now.

A smog cloud appeared, signalling Europe. Near the coast by Oporto, Kurt said, 'See there. The bows of the *Jacob Maersk*, Danish tanker – blew up in the mouth of the harbour.' I could see the light blue shell of her ruined snout pointing skywards. 'Terrible. The crew's wives and children were watching from the quay when it happened.'

Bjarne said, 'All the engine room men were lost. Burnt. The pilot was first over the side, they said.' I couldn't see that the pilot had been wrong.

426

We entered Leixoes harbour basin, skirting a nest of fishing boats, and at last slid alongside among a nodding cluster of high, rattling cranes. The company's agent was here and came aboard to huddle with Kurt, bringing news that the *Pep Sirius* must now go to Dover. The officers took the mail the agent had brought them and quickly slipped off to read it in private.

Like the glorious answer to a feeble prayer two cables were delivered in quick succession to the *Pep Sirius*. They were both from Andrew Bell. The first said:

> Am trying to make arrangements for your onward passage Leixoes Watchet (North Somerset) on a Chas Willie ship, they have a regular service on this route. Unfortunately they have no spare accom – not even a spare berth. Suppose even you would prefer not to use a sleeping bag in an alleyway to complete your odyssey. Hope to have more info. Andrew Bell.

And the second:

> Chas Willie (Cardiff) able offer you a berth on *Kaina* from Aveiro to Watchet. This ship was built Holland 1967 and although Panama flag at the moment was British flag until July 1982. Please let me know if you want to use her so that we can make appropriate arrangements with charterers. Andrew Bell.

Saint Andrew Bell, I thought. I cabled back from the *Pep Sirius*'s agent that I was ready to present myself at Aveiro, wherever that was, at the earliest moment. While I was shaking hands with the Danes and Marcos, Bjarne came up with a final message from Andrew Bell that capped the two earlier ones: 'All fixed. Ship sails for Boulogne, then to Plymouth in ballast.'

The port of Aveiro, not far to the south, lay across mudflats wreathed in fog. The Willie office was one of a handful of identical small huts, but it stood out from the others because over it flew the green and white flag of Wales with its red dragon and the name 'Willie' in black letters. The little ship lay in the river nearby. She was, as they used to say, no oil painting, but what was that to me, with 'home' in my game of Grandmother's Footsteps so close?

427

The white-haired Captain was a Cardiff man called Tom Newby. 'There's no problem,' he said. 'She's not the *Queen Mary*. Go anywhere on her you like. Dig in. Be at home.' The first officer and the crew were Estonian mainly, he said. But there were very few crewmen, I discovered; I only remember two or three deckhands and there certainly wasn't room for many more.

'It's noisy, too,' said a voice at my elbow when I was on board. Looking round, I saw a middle-aged man with a long nose the colour of a loganberry. 'Keith's the name.' He jerked a finger at a companionway. 'See my bloody little bolthole. Small? I'll say she's small. Just come and listen to the bloody generator next me 'ead.' We both laughed. 'Don't expect no bloody washin' machines here, Gav,' he said. 'It's not that sort of ship. I can tell you. The washbasin – that's the washin' machine.' He took my arm and steered me into a corner of the deck. 'Look, the cook's a bloody woman. Estonian. Just watch your time. This morning I came to breakfast at eight o'clock, and the old dragon refused to serve me.'

Keith nodded his head at the red dragon of Wales flapping near the *Kaina*'s funnel. 'There's two bloody dragons on this ship, Gavin. I'm tellin' you. Mark my words.'

Landfall

So He bringeth them to the haven where they would be.

Psalm 107

Thirtynine

What did the chill of a brash east wind matter now? Sula, the square-bodied Estonian chief officer, flapped his arms and scowled across the salt flats at a rising sun that looked as cold as his nose. Both sun and nose looked beautiful to me. This was the last leg; home in a few days. We stood on the *Kaina*'s bridge waiting to sail.

'Roll on a week from now,' Keith Lear said with a gloomy smile. It was the third time he'd said it since we'd sat over fried eggs, a rasher each of bacon, rolls and tea under the contemptuous glare through her hatch of Magda, the dragon-lady cook.

'Off to Boul-og-nee,' he said now. The long nose above his white high-necked sweater made him look like a man peering over a white wall. But we didn't move.

Captain Newby, relaxed in green sweater, white shirt and dark blue trousers, looked out across the flats. 'Well, we'll have the wind offshore. All we need is the *pilote*.' We waited. He hummed a song from *Fiddler on the Roof*.

One hour and five minutes late the Portuguese pilot appeared, a stout man, puffing a bit. 'Where's the *pilote*, *amigo*?' Captain Newby hailed him cheerily.

'Sorry, captain.'

'Oh, okay,' said Newby.

'Let go forrard!'

Boulogne, Boulogne! Roll on, Bou-log-nee.

Through bifocals Newby's gentle, attentive schoolmaster's eyes watched the *Kaina*'s bows swing out into the stream as calmly as if he were supervising a simple experiment in the chemistry lab.

'Slow ahead,' came the pilot's voice.

431

'Slow ahead,' Newby echoed, winking at me. 'And away she goes like a scalded cat!'

'More speed, captain!'

'More speed! Ah-ha!'

Newby carolled over the telegraph and we twisted past idle trawlers and a brand-new, brightly painted German tanker, so modern that Newby took the trouble to point out to me the fact that her bridge could be mechanically raised and lowered to negotiate low bridges.

'I remember you,' Newby said to the pilot, 'in the *Lady Sylvia*.'

'Ah, yais. *Laddy Sylvia*. Yais.'

The little river snaked, and soon its banks fell away and the sea advanced on us in thick, steep, rolling yellow-green waves. The *Kaina* began to dip and heave; I felt the planking of her wheelhouse shake under my feet; the feeling of movement, of the sea, of moving north, was exciting.

The *Kaina* was a good ship for my last leg home. She reminded me of the *Northgate*, a Hull coaster I had boarded one January night at Fowey in southern Cornwall, aged seventeen and thrilled to be sailing up the Channel to Antwerp. The *Northgate* tried to drown me in the worst Channel storm for a decade and we were forced to anchor off Dungeness with a fleet of other vessels, thrown about so badly that even the captain was seasick. The *Kaina* was about the *Northgate*'s size and she had the same down-to-earth, take-it-or-leave-it look.

Keith interrupted my reverie. 'All right, then – let's go and have some vino,' he was saying. 'And a little bit of *mangare*, too. If it's eatable. It almost never is, I'm warnin' yer.' Keith was one of a race of congenital grumblers. Yet, however much he moaned about nearly everything else, he approved of Captain Newby.

'He's quite old,' he said. 'Well, very old, really. Seventy or more, likely.'

'A very good seventy, then.'

'Oh, very good. Marvellous for his age.' Coming from Keith, I realize now, there could not have been a more glowing testimonial.

Marvellous for his age or any other Newby certainly was. He was a seaman of great experience who had started out to sea as a boy in old Cardiff tramps after his father had been killed while serving in the Glamorgan Yeomanry under Allenby in Palestine during the First World War. Of course, the Royal Navy had duly grabbed young Newby.

'Small navy ships – they were my lot in the war – the Second War, mind. Minesweepers, corvettes, torpedo boats – that sort of thing. In '43 I was around the Middle East a lot – Tobruk, Mersa Matruh, Port Said. I was never sunk. Luckily.' He laughed and gave a little whistle. 'Phew! 1943. Forty years ago and it doesn't seem like it. Yet it's all gone, hasn't it, that forty years? In a flash. Frightening, really. The Royal Navy sent me to Hamburg at the end of the war to try to get the port running again. Terrible mess, it was. Took two years.' Even while reminiscing, he stooped his white head over the auto-pilot, checked the compass bearing, ran his finger over the chart. 'I don't know,' he said, peering into the radar, 'I tell young men to make the most of their time – it'll go like a flash, I say, although you don't think so now. That's what I tell 'em. Remember how the weeks at school used to drag?' Newby went on. 'You thought term would never end!' He was never still … pacing … snatching up binoculars to stare at ships … checking … checking. Forty years ago he had been a man at war in the Middle East. Forty years....

'Ay, you thought the months would never end,' Tom Newby said, bending over the chart.

As the *Kaina* ploughed northward towards the chillier Biscay seas the imminence of home drowned any anxiety about the weather, a feeling heightened by the homely good nature of the men around me. Above all, by the way they talked. Keith sprinkled his conversation quite unself-consciously with English rhyming slang – 'Harry Tate' and 'China Plate' both meant 'Mate', and 'Jack the Ripper' meant 'Skipper'. When I asked the skipper himself how he'd describe the present bumpy sea, Newby replied, 'Oh, I'd say it's "rather rather" at the moment. Slightly better than "rough".' And looking astern at a smaller, Russian ship making heavy weather he said, 'I think we've got the legs of the Sovietsky, eh? Ay, I think so.'

Frank, the second engineer, was another sceptical veteran of years in ramshackle ships. His looks reminded me of a rough-and-ready version of the White Queen in *Alice in Wonderland*: a doughy face as deeply creased as a crumpled pillow; thick eyebrows rearing up like questing black caterpillars; quiet, unenvious eyes. After the first day, we met regularly in Keith's cramped, noisy berth to drink his vino or my whisky. Frank drank nothing. 'Old Frank's had half his stomach cut out,' Keith explained. 'Ulcers. All the rotten food he's eaten on ships.

There's cooks on ships as cooks nothing but fried stuff. All fried. Or boiled. Terrible. Rots the stomach after years of it. It rotted old Frank's.'

'Tha's right,' said Frank in a matter-of-fact tone.

They suited each other like a stage partnership. Even in the short time I was on the *Kaina* I came to recognize a scene or two from their act. Frank would forever wipe his thick glasses, play-acting crotchety, complaining, 'Ah can't see a bloody thing,' and Keith would laugh at him, ''Course not. They're coated with dirty bloody grease from your bloody engine room' – or words to that effect. 'Fook off.' That was Frank's way of signing off.

They were delightfully, seedily British, almost of an earlier, harder, less neurotic age. From their bad teeth and unhealthy complexions to their coarse, deadpan humour, from Frank's baggy, wide-stitched cardigans and old stained grey trousers to Keith's dark blue pea-jacket and old-fashioned sailor's blue cap, they called to mind stories by W. W. Jacobs of foggy ports and erring captains' daughters, and lines by Masefield on tramps in dirty Channel weather carrying cargoes of iron-ware and cheap tin trays. They brought back to me an early twentieth-century world in which sailors still carried ditty-boxes and parrots in cages; a world of greasy mess room plates, the cook's thumbprint in the gravy, piled with fatty pork and waterlogged spuds and peas that had first been dried like dead men's eyes and then drowned like unwanted puppies; of thick chunks of bread called 'doorsteps' smeared with beef dripping; of suet pudding called 'spotted dog' you could have thrown overboard and anchored a Swansea collier to. A dingier world, maybe, but not one that, compared to today, need feel ashamed of itself. This was the way to come back to Blighty. Not on some spick-and-span, soulless, automatic container ship.

'We'll have to see what Biscay will do with us, eh?' Keith said. 'Can be bloody awful. Just my luck. But y' never know.'

In the event, the much-feared Biscay was little more than a cold, grey, bumpy pond. From the course pencilled daily by the captain or the mate on the wheelhouse chart I watched our progress across that temperamental chunk of water, from the north-west corner of Spain to the great lion-head boss of Cape Finisterre that guards the approach to the English Channel. I inspected the barometer for disastrous falls, searched the skies for malignant clouds, but the waters of Biscay continued 'rather rather'. Through the monotonous hiss of our unexceptional bow-wave, France and Boulogne drew nearer.

'Bou-log-nee. I must be up early to see that approach,' said Keith. '"Not a whore in the house washed and the street full of randy sailors."'

'What on earth is that?'

'Search me. Just a seaman's expression meaning "very early".'

So many ships were dodging about in these cluttered seas that we seemed to be part of a northbound convoy; an unmistakable sign that home was near. I began to feel impatient for the end, and understood why Wordsworth wrote an irritable poem about being sidetracked to Boulogne when he was particularly anxious to return to England –

Why cast ye back upon the Gallic shore,
Ye furious waves! a patriotic son
Of England – who in hope her coast had won,
His project crown'd, his pleasant travel o'er ...?

Up the Channel. Beacons and buoys and the skinny arm of a sea wall: Boulogne wavered before us in a haze. Tom Newby said to Keith at the wheel: 'Keep her straight, if you have the strength. Oh, I forgot, Gavin. Don't bother to wear a bow tie with your suit when we arrive. It's not Sunday, don't forget.'

'You'll be putting up your gold stripes, though?'

'Oh, ay. The steward's polishing 'em now.'

We advanced on Boulogne behind a huge tanker, *Calliope E.*

'Last time I was in Boulogne,' Newby continued, 'it was the first day of the liberation of the port from the Germans. I remember standing on the jetty watching the first Allied cargo ship coming in. She hit a magnetic mine and up she went. Pilot killed, and the captain. Two bodies in the water.' He examined the sky. 'Mild, isn't it?'

In a fine aura of spray, a cross-Channel hovercraft – the ferry from England – contoured the swell ahead of us, sidling into the opening between the nutcracker jaws of two harbour walls. Beyond, the dockside cranes of Boulogne nodded their heads as if performing some solemn ritual for the church on the hill. Suddenly my mind saw England, and the London I left for Shanghai. How easy it would have been to leave the *Kaina* here and buy a ticket on a Channel ferry to England. There was no need to go all the way to Plymouth, after all. But it would have been a poor, half-cock ending. Anyway, I was not in a mood to abandon ship.

Boulogne was a long walk away from the wharf, so we ate on board. A damp, vegetable smell drifted from the galley in the sweatbox of the mess.

'I'm bloody glad I'm not married to bloody Magda,' Keith said over chicken, potatoes and cabbage. 'I'd soon be doin' time for bloody murder.'

Framed in her serving hatch, Magda the cook stared at him through the steam as if she might cut off his head.

'You thing!' she shouted.

That afternoon, because everyone else was busy, I found myself alone with Magda in the galley, cadging an extra cup of tea.

'No. I do *not* like working on ships,' she said tartly when I asked her. 'But there's not so much work ashore.' Her English was perfect and her accent barely noticeable.

'It's the people,' she said. 'Just a lot of drunks.'

'Lonely?'

The question seemed to surprise her. 'I have crosswords. Sometimes reading.' She put a piece of toast in front of me and added a lump of butter. 'I speak languages. English, Estonian and German, Portuguese, Spanish and Italian, too.' The kettle whistled.

'When I came three weeks ago the kitchen was very dirty, smelling. Men are dirr-ty pigs. They just want to sit around and drink beer.' She spoke roughly but there was the hint of a smile now. She poured boiling water into a teapot.

'Keith says —' I started.

The smile vanished. 'That thing!' she snapped and whipped the butter dish back into the fridge, slamming the door.

Captain Tom Newby said, 'I don't expect you've ever met Estonians before. There's quite a community of them in Cardiff. They're all right. Only thing, they've not much sense of humour.' He smiled. 'Magda's a bit, er, abrasive, of course. But she's a good cook.'

We were sitting in Newby's odd coffin of a cabin. 'We should be away to Plymouth tomorrow some time. The forecast says force six to seven south-westerly gales, so we'll be lucky to make it alive!'

436

His mother-in-law would be a hundred and three in June. 'She could read and hear and watch the telly until a year ago. Her hundredth birthday was a great party. Dozens of cards – one from the Queen, of course.' He himself had retired from the sea after the Hamburg experience, but even now, he said, he liked to take temporary command of ships like the *Kaina* – just for a few weeks, not more. You need money to keep an old mother-in-law.

Keith, Frank and I made our way over an obstacle course of concrete moles, cement barriers and a busy main road to the hovercraft terminal's snack bar for a beer or two and a stretch of the legs. 'Ha,' Keith said, looking at a chef stirring soup with a cigarette in his lips. 'Fag-ash soup! I've had *that* many a time on ships.'

Three beers later I mentioned the gale warnings. 'We'll be shaken to bloody bits,' said Keith.

'She might even fall apart,' Frank said.

Keith looked at him. 'Well, one thing – *you'd* be drowned in the bloody engine room, like a rat in a fookin' trap.' He raised his beer can. 'And serve you right, you measly old bastard.'

'Ah'd coom oop and claw yer fookin' down with me, youse....'

They narrowed their eyes at each other affectionately and laughed. The tannoy was calling passengers, in French and English, to present themselves at emigration control. The fourth beer came.

'Well,' Keith said, watching the hovercraft moving sedately down its ramp to the sea, 'it'd make a dramatic end to your book.'

'It certainly would.'

Frank made the face of a drowning man. 'Glug, glug!' he said.

Next morning, with dew on her hatches, the *Kaina* moved out of the brownish haze of Boulogne's industrial zone and followed the break-water round to the flashing white light at its tip. Our course lay across the Channel, then down the English coast, westwards, towards Devon. Past the flashing light the *Kaina* began to rear and sway. Seagulls screamed at us as though we were mad.

'Steady the Buffs.' Captain Tom Newby moved swiftly about the bridge, from automatic navigator to radar to chart, singing '"Oh, the hee-eells are on fay-ah with the sound of mew-sic...."' Then: 'How about some Rosie Lee? Settles the stomach, tea. The weather'll be "rather rather" to "rough" today, I really do think.'

Alf Sula raised his round white moon-face from a plate of bacon, a mug of tea beside him. 'I've got some pictures,' he said, groping into a wallet. 'Good old friends.'

One photograph was of a happy reunion. Round a table, laughing men and girls leaned towards the camera's flash.

'Estonian. 1951. A reunion in London. There's me. That one's a ship's captain now. That one's in Canada. That one ... I don't know.'

The small, sad pile of photographs lay beside his plate of bacon rinds. I saw two kids in cowboy hats; his sons. 'They're nineteen or twenty now. They still speak the old language.'

Magda listened from her hatch, craning her neck, her expression almost tender.

The weather, after all, was kind. Rain and sea water swept us from bows to stern and mist hid the cliffs of the English coast, but there were no gales, even though it was evident that my final landfall was not going to be blessed with even the palest of welcoming suns. Instead there were BBC news bulletins and *Coronation Street* on the ship's telly. I thought of other, less appealing, signs of home. Newspapers, for instance, their pages crammed with the trivia of a self-pampering society – yet another inquiry into teenage sex; a breathless report on next summer's swimsuits; and columns filled with the petulance of a people who feel cheated because their affluent life falls short of perfection.

Keith confessed, 'I'm in what is commonly known as a Kiss-me-arse Latitude, when you're just about to pay off and you've got to the stage when you don't give two monkeys' fucks for anything.' He stopped and gave an exaggerated start of alarm. 'Oh, God, Francis, what 'ave *you* been doin'?' Frank's dishevelled head had suddenly thrust towards us round the door.

'Playin' pontoon in t'engine room.' Frank grinned and went on: ''Ey, 'ave you 'eard this one? The man says: "Look, missus, ah'd like a good goose for Christmas, wouldn't you?" She says: "Ooh, yes, ah would." So 'e says: "Well, take yer knickers off!"'

'Time we parted, Frank,' Keith said sadly. 'Oh, Francis, Francis, I do worry about you. I really do.'

Parachute flares trickled down through the mist over a British warship off the Salcombe River, reminding me of the Falklands. A sleek white motor yacht with a smart yellow funnel danced by and two men in smart caps and a woman in a heavy sweater waved. They looked cold and damp.

'Lovely summer's eve,' Tom Newby said. 'Rig of the day on arrival: Red Sea rig, eh? Red Sea rig. Any sign of the Plymouth pilot?'

Keith, at the wheel, said, 'He's just been on the radio saying, "Berth at once. Pilot at the breakwater."'

'Oh, ay. Jolly good.'

Round the point at the approach to Plymouth odd puffs of cloud hung about like gunsmoke. A long breakwater cut the harbour entrance in two.

'Where's the *pilote*? Where's the *pilote*?' Newby sang out to no one in particular, and soon a jolly pilot with a Devon accent was stamping about the bridge. Under his direction we moved on towards Georgian houses, church steeples, the Hoe, and the black gun slits of wartime bastions on the slopes above the harbour.

'Stop 'er. 'Ard a-port, sir.'

We turned, very slowly, into a dock that seemed unusually narrow.

''Ard a-port, is she? The tide'll bring 'er round.' We edged further into the dock, almost shaving the rust off the sides of a Greek freighter.

'Give 'er a bit of starboard, sir. Just a bit. She'll do the rest.'

At the entrance to the little dock was a high dead wall with a gate in it. Rain stood in oily puddles on the cobbles. In the late January afternoon drizzle everything looked very old, tired and dismal. In what other life had I dozed in the sun by that grave on a hillside at Hiva Oa? On what planet had Emma, on a sugary beach with a red hibiscus in her hair, yearned for New Zealand, and Amosa, the wood demon, darted through the giant colonnades of Mount Vaea, calling until the forest echoed like an aviary? Where had I seen the Snow Queen's Palace and the windswept isle from which Tony, the shaggy dog of Cape Horn, had tried to repel single-handed this British invader?

For the last time I heard 'Finished with engines' – and as usual it sounded like a death sentence. Old Tom Newby looked at me in wonder. 'Gee whizz!' he said. 'We made it.'

From Plymouth there would be a general dispersal. Captain Tom would go to Cardiff by train after what might prove to have been his last voyage – who could tell? 'I wouldn't mind, Gavin. No, I wouldn't mind. Depends a bit on the old mother-in-law. A hundred and three! Just imagine.'

Sula, Magda, and the others would stay with the ship and after a day or two spent loading china clay they would go south with her again to Morocco; with any luck they would find a bit of sun and good cheap wine.

Frank would go with them. 'Well, joost for now,' he said.

Barry, the young ordinary seaman, was off by train to Liverpool where his family was waiting to give him a twenty-second birthday party. There was to be a train to Liverpool for Keith, too, taking his dicky heart back to Moreton on the Wirral. He'd be walking his dog on the promenade in a day or two, unable to take his eyes off the sea he so loved and hated. 'Gettin' shot of this old rattle-trap, thank Christ!' he crowed to Frank and me.

'Ah'll be seein' youse back at sea in no time flat,' Frank assured him amiably. 'Ah'll fookin' bet yer that.' In a cloud of fond obscenities, they scrubbed and dressed up for the farewell night's run ashore.

'Come on,' said Keith knowledgeably. 'The Breakwater Inn's the best place. No trains to catch tonight.'

I realized that for the first time for what seemed like a decade I was in no hurry to go anywhere. Oh, no – no trains tonight. Time enough to catch a London express tomorrow.

It turned out to be a remarkably decorous farewell to a year of travel halfway round the world. We drank beer and then whisky in the Breakwater Inn, creeping, with the publican's permission, into a small back room to escape the noise of a pop group called the Spare Parts.

440

'I'll give 'em spare parts,' said Keith. 'They should send 'em to the Falklands.'

'Falklands, hell! Argentina more like,' Frank growled.

We said goodnights and goodbyes outside my cabin.

'Ta-ta, then,' said Keith. 'Don't forget, if you come Wirral way....'

'Good luck, Gav,' said Frank with his doughy, innocent grin.

I felt I had known them half my life. Neither was young any more. They were Ancient Pistol and Corporal Nym. They were old-fashioned, skiving British sailors, free from illusion and ambition. I would miss them, but it wouldn't do to say so.

I didn't see them again. Next day things were different. Dock workers, agents' men and customs officials took over the ship. Loading would begin almost at once. With new men aboard and a new destination ahead of her, the *Kaina* had become a stranger; she had no time for me any more.

I took a final mug of tea with Magda in her spotless galley – she actually twisted her grumpy mouth into a smile for me as she poured it. Then I went to say goodbye to Tom Newby. A radio handset fizzed at his elbow, and a rough Plymouth voice snarled from it '... and tell 'er she can get stuffed!'

'Oh dear,' Captain Tom said, smiling and switching it off. 'Sounds like the B B C.'

He held out his hand. 'The end of the line, eh?' he said in his soft Welsh voice. 'Ay, the end of the line.'

I took this good man's outstretched hand; and that was that.

The end of the line came swiftly now, and with it came the deep, cold ache of something loved and lost. A taxi dumped me at Plymouth station. The express train to London normally had a dining-car, but today when it pulled into the station the ticket collector told me that the station staff had forgotten – *forgotten*! – to attach it. So I sat with an empty stomach, staring through the carriage window at the weeping English countryside, and thought once more of that distant beginning. The dusty books of adventure high up in my grandmother's old attic in Bude with its view of the Atlantic Ocean had tantalized my mind with Stevenson's dream of

Tales, marvellous tales
Of ships and stars and isles where good men rest.

That dream had beckoned me away to sea as a boy and I had resisted it almost too long. Now at last I had returned to tell the tale and the dream was fulfilled.